The World Economy

Second edition

As globalization continues apace, lines of communications are shortening and the boundaries between nations are becoming increasingly blurred. We rarely view things now solely from the point of view of our country of residence and instead adopt a global perspective on an increasing range of issues. This is particularly true in economics – the global economy has some of the characteristics of an interlinking jigsaw and no single nation can truly exist in isolation.

The tendency of most textbooks in international economics is to look at the world economy from the point of view of one country. The second edition of Horst Siebert's *The World Economy* rebels against this tendency and treats the world as a single entity. The key issues that have affected the world trade system since the turn of the millennium are thus very much to the fore, including:

- globalization and the increasing role of bodies such as the WTO and IMF
- the roots of financial and currency crisis (the Asian and Latin American experience)
- regional integration in the world economy including NAFTA and the EU
- conflicts between the national interest and global concerns (protectionism, competition between governments, environmental issues, the world order)

This book should be equally essential to those studying the world economy from the perspective of economics, finance and business. It includes a massive range of up-to-the-minute data in the form of tables, figures, graphs and pie charts and, as well as fulfilling the role of a textbook, should provide a valuable reference guide.

Horst Siebert is President of the Kiel Institute of World Economics, Germany.

The World Economy

Second edition

Horst Siebert

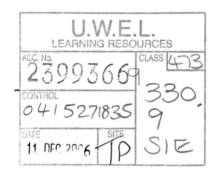

London and New York

First published 1999
by Routledge
11 New Fetter Lane, London EC4P 4EE

Simultaneously published in the USA and Canada
by Routledge
29 West 35th Street, New York, NY 10001

Reprinted 2000

Second edition first published 2002

Routledge is an imprint of the Taylor & Francis Group

© 1999, 2002 Horst Siebert

Typeset in Times by RefineCatch Limited, Bungay, Suffolk
Printed and bound in Great Britain by
TJ International Ltd, Padstow, Cornwall

British Library Cataloguing in Publication Data
A catalogue record for this book is available from the British Library

Library of Congress Cataloging in Publication Data
A catalog record for this book has been requested

ISBN 0–415–27183–5 (hbk)
ISBN 0–415–27184–3 (pbk)

Contents

List of figures   vi

List of tables   x

Preface   xii

1   The global view   1

Part I
The World Goods and Factor
Markets and Economic Growth   21

2   The world product markets   23

3   The factor markets in the world
economy   51

4   Growth processes in the world
economy   69

Part II
Monetary and Financial Markets   93

5   Global money and currency markets   95

6   Financial crises   111

7   Currency crises   123

8   How to prevent a monetary–financial
crisis   139

Part III
Regional Dimensions of the World
Economy   161

9   Developing countries   163

10   The transformation countries   181

11   Regional integration in the world
economy   199

12   The European Union   209

Part IV
National Economic Policy versus a
World Economic Order   233

13   National protectionism versus
worldwide free trade   235

14   Locational competition   253

15   Using the national and global
environment   267

16   An institutional order for the world
economy   273

References   301

Index   309

List of figures

1.1 Economic growth in the centrally planned economies of Eastern Europe, 1950–1990   3

1.2 Economic growth in selected regions of the world, 1950–1998   4

1.3 The Kindleberger spiral   5

1.4 The world oil price   7

1.5 Costs of transport and communication   9

1.6 World industrial production, world trade and foreign direct investment, 1973–2000   11

1.7 Regional structure of the world's gross domestic product, 2000   14

1.8 Regional structure of world trade, 2000   15

1.9 Growth in the world economy, 1980–2000   16

1.10 Shares of world export, 1975–2001: industrial countries and developing countries   16

1.11 Shares of world export, 1975–2000: United States, Germany, Asian 'tigers'   17

2.1 World oil market   25

2.2 World supply curve for hard coal   26

2.3 World transformation curve and world market equilibrium   27

2.4 Relative price of the equilibrium   27

2.5 Equilibrium with the Marshall–Mill offer curves   28

2.6 Trade barriers and world transformation curve   29

2.7 Increased labor supply and world transformation curve   31

2.8 Increased labor supply and relative price   31

2.9 Increased labor supply and welfare in industrialized and newly industrializing countries   33

2.10 A change in factor endowment   34

2.11 Commodity price ratio and factor price ratio   35

2.12 Chain of effects of an increased labor supply   36

2.13 The European model of unemployment and the American model of employment   37

2.14 Demand shift and international trade   39

2.15 Relative price between tradable and non-tradable goods   40

2.16 Falling average costs   41

2.17	Commodity axis and firms	42
2.18	The incumbent and the newcomer	45
2.19	Technology intensity and comparative advantage, 1999	47
2.20	Exports and the real exchange rate: the US	48
2.21	Exports and the real exchange rate: the UK	48
3.1	The world market for labor	52
3.2	The supply curve of the world market for labor, 1992	53
3.3	Transformation in time	55
3.4	The world market for capital	58
3.5	Optimal allocation of capital	59
3.6	Current account balances and national capital markets	62
3.7	Savings rates and investment rates in selected countries, 2000	64
3.8	Debt cycle of the US	66
3.9	The factor price frontier	67
4.1	Development of real per capita income and export ratio in the early industrialized countries, 1820–1990	70
4.2	Growth and business cycle in the OECD countries	72
4.3	Optimal accumulation of capital	74
4.4	Optimum capital accumulation, time preference and population growth	75
4.5	Long-term equilibrium	76
4.6	Long-term equilibrium with capital import and capital export	78
4.7	Growth path of a capital-importing country	79
4.8	Growth path of capital importer and capital exporter	80
4.9	Real per capita growth and foreign trade in the early industrialized countries, 1870–1990	81
4.10	Investment shares and growth rates in selected countries, 1980–2000	84
4.11	Convergence of the OECD countries, 1870–1993	87
4.12	Convergence in the European Union	88
5.1	Money expansion and inflation, Argentina, 1970–2001	96
5.2	Equilibrium of the quantity of money in the world with two currencies	97
5.3	Monetary equilibrium, purchasing power parity and the foreign currency market	100
5.4	Inflation and the exchange rate change (in percent), Argentina, 1970–2001	101
5.5	Interest rate parity and purchasing power parity	103
5.6	Russia: interest rate and exchange rate with respect to the US, 1997–2001	105
5.7	Korea: interest rate and exchange rate with respect to the US, 1997–2001	105
5.8	Exchange rate DM/$ and purchasing power parity	106
5.9	Exchange rate DM/lira and purchasing power parity	107
5.10	Inflation and exchange rate changes of some important currencies, 1974–1998	107
5.11	US dollar, deutsche mark and yen	108
6.1	The stock market bubble and the Great Depression	113
6.2	Money expansion in Japan	117
6.3	Interest rates in Japan	118
6.4	The Japanese bubble	118
6.5	The impact of the bubble on economic growth	119
6.6	Share prices in Japan and in the US	120
7.1	The real exchange rate and the current account	127

7.2   Real exchange rate of the
       deutsche mark and the US dollar   129

7.3   Czech Republic: nominal and real
       exchange rate and current account   131

7.4   Mexico: real and nominal
       exchange rate and current account   132

7.5   South Korea: real and nominal
       exchange rate and current account   133

7.6   Thailand and Indonesia: nominal
       exchange rates of baht and rupiah
       and current account   134

7.7   Brazil: real and nominal exchange
       rate and current account   135

7.8   Turkey: real and nominal exchange
       rate and current account   136

8.1   IMF credits in percent of recipient
       country's GDP   144

8.2   Exchange rate within a range of
       fluctuations   155

8.3   Exchange rates in the EMS   156

9.1   The development trap   166

9.2   Vicious circle of underdevelopment   168

9.3   GNP per capita of Latin American
       countries and Asian and African
       countries, absolutely and relatively
       to the US, 1975 and 1998   170

9.4   Annual changes in the absolute
       GNP per capita and the relative
       position to the US between 1975
       and 1998   171

9.5   Debt of Argentina, Brazil and
       South Korea, 1970–1999   173

9.6   Debt of Thailand and Indonesia,
       1970–1999   174

9.7   Money expansion, inflation and the
       exchange rate change, Brazil,
       1970–2000   176

9.8   Money expansion, inflation and the
       exchange rate change, Mexico,
       1970–2000   177

9.9   Budget deficits of Argentina, Brazil
       and Mexico, in percent of GDP   178

9.10 The real exchange rate   180

10.1 Areas and sequence of reforms   182

10.2 The J-curves in Central Europe
       (gross domestic product in real terms)   184

10.3 The J-curve in Russia and the
       Baltic States (gross domestic
       product in real terms)   185

10.4 'Big bang' versus gradual adjustment   186

10.5 Budget deficits of selected
       transformation countries (in
       percent of GDP)   189

10.6 Current account deficits of
       selected transformation countries
       (in percent of GDP)   190

10.7 Rouble–dollar rate and rate of inflation   192

10.8 Polish zloty: nominal and real
       exchange rate *vis-à-vis* the US dollar   192

10.9 The J-curve in East Germany,
       industrial production 1988–2001   195

10.10 Growth of real GDP in China   196

11.1 Trade-creating and trade-diverting
       effects of a customs union   203

11.2 Regional integration and free trade   206

12.1 EU: population shares and shares
       of votes in the council after the
       Treaty of Nice   217

12.2 Set-up of the ECB   220

12.3 Labor productivities in Euroland, 2000   226

13.1 Tariffs and world trade in economic
       history   237

13.2 Effects of a tariff on imports   237

13.3 Subsidy for import substitutes   239

13.4 Quota   240

13.5   Tariff effects on the terms of trade   243

13.6   Tariff effects on a country's welfare   244

13.7   Tariff war   244

13.8   A country's advantage from free trade   247

13.9   Welfare gains for the world   248

13.10 The welfare effect of external trade   249

14.1   Levels of locational competition   254

14.2   The impact of a source tax on capital   258

14.3   Marginal benefit and marginal cost of infrastructure   259

15.1   The economic system and the environment   268

16.1   Gains from trade with strategic behavior   274

16.2   Trade benefits area   275

16.3   Different concepts of trade policy   277

16.4   The decision structure of the WTO   281

List of tables

1.1 Growth rates of world industrial production, world trade and foreign direct investments, 1985–2000   12

1.2 World domestic product, production approach by sectors (2000), in percent of the world domestic product   13

1.3 World domestic product, expenditure approach (2000), in percent of world domestic product   13

1.4 The ten largest countries of the world   14

1.5 GDP growth rates, 1980–2000   15

1.6 Growth competitiveness ranking   18

2.1 Intra-industry trade   43

3.1 Intertemporal mechanism of balances   62

3.2 Gross capital inflows (in billion US dollars)   63

3.3 Inflow of direct investments, as percent of gross investment   65

4.1 Time required for convergence   86

6.1 Balance sheet of a commercial bank   115

6.2 Capital losses in Japan, 1990–1996 (in trillion yen)   119

8.1 Official creditors' long-term debt outstanding and disbursed in countries in crisis (in billion US dollars)   144

9.1 The 10 poorest countries in the world (gross national product per capita in US dollars, 1999)   164

9.2 The newly industrialized countries, 1999   169

9.3 Foreign debt of selected countries, 1998   174

9.4 Macroeconomic instability, 1985–2000   175

10.1 Important economic variables in the transformation process   187

10.2 Privatization of production and government expenditure of the state in distribution in percent of GDP, 1999   189

11.1 EU, NAFTA and Japan, 1999   205

11.2 Share of intra-regional trade (exports plus imports) as percentage of each region's total trade, 1948–1999   207

12.1 Degree of centralization   212

12.2 Required majorities   215

12.3 Allocation of votes in the EU   216

12.4 Candidate countries, 2000   230

16.1 The prisoners' dilemma: welfare levels with free trade and tariff policy   276

16.2 Pay-off matrix of protectionism and liberalization of the EU and North America   276

16.3 GATT/WTO membership, 1948–2001   279

16.4 Liberalization rounds and protectionist counters   280

16.5 Elements of an institutional order for the world economy   298

Preface

· ·

The topic of this book is the world economy. It provides an analysis of the global economic structures and processes in the world. It looks at the economy of the planet Earth as if the world were observed from outer space. In a time when the communication system is organized globally, when we can communicate from Buenos Aires to Kiel over the Internet and when huge quantities of data can be exchanged between Cambridge and Hangzhou, when CNN broadcasts news worldwide, when transport costs and distance are becoming less and less important and when more and more people are becoming accustomed to finding their jobs in all parts of the world, such a world view of the economic processes and structures appears to be imperative.

In this book, we study the world's product, its composition by sectors and the main components of world aggregate demand. We look at economic growth, including some historical evidence. We analyze the world markets for goods, the adjustments to disturbances of equilibria on the commodity markets and the role of trade. Moreover, the world market for factors for production, for labor and capital, are examined.

Specific issues are the world monetary and financial markets and monetary and financial crises. A global monetary equilibrium with different monies and exchange rates is discussed, including approaches explaining the exchange rate in the long and the short run. Purchasing power parity, interest rate parity, exchange rate overshooting, optimal asset portfolios, financial bubbles and recent currency crises are the topics. The volatility of financial and currency markets has an impact on the real sphere of the economy, and a crisis may jump from one country to another. An important issue is how financial crises can be prevented, what role the IMF should play and whether exchange rates can be stabilized.

In a further step, the book looks at the regional dimension of the world economy, namely at developing countries and the new market economies (transition countries). It also analyzes approaches to regional integration in the world including the European Union.

The book also addresses potential conflicts between the national interest and global concerns. This relates to national protectionism versus free trade. It also refers to the concept of locational competition which means that the immobile factors of production, that is labor, compete for the mobile factors, that is capital and technological knowledge.

Locational competition is competition between governments, including competition in taxation, in the supply of public goods and in the institutional design of countries. Using the national and the global environment can be interpreted as another area where national and global interests can clash. In order to prevent strategic (i.e. non-cooperative) behavior, an institutional order is required for the world economy for the international division of labor.

The book has developed from my regular lecture on the world economy at the University of Kiel, from my research at the Kiel Institute of World Economics and from the discussions with my research colleagues. If one works at a research institute like the Kiel Institute for World Economics where many ideas are floating around, one is permanently exposed to a shifting frontier of knowledge. New areas of problems have to be recognized quickly. Many international visitors stimulate imagination and require answers to pressing problems. Moreover, I had to present the Kiel ideas in international conferences, in lectures at Zhejiang University in Hangzhou, China, and at the Instituto Universitario Banco Patricio in Buenos Aires, at the Fundación Mediterránea, at Córdoba in Argentina, the Uruguay–German Chamber of Commerce in Montevideo, at the UN Commission for Latin America and the Caribbean in Santiago de Chile and in the newly established Group of Economic Analysis of the European Commission. Some of the paragraphs of this book have indeed been written in these and other parts of the world, often of necessity ignoring the tourist attractions.

In this second edition, I have rewritten Part II on 'Monetary and Financial Markets' now presented in four chapters instead of two. The chapter on the European Union has been redone as well. The text has been scrutinized throughout, the presentation has been improved where the previous text was unclear or too complex. All tables and figures have been updated.

I am grateful to many who have criticized the manuscript in its different stages and who have influenced my thoughts. I have continuously discussed the topic of the international division of labor with my colleagues at the Kiel Institute, especially with Gernot Klepper, Henning Klodt, Rolf J. Langhammer, Joachim Scheide, Rüdiger Soltwedel, Harmen Lehment, with my colleagues at the Economics Faculty of Kiel University, especially Gerd Hansen, Johannes Bröcker, Horst Raff and Thomas Lux, and with my colleagues at the German Council of Economic Advisors, who have sharpened my grasp of economic problems and of approaches to problem solving. Last but not least, my students at Kiel, and also at the Universities of Konstanz and Mannheim where I had taught before, have been a permanent challenge to presenting the fascinating issues, avoiding the boring and not too hesitating to state the obvious.

Claudia Buch and Christian Pierdzioch have criticized Chapters 5–8, Rolf Langhammer has given valuable hints at Chapter 16. With Oliver Lorz I have discussed frequently issues of model building. Matthias Deschryvere, Jann Lay, Leandro Navarro and Susan Steiner have updated the tables and figures, and they have gone through a large part of the chapters.

A manuscript like this one is born slowly, and under pain with many roundabout processes which, unfortunately, are not always productive. In typing the manuscript, Hannelore Owe and Nicole Rimkus have accompanied this process of creative construction with composure and professionalism.

I also acknowledge the following for permission to reprint illustrations used in the book: the World Bank for figures from the *World Development Report 1995*, 'Workers in an integrating world', pp. 51 and 121; the Centre for International Economics and Dr Andrew Stoeckel for a table from *Western Trade Blocs*, 1990, p. 69; dtv (Deutscher Taschenbuchverlag) and Charles P. Kindleberger for a figure from *The World in Depression, 1929–1939* (Routledge, London and New York, 1973, p. 172) and Bernhard Heitger and Leonard Waverman for figures from *German Unification and the International Economy*, 1993, pp. 76–77.

Horst Siebert

Chapter 1

The global view

∙∙∙

What you will understand after reading this chapter

The world economy is an exciting topic. The collapse of the centrally planned economies, the oil crisis, the Great Depression in the 1930s, the failure of Latin America in the lost decade of the 1980s and the success of the Asian 'tigers' in spite of the temporary financial disturbance in 1997/1998 – these are all fascinating issues (section 1.1). The world economy is becoming more global. The segmentation of markets is being reduced; new regions, which have until recently scarcely been involved in world trade, are pushing into the international division of labor (section 1.2). The reader will be familiarized with the most important variables of the world economy, notably world product and its composition from the production and the expenditure side as well as its regional structure (section 1.3). The world economy is in a process of continuous change. Thus, the newly industrializing countries have succeeded in becoming much more integrated into the international division of labor (section 1.4). Meanwhile some of them have reached remarkable places in the ranking of competitiveness (section 1.5). For these and other problems we have to take a global view, as if the world is being analyzed from outer space (section 1.6).

1.1 Seven pictures of the world economy

Picture 1

Let us turn back the clock some 140 years. At that time, Japan was a closed economy without significant international relations in either the economic or the cultural field. During the Meiji Revolution in 1868, Japan opened itself consciously to the outside world. For the early periods of the opening process and of its development, it is reported that Japan started to produce spokes for imported bicycles and in this way pursued a policy of import substitution. At the end of the 1920s, Japan had become an important exporting country with a share of the world export volume of approximately 3 percent. After Japan's breakdown owing to the Second World War, Japan had to start building the economy up again. In 1950, Japan had a relatively insignificant position in the world economy; its share of the world export volume was 1 percent. Today, Japan provides nearly one tenth of the world export volume, and its efficient industry is, in spite of some problems in the 1990s, challenging North America as well as Europe.

How does a country manage to integrate itself successfully into the international division of labor? How does an open country efficiently use its resources so that it reaches a maximum of welfare gains from trade? Which mechanisms cause an economy to produce those export goods that are demanded in the world? What does a policy concept with a consistent international orientation look like? Where are the limits of the process of economic growth through trade? Does continuing success with export goods mean that worldwide demand for the currency of the country is growing considerably, eventually culminating in an appreciation so that price competitiveness is partly eaten away? Has Japan run into structural problems in the 1990s that will severely affect its growth potential? What experience on catching up do we have for other countries?

Picture 2

After 1945, the centrally planned economies of Eastern Europe could not reduce their development gap to the US. Whereas during the 1950s and the 1960s relatively high real growth rates of the communist countries could still be recorded, the 1970s are characterized by very low growth rates. During the 1980s, the communist systems collapsed. They could not adequately provide their citizens with goods. In Figure 1.1, the relative distance to the US level of GDP per capita is denoted on the horizontal axis, growth rates are depicted on the vertical axis. High growth rates in a decade would move a country to an improved relative position to the US. Note that purchasing power parities are used; nevertheless comparisons may be distorted.

What are the reasons for this failure of the communist system? Apart from an inefficient planning system, lacking property rights and setting wrong incentives, how important was the so-called 'division of labor planned from above' for the miscarriage? How relevant was the attempt of the centrally planned socialist economies in the COMECON (Council of Mutual Economic Assistance) in Eastern Europe to exploit economies of scale in production by an explicit process of specialization? Buses for the COMECON countries were produced in Hungary, tramcars in former Czechoslovakia, and railway cars in former East Germany. This specialization, planned from above, eliminated competition between the COMECON economies which were exempted from international competition anyway.

How can we explain why economies do not catch up, cannot keep up their prosperity level or even suffer a self-inflicted erosion of their economic competitiveness relative to other countries? How long can governments conceal such processes from their population? When do people, drawing comparisons with other countries, become aware of their deteriorated economic situation? How can the post-communist reform countries be integrated into the international division of labor? Under what conditions will countries fall behind?

Picture 3

The story of economic growth of different regions of the world is told in Figure 1.2. Latin America recorded weak economic growth in the five decades from 1950 until 1997 and had a negative growth rate in the 1980s, its 'lost decade'. It pursued an economic policy that was not successful. By means of an import substitution policy, it partly excluded itself from the international division of labor. Imports were hindered, and domestic sectors were not exposed to international competition. Until the 1980s, for example, Mexico had a system of import licenses where, as a rule, an import license was linked to a stronger peso in a system of split exchange rates. In this way, license holders could buy imported goods at a preferential price. This system was governed by a bureaucracy which made it possible for the politicians in charge to exert political power. Mexico did not give up this policy until the 1980s and joined the GATT only in 1986. The positive growth rates of Latin American countries in the 1950s, 1960s, 1970s and 1990s were not sufficient to reduce the income gap relative to the US, where the growth rate was higher.

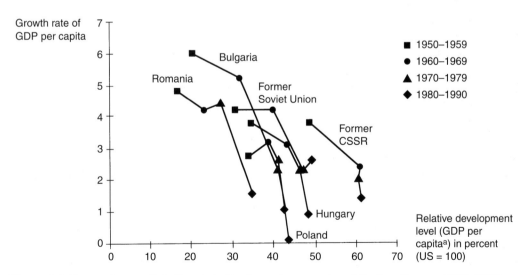

Figure 1.1 Economic growth in the centrally planned economies of Eastern Europe, 1950–1990

[a] Calculated with purchasing power parity.
Source: Heitger (1993), according to data from Summers and Heston (1988, 1991).

3

The development of the Asian countries on the Pacific rim took a different course. They were basically characterized by an international orientation of their economic policy and exposed their economies to competition from abroad. On average, discrimination in favor of the domestic relative to the external sector was not prevalent. Until the Asian financial crisis of 1997/1998, the four 'tigers' (Hong Kong, South Korea, Taiwan, Singapore) had real growth rates of 6 percent (and higher) for five decades.

The COMECON countries had negative growth rates in the 1980s. On average they have fallen behind in their income position relative to the US. In the 1990s, this result is especially due to the developments in Russia, Belarus and the Ukraine; the Eastern European countries have been more successful in the transformation process.

Western Europe has caught up with the United States in the four decades since 1950,

but fell back a little in the 1990s when the growth process in the US economy became stronger again and when capital accumulation proceeded there at a higher pace than in Western Europe.

What are the necessary ingredients for a successful growth process? Why do countries stagnate relative to others, why do some fall back? Did those countries pursuing a policy of import substitution and protection from foreign trade deprive themselves of possible development prospects and potential welfare gains? What is the relationship between international orientation and economic growth? Do open economies experience stronger growth?

Picture 4

At the time of the Great Depression at the beginning of the 1930s, the world economy experienced a massive breakdown. The

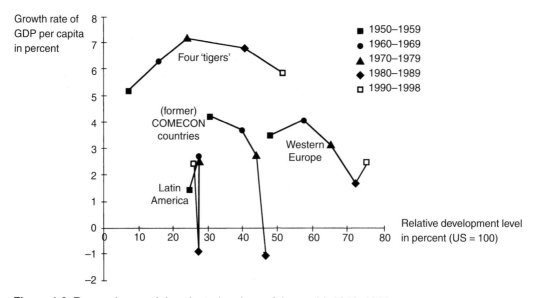

Figure 1.2 Economic growth in selected regions of the world, 1950–1998

Source for data: Heitger (1993); IMF, *International Financial Statistics*, CD-ROM, 2000; World Bank, *World Development Indicators,* CD-ROM, 2000.

volume of world trade fell to one third of its former level within four years. The so-called Kindleberger spiral shows how the world import volume of 75 countries, which can be regarded as a world trade indicator, dwindled from month to month (Figure 1.3).

What would be the effects of such a break-down of world trade today? For instance, the US is exporting 10 percent of its GDP; a fall of its exports to one third would mean a reduction of 3 percent of aggregate demand – a severe recession. Or take Germany which exports about one third of its GDP. Here, a drop in the export volume to one third would

represent an 11 percent drop in aggregate demand and a devastating depression. Related questions are: Can monetary and financial crises spread into the real sphere of the economy? Under what conditions can a regional crisis like the Mexican crisis in 1994/1995 and the Asian crisis in 1997/1998 be contained? Under what conditions is contagion inevitable?

Picture 5

During the two oil price shocks in the 1970s the oil price increased nearly twentyfold

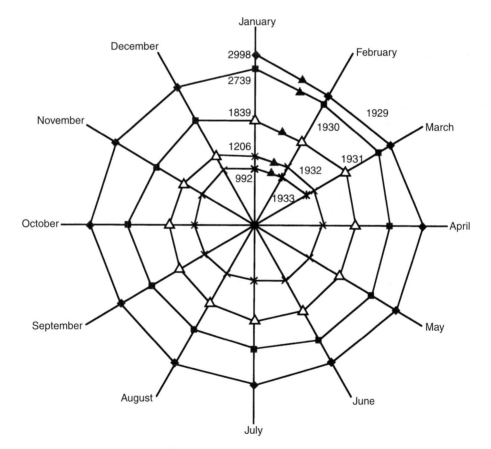

Figure 1.3 The Kindleberger spiral[a]

[a] World import volume in million US gold-$.
Source: Kindleberger (1973, p. 172).

compared to the 1960s (Figure 1.4). Whereas in the 1960s the oil price was significantly below US$2 per barrel of crude oil, it increased fivefold to approximately US$10 during the first oil crisis in 1973/1974. During the second oil price shock in 1979/1980, the price per barrel rose from US$12 to nearly US$40. The reason for this development was that the resource countries claimed the property rights to the crude oil reserves in their soil. In this way the seven big international oil companies were cut off from their supply sources. Under the terms of the concession contracts that were used until then, the oil firms had to pay a given percentage of their proceeds for the extracted amounts of oil (royalty). De facto, they were in charge of the oil extraction and also had the right (often for a period of up to 70 years) to tap new oil wells. At the beginning of the 1970s, the oil exploitation rights moved to the resource countries. As a consequence, the world's oil supply could no longer be allocated in the vertical hierarchy of the enterprises (extraction, refinery, transport, distribution). Instead, markets – especially the Rotterdam spot market, but later on also forward markets – increasingly took over the allocation of oil.

The impact of the oil crisis was that the capital stock, geared to the low oil prices of the 1960s, became partly obsolete, especially the machines in the production processes and the engines of the means of transport. The productivity of existing capital fell, and this had effects on production, employment and growth. At the same time, a redistribution of real income in favor of the oil-producing countries took place. The countries without oil resources, particularly the industrialized nations, had to give away more export goods per barrel of imported oil than before, their terms of trade deteriorated. In the end, the oil-producing countries had considerable petro-dollar earnings at their disposal which could not be completely absorbed by their imports. A petro-dollar recycling took place which later became the germ cell of the debt crisis of the developing countries.

How does the world economy cope with such a sudden shortage of a production factor? What adjustment processes have to take place? Are economies that depend strongly on the import of a natural resource able to reduce their demand for this resource in the middle and long run? Is it possible, at least partially, to substitute those resource inputs which become more expensive by other production factors? Is import demand inelastic? How is the income distribution between the production factors affected by such an adjustment process? How does the political process of a country deal with such a shortage?

Picture 6

Since the 1960s, consciousness concerning scarcity in the environment has been growing, especially in the industrialized nations. In contrast to the oil crisis, this has not induced a sudden cutback of the supply of a resource but the beginning of a long-term and lengthy process in which countries change the framework for using the environment by defining new property rights. The environment is not only a national factor of endowment requiring national policy approaches; some aspects of the environment represent an international public good for which worldwide user rights have to be developed.

What effects does such a long-term redefinition of the institutional framework for environmental use have on the international division of labor? Do particular countries lose competitiveness in specific economic branches? Do other countries gain comparative price advantages? How are trade flows and capital flows adjusted to environmental scarcity? What solutions are offered for global environmental activities like the protection of the ozone layer?

Picture 7

After the opening up of Central and Eastern Europe and with the integration of China into the international division of labor, a huge and radical change is taking place in the world economy. Countries well endowed with the production factor of labor are starting to participate in the international division of labor. The integration of China alone, with 1.2 billion people, means that the effective supply in the world labor market increases by one fifth.

What impact does such an increase in the effective labor supply have on the world economy? Is it true that prices of labor-intensively produced goods will have to fall?

Will the incomes of workers that have produced these goods in industrialized countries up to now have to fall as well? Will countries now take refuge in protection? To what extent will the regions being newly integrated into the world economy represent attractive markets? What stimulating effects will originate from these additional markets? Are these stimulating effects strong enough to compensate the industrialized countries which may lose in labor-intensive goods? Will the industrialized countries as a whole gain or lose?

The common element of these seven pictures is that change is taking place in the world economy. This could be a sudden shock for the world economy, like the oil price shock or the collapse of world trade and production in the Great Depression of the 1930s. But change can also be a long-term, 'historical' process that develops gradually such as the gradual decline of the economies in Eastern Europe, the poor performance of Latin America in the decades from 1950 until 1990

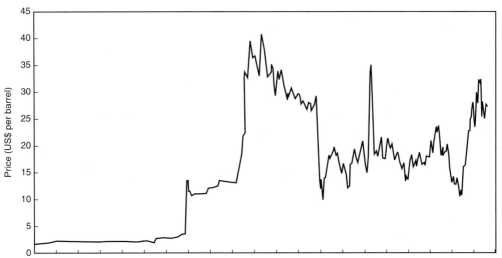

Figure 1.4 The world oil price

Source for data: IMF, *International Financial Statistics*, CD-ROM, 2000.

and the slowly increasing awareness of the environmental problem.

1.2 *What does globalization mean?*

In the 1990s, globalization has become a key word. By 'globalization' we mean a reduction of market segmentations and an increasing interdependence of national markets. We shall now look at the catalysts for globalization and at its impact.

Reasons for globalization

In the world economy we can observe a whole string of tendencies that lead to globalization:

- Transport and communication costs have fallen significantly in recent decades. This holds for the traditional costs of covering distances by sea and air (which have been reduced to approximately one fifth since the 1920s and 1930s respectively) as well as for the costs of telecommunication (Figure 1.5). For instance, a three-minute telephone call from New York to London in 1930 cost US$250 (in constant prices of 1990), in 1950 it was US$50 and in 1990 just US$3.32; the price for processing information fell from US$1 per instruction per second in 1975 to one cent in 1994 (World Bank, *World Development Report 1995*, p. 45). The costs of using satellites have also fallen dramatically.
- With regard to information technology, the world is experiencing a revolution. The World Wide Web represents a powerful global information network. In 1998, 180 million Internet stations participated in this worldwide network. According to industry estimates, it will probably increase to half a billion in 2002.
- The reduction of political tensions (e.g. the

Cold War, apartheid in South Africa), regional efforts towards integration, for example in Europe, and the strengthening of multilateral trade agreements also have eliminated impediments to trade.

- The radical change in the former centrally planned economies of Central and Eastern Europe and the opening of China have integrated important regions of the world into the international division of labor. Taking India into account as well, a historical process is taking place, in which more than 40 percent of the world's population is additionally integrated into the world economy. This implies that the limitation of the size of markets, which was a possible barrier for the extension of the international division of labor in the past, will be less important in the future.
- Most developing and newly industrializing countries have changed their strategies for development and foreign trade and are now much more open. Sixty-seven countries have joined the WTO from early 1985 to 2001 including China.
- Apart from measures which explicitly restrict trade, national regulations are increasingly being reviewed. They are continuously adjusted in a process of institutional competition, thus resulting in fewer impediments as well.

The impact of globalization

Globalization means that market segmentations in product and factor markets are reduced and that national markets become more interdependent. The allocation mechanism is working globally, so that international differences in prices will lead to arbitrage. Globalization means that differences in supply and demand conditions of different countries can be leveled out more easily by international exchange. Market participants have to adjust to this global mechanism of allocation. Firms maximizing their profits have to consider essential repercussions in worldwide markets.

Globalization of markets must not be confused with the centralization of decision processes. The increasing interdependence does not imply a centralization of decisions. Decisions are still, or even more so, made in a decentralized way. The globalization of markets and the decentralization of decisions are supported and stimulated by new technologies for organization and communication, e.g. CAD (computer-aided design), CIM (computer-integrated manufacturing), by software that allows immediate control of the decentralized units, by groupware that can be

used by several users simultaneously. But decisions now have to be made under different restrictions, because the options of globalized markets and of a high mobility of factors of production have to be taken into account. A highly integrated world economy, above all the decreasing costs for transport and communication, increases the possibility of a fragmentation of production. An increasing fragmentation of production also means that locations can be changed more easily.

In combination with the fragmentation of production, the increasingly global orientation of firms will go hand in hand with growing intra-firm trade. Direct investment (see below) as a predecessor of future trade flows will gain in importance.

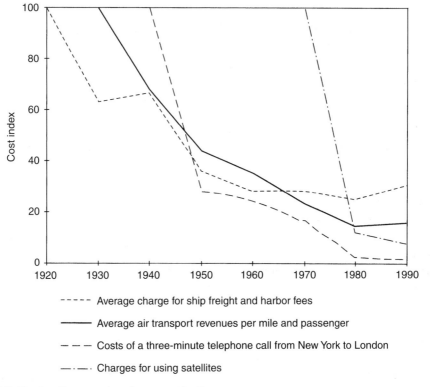

----- Average charge for ship freight and harbor fees

⸺ Average air transport revenues per mile and passenger

— — — Costs of a three-minute telephone call from New York to London

—·—· Charges for using satellites

Figure 1.5 Costs of transport and communication

Source: World Bank, World Development Report 1995, p. 51.

The reduction of market segmentations will not only strengthen the commodity arbitrage between different supply conditions in the traditional sense of inter-sectoral trade, but it will also allow different product preferences of consumers to come into play. Product variety is an important aspect of trade. In this respect, intra-sectoral trade will become more important.

Services

The increasing integration of the world economy changes the conditions for the trade in services. By 'trade in services' we mean several quite diverse phenomena: a service like an international telephone call may actually cross a border ('cross-border supply'), consumers or firms of one country may use the service in another country ('consumption abroad'), a service may be supplied in another country ('commercial presence') or individuals may travel to supply their service in another country ('presence of natural persons'). The diversity of services becomes apparent by the WTO classification list with seven main categories (and 62 subcategories), namely distribution services, education services, communication services (including telecommunication services, audio-visual services such as motion picture production and distribution, radio and television services), healthcare services, professional services (including legal services, accounting services, data processing, business consultancy, advertising services, architecture, engineering), transportation services, and travel and tourism services. In addition, there are also other areas such as financial services (bank services, trade in stocks and shares, the insurance business).

A major distinction of service categories is between border-crossing and local services, analogously to tradable and non-tradable goods. Applying these categories, another distinction becomes relevant, namely between 'person-disembodied' and 'person-embodied' services (Bhagwati 1984; Klodt *et al.* 1994). Disembodied services, like detail engineering using computer programs, the development of software or accounting data processing are not 'embodied' in persons. They do not require business partners to meet locally when the service is carried out. For the international trading order, these services (cross-border supply) are not very different from tangible goods. Just as commodities are carried by the transport system, disembodied services cross national borders by means of communication media.

The increased importance of trade in services has not been observed for the last 20 years (Siebert and Klodt 1999). Although approximately 20 percent of world trade is trade in services, this ratio has stagnated since 1975. However, the new communication technologies are likely to make trade in disembodied services grow ever more intensively. The stronger the tertiarization processes are in the industrialized nations, i.e. the increase of the share of services in GNP, the more important international trade in services is going to be. Moreover, extending the WTO rule system to services should be favorable to the trade in services.

Increasing interdependence of factor markets

The reduction of impediments to international mobility not only refers to commodity markets but also to factor markets. In particular, capital mobility is becoming more important, and foreign direct investment plays an important role for capital movements across borders. Different motives are relevant. For example, it may be desirable to be present in an expanding market, to avoid transaction costs or to circumvent the political segmentation of markets due to foreign trade policy. But direct investment also follows comparative cost advantages, where expected locational advantages are anticipated. In this respect, direct investment today is the predecessor of trade in commodities tomorrow.

Since the 1980s, foreign direct investment has grown considerably faster than world trade (Figure 1.6, Table 1.1) and, if one neglects recessions, world trade measured in real terms has grown considerably stronger than world production. World industrial production increased with a real growth rate of approximately 2 percent per year from 1985 until 1997 and the world trade volume by 6 percent, as measured by the real world export volume. Foreign direct investment, though extremely volatile, rose by 13 percent. These figures indicate a growing interdependence in the world.

Labor markets are becoming substantially more global for those with high qualifications, e.g. management. Apart from this, for the most part labor markets remain nationally segmented. But this does not imply that there is no international competition between workplaces. Interdependence has an indirect effect; for instance, via trade flows and capital mobility.

International interdependence of financial markets

Besides foreign direct investment, portfolio capital has become extremely mobile; it now can be moved immediately worldwide from one financial market to another.

1.3 *World gross product*

The world gross product amounted to approximately US$30.2 trillion in 1999

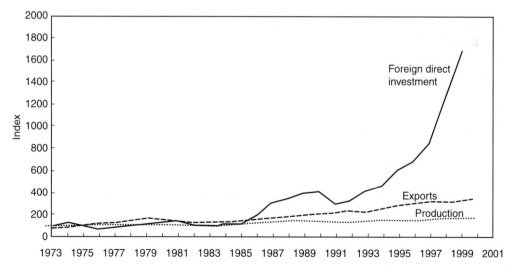

Figure 1.6 World industrial production, world trade and foreign direct investment, 1973–2000[a]

[a] Indices; 1973 = 100. Exports without services. Foreign direct investments adjusted with the US industrial goods price index.
Source for data: IMF, *International Financial Statistics*, CD-ROM, December 2001; World Bank, *World Development Indicators*, CD-ROM, 2000; own calculations.

Table 1.1 Growth rates of world industrial production, world trade and foreign direct investments, 1985–2000[a]

Year	World industrial production	World trade[b]	Foreign direct investment
1985	2.4	0.9	3.8
1986	1.2	13.1	60.6
1987	4.1	15.1	56.2
1988	5.0	10.4	12.0
1989	3.6	3.6	17.7
1990	1.6	9.6	−0.6
1991	−0.8	2.0	−24.5
1992	−0.7	5.6	7.4
1993	−1.0	−1.2	28.3
1994	3.9	12.2	10.8
1995	3.7	15.0	32.7
1996	2.4	2.8	12.8
1997	4.5	3.2	23.7
1998	0.7	0.7	48.2
1999	2.4	2.0	32.4
2000	5.2	5.5	n.a.

[a] All rates measured in percent.
[b] Exports.

Sources: IMF, *International Financial Statistics*, CD-ROM, July 2001; World Bank, *World Development Indicators*, CD-ROM, 2000; World Bank, *World Development Report 2000/2001*; own calculations.

(World Bank, *World Development Report 1999*, Table 12). Lower income countries had a GNP per capita of less than US$755. Countries with higher income had a GNP per capita larger than US$9,265 (1999). Medium income countries were between US$756 and US$9,265 (World Bank, *World Development Report 2001/2002*).

With respect to the term 'world gross product', a note to the reader is required. When we look at a single country, we distinguish between two concepts: gross domestic product (GDP) and gross national product (GNP). Gross domestic product is the product generated by the factors of production located in a country including foreigners working in the country and capital in the country even if owned by foreigners. Gross national product is the income accruing to all citizens of a country including income from work (for instance of expatriates) and capital income earned in foreign countries.

On the world scale, GDP and GNP yield the same total when summed up over all countries, as (at least so far) no factor of production is active far outside the planet Earth. In this regard we could use the term 'world product'. However, since we have become used to the term 'GDP' (gross domestic product) and since we will continuously be comparing the country view to the world view in this book, we will use the term 'world gross domestic product', or 'world GDP'. Where GDP data are not available, GNP data will be applied.

Viewed from the production side, services, with a share of 63 percent, are the most important sector of the world domestic product. The industrial sector contributes

31 percent and agriculture 5 percent (Table 1.2). Countries with a lower per capita income (according to the World Bank classification, those countries with a per capita income of less than US$756 per year) are heavily specialized in agriculture. Countries with high income (US$9,265 or more per year) have a relatively large share in services.

From the expenditure side, private consumption contributes the biggest share to the world gross domestic product, with more than 60 percent. Gross investment is at about 23 percent and government consumption at 15 percent (Table 1.3). Countries with a medium income show a higher share in gross investment. In all three groups of countries investment is financed from domestic savings and not through a negative current account.

The regional structure of the world domestic product is shown in Figure 1.7: the gross domestic products of the economies with a lower, medium or higher income are US$1.0 trillion, US$6.6 trillion and US$24.7 trillion, respectively. The US contributes 31 percent to the world domestic product, Japan 15 percent, Germany 6 percent. The share of the other OECD countries is of a similar dimension to that of the US (29 percent – without Germany and Japan). China accounts for 3 percent of the world domestic product. The world market share (Figure 1.8) differ from the production share.

With its US$10 trillion economy, the United States is the largest country of the world measured in terms of gross national product. China is the largest country measured in terms of population (Table 1.4).

1.4 Economic change in the world economy

The world economy is in a process of permanent change. Since 1980, economic growth

Table 1.2 World domestic product, production approach by sectors (2000), in percent of the world domestic product[a]

	Agriculture	Industry	Services
Countries with lower income	23	33	44
Countries with medium income	11	36	54
Countries with higher income	2	31	67
World	5	31	63

[a] World Bank, *World Development Report 2000/2001*, Table 12.
Source: World Bank, *World Development Report 2002*, Table 3.

Table 1.3 World domestic product, expenditure approach (2000), in percent of world domestic product

	Government consumption	Private consumption	Gross investments	Gross savings	Current account
Countries with lower income	11	69	21	21	0
Countries with medium income	12	62	25	26	1
Countries with higher income	16	62	22	23	1
World	15	62	23	23	0

Source fore data: World Bank, *World Development Report 2001/2002*, Table 3.

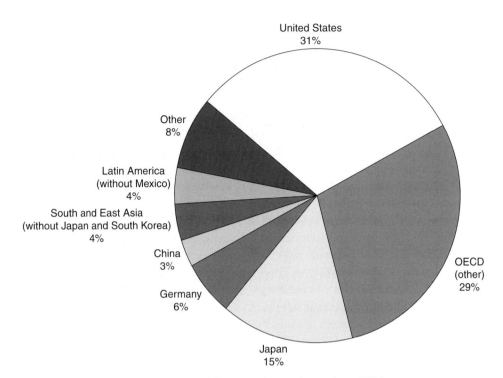

Figure 1.7 Regional structure of the world's gross domestic product, 2000

Source for data: World Bank, *World Development Report 2001/2002*, Table 3.

Table 1.4 The ten largest countries of the world

GNP (billions of US$, 2000)			Population (millions, 2000)		
1	United States	9,883	1	China	1,261
2	Japan	4,677	2	India	1,016
3	Germany	1,870	3	United States	282
4	France	1,413	4	Indonesia	210
5	United Kingdom	1,286	5	Brazil	170
6	Italy	1,069	6	Russia	146
7	China	1,080	7	Pakistan	138
8	Brazil	690	8	Bangladesh	130
9	Canada	588	9	Japan	127
10	Spain	555	10	Nigeria	127

Source for data: World Bank, *World Development Report 2000/2001*, Table 1.

has been roughly at 3 percent per year; in the 1990s it was at 2.5 percent (Table 1.5). Quite a few of the developing countries are growing at a higher rate; for instance, the four Asian 'tigers' (Hong Kong, Korea, Malaysia, Singapore) at 6 percent and more before the financial crisis of 1997/1998 (Figure 1.9). The industrialized countries have a lower growth

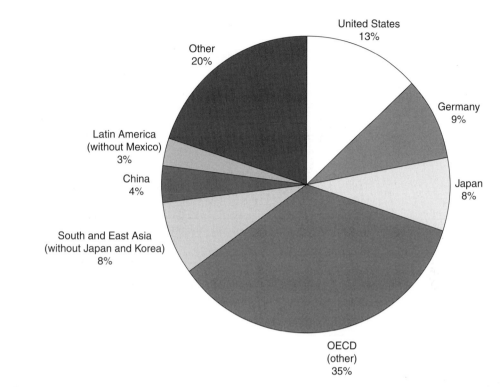

Figure 1.8 Regional structure of world trade, 2000

Source for data: IMF, *International Financial Statistics*, CD-ROM, May 2001, World Tables, Exports (DZF).

Table 1.5 GDP growth rates, 1980–2000

	1980–1990[a]	*1990–2000*[b]
World	3.2	2.6
Low-income countries	4.4	3.4
Middle-income countries	3.2	3.6
High-income countries	3.1	2.4

Sources:
[a] World Bank, *World Development Report 2000/2001*, Table 11.
[b] World Bank, *World Development Report 2001/2002*, Table 3.

rate of 2–3 percent. The transformation countries in Central and Eastern Europe have experienced negative growth rates during the period of transformation. Russia still has negative growth rates. Note that the process of economic growth in the world economy is influenced by business cycles.

Since 1970, the developing and newly industrializing countries as a whole have succeeded in integrating themselves into the international division of labor. Their contribution to world trade has grown from 18 percent in 1975 to 30 percent in 2000 (Figure 1.10). The newly industrializing countries of

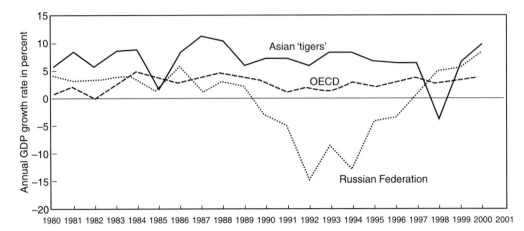

Figure 1.9 Growth in the world economy, 1980–2000[a]

[a] Asian 'tigers': Hong Kong, Singapore, South Korea and Taiwan.
Source: World Bank, *World Development Indicators*, CD-ROM, 2000; World Bank, *World Development Report 2000/2001*; OECD-DATABASE, Datastream, December 2001.

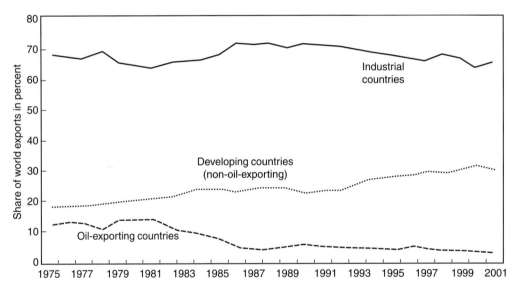

Figure 1.10 Shares of world export ,1975–2001: industrial countries and developing countries

Source for data: IMF, *International Financial Statistics*, CD-ROM, August 2001; oil-exporting countries in 2000 and all 2001 data: preliminary estimates.

Asia on the Pacific rim, especially managed to realize high gains. They significantly increased the share of industry products in their exports, e.g. Singapore from 34 percent (1965) to 84 percent (1996). The world market share of the four 'tigers' (Hong Kong, Singapore, South Korea and Taiwan) grew from approximately 3 percent in 1975 to approximately 10 percent in 1999 (Figure 1.11). In comparison, the African continent south of

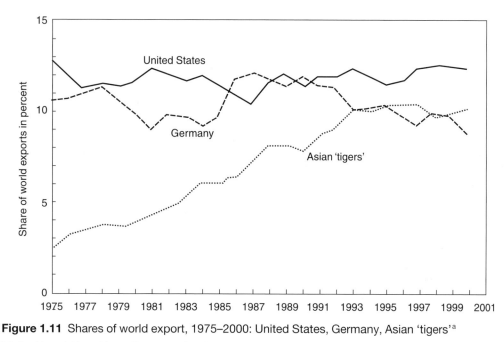

Figure 1.11 Shares of world export, 1975–2000: United States, Germany, Asian 'tigers'[a]

[a] Asian 'tigers': Hong Kong, Singapore, South Korea and Taiwan.
Source for data: IMF, *International Financial Statistics*, CD-ROM, December 2001.

the Sahara, with a world market share below 2 percent, remains the poorhouse of the world for the time being.

1.5 A ranking of competitiveness

Several organizations compile rankings of competitiveness for all countries of the world. For instance, the World Economic Forum (2000) has developed a ranking of competitiveness for 59 countries from surveys and statistical information. The index underlying the ranking is composed of three sub-indices: the Economic Creativity Index measuring economically effective innovation or effective transfer of technology; the Finance Index measuring an efficient financial system with high rates of saving and investment; and the International Growth Competitiveness Index measuring greater economic integration of the country with the rest of the world. In this

context, the Growth Competitiveness Index itself measures factors that contribute to a high rate of growth in GDP per capita. The small open economies are positioned at especially high places. It is somewhat surprising to find Germany ranked only at position 15 (Table 1.6).

1.6 The global dimension

The subject of this book is the world economy. The book does not concentrate on a single open economy, i.e. an economy linked to other countries through trade or capital flows. Instead, it provides a global analysis of the structures and processes in the world economy, as if the world were looked at from outer space. In a time when the communication system is organized globally, when we can communicate from Buenos Aires to Kiel over the Internet and when huge quantities of

Table 1.6 Growth competitiveness ranking

Country	Competitiveness ranking 2000	Country	Competitiveness ranking 2000	Country	Competitiveness ranking 2000
United States	1	Japan	21	China	41
Singapore	2	France	22	Egypt	42
Luxembourg	3	Portugal	23	Mexico	43
Netherlands	4	Iceland	24	Indonesia	44
Ireland	5	Malaysia	25	Argentina	45
Finland	6	Hungary	26	Brazil	46
Canada	7	Spain	27	Jordan	47
Hong Kong	8	Chile	28	Peru	48
United Kingdom	9	Korea	29	India	49
Switzerland	10	Italy	30	El Salvador	50
Taiwan	11	Thailand	31	Bolivia	51
Australia	12	Czech Republic	32	Colombia	52
Sweden	13	South Africa	33	Vietnam	53
Denmark	14	Greece	34	Venezuela	54
Germany	15	Poland	35	Russia	55
Norway	16	Mauritius	36	Zimbabwe	56
Belgium	17	Philippines	37	Ukraine	57
Austria	18	Costa Rica	38	Bulgaria	58
Israel	19	Slovak Republic	39	Ecuador	59
New Zealand	20	Turkey	40		

Source: World Economic Forum, *The Global Competitiveness Report 2000*, Table 1.

data can be exchanged between Cambridge and Hangzhou, when CNN broadcasts news worldwide, when transport costs become less and less important and when more and more people become accustomed to finding their jobs in all parts of the world, such a world view of the economic processes and structures appears to be imperative.

Thus, the paradigm prevailing here is an analysis of the world as a whole. The world is first of all interpreted as an entity. This is true for the macroeconomic aggregates of the world economy, like the world's domestic product and the main components of world aggregate demand. It also refers to macroeconomic approaches to explain processes in the world economy, like cyclical movements or economic growth. In contrast to such a macroeconomic view, other aspects are rather microeconomic; for instance, an analysis of the world markets for goods, including adjustments to disturbances of equilibria on the commodity markets. In a similar way, this also holds for the world market's factors of production. A specific issue is the world money market and the financial markets. The volatility of financial and currency markets has an impact on the real sphere of the economy, and a crisis may jump from one country to another. An important issue is how a financial crisis can be prevented. In a further step, this global view can be abandoned to analyze different regions of the world, like developing countries and the new market economies (transition countries). In a more disaggregated outlook, processes of regional integration, including that in the European Union, are also of interest. Finally, it is interesting to examine the role which is left for national economic policy in the world economy today, to look at potential conflicts between the national interest and global concerns and to study the institutional arrangements which should be developed for the world economy.

Part I

The World Goods and Factor Markets and Economic Growth

···

Being interested in the world economy, we have to answer the question how the division of labor is carried out and how development and growth processes can be explained. We first analyze the division of labor under static conditions. In a paradigm of allocation, markets are important, notably product markets (Chapter 2) and factor markets (Chapter 3). Second, we study how the division of labor in the world changes over time and how the process of economic growth can be explained (Chapter 4).

The world product markets

· ·

What you will understand after reading this chapter

The reduced costs of economic distance and the integration of the newly industrializing countries as well as of the new market economies have changed the equilibrium of the world product markets. The supply of commodities has increased and at the same time new markets have arisen. In order to examine these effects, we first look at world product markets (section 2.1) and the world market equilibrium on the product markets (section 2.2). Then the effects of the reduction of trade barriers and the rising labor supply will be discussed (sections 2.3 and 2.4). The impact of a labor supply increase on factor income and on employment is a major point (section 2.5). The most important theorems on the international division of labor will be briefly summarized (section 2.6). Shifts of demand and a changed demarcation line between tradable and non-tradable goods also play their role (sections 2.7 and 2.8). Some world markets are characterized by imperfect competition (section 2.9); imperfect competition is associated with intra-sectoral trade (section 2.10). The question is raised whether markets are contestable when economies of scale exist and different preferences have to be taken into account (section 2.11). Markets are discussed as approaches to the inter-national division of labor (sections 2.12 and 2.13). The export structure of countries is reviewed (section 2.14). We also discuss the influence of the real exchange rate on exports (section 2.15).

2.1 The world product markets

From an international perspective, it is interesting to study world product markets, for instance the world oil market or the world coal market (see case studies). The analysis of these and other product markets would lead us to answer questions like the following: To what extent is such a market integrated worldwide and to what extent is it segmented? Where does production take place? Do we have a vertical structure of production? Is the value-added chain of production sliced up? What are the backward and forward linkages of production? To what extent is production separated spatially from demand? Is the industry vertically integrated? Or do markets perform the allocation of production and investment decisions? What are future trends of an industry? And which major factors influence these trends?

2.2 The world market equilibrium

The concept of the world market equilibrium

The world product markets are in equilibrium if there is no excess demand. The prices on the markets must adjust in such a way that this condition is satisfied. We express this condition with

$$E_i^W = C_i^W - Q_i^W = 0 \qquad (2.1)$$

Excess demand (E_i^W), that is the difference between demand (C_i^W) and supply (Q_i^W), must be equal to zero for each good i. Then, the world market is cleared. When supply or demand conditions on a world market change, the price has to change as well.

In a world market equilibrium not only has the excess demand for a commodity to be equal to zero. In addition, it must hold that firms have found their profit maximum with their supply and households their utility maximum with their demand. For firms, this condition is fulfilled if the commodity price ratio corresponds to the marginal costs ratio. To clarify this, we introduce the concept of the world transformation curve (curve *VWX* in Figure 2.3). It indicates – for a given factor endowment and technology – the maximum production quantity of good 1 for a given production quantity of good 2. The marginal rate of transformation (slope of the transformation curve) dQ_2/dQ_1 indicates the opportunity costs of producing an additional unit of good 1, measured in units of good 2 forgone. It shows to what extent it is possible from the production side to produce more of a good by means of diverting the factors of production away from the other good. The marginal rate of transformation corresponds to the ratio of marginal costs. The commodity price ratio p also indicates the relative valuation of the two goods by the households. From the supply side of the economy an equilibrium exists if the commodity price ratio corresponds to the inverse ratio of the marginal rate of transformation $p = p_1/p_2 = |dQ_2/dQ_1|$. In Figure 2.3, the commodity price ratio p is given by a straight line with the angle α. It corresponds to the quantity ratio Q_2/Q_1 (where Q_i *denotes units of good i*), in this way indicating how many units of good 2 can be exchanged for one unit of good 1.

The quantities of the two goods produced at point *W* amount to the world domestic product. Valued with the relative price p and measured in units of good 1, the world domestic product is given by the distance *OT*. Measured in units of good 2, the world domestic product is shown by the distance *OY*.

The point of production on the world transformation curve depends on the demand conditions, because demand and supply together determine the relative price that clears the market in accordance with equation 2.1. The relative price of the equilibrium can be determined with the usual demand–supply

Case studies

As an example of a world good market, the world crude oil market with the observed prices for a barrel of oil and the traded quantities is shown in Figure 2.1. In the 1960s, demand increased and supply expanded; the price remained nearly constant. In the two oil crises of 1973/1974 and 1979/1980, supply remained constant and even declined during the second crisis, whereas prices jumped. In the early 1980s, prices fell. In 2000 and 2001, the oil price increased again while the quantity remained constant.

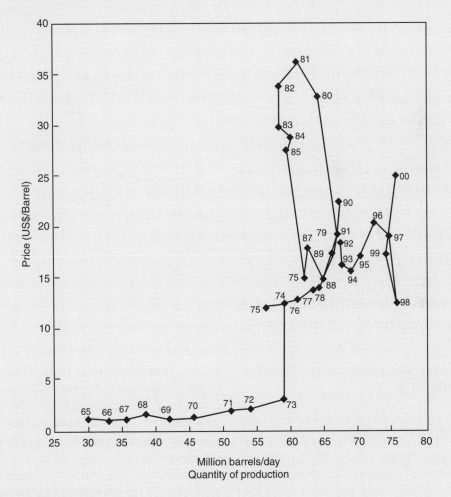

Figure 2.1 World oil market

Source for data: OECD, *Economic Outlook*, July 2000.

Figure 2.2 shows another example of a world product market, the long-term world supply curve for hard coal. On the horizontal axis the mining capacity is shown. The mining costs vary significantly between different suppliers from US$12 per (metric) ton in China to US$195 per ton in Germany. In this context, we have to distinguish between extraction costs for open-pit mining (o) and for underground mining (u). The supply curve shown comprises 85 percent of the worldwide mining capacity.

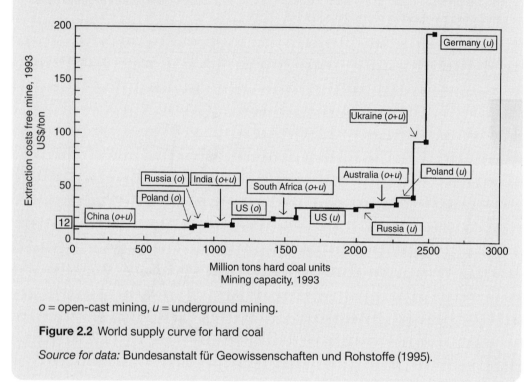

o = open-cast mining, u = underground mining.

Figure 2.2 World supply curve for hard coal

Source for data: Bundesanstalt für Geowissenschaften und Rohstoffe (1995).

diagram or with the help of the Marshall–Mill offer curves.

Demand–supply diagram

In Figure 2.4a, the relative price $p = p_1/p_2$ is shown on the vertical axis in the usual market diagram. The quantity of good 1 is depicted on the horizontal axis. If the relative price p is high the demand for good 1 is low; with the relative price going down demand for good 1 increases (demand curve $C_1^W(p)$). The supply curve can be derived graphically from Figure 2.3. The point of the maximum production of

good 1 corresponds to the point V' (point V of the transformation curve in Figure 2.3); the point of zero production of good 1 corresponds to the point X' (point X in Figure 2.3). The positive slope of the supply curve represents the increasing marginal rate of transformation, that is the increasing marginal costs of the production of good 1. The movement along the supply curve corresponds to the movement along the transformation curve. The relative price of the equilibrium is determined by point W at the intersection of the supply and the demand curve. In Figure 2.4b, the excess demand for

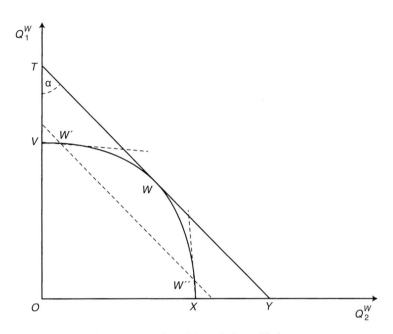

Figure 2.3 World transformation curve and world market equilibrium

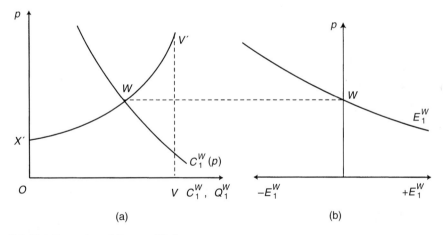

(a)   (b)

Figure 2.4 Relative price of the equilibrium

good 1 is derived from the horizontal difference between quantities demanded and supplied.

Offer curves

The world market equilibrium can also be described by the Marshall–Mill offer curves.

For this analysis, the world market is divided into two regions, home and foreign. In Figure 2.5 the home and foreign offer curves are shown (in this context good 1 is the home export good and good 2 the foreign export good). The offer curve of a country indicates how many units of the import good have to

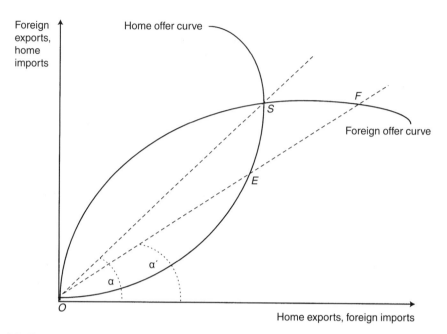

Figure 2.5 Equilibrium with the Marshall–Mill offer curves

be offered to a country in exchange for its export good. The shape of the offer curve of a country is explained by the following:

- The increasing marginal production costs of a good: the increasing marginal rate of transformation when moving along the transformation curve of a country indicates that the opportunity costs of a good increases with the amount being produced. Therefore, the offer curve is upward sloping.
- The substitution effect: with an increasing relative price of a good (the export good) demand for this good decreases and demand for the other good (the import good) rises correspondingly. This effect also causes a positive slope of the offer curve.
- The income effect: the rising relative price p means an increase in real income for the home country, because it gets more units of the import good for one unit of its export good, i.e. its terms of trade improve. With

higher income, demand for each of the two goods increases. In this way, the income effect runs contrary to the substitution effect.

The equilibrium is reached at point S with a relative price p that is given by the tangent of the angle α. At point S, excess supply of the export good of the home country and excess demand of the import demand of the foreign country are identical. The market is cleared. Along the straight line with the gradient α', however, the points E and F signal that at the given relative price the home country's trade offer does not correspond to the offer of the foreign country. There is excess demand for good 1 and excess supply of good 2. Consequently, the relative price p must rise.

The law of one price

The world market is characterized by the law of one price. If no trade barriers exist and if transport costs equal zero, that is if markets are not segmented, the same price must be observed everywhere for a homogeneous good. This is a significant simplification, of course, but it helps to make an important aspect perfectly clear, namely spatial arbitrage. As long as there are price differentials it is worthwhile to arbitrage them away by moving goods from one location to another.

2.3 The reduction of trade barriers and the world market equilibrium

The reduction of trade barriers, for example as a result of lower transport and communication costs, means that arbitrage is intensified and that the efficiency gains rise. The world transformation curve moves outward.

The world transformation curve results from the transformation curves of each individual country. Figure 2.6 shows the special case of two countries. In order to keep the argument simple we assume that initially both countries are in autarky. Alternatively, the initial situation may be interpreted as having some trade, but the level of trade can be expanded if market segmentations are reduced. The transformation curves are drawn in such a way that the production points A and A^* of the two countries coincide in one point. In this case, world production is given by point O^*. But the states of autarky A, A^* in the two countries do not represent a world market equilibrium, because relative prices differ and because without trade barriers it is worthwhile for the home country to produce more of good 1 (moving in the direction of an increasing production of good Q_1 on its transformation curve). At the same time, it is worthwhile for the foreign country to produce more of good 2 until the price ratios in the two countries are brought in line with each other. This is the case at point P in Figure 2.6. The marginal rates of transformation in the two countries correspond to each other, and they correspond to the uniform

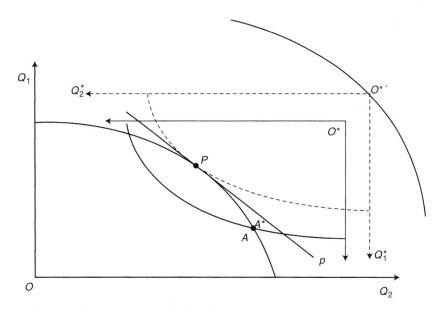

Figure 2.6 Trade barriers and world transformation curve

price ratio in the world economy (straight line *p*). Point *P* means a higher output in the world economy (*O**). In this way the world as a whole gains from the transition from autarky (or from a low level of trade) to trade (or to more trade).

The world as a whole gains from the more intensive arbitrage that is made possible by the reduction of market segmentations. It can also be shown that each country gains from the higher level of trade. Take the home country and compare its budget space in the initial situation *A* and in the new situation *P*. In autarky, the home country has no other choice but to consume in point *A*. With free trade, the home country consumes on a point along line *p*. Its budget space has increased; it enjoys a higher welfare. Trade is an option to supply or demand goods at the given world market price. It offers welfare gains; otherwise, a country could always choose the state of autarky. Gains from trade will even occur if the other country behaves in a protectionist way (Free Trade for One theorem).

After the most important characteristics of the world market equilibrium have been discussed, it will be explained in the following how the world market equilibrium adjusts to disruptions.

2.4 Increase of labor supply and world market equilibrium

World market equilibrium will be disturbed, if the supply of a production factor changes. Factor abundance may also change gradually; for example, if the pollution of the environment is increasingly taken into account. Another relevant case is that the world labor supply increases. That is the present situation with the integration of China and the former centrally planned economies into the world economy. Assume that these countries were completely segmented in an initial situation. Let them then participate in the international division of labor. Then, integrating them in the international division of labor means that the world transformation curve shifts outward more in favor of the labor-intensively produced good 2 than in favor of good 1 (Figure 2.7). Consequently, more of this good can be produced.

Let us conduct a thought experiment. Assume that the relative price *p* between the two goods remains constant for the moment; the world market equilibrium then moves from point *W* to point *W″*. The production of good 1 falls, the production of good 2 increases. If consumers associate an increase of good 2 with a lower marginal utility of a unit of good 2 and a decrease of good 1 with a higher marginal utility of a unit of good 1, then the relative price of the initial position will not be a market equilibrium. In other words, at the old price there is an excess supply of good 2 and an excess demand for good 1. The price of good 2 must fall (by a little), the price of good 1 must rise (by a little). The relative price *p* has to rise and in this way a new point of equilibrium *W′* will be realized. This point must be situated to the right of the initial equilibrium *W* if the transformation curve moves in favor of good 2. (If homothetic preferences are assumed, the quantity ratio $Q_1 : Q_2$ decreases compared to the initial position.)

In the demand–supply diagram, the increased labor supply can be expressed by a downward shift of the supply curve of the labor-intensive good, in relation to the relative price of this good (Figure 2.8). The relative price of the labor-intensive good 2 is $p_2/p_1 = 1/p$, which is the reciprocal value of the relative price of good 1 that has been used as a numeraire. With a given relative price *OW* there is an excess supply *TW* of good 2.

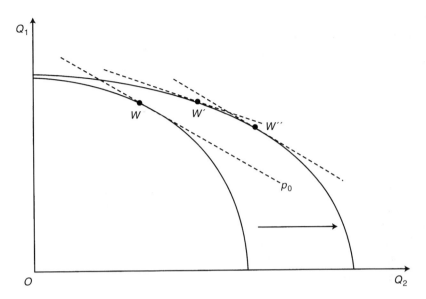

Figure 2.7 Increased labor supply and world transformation curve

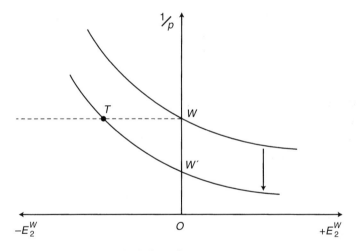

Figure 2.8 Increased labor supply and relative price

Therefore, this cannot be an equilibrium and the relative price $1/p$ must fall to OW'. When determining the new equilibrium point W' it must be taken into account that besides the additional supply or production effect an income effect is relevant as well. The income effect results from the rise in world domestic product. This means that income increases and that the demand for good 2 rises (the demand curve moves upwards). Assuming that the production effect dominates the income effect, the excess demand curve moves downwards and relative price changes to the disadvantage of the labor-intensively produced good and in favor of the non-labor-intensively produced good.

In order to show the adjustment process in the separate regions of the world economy, let us divide the world into relatively capital-abundant industrialized countries and newly industrializing countries with relative labor abundance. According to their comparative advantage, the industrial countries export the capital-intensively produced good 1 and import good 2. For the representative industrialized country the increased labor supply means that its terms of trade improve (p rises). The situation analyzed here differs from the oil crisis. There is not a shortage of an important foreign production factor, with the supply deficit negatively affecting the terms of trade of the industrialized country. Instead labor supply increases.

The industrial country specializes even further in the production of the capital-intensive good. The point of production moves from P to P' (Figure 2.9a). The new trade triangle indicates the more favorable terms of trade. The country reaches a higher utility level (the indifference curve in point C' is further away from the origin than the indifference curve in point C).

The newly industrializing country (China) gains as well. It moves its production point from autarky (point P^{**} in Figure 2.9c) to $P^{**\prime}$ and reaches consumption point $C^{**\prime}$. Note that demand for the labor-intensive product is increased, that more of this good is produced and that wages rise in the newly industrializing country.

Consider now a third group of countries: the newly industrializing countries without China. The terms of trade of this group of countries decreases. By assumption they export labor-intensively produced goods and they get competition from the newcomer China (Figure 2.9b). Note that the trade triangles of this group of countries ($P^*B^*C^*$) and of the industrialized countries (PCB)

must be identical in the initial situation. Note also that p falls for this group of the newly industrializing countries by moving their production point from P^* to $P^{*\prime}$.

If we do not only look at an isolated labor supply increase, other factors can improve the real income position of the newly industrializing countries; for example, if there is technological progress in the production of the export good 2 or if demand for the export good of the newly industrializing countries increases strongly owing to world economic growth.

2.5 Increase of labor supply and factor income

Globalization does not only mean that segmentations of commodity markets are reduced and that the law of one price holds for goods. In addition, the factor markets are also moving closer together. At any rate, this is valid for production factors that are mobile internationally, but it can be shown that the law of one price is also valid for the immobile factors including labor.

Adjustment of production quantities and factor demand

Given a set of assumptions, factor prices will be brought into line with each other by trade, even if the factors are internationally immobile. Again, we start with the assumption that important population-abundant regions of the world are integrated into the international division of labor. This is equivalent to an increase of the world factor supply. In Figure 2.10, the rectangle $OCO'B$ characterizes the factor endowment of the world (industrialized countries plus developing countries) before the integration of Central and Eastern Europe and China. In this

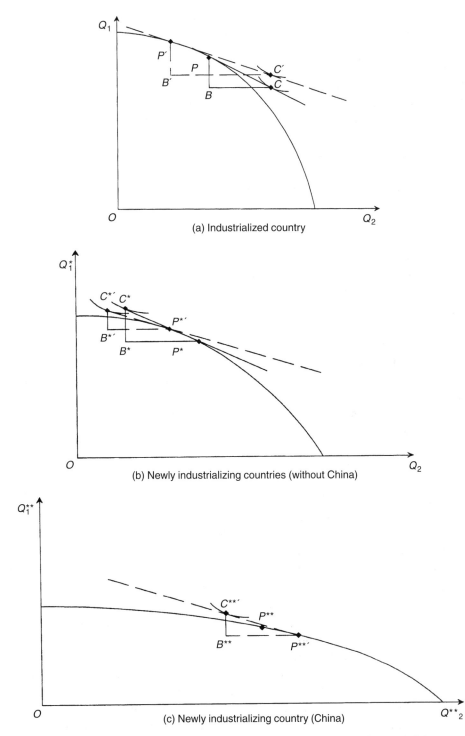

Figure 2.9 Increased labor supply and welfare in industrialized and newly industrializing countries

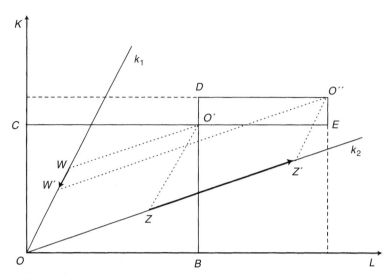

Figure 2.10 A change in factor endowment

endowment box (Edgeworth box), the slopes of the lines k_1 and k_2 show the capital intensities of the two sectors 1 and 2. The capital intensity defines how many units of capital are used per unit of labor in the production of a good. These factor intensities are determined by the wage–interest ratio, that is by the factor price ratio. The lengths of the lines (OW and OZ) are proportional to the production volumes of the two goods.

By integrating new regions into the world economy the factor endowment box of the world is enlarged by the rectangle $O'DO''E$. If we assume that the wage–interest ratio – and along with it the factor intensities – remains constant, then the additional labor supply causes an extension of the production of good 2 from Z to Z'. The production of the capital-intensive good is reduced from point W to W'. If we only take an increase of the labor supply into account (and not an increase of the capital supply as well), then, if a constant relative price of the goods is assumed, the production of the capital-intensive good will clearly decrease. This is

the Rybczinski theorem. If the regions that have been newly integrated into the world economy possess a capital stock in addition to their labor supply, the change in the production of good 1 is not clear if a constant relative price of the goods is assumed. However, as the newly integrated region is relatively labor-abundant compared to the rest of the world, the relative production $Q_1 : Q_2$ falls (from $OW : OZ$ to $OW' : OZ'$).

Adjustment of relative factor prices

Until now our argument has followed the Rybczinski theorem and assumed that the wage–interest ratio remains constant. This implies that the capital intensities in both sectors remain constant, too. However, as shown above, an increase in the world labor supply results in an increase in the supply of the labor-intensive good 2. As a consequence, the price of good 2 must fall and the relative price p must rise. As the relative commodity price and the factor price ratio are connected with each other this means that the wage–

interest ratio must fall (if good 2 is the labor-intensive good).

We can explain this relationship with the help of the Harrod–Johnson diagram which is based on the Heckscher–Ohlin model (Figure 2.11). Let us assume perfect competition and a linear-homogeneous production function. Then the capital intensity rises with an increasing wage–interest ratio. Labor will be replaced by capital with an increasing wage–interest ratio. This relationship is valid for both sectors. In Figure 2.11, sector 1 is more capital-intensive than sector 2. Let us assume that the wage–interest ratio rises. Then, the relative production costs for the labor-intensively produced good 2 increase. Consequently, the relative price p falls.

We can also argue in another way: let us assume that demand changes in favor of good 2. This increases the incentive to produce more of the labor-intensive good 2. Demand for labor increases and the wage–interest ratio rises. Therefore, the Harrod–Johnson diagram has the shape that is shown in the lower part of Figure 2.11. These relationships are valid in both countries, because we assume that the same technology is used everywhere.

The distance OW in Figure 2.11 characterizes the wage–interest ratio in the world economy in the initial position. This wage–interest ratio corresponds to the commodity price ratio OB. If the labor supply in the world increases when labor-abundant countries are integrated into the international division of labor, the labor-abundant countries find it favorable to produce more of the labor-intensive good. For the capital-abundant country it is favorable to specialize more strongly in the production of the capital-intensive good. On balance, the wage–interest ratio must fall to OW'. The relative price p rises to OB', that is the labor-intensively produced good becomes relatively cheaper.

If the world market equilibrium is disturbed by an increase of the labor supply the system will adjust until a new equilibrium is found. With the new uniform relative price, the world consumption point and the world

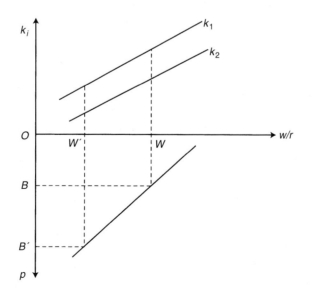

Figure 2.11 Commodity price ratio and factor price ratio

production point on the world transformation curve are determined. It is further determined which commodities are traded between the different regions of the world, in this way evening out the differences in the factor endowments. The relative price is determined on the commodity markets. The new factor price ratio is found as well, and the factor intensities that characterize production in the world are determined (Figure 2.12). In this way we have a new 'integrated' world market equilibrium.

Important aspects in economic reality

In reality, there will never be a perfect equalization of commodity prices and factor prices. There will always remain some arbitrage possibilities, because not all segmentations of markets will be eliminated. However, there is a process in which relative prices tend to become more equal. Besides remaining segmentations, other aspects have to be taken into consideration which are not included in the very simplified Heckscher–Ohlin model that is used here. This is true for the assumption of the same technology in the two regions of the world as well as for the assumption of homogeneous production factors. In the real world, countries have different technologies (embodied in the capital stock). Moreover, labor is not homogeneous, because in the real world labor represents different levels of technological knowledge (human capital). Therefore, labor productiv-

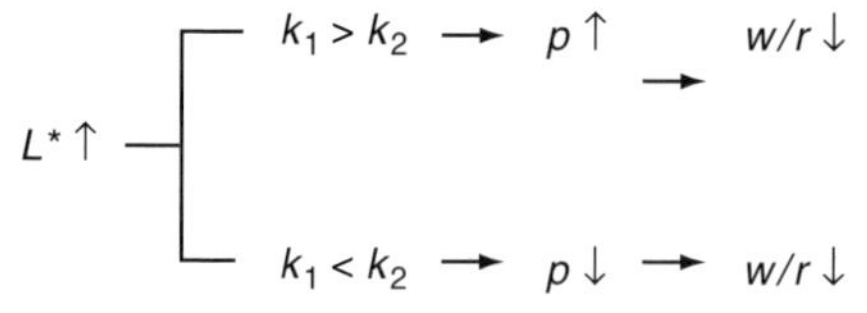

Figure 2.12 Chain of effects of an increased labor supply

ity (for example, in the industrialized countries) is higher than elsewhere. Consequently, there cannot be a perfect wage equalization.

The approach used here looks only at a comparative-static change of an increased labor supply. Other approaches have to complement this picture. For example, the newly industrializing countries could succeed in building up a capital stock and in attracting capital and technology from abroad, which improves the productivity of labor, if they pursue a suitable policy. Then a growth process starts and, as a consequence, real income and real wages in the newly industrialized countries rise. This is in addition to the effect of the increased demand for labor due to specialization in the newly industrialized countries. As empirical surveys show, real wages in these countries rise (World Bank, *World Development Report 1995*, Figure 2.2).

Finally, the Heckscher–Ohlin approach merely explains the inter-sectoral division of labor. Under comparative-static conditions, one sector of a country expands, whereas the same sector of the other country shrinks. According to the paradigm of intra-industry trade, this need not be the case (see below).

Quantity adjustment with rigid factor prices

If the factor price ratio does not react to the changed scarcity conditions, the factor quantities, particularly employment (and unemployment), have to adapt. This is the 'European' model of the labor market (or the 'Continental' model, as it applies especially in France, Germany and Italy) with relatively rigid factor prices. As a simplification, we look at only three regions of the world: (i) the labor-abundant countries that are newly taking part in the international division of labor, where the wage rate rises due to the specialization in labor-intensive products; (ii) the

US, where wages adapt flexibly so that full employment is achieved; (iii) Continental Europe with its inflexible labor markets and a rigid relative factor price, where (as a consequence) the adjustment process is carried out via employment changes.

If there is an excess supply on the world labor market, this imbalance is 'corrected' by the quantity effects in Europe. Figure 2.13a shows the European endowment box. The factor price ratio and therefore the factor intensities remain constant. Europe has to

reduce the production of the labor-intensive product 2 by $H'F'$. If at the same time the capital-intensive production is expanded by HE, then this results in unemployment EO'.

In contrast to the European model, the relative factor price adjusts in the American model (Figure 2.13b). Here, the wage–interest ratio (w/r) falls (in reality the wage of the less qualified goes down relatively). The capital intensity in the two sectors falls from k_1 (k_2) to k'_1 (k'_2) and full employment is reached.

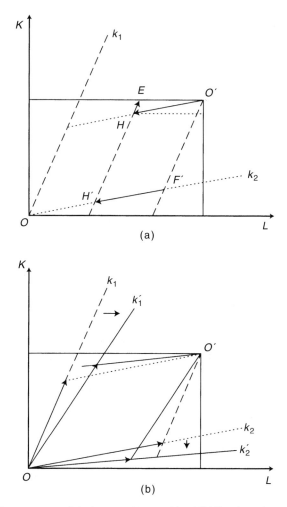

Figure 2.13 (a) The European model of unemployment and (b) the American model of employment

2.6 The most important theorems

The adjustment process in the world economy can be summarized by the following theorems. Originally, these theorems were related to the transition from autarky to trade; in our context we apply the theorems to the change from an initial position with foreign trade to a new situation where an increased labor supply is integrated into the world economy. It is assumed that full employment is reached by flexible factor prices.

- *Jevons's law of one price.* If transaction costs are left out of consideration, then there will be a uniform price for one good in the world market. The characteristic of the world market equilibrium is that the product markets are in equilibrium and that therefore the profit-maximum product supply corresponds to the utility-maximum product demand. This equilibrium is established by a uniform relative price ratio.
- *Heckscher–Ohlin theorem.* A country has a comparative advantage to export the good that uses its relatively abundant factor of production intensively. An increased labor supply in a labor-abundant region of the world means that this region exports the labor-intensive good and expands the production of this good; the capital-abundant region exports the capital-intensive good and expands the production of that good relative to the labor-intensive good.
- *Rybczynski theorem.* With given relative product prices, the increase of a factor supply leads to an increase in the production of the good whose production is relatively intensive in that factor. This result illustrates one aspect of the Heckscher–Ohlin theorem. The incidence of an exogenous increase of a production factor is described by a partial equilibrium analysis.
- *Stolper–Samuelson theorem.* The rise of the relative price of one good results in an increase of the real price of the factor that is used intensively in the production of the good. The real price of the other factor falls. In the labor-abundant region of the world, the demand for labor increases and the wage rate rises. In the capital-abundant industrialized nations, the real interest rate rises and the real wage falls. The income share of labor in the labor-abundant region rises. In the typical industrialized country, the income share of capital increases.
- *Factor price equalization theorem.* Trade of final products leads to a complete equalization of the factor price ratio. The real factor prices adjust as well. Relative product prices adjust. The factor prices adjust as well. The labor-abundant country exports more labor-intensive products and this drives up wages. The capital-abundant country exports more capital-intensive products and this drives up the interest rate.

2.7 Demand shifts and world market equilibrium

If the preferences in the world move in favor of good 1, this will have an impact on the trade equilibrium. Let us assume that a change in preferences in favor of good 1 disturbs the old equilibrium at point G (Figure 2.14). At the old relative price $(p : OG)$, excess demand in the world for good 1 is positive, the market is not cleared. Point G', reflecting the increased preferences, cannot be realized. Since there is a positive excess demand $E_1^W(p)$ > 0 in G', the relative price must change. The relative price of good 1 must rise in order to reduce demand for good 1 and increase the

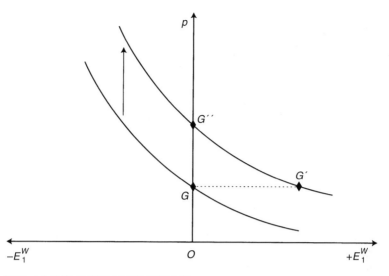

Figure 2.14 Demand shift and international trade

production incentive for this good. A new equilibrium will be realized at point *G″*.

This new equilibrium means a higher relative price *p*. If we assume good 1 to be the capital-intensively produced good, then the wage–interest ratio must fall correspondingly. The income share of labor declines.

2.8 Globalization of commodity markets and non-tradable goods

Apart from internationally tradable goods there are non-tradable goods. These are goods that, by definition, must be produced in the country where they are consumed. For these goods there can be only a national (or regional) market equilibrium; national excess demand or national excess supply do not represent feasible equilibria. If we combine the export goods and the import substitutes of a country into a composite tradable good (which is possible if the relative price between the export goods and the import substitutes remains constant), then an economy can produce tradable (Q_T) and non-tradable (Q_{NT})

goods *(transformation curve TT* in Figure 2.15). If the relative price p_T/p_{NT} between tradable and non-tradable goods is given (by tan α), then the point of production *P* is determined. The market equilibrium for non-tradable goods requires that the quantity supplied (*OB*) correspond to the quantity demanded. This is the case for the straight line *BD* in Figure 2.15. If the country obtains a credit *PD* from abroad (budget line *p′*) it can realize a higher point of consumption on the straight line *BD*. Note that in this diagram a trade triangle cannot be drawn.

Globalization applies only to the goods that are tradable. Globalization is not valid for the non-tradable goods that are produced for purely national (or regional) demand. Here international competition can only have indirect effects; in fact, there are two relationships. First: non-tradable goods define the opportunity costs of the tradable goods, because they need production factors that could otherwise be used for the production of the tradable goods. If the preference for non-tradable goods increases, the production

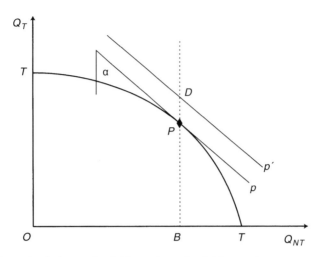

Figure 2.15 Relative price between tradable and non-tradable goods

point *P* moves to the right, and therefore fewer production factors are available for tradable goods. Depending on the factor intensity of the non-tradable goods, there are effects on the comparative advantages of the country. Second: owing to decreasing transport costs and declining barriers to trade, more non-tradable goods turn into tradable goods; thus goods that were previously non-tradable can be exported owing to lower transport and communication costs. This is even the case for a whole lot of disembodied services (like engineering services). Therefore, globalization means that the line of distinction between tradable and non-tradable goods is shifted. This implies that the transformation curve is moved outward with a bias: the area of Q_{NT} shrinks and the area of Q_T expands (this effect is not shown in Figure 2.15).

2.9 Imperfect competition

Until now the analysis has been characterized by the assumption of perfect competition: market participants on the world commodity markets are so numerous that the individual firm in a country cannot influence the price and must accept it as given. This premise becomes doubtful if the average costs of production fall with an increased quantity of production and if product preferences bring about specific market segments.

Increasing returns to scale

Constant average costs are the result of constant returns to scale, i.e. of a linear-homogeneous production function. By multiplying the use of all production factors by a factor λ (for example by 2), the production result is also multiplied by λ (by 2). If the production activity is compared to putting a flower in a flowerpot, then any number of flowerpots can be put side by side, and the production is multiplied according to the number of flowerpots. Adding an identical second factory to an existing factory therefore leads to a doubling of output. This relationship no longer holds if there are increasing returns to scale, i.e. if $Q\lambda^a = F(\lambda K, \lambda L)$ with $\alpha > 1$. Then a doubling of the inputs multiplies output by more than 2. Therefore, in the case of increasing returns to scale the production becomes less costly if the quantity produced increases. The firm moves downwards along the falling average costs curve (Figure 2.16).

Increasing returns to scale or falling average costs can be explained, for example, by a learning curve (learning by doing). Empirical studies, e.g. for the construction of large airplanes, show a learning rate of 0.2, which means that unit costs are reduced by 20 percent if the accumulated output is doubled. But falling average costs are also caused by production processes requiring a minimum input of production factors, for example, because the input of capital must exceed a minimum size due to the characteristics of the production process. In all these cases, there are fixed costs of production which are more profitably spread over the units of output with an increased production quantity. Falling average costs may apply to specific production units (shop level) or they may appear on the plant level because with several shops it is possible to fragment the production process or to have a better risk-spreading. Finally, increasing returns to scale can be linked to the firm level; minimum advertising budgets or better liquidity can be mentioned as examples.

Increasing returns to scale can also be explained by positive spillovers. Let K^j, L^j represent factor inputs of firm j. Then output Q^j of firm j may also depend on the capital stock K of the industry (of all the firms) with $Q^j = F^j(K^j, L^j) \cdot K^\xi$ where K may represent the capital stock as a measure of accumulated experience from learning by doing or knowledge capital. ξ indicates the impact of the industry's capital stock. Whereas the part F^j of the production function may be linear-homogeneous, the function as a whole can exhibit economies of scale. The marginal productivity of capital in firm j then also depends on the industry factor K with $F_k^j(K^j, K)$.

The spatial dimension of knowledge capital is an important question. (i) If it is industry-specific, each firm of an industry in a country benefits from the knowledge capital of other firms in the same industry. (ii) If it is localized, then firms in a region benefit from the knowledge capital accumulated in the region, but knowledge capital may extend to many sectors. An example is a qualified regional labor pool that may be used in different countries. (iii) Spillovers may also occur worldwide. Then K relates to knowledge capital existing in the whole world.

Increasing returns to scale and of falling average costs imply that perfect competition changes into imperfect competition: a firm may become a monopolist or an oligopolistic structure may arise.

The limits of increasing returns to scale

The argument of increasing returns to scale should not be overestimated. It should not be forgotten that central planning in Eastern Europe was based on the supposed relevance of increasing returns to scale, but in the end the strategy to make use of increasing returns to scale failed. There are quite a few reasons why increasing returns to scale do not grow without limit. With larger organizational units, flexibility will be lost and management

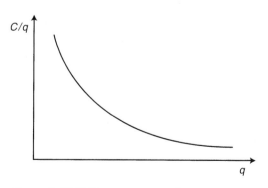

Figure 2.16 Falling average costs

costs will rise. Moreover, important restrictions can weaken the advantages of large dimensions, for example missing opportunities to expand at the actual location or lack of employees with the necessary qualifications. In the end, missing competition leads to a loss of efficiency.

Different product preferences

Apart from increasing returns to scale, product preferences are a second reason why world markets can be imperfect. People do not have the same preferences everywhere. They do not all want the same homogeneous product. These product preferences mean that market segments are defined by households with a preference for a specific product. Consumers are prepared to pay a relatively higher price for the specific good they want best ('ideal variety'). Arrange households *a–h* along a commodity axis indicating proximity or distance between goods according to individual preferences (Figure 2.17). Assume all households have the same income. Then the continuum *a–h* indicates the demand side of a market with different product preferences. Consider two firms *x* and *y* which produce goods *c* and *g*. Firm *x* may also cater for preferences *a*, *b*, *d*, *e* and *f*, but it cannot produce these goods with the same quality *c*; it may compete with firm *y* with respect to products *d*, *e* and *f*. Depending on the average cost curve of firms and on distance costs in terms of product quality, firms may serve a larger or a smaller market segment. In reality, preferences of consumers may be concentrated on some goods. Also, goods with similar characteristics may be easily substituted against each other so that they form a cluster of relatively similar goods. On the commodity axis, there may be substitution gaps between groups of goods; according to preferences, goods may not be sufficient substitutes. Consequently, the market form of imperfect competition prevails under such conditions.

2.10 Intra-sectoral trade

The combined effect of economies of scale and preferences for different goods on the size of markets is ambiguous. Economies of scale pull in the direction of large markets because average costs fall; preferences for different products pull in the other direction working towards market niches for specific products and for market segmentation. This means that large production units are not necessarily the outcome of both forces. This also has implications for location and trade.

While increasing returns to scale work towards a situation where the production would be concentrated at a few places or even at one single spot, product preferences have the consequence that market segments are defined and that these market segments limit the exploitation of increasing returns to scale. Product preferences thus prevent production from concentrating in a single spot; on the contrary, product preferences of consumers spread production over many firms and thus over a wide area. Then, intra-sectoral trade takes place because the individual firms, each filling a certain market segment, produce for

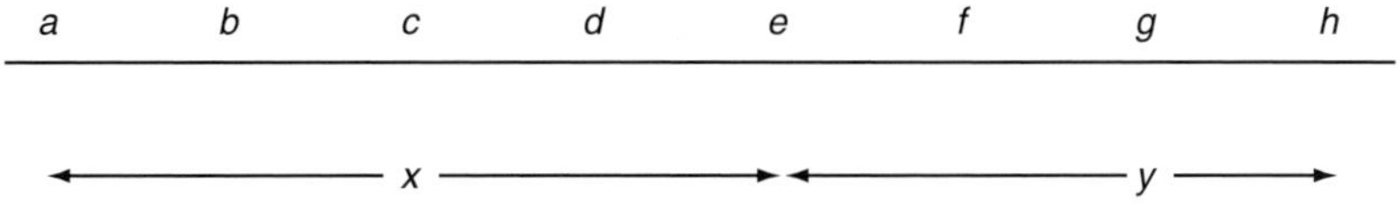

Figure 2.17 Commodity axis and firms

their own country as well as for abroad. Exploiting increasing returns to scale is limited by the demand for different product varieties and distance costs.

A significant part of the product flows between countries with a high per capita income is not an exchange of products between different sectors, but exchange within the same sector. Italians import German cars and Germans import Italian cars. Increasing returns to scale and product preferences are two reasons why we can observe such intra-industry or intra-sectoral trade.

More than half of the trade between the industrialized nations is intra-sectoral trade. With a wide delimitation of sectors on the two-digit level, intra-industry trade reaches nearly 70 percent for the US and slightly more for Germany (Table 2.1). Historically, intra-industry trade has grown strongly. In regional integrations an increasing importance of the intra-industry trade can be observed.

Two different approaches to explaining trade

Consequently, there are two very different approaches to explaining the international exchange of goods. The hypothesis of the inter-industry trade in the sense of the Heckscher–Ohlin approach explains the exchange of different goods, the exchange of

wine and cloth, or of crude oil and machines, that is the trade between sectors. Trade is therefore predominantly dependent on the differences in the production conditions, especially the factor endowments. The hypothesis of intra-industry trade, on the other hand, emphasizes the exchange of similar products, for example the exchange of cars for cars or of wine for wine. Here, trade is based on increasing returns to scale and on differences in product preferences.

The perspective of intra-industry trade increases the acceptance of the international division of labor: while in inter-industry approaches countries can only gain advantage from the international division of labor by allowing sectors with a relative price disadvantage in the country to shrink, intra-industry trade means that the same sector can expand in different countries owing to an intensified division of labor. Although single branches must also shrink in this approach, other branches of the same sector can grow. This makes adjustments less painful.

2.11 Contestable markets

Monopolies and international oligopolies

Increasing returns to scale mean that, in theory, large production facilities arise. This

Table 2.1 Intra-industry trade[a]

	1961	1971	1981	1986	1991	1996	1999
Germany	0.4102	0.5735	0.6115	0.6597	0.7500	0.7277	0.7382
Japan	0.2453[b]	0.2743	0.2010	0.2463	0.3385	0.4310	0.6938[c]
US	0.4695	0.5271	0.4953	0.5361	0.6556	0.6721	0.4456

[a] Intra-industry trade of each country with the world, calculated with the Grubel–Lloyd index, two-digit level

$$GL = \left[\sum_i [(Ex_i + Im_i) - |Ex_i - Im_i|] \middle/ \sum_i (Ex_i + Im_i) \right].$$

[b] 1962.

[c] 1988.

Source for data: OECD, *International Trade by Commodities Statistics.*

implies at the extreme single suppliers (monopolies) or few suppliers (oligopolies). Oligopolistic firms can either be in a Cournot quantity competition (with, as a rule, a homogeneous product) or in a Bertrand price competition (with a heterogeneous product). In this context, the assumptions about the strategy variable of a supplier, especially how he or she reacts to the actions of the other supplier, is relevant. In the Cournot quantity oligopoly, each supplier takes the quantity supplied by the other producer as given and decides on their own supply quantity. In the Bertrand oligopoly, the price of the other suppliers is taken as given and then one decides on one's own price. In a two-stage game, the production capacity is determined first; then price competition starts. Oligopolistic market forms are the starting point for strategic trade policy (Chapter 9).

Barriers to market entry

Most of the capital that has been invested in a firm is no longer malleable and cannot be used in any other way. This capital represents sunk costs. Firms that are established on a market have two strategic advantages in comparison with a potential newcomer: as part of their capital used has sunk, they no longer necessarily have to take these capital costs into account in order to calculate their prices. The new entrant, however, must first of all incur these fixed costs before they can actually enter the market. Sunk costs give the established firm a short-term competitive advantage. Apart from sunk costs, the established enterprise can have an advantage because it has gained production experience and has moved downwards on the average costs curve, e.g. owing to learning effects. This stresses the advantage of an early start. Enterprises that are established early on the world market have the opportunity to gain experience, to make use of learning effects and to attain lower average costs with their accumulated production.

The contestability of markets

Markets are contestable in the sense that a market entry of a new supplier could be imminent. This limits the maneuvering space of an incumbent firm in its price setting. In Figure 2.18 the position of a monopolistic supplier with a falling average cost curve is shown. If the firm is in a monopolistic position it may produce at point M on its average cost curve with a monopoly profit MF. Point M is determined by marginal revenue (not shown in Figure 2.18) and marginal costs being equal. If a newcomer enters the market, the firm can no longer capture demand alone. For the monopolistic supplier, the demand function rotates downward. If the market is sufficiently contestable, profit will be driven to zero (point S').

Whereas a new supplier must finance the use of fixed capital, whereas the established supplier does not have to consider their sunk costs in the short term, there are no sunk costs in the long term. That is because in the long term the established firm must renew its capital. Then it has to decide whether to redirect the earned depreciations to another investment purpose. That means that the renewal of the depreciated capital must pay off. Besides sunk costs, a newcomer must take into account the lower average costs of the incumbent supplier owing to the production experience it has gained. But if the established firm exceeds its scope for setting its price, a newcomer can successfully enter the market. Therefore the established enterprise is restricted in the use of its monopoly position by the imminent market entry of a potential

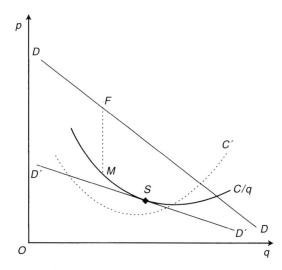

Figure 2.18 The incumbent and the newcomer

competitor. In addition, it is possible for the newcomer to undermine the pre-eminence of the established enterprise with a better technology (for example, Microsoft and other software and PC firms with respect to the dominant player IBM, supplier of telephone services).

It is difficult to come up with examples for monopolistic or oligopolistic world product markets that are actually not contestable. Unambiguously there is an oligopoly with high barriers to enter the market in the construction of large-capacity airplanes with the two suppliers Airbus and Boeing–McDonnell-Douglas (the latter came into existence by a merger in 1996). Other world markets, however, can be characterized as contestable markets; for example, the world automobile market or the semiconductor market. It is important to note that the lifespan of the products has decreased significantly, for instance in the semiconductor market. This implies that new entrants get a chance and competition is intensified.

The race for the technological lead

Markets are also contestable if enterprises compete for new knowledge, i.e. if they engage in a research and development race (Grossman and Helpman 1991a). Enterprises of individual countries try hard to find new products and new production technologies by means of research and development in order to become the market leader in the corresponding markets. Research and development may be interpreted either as an independent industry or as an element of industrial firms of the high-technology field. The output of the research and development industry, i.e. new products and new technology, can be regarded as an input to the manufacturing industry. The research and development process is driven by the profit prospects in the industry. This means that new technological knowledge is generated in a competitive process. Technological progress is endogenous, being the result of competition.

In such an approach, firms compete with their research and development expenditures

45

for world market shares. This has implications for trade. The manufacturing industry can be subdivided in this context into a high-technology field and a traditional industry. The high-technology industry is characterized by the market form of an international oligopoly with profit prospects owing to technological leads or by the market form of monopolistic competition, whereas the traditional industry can be characterized by perfect competition with constant returns to scale. While in the high-technology field in essence intra-industry trade takes place, the traditional industry is the basis for inter-industry trade. Besides inter-industry and intra-industry trade, international trade also encompasses the exchange of technological knowledge.

mechanisms are responsible for this effect: some economies, for instance the newly industrializing countries, succeed in improving their factor endowments (acquired comparative advantage instead of natural comparative advantage). For example, the savings rate and the investment rate of some newly industrializing countries of South-East Asia amount to 35 percent or more, which results in a strong increase of the capital stock. Apart from physical capital, also the endowment with human capital can be strengthened in the course of time, by investing in education. As a third factor, the infrastructure can be improved by building new roads, airports and better telephone networks. In addition, the diffusion of new knowledge causes an improvement of the locational conditions in developing countries.

At the same time, processes take place in

2.12 *Hierarchy versus markets*

Goods and resources can be allocated through markets or within firms. Markets can replace firms; that is, there are hierarchies or vertical integrations. A firm can be interpreted as a network of contracts that combines different production factors. A firm can also be defined in the sense of institutional economics as an organizational unit with lower transaction costs than on markets: a transaction will be carried out within a firm if the transaction costs within the firm are lower than on the markets. The dividing line between firms and the market therefore is determined by the level of the transaction costs.

Firms can be integrated vertically by including production levels that precede or follow the production process within the firms. For example, the large crude oil companies (the 'seven sisters') were integrated vertically before the first oil crisis; concession contracts, often for a period of 50 to 70 years, guaranteed their access to the natural resources, also to the undiscovered resources of the resource countries. The firms had transport capacities at their disposal, and they owned refineries and distribution networks in the industrialized countries. In the 1970s, the extraction rights were passed to the resource countries and therefore the vertical integration of the enterprises was broken up. The spot markets (for example, in Rotterdam) gained in importance and forward markets were established. Markets replaced vertically integrated firms.

2.13 *Shifting comparative advantage and relocation*

In the course of time, locational conditions and therefore trade flows change. Different

the industrialized countries that reduce the competitiveness of some sectors. The desire for a higher labor income causes some labor-intensive products to become unprofitable. The extension of the social security systems leads to a rise of labor costs. Moreover, a society can get lethargic: for example, people could shy away from taking entrepreneurial risks or from opening the educational system to competition.

2.14 Export structure and market share of countries

If we aggregate a country's position on all these specific product markets of the world we obtain a picture of a country's specialization. This includes information on whether a country is heavily specialized on a few specific export goods and thus is exposed to risks in these markets or whether its product structure of exports is more evenly balanced.

Information on the export structure may also relate to the issue whether exports are in the high-tech, medium-tech or low-tech category. Technology intensity is defined as a part of R&D expenditure relative to product

sales (high tech: >10; medium tech: 4.9–0.9; low tech: <0.7). Figure 2.19 exhibits this information for the US, Germany, Japan, France and the United Kingdom. The export position has been calculated using RCA coefficients, i.e. revealed comparative advantages.[1] Whereas the US specializes in high-tech exports, Germany and Japan have their comparative advantage in medium-tech products.

2.15 Exports and the real exchange rate

Exports are influenced by many factors such as the income level and income growth abroad. Another determinant is the exchange rate (e) which is defined as the price of the foreign currency: How many units of the home currency, for instance euro (€), have to be given up for one unit of dollar ($), i.e. $e = $ €/$. $\hat{e} > 0$ means a devaluation of the home currency, $\hat{e} < 0$ means an appreciation. Exports are also influenced by

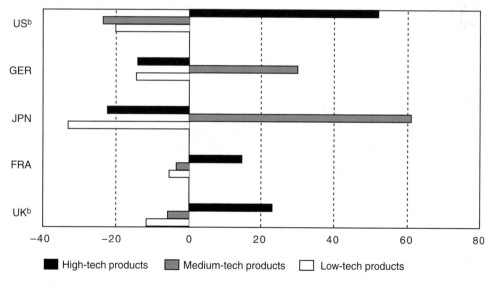

Figure 2.19 Technology intensity[a] and comparative advantage, 1999
[a] RCA indices according to technology intensity [b] 1998.
Source: Siebert (2001b, Table 3.1).

price differentials between countries. Consequently, it is the real exchange rate

$$e_R = eP^*/P$$

that influences exports.

Real exports change in line with the real exchange rate. Thus, US exports fall with a real appreciation of the US dollar in the early 1980s, and they increase with a real depreciation in the late 1980s (Figure 2.20). In the

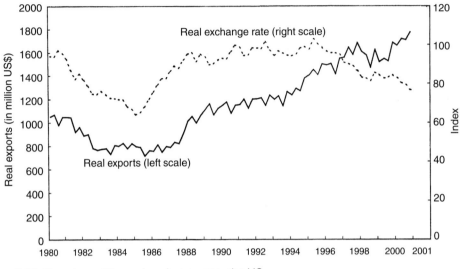

Figure 2.20 Exports and the real exchange rate: the US

Source: International Monetary Fund, *International Financial Statistics*, CD-ROM, July 2001.

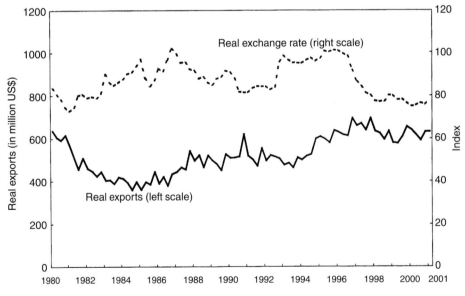

Figure 2.21 Exports and the real exchange rate: the UK

Source for data: International Monetary Fund, *International Financial Statistics*, CD-ROM, July 2001.

1990s, real exports increase whereas the real exchange rate remains constant and even falls (the US dollar appreciates in real terms) in the late 1990s. This indicates that the US has gained competitiveness.

Figure 2.21 exhibits exports of the UK and the real exchange rate of the British pound. The interdependence seems less pronounced than in the case of the US. The pound devalues in the period 1981–1987, but real exports rise only after 1984. The real devaluation of the pound in 1992 has had a positive impact on real exports. The real appreciation in 1995 was followed by more or less stagnating real exports.

Note

1 The RCA index of a sector i compares exports and imports of a sector i with the exports and imports of all sectors. It is defined as

$$RCA_i = \left[\frac{x_i - Im_i}{x_i + Im_i} - \frac{\Sigma(x_i - Im_i)}{\Sigma(x_i + Im_i)} \right]$$

A positive value indicates that a sector has a comparative advantage relative to the other sectors of countries which are used as a norm.

Chapter 3

The factor markets in the world economy

....

What you will understand after reading this chapter

Besides the markets for goods, the factor markets play a decisive role in the paradigm of the world economy. Equilibrium of the world economy also requires the factor markets to be in equilibrium. If this equilibrium is disturbed, the world economy has to adjust. The adjustment processes in the world factor markets are thus of great importance. The world labor market (section 3.1) and the world capital market (section 3.2) are discussed in particular. Important questions are whether national capital markets are segmented and how close is the relation between national investment and national savings (sections 3.3 and 3.4). Historically, some countries have developed from net debtors to net creditors. This is the debt cycle hypothesis (section 3.5). For a given production technology, the prices of the production factors are related to each other and a factor-price frontier exists (section 3.6). Finally, the world market for natural resources and disturbances on the factor markets are dealt with (sections 3.7 and 3.8).

3.1 The world market for labor

Migration and wage equalization

Applying the concept of a world market for labor as a production factor, as we did for goods, we have to compare the world demand for labor and the world supply of labor. A simple interpretation of the world labor market is obtained under the following assumptions. Assume labor to be perfectly mobile internationally and to be homogeneous especially as far as qualifications are concerned. Furthermore, the labor supply is assumed to be exogenously given and constant over time. Under these assumptions, the world market for labor can be represented as shown in Figure 3.1. *OO** is the world supply of labor, allocated between the home country, or Home (*OC*), and foreign countries, or Foreign (*O*C*). Home's labor demand curve (*F_L*)

shows a higher marginal productivity than the corresponding curve of Foreign (*F_L**). The two markets are assumed to be segmented; the home wage of *CA* is higher than the foreign wage *CB*.

If the wage difference *BA* is sufficiently high, foreign workers find it worthwhile to migrate into the home country. Consequently, world production can be extended. Migration generates additional production represented by the triangle *BAG* (Harberger triangle). Home's additional production is *AGDC*, whereas Foreign's production is reduced by *BGDC*. Owing to the migration, the factor endowments of the two countries change; Home increases its supply of workers, requiring the Home wage to fall. In the new equilibrium (point *G*), all home workers receive a lower wage. Foreign loses labor, and all foreign workers receive a higher wage.

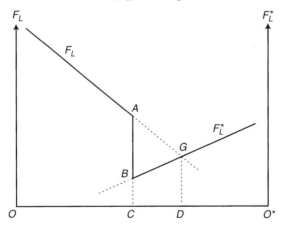

Figure 3.1 The world market for labor

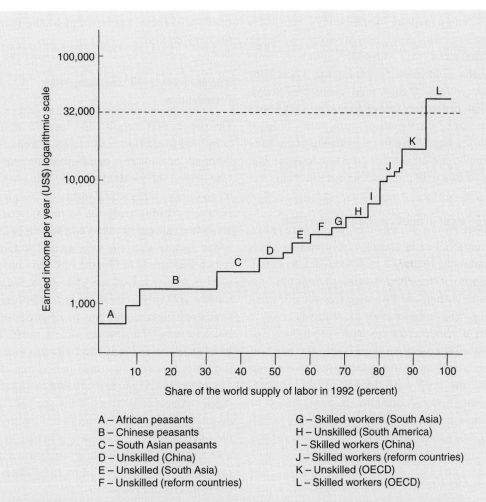

A – African peasants
B – Chinese peasants
C – South Asian peasants
D – Unskilled (China)
E – Unskilled (South Asia)
F – Unskilled (reform countries)

G – Skilled workers (South Asia)
H – Unskilled (South America)
I – Skilled workers (China)
J – Skilled workers (reform countries)
K – Unskilled (OECD)
L – Skilled workers (OECD)

Wages logarithmically scaled, in prices of 1995. The share of the labor supply segments is given by the length of the horizontal part. Unlabeled horizontal parts represent labor supplies that make up for less than 2.5 percent of the world supply of labor.

Figure 3.2 The supply curve of the world market for labor, 1992
Source: World Bank, *World Development Report 1995*, Figure 18.1.

world can be developed (Figure 3.2). In this concept, labor supply depends on the annual income in US dollars, the segments of this curve being valid only for particular regions of the world. For each segment, labor is homogeneous, receiving the same real wage. Chinese peasants supply labor for an income of approximatly US$1,000: skilled workers in OECD countries supply labor for an income of about US$34,000. The horizontal distance between the particular lines indicates the size of the labor supply of the relevant regions in the overall world labor supply.

Segmentation and wage differences

If workers are spatially immobile internationally and inhomogeneous concerning their qualification, then national labor markets are segmented, and wage differences exist. But besides differences in qualification, or human capital, workers in a particular country can also benefit from a better endowment with physical capital or from locally immobile technological knowledge that enables them to be more productive. Such differences of endowment conditions have to be distinguished from policy-induced market segmentations, e.g. immigration laws. Finally, preferences for a certain location can be so strong that people accept lower wages.

Movement of goods instead of migration

Even if labor is completely immobile internationally, there can be a tendency to equalization of real wages through international trade, with goods assuming the role of migration. The country that is relatively rich in capital specializes in the production of capital-intensive goods, causing the price of capital goods, i.e. the real interest rate, to rise and the real wage to fall. Under appropriate model conditions, a convergence or even a complete equalization of real wages occurs (see Chapter 2).

3.2 The world market for capital

On the world capital market, the equilibrium between savings and investments is determined. Savings means abstaining from consumption, investment means accumulating capital. Demand and supply of new capital meet on the world capital market. The share of gross savings and gross investment is approximately 23 percent of the world national product (Table 1.3). With a world domestic product of approximately US$30 trillion (*World Development Report 1999*, Table 12), the world capital market consequently has a volume of about US$6.9 trillion per year. Since we are here looking at savings and investment this sum does not refer to financial markets but to the market for 'real' capital.

The productivity of abstaining from consumption

On the capital supply side, people abstain from consumption, i.e. they save. The demand for capital is determined by production. From the production side, it is possible to produce additional units of goods in period 1 through capital formation in the preceding period 0. Not consuming a cow today means that the cow is still available for consumption tomorrow and that on top of this it has calved as well. As Robinson Crusoe abstains from walking to the remote source of fresh water, and as he produces a bucket during the time, he suffers thirst. But he also spares himself the frequent walk to the water source in the next period and then has more water per unit of time at his disposal. Abstaining from consumption, i.e. investing, has a positive productivity. In the next period, $1 + F_K$ units of a good are available instead of one unit, F_K indicating the marginal productivity of capital (of abstaining from consumption).

In Figure 3.3, the transformation curve shows the possibility of transformation over time. The marginal rate of transformation $|dQ_1/dQ_0|$ indicates how many additional units of output are possible in the second period (distance *HI*) if one unit of consumption is abstained from in the first period (distance *TH*). The marginal rate of transformation in time results, on the one hand, from a unit of a good not consumed today being preserved and being available for consumption in the next period (storing). But, on the other hand, abstaining from consumption is also linked to a productive detour or a roundabout method (Marshall 1890),

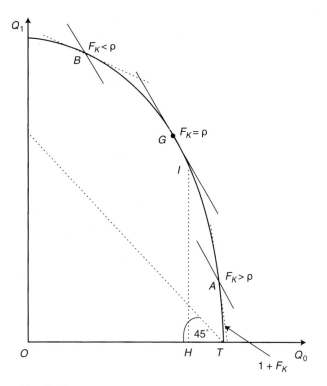

Figure 3.3 Transformation in time

yielding a positive marginal productivity per unit of consumption abstained from.

The transformation curve ranks all investment projects in the world according to their marginal productivity of capital F_K. Those projects with the highest marginal productivity are located on the lower part of the transformation curve, so that the first unit of capital invested has the highest marginal productivity. The more capital is invested, the lower is the marginal productivity of an additional project. The increasing marginal rate of transformation thus indicates the declining marginal productivity of additional units of capital. The opportunity cost of abstaining from consumption rises. The rate of return of investment (i.e. of non-consumption) is F_K. Through non-consumption, $1 + F_K$ units of the good are available in the next period. This

is the benefit of waiting. The marginal rate of transformation in time $|dQ_1/dQ_0|$ must correspond to the relative price of the two goods in time, p_0/p_1; this relative price is of the dimension Q_1/Q_0. It shows in which quantitative relation a good is intertemporally exchanged on the market. Thus, from the production side of the world economy,

$$\left|\frac{dQ_1}{dQ_0}\right| = 1 + F_K = \frac{p_0}{p_1}$$

has to hold.

The cost of abstaining from consumption

Abstaining from consumption involves costs of waiting. These opportunity costs are generated by shifting consumption to the future. If the household had only the one unit of a good at its disposal tomorrow that it abstains

55

from today, and if it would assign the same utility to this situation as to the initial situation, it would have no preference for the present period.[1] But if it values this unit less, because it will be consumed only in the future, the future consumption has to be discounted with the rate of time preference, ρ. The rate of time preference indicates how the future consumption is evaluated in comparison to consumption today. It is the factor used to discount consumption in the future in comparison to consumption today. For the rate of time preference,

$$\rho = \left|\frac{dC_1}{dC_0}\right| - 1$$

holds, where $|dC_1/dC_0|$ is the marginal rate of intertemporal substitution. It measures the quantity of consumption necessary in the second period to compensate the household for abstaining from one unit of consumption in the first period.

The time preference rate of consumption ρ is not identical to the utility discount rate δ. The preference rate of consumption in time ρ expresses how the future consumption has to be discounted, whereas the discount rate of utility δ expresses how the future utility has to be discounted. This is the 'impatience'. The discount rate of utility is, as a rule, assumed given as constant over time, whereas the rate of time preference varies with the consumption level. If future consumption is higher than present consumption, an additional unit of consumption yields less satisfaction in the future than it creates in the present.

The rate of time preference ρ is thus determined by two factors. One is the impatience of households. A household generally values future satisfaction of its needs lower than the immediate satisfaction. This impatience is represented by the discount rate of utility δ. The second factor is intertemporal consump-

tion smoothing: because of a diminishing marginal utility of consumption, a household wants to stretch consumption over time. In a long-term growth equilibrium, where consumption does not change anymore, the rate of time preference ρ equals the discount rate of utility δ. Thus (in models where consumption increases over time) the discount rate of utility can be regarded as the lower limit of the rate of time preference. Therefore, the literature often speaks only of the discount rate.

What does this mean for the consumption and saving decision of households? Consumers are indifferent about consuming today or tomorrow if the utility of a unit consumed today and the present value of the utility of a unit consumed tomorrow are equal in their judgment. For households, the relative price has to correspond to the marginal rate of substitution in time and thus be equal to the ratio of the marginal utilities in both periods.[2] The marginal rate of substitution in time thus measures the consumption quantity that is necessary to compensate the household for abstaining from one unit of consumption in the first period. Thus, from the consumption side of an economy, the price ratio between consumption today and consumption tomorrow has to be equal to the marginal rate of substitution

$$\left|\frac{dC_1}{dC_0}\right| = 1 + \rho = \frac{U'_0(C_0)(1+\delta)}{U'_1(C_1)} = \frac{p_0}{p_1}$$

Equilibrium between the benefits and the costs of abstaining from consumption

Summing up the conditions for the production and consumption sides, it follows that

$$\left|\frac{dQ_1}{dQ_0}\right| = 1 + F_K = \frac{p_0}{p_1} = \frac{U'_0(C_0)(1+\delta)}{U'_1(C_1)} = 1 + \rho = \left|\frac{dC_1}{dC_0}\right|$$

The marginal rate of transformation (tangent to the transformation curve) and the marginal rate of substitution (tangent to the indifference curve) have to be equal (point G in Figure 3.3; the indifference curve is not shown).

In Figure 3.3, point A cannot be an optimal point, as the marginal productivity of capital is higher than the rate of time preference ρ. The benefit of waiting, i.e. the additional production, is higher than the costs of waiting, i.e. the loss of utility through abstaining from consumption. Analogously, point B is not an optimal point, as the marginal productivity of capital is smaller than the rate of time preference. Here the benefit of waiting is less than the costs of waiting. The optimum is reached in point G.

The position of the optimal point G varies with the rate of time preference. If the rate of time preference ρ is high, abstention from consumption is relatively low. Then, the equilibrium point G moves downward on the transformation curve. If the rate of time preference is low, abstention from consumption is higher. Then, the equilibrium point G moves upward.

Marginal productivity, time preference rate and market interest rate

The marginal productivity indicates how, from the supply side, investing yields a return (through a productive detour or a roundabout process); the time preference rate expresses what, from the consumption side, the consumers demand for abstaining from consumption. The relative price p_0/p_1 for the product in the two periods expresses the intertemporal relative price. For this relative price, $p_0/p_1 = 1 + r$ holds, where r is the market interest rate. The equilibrium for capital formation in the world capital markets thus requires $F_K = \rho = r$.

In equilibrium, the market interest rate r has to be equal to the marginal productivity and the rate of time preference. As we shall see later on, in intertemporal approaches and also in models of growth, we distinguish between long-term equilibria and adjustment paths to long-term equilibria (Chapter 4). The market for capital has to be in equilibrium in the long-term situation as well as during transition.

The demand–supply diagram of the world market for capital

The relationship between the benefits and the costs of waiting can also be illustrated in a different representation of the world capital market (Figure 3.4a). On the vertical axis, the marginal productivity of capital (F_K), the rate of time preference ρ and the (real) interest rate r are shown. On the horizontal axis, the levels of investments (I) and savings (S) are shown. The demand curve for new capital contains projects with different marginal productivities. Projects with a particularly high marginal productivity are located in the upper part of the F_K curve. When these projects are complete, projects with a lower marginal productivity of capital become worthwhile. The F_K curve is thus the demand curve for new capital in the world economy. It results from the demand curves of the individual countries. The curve is obtained by horizontally adding the curves of the individual economies. Regarding the world market, all feasible projects in the world are ranked according to their profitability on this curve. It represents the demand side of the capital market with different investment prospects.

The supply curve shows the abstention from consumption that the households of the world are ready to accept at different

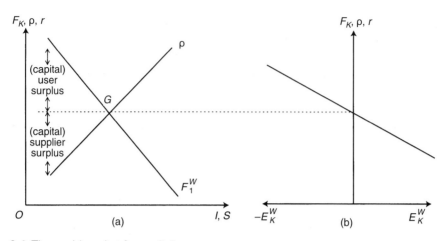

Figure 3.4 The world market for capital

world-market interest rates. One may also imagine that this supply curve for new capital represents households or countries with different rates of time preference. Countries or households with a low rate of time preference offer abstention from consumption, i.e. real savings, even at a very low real interest rate. If the real interest rate rises, more households or countries supply savings.

The equilibrium lies in point G, where an equilibrium real interest rate is determined and the demand for new capital equals the supply of new capital. Investment projects with a lower marginal productivity are not carried out whereas the investment projects with a higher marginal productivity receive a capital user (demand-side) surplus. They have a marginal productivity that is higher than the real interest rate required in the market equilibrium. Concerning the supply curve, the potential savings of households or countries requiring a time preference rate (respectively a discount rate) higher than the market-clearing real interest rate do not become effective. Countries or households with a lower time preference receive a supplier surplus.

These relations can also be represented as a

curve of excess demand for new capital depending on the interest rate (Figure 3.4b). At high real interest rates, excess demand is negative, i.e. there is too much abstention from consumption; at low real interest rates, excess demand is positive, i.e. too much capital is demanded.

In Figure 3.4, the flows of a period are taken into account, i.e. the investments, the abstention from consumption, the savings. This figure can also be applied to the aggregated demand for capital over all periods and the aggregated savings over all periods. In this interpretation, the capital stock is indicated on the horizontal axis. If capital already in existence can be employed flexibly, both representations are equivalent.

Tobin's q

Tobin's q represents an evaluation of a country's capital goods (or of its existing stock of capital). In the above model, the stock of capital is determined by the condition $F_K = r$, assuming that capital can be reallocated at negligible costs. In the long run, this may indeed be the case. In the short run, however, adjustment costs arise with the reallocation of capital. This has effects on investment behavior. Consider a firm maximizing its profit over a time period and facing adjustment costs for its capital. Then, the installed capital enters the investment calculation of the firms at a shadow price with adjustment costs playing a role. Tobin's q can be regarded as an expression of this shadow price. It is defined as

$$q = \frac{\text{market value of the capital installed}}{\text{replacement cost of the capital installed}}$$

If $q < 1$, the market value lies below the replacement costs, and it does not pay off to replace the capital good once it is depreciated. It is not worthwhile for a firm to take up new capital from the capital market. The firm reduces its capital stock. If $q > 1$, it is worthwhile to renew a capital good. Then it pays off to use more capital and to attract it from outside.

Tobin's q permits us to link the investment decision to the stock market, as the market value of the capital installed can be indicated by the valuation of shares. The replacement costs of the installed capital are given by the price index for investment goods. Thus the rate of change $\hat{q}$ of Tobin's q is

$\hat{q}$ = share index (e.g. Dow Jones) rate of change – rate of change of the price index for investment goods

If, for example, the share index rises, perhaps because optimism spreads in an economy, because of lowered corporate taxes, a technological breakthrough recorded or more favorable export opportunities, the rise of Tobin's q signals better investment opportunities. The formulation with Tobin's q is perfectly compatible with the neoclassical approach of marginal productivity. If the marginal productivity rises through technological progress, the market value of capital will increase, q exceeds 1 and it pays off to invest. With positive expectations, q rises as well. The appeal of the q approach is that the investment behavior of firms is linked to the valuation of the firms through the stock market.

Capital allocation for two countries

An alternative representation of capital accumulation on the world market for capital explicitly considers two regions of the world (two countries; Figure 3.5). It is assumed here that the marginal productivity of the capital

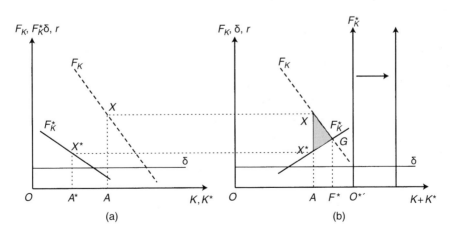

Figure 3.5 Optimal allocation of capital

stock in the two countries is higher than the discount rate δ (which is relevant in the long run). We assume the two countries to have a uniform discount rate. Figure 3.5 shows the curves for the marginal productivity of capital for the home and foreign countries. It is assumed that due to technological knowledge the home country has a higher marginal productivity of capital. It has accumulated the capital stock *OA* with the corresponding marginal productivity of capital *AX*. The foreign country has a less favorable productivity curve, a smaller capital stock *OA** and a lower marginal productivity of capital *A*X**. The capital productivities of the two countries are higher than their discount rate δ.

The information contained in Figure 3.5a is rearranged in Figure 3.5b. The curve for the marginal productivity of the home country has been duplicated from Figure 3.5a, the home country has realized a marginal productivity according to point *X*, and it has accumulated the corresponding capital *OA*. The curve of marginal productivity for the foreign country is arranged in the 'inverse' direction, originating at point *O**. Figure 3.5b is drawn such that the straight line *OO** represents the sum of the capital stocks *OA* of the home country and of the foreign country *O*A*. With the present capital allocation between the two countries, a gap between their marginal productivities results. The points *A* and *A** can thus not be a world market equilibrium. Similarly to the market for goods, the possibility of arbitrage exists. This is expressed by the Harberger triangle *XGX**. It is worthwhile to transfer capital from the foreign country to the home country. The equilibrium point is reached in point *G* in Figure 3.5b, the foreign country having transferred an amount AF of capital to the home country.

Point *G* balances the differences in the marginal productivities of capital. It represents, however, only a short-term equilibrium, as the marginal productivity of capital exceeds the discount rate. It is thus worthwhile to accumulate capital. The total stock of capital *OO** rises. Capital accumulation can occur in the home country as well as in the foreign country. For simplicity, let us assume that the capital stock rises only in the foreign country, equal to an amount of the straight line *O*O*'*. Notice that the position of the foreign country's curve of marginal productivity F_k^* moves to the right, along with the point of origin *O*'*. The equilibrium is attained at the intersection of the curves of marginal productivity on the *d* line (not shown in Figure 3.5b). The point of origin *O*'* moves until the marginal productivity in both countries equals the discount rate δ.

3.3 Global demand for capital interpreted as national excess demands

In the previous analysis, we started out from the assumption of a uniform world market for capital. An alternative concept is to assume that, as a first step, single countries attempt to achieve a balance between the demand for new capital and the abstention from consumption. If there is excess demand for capital in a country, this excess demand then, as a second step, becomes effective on the world market. The world demand for new capital is then the sum of the countries' excess demand for new capital (E_I) and thus $D_I^W = \sum_j E_I^j$ for $E_I^j > 0$. Correspondingly, the supplied savings s_I^W are the sum of all countries' excess supply, and thus $s_I^W = \sum_j E_I^j$ for $E_I^j < 0$.

In principle, this formulation leads to the same result as a uniform view of the world market for capital. The formulation is helpful because it can be specified with the help of the particular countries' current account balances. A current account deficit means that an economy receives more goods, services, property income and unilateral (free) transfers in one period than it gives away. Thus, resources amounting to the level of the current account deficit are transferred into the country. Capital imports take place. A current account surplus means that a country gives away more goods, services and transfers than it receives in one period. Resources are exported. Capital export takes place.

Looking at a current deficit from a financing point of view, a current account deficit means that a country uses more goods than it produces. Absorption exceeds production; this has to be financed from abroad (Siebert 2000a: Chapter 11). The financing restriction can be explained as follows. Let us start with the equation for national income $Y = C + I + G + X - Im$ (C: consumption; I: investment; G: government expenditure; X: exports; Im: imports). Adding the transfer balance, Tr, on both sides, we have

$$Y + Tr = C + I + G + X - Im + Tr$$

If taxes T (which are supposed to contain the indirect taxes as well) are subtracted from both sides, it follows that the current account balance $X - Im + Tr$ equals $S - I + (T - G)$. The current account balance thus equals the surplus of savings over investments. Taking into account government savings (i.e. the government budget surplus), we have:

$$S - I + (T - G) = X - Im + Tr$$

This is the financing restraint of an open economy. The current account balance and the capital account balance are determined simultaneously; they are two sides of the same coin. A country with a current account deficit does not have enough savings to finance its investments. A country with a current account surplus saves more than it intends to invest.

If the world consists of two countries only, the home country and the foreign country, the balances of the two countries' current accounts must add up to zero in each and every period. If Home has a current account deficit in period 0, meaning that it is not able to fully finance its investments and therefore it has to import capital, indebting itself, Foreign has to have a current account surplus of a corresponding amount in the same period, exporting capital and granting a loan. Let us now introduce the time aspect and assume that there are only two time periods. Then Home has to obtain a current account surplus in period 1 to be able to repay its debt. Home's current account is thus intertemporally balanced, but it has been able to consume more goods in period 0 than it would have been able to, based only on its own production capacity. In return, it has to pay goods back in period 1. Correspondingly, this results in a current account deficit for Foreign in period 1, as it can now live off means received from credit loan repayment. For Foreign, the current account is intertemporally balanced as well. This intertemporal mechanism of balances is represented in Table 3.1.

In Figure 3.6, the national markets for capital are shown. In autarky (point A), Home's interest rate is relatively low, whereas Foreign has a relatively high interest rate (point A^*). With free movement of capital, a uniform world market for capital exists. Home exports capital (EX) and has a current account surplus. Foreign imports capital (MP) and has a current account deficit.

Table 3.1 Intertemporal mechanism of balances

	Home	Foreign
Period 0	Current account deficit, import of capital, indebtedness	Current account surplus, export of capital, loan
Period 1	Current account surplus, export of capital, debt repayment	Current account deficit, import of capital, debt repayment received

3.4 The relationship between national investment and national savings

The world market for capital as a peak balancing device

One approach to determining world excess demand for capital is to add up national excess demand. The volume of the excess demand for new capital can be observed from the sum of the negative current account balances. Summing up the negative current account balances of the 125 countries featured in the *World Development Report*, the total deficit for the year 1998 amounts to US$365 billion. Putting the current account deficits into relation with the world national product yields a value of only 1.24 percent of world GNP. According to this, the peak balancing function of the world capital market, measured against the current deficits, makes

up for only a small portion of the world national product. Gross savings, however, amount to 22.4 percent of the world domestic product. Thus, according to this approach, only 6 percent of gross investment in the world economy is financed through international (real) capital movements. Data of foreign direct investments are reported in Table 3.2; they suggest a somewhat higher, but basically similar, dimension for the annual average 1991–1999. In individual countries, the current account deficits regularly reach a maximum of 2–3 percent of GDP (see Bosworth 1993). For example, the US (US$370 billion, 3.7 percent of GDP), and the United Kingdom (US$27 billion, 1.9 percent) show relatively high current account deficits for 2000. In rare cases higher deficits of up to 5–6 percent are observed (see Chapters 9 and 10).

Capital flows run mainly between the industrialized countries. About 68 percent of

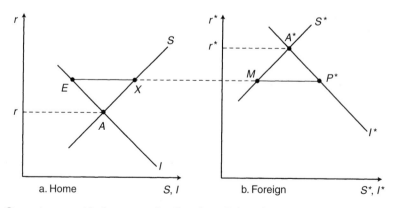

Figure 3.6 Current account balances and national capital markets

Table 3.2 Gross capital inflows (in billion US dollars)

		1991	1993	1995	1997	1998	1999	Annual average[a]
World	Direct investments	154.4	218.6	329.2	418.1	674.1	911.2	419.0
	Portfolio investments	466.4	754.4	595.1	1,002.2	993.8	1,632.4	853.0
	Other investments	104.4	438.7	775.2	1,276.9	477.7	382.5	578.7
	Total	725.2	1,411.7	1,699.5	2,697.1	2,145.5	2,926.0	1,645.1
Industrialized countries	Direct investments	113.7	143.3	207.4	235.9	474.8	692.2	283.3
	Portfolio investments	418.3	620.7	538.4	847.9	904.2	1,476.1	739.2
	Other investments	36.7	359.0	568.0	1,154.1	537.7	421.2	504.2
Developing countries	Direct investments	40.7	75.3	121.8	182.2	199.2	219.0	135.7
	Portfolio investments	31.0	117.1	47.2	127.6	50.5	125.6	93.7
	Other investments	64.1	74.8	165.3	91.0	−114.4	−51.1	48.3
Latin America	Direct investments	13.1	14.3	30.7	61.5	71.1	89.2	43.8
	Portfolio investments	26.0	74.2	5.9	31.5	30.5	12.9	40.8
	Other investments	4.5	−5.1	44.7	3.7	10.6	5.3	6.2
Asia[b]	Direct investments	20.8	46.2	64.8	80.0	85.5	90.6	63.9
	Portfolio investments	3.7	28.5	30.6	25.8	−1.9	87.5	31.2
	Other investments	36.9	35.3	72.6	55.5	−184.5	−90.6	6.2
Eastern Europe[c]	Direct investments	2.7	5.7	17.3	22.9	22.2	25.0	14.3
	Portfolio investments	0.8	10.7	6.0	53.8	10.1	8.4	13.0
	Other investments	3.7	20.7	24.5	14.7	26.3	19.2	16.2

[a] Annual average: for the years 1991–1999.   [b] Asia: not included are Hong Kong and Taiwan.
[c] Eastern Europe: including Malta, Turkey and Cyprus. Figures rounded to one digit.
Source for data: IMF, *Balance of Payments Statistics Yearbook* (1998); IMF, *Balance of Payments Statistics*, December 2001.

the world's foreign direct investments are capital inflows into the industrialized countries (1999). However, the share of the newly industrializing countries has risen considerably in the 1990s (Table 3.2). The portfolio investments (transactions in shares and bonds and also in money market instruments and derivatives) show a similar picture. Portfolio investments differ from direct investments in the way that the investor is not durably interested in the firms in which he or she is investing.

Considerable capital inflows for particular countries

Even if the world market for capital in general only seems to balance peaks between savings and investments, capital inflows can gain a considerable importance for particular countries and in particular periods. The share of direct investments in gross investment attains 20 percent and more in Chile and Hungary in a number of years (Table 3.3).

3.5 *The debt cycle: from net debtor to net*

The debt cycle

In its historical development, an economy can go through a debt cycle (Siebert 1987, 1989). It begins as a 'young' debtor because capital import is worthwhile due to $F_K > r$. The

The close relation between national investments and national savings

Feldstein and Horioka (1980) found out that the national capital markets are of considerable importance for the clearing between capital demand and capital supply. For a panel of 21 OECD countries and the time from 1960 to 1974, they found a high correlation between the national savings rate and the national investment rate with a regression coefficient close to 1. The rates were calculated as averages for the total period of 15 years and also for subperiods of five years. The simple OLS (ordinary least squares) regression $(I/Y)_i = \alpha + \beta (S/Y)_i$ for the 21 countries $(i = 1, \ldots, 21)$ and the 15-year period yields a regression coefficient β of 0.89 for gross savings and of 0.94 for net savings. Similar coefficients were found for the five-year period. These coefficients can be interpreted as savings retention coefficients. With perfect capital mobility one would have expected no relation at all between the savings rate and the investment rate, β thus equaling zero. However, since the coefficient is closer to 1 than 0, the hypothesis $\beta = 0$ has to be rejected. The results of Feldstein and Horioka suggest that national capital markets have considerable weight and that only small excess demands and supplies are balanced on the world market for capital. Perfect capital mobility does not exist.

Recent tests show that the close relation observed by Feldstein and Horioka has become less tight in recent times. Based on annual data for 1960–1988, Sinn (1992a) has shown for 23 OECD countries that the long-term average of the relationship between the national rates of savings and investment has declined considerably, especially since 1973 (the coefficient of the regression equation is 0.68 for the 1980s); international capital mobility has thus increased.

In Figure 3.7, savings rates and investment rates in 2000 are shown for selected countries. As can easily be observed, the values for most countries lie close to a straight line with an angle of 45°.

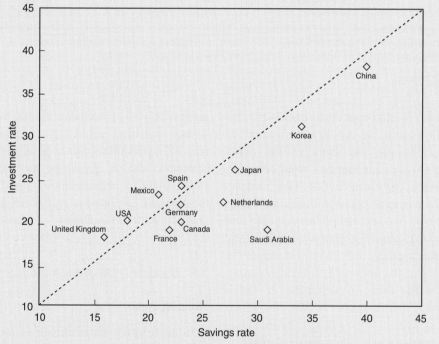

Figure 3.7 Savings rates and investment rates in selected countries, 2000

Source for data: World Bank, *World Development Report 2001/2002.*

Further reading

Feldstein, M. and C. Horioka (1980). Domestic Saving and International Capital Flows. *Economic Journal*, 90: 314–29.

Sinn, S. (1992a). Saving–Investment Correlations and Capital Mobility: On the Evidence from Annual Data. *Economic Journal*, 102: 1162–70.

Table 3.3 Inflow of direct investments, as percent of gross investment

	1986–1990	1991	1992	1993	1994	1995	1996	1997	1998	1999
Czech Republic	0.3	n.a.	n.a.	6.6	7.4	15.4	7.8	7.9	17.3	35.8
Hungary	n.a.	20.9	20.0	32.1	13.7	50.2	23.5	21.3	18.3	n.a.
Poland	0.2	1.9	4.8	12.4	10.5	15.5	15.1	14.5	15.9	18.4
EU-15	5.9	5.1	5.0	5.8	4.9	6.8	6.6	8.2	14.7	22.1
Argentina	3.2	8.7	11.6	6.2	7.1	12.1	14.1	16.1	11.5	47.2
Brazil	1.2	1.2	1.8	0.7	1.8	3.4	7.5	12.2	20.6	32.4
Chile	16.3	11.9	10.0	9.3	21.8	19.0	27.1	27.1	24.4	62.2
Mexico	6.1	8.1	6.2	5.9	13.4	20.4	15.5	16.4	12.8	11.6
Korea	1.5	1.0	0.6	0.5	0.6	1.0	1.2	1.7	5.7	8.2
Malaysia	10.3	22.4	23.9	19.2	14.5	10.8	11.9	11.7	11.1	8.9
Thailand	5.0	4.9	4.8	3.6	2.4	3.0	3.1	7.4	29.1	25.3

[a] Czech Republic, 1986–1990: Czechoslovakia.

Source: IMF, *International Financial Statistics*, CD-ROM, May 2001.

marginal productivity of capital exceeds the world market interest rate, for instance when considerable investment opportunities exist in a country. By capital imports, a stock of capital is built up in the debtor country. This increases the production possibilities. From the additional production, interest payment and debt repayment can be financed so that debt decreases in the course of time. At some point in time, the country moves into a creditor position.

Debt half-cycle

An economy will not always succeed in going through a full debt cycle from debtor to creditor. The expected marginal productivity of capital may be overestimated, or the foreign debt may not be used for capital formation, but to finance the government budget and, in the end, for consumption, e.g. to finance social programs or election promises. Then the commitment of the foreign debt weighs heavily on the economy. From a country's budgetary restriction $\dot{V} = I - S + rB$ (with V: debt; $\dot{V} > 0$: new indebtedness) it follows that reducing debt ($\dot{V} < 0$) at a given investment level (I) and given interest payments (rV) requires high savings if a country has accumulated high debt. This is equivalent to the statement that there has to be a high export surplus for a country to be able to pay interest and repay its foreign debt.

Case studies: the US and the UK

One example for such a development is the US. Especially during the time of the railroad boom (1840–1870), the US attracted foreign capital. At some point foreign debt was more than 20 percent in relation to its gross domestic product (Figure 3.8). The debt amount was then reduced and the US became a net creditor from 1914 onwards before moving into a net debtor position again in 1985. In Figure 3.8, two different statistical sources are used for the US, but their results show similar tendencies. The United Kingdom had a net creditor position in the world economy until the beginning of the 20th century; afterwards it got into a net debtor position which was partially reversed by the oil discoveries in the North Sea.

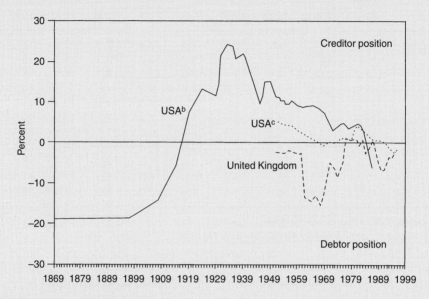

Figure 3.8 Debt cycle of the US[a]

[a] Debt in percent of gross domestic product. [b] Holtfrerich and Schötz, 1988. [c] All other data: IMF, *International Financial Statistics*, CD-ROM, May 1997.

3.6 The factor-price frontier

Owing to the production function, a unique relationship exists between prices of the different production factors. Intuitively, a factor's marginal productivity under a given production function can increase if less of this factor and more of the other factor is employed; the marginal productivity of the increasingly employed factor then falls. The real factor prices correspond to the marginal productivities. Taking the price of one factor as given determines the price of the other factor because of the production function. The factor-price frontier describes this relationship. It is the locus of all combinations of real factor prices which are conceivable with a given production function and thus with a given technology. For a substitutional, linear-homogeneous production function, the factor-price frontier is shown in Figure 3.9.

Assuming a production function for the

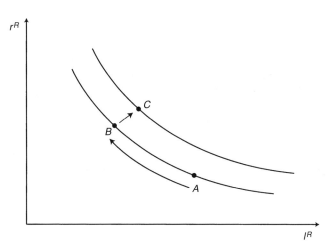

Figure 3.9 The factor price frontier

world, there is an interdependence between the real interest rate (r^R) and the real wage (L^R) under given conditions of production. In factor market equilibrium, one distinct combination of the conceivable combinations is realized on both factor markets (point *A*). Assume that the real factor prices are just high enough for full employment of both factors in the world. If the labor supply now rises in the world and the equilibrium wage falls due to this rise, the real interest rate rises (from point *A* to point *B*). The change of real factor prices already described in Chapter 2 occurs. The integration of economies rich in labor, like China, thus changes both absolute and relative factor prices.

If we take into consideration that technological progress is stimulated by globalization, the factor-price frontier moves outwards. The real wage can thus rise (from point *B* to point *C*).

The factor-price frontier is also valid for single economies or regions of the world. Depending on the production technologies, the frontier may be different for different countries. With the factor-price frontier we may also show what it means for a country if capital moves out of a country: the real inter-est rate rises, the real wage falls. Locational competition for the mobile capital thus has consequences for labor as a production factor.

3.7 *The world market for natural resources*

The previous considerations can analogously be applied to natural resources as a production factor. Taking natural resources (R) into account as an additional production factor in the production function $Q = F(L, K, R)$, the demand for resources is determined by the real resource price (nominal resource price w divided by the product price p) being equal to the marginal productivity of the resource (F_R): $w/p = F_R$. Thus, the world market for resources can be represented similarly to Figure 3.1.

A sudden resource shortage (for example, during the oil crisis in the 1970s) can be interpreted as a shift of the factor-price frontier (in Figure 3.9) to the left. The existing capital stock being adjusted to low oil prices becomes partly obsolete as oil prices rise. The marginal productivity of capital and labor falls. This means that the real factor incomes for capital and labor are reduced. In the course of time, this movement of the factor-price frontier to the left can be partly reversed if technological progress, e.g. opening up new energy resources and saving energy, moves the factor-price frontier outwards again.

A special problem with natural resources is depletion. We distinguish between non-renewable resources (oil) and renewable resources (wood, fish populations). When non-renewable resources are in finite supply and when substitution is not possible, they may eventually be exhausted. The optimal rate of resource extraction over time is therefore a decisive issue. When resources are renewable, the issue is how the rate of renewal and the rate of withdrawal have to interplay in order to secure an optimal pattern of resource use over time. Another issue is allocating the environment for competing uses (Chapter 15).

3.8 Changes on factor markets and world market equilibrium

A new equilibrium in the world factor markets has to be found when conditions change. Here are some cases:

- A technological breakthrough leads to an increased demand for capital. The capital demand curve on the world market for capital moves upwards. The interest rate rises. The same effect can be observed in the case of stronger growth, e.g. due to a higher growth path or during a recovery in the business cycle.
- A shortage of natural resources (oil) reduces the marginal productivity of capital. The interest rate falls.
- Institutional changes can influence the factor markets as well. In Western Europe, a high level of unemployment has developed over the past 30 years owing to the institutional setting of the labor market.

Another example of the impact of institutional arrangement is the introduction of capital-funded old-age insurance systems in the world; this stimulates savings and reduces the interest rate.

Note

1 In the figure given here, let BD be equal to DA, i.e. let the straight line have a slope of 45°. Then BC indicates how much is necessary to keep the household indifferent relative to point A and CB/DA is the preference rate (of consumption) in time. For consumption, the marginal rate of substitution in time results from totally differentiating the utility function

$$U = U(C_0) + \frac{1}{1+\delta} U(C_1)$$

at a constant utility (the so-called Euler equation):

$$\left| \frac{dC_1}{dC_0} \right| = \frac{U'_0(C_0)(1+\delta)}{U'_1(C_1)}$$

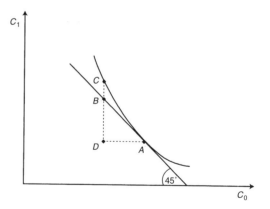

2 From the intertemporal utility-maximizing calculus

$$\max U = U_0(C_0) + (1+\delta)^{-1} U_1(C_1)$$

subject to

$$C_1 = Y/p_1 - (p_0/p_1)C_0$$

It follows that

$$(1+\delta)^{-1} U'_1(C_1) - U'_0(C_0)p_1/p_0 = 0$$

or

$$\frac{p_0}{p_1} = (1+\delta) U'_0(C_0)/U'_1(C_1)$$

Chapter 4

Growth processes in the world economy

....

What you will understand after reading this chapter

Previous chapters have analyzed the world markets for goods and for factors of production, this chapter continues the global economic view, looking at the way growth processes take place in the world economy. The historical record of the last two centuries shows a continuous upward movement in income per capita interrupted by two world wars and the hyper-inflation of the 1920s and the Great Depression of the 1930s (section 4.1). Growth processes overlap with cyclical movements (section 4.2). The driving force of economic growth is the augmentation of production factors, comprising capital accumulation, population growth and technological progress (section 4.3). Capital exports and imports play a decisive role in the growth processes of open economies (section 4.4). We discuss why openness is important (section 4.5). Localization factors are surveyed in section 4.6. Empirical evidence suggests the relevance of capital accumulation for growth (section 4.7). An intensely discussed topic is whether economic processes are characterized by divergence or convergence (section 4.8). Economic growth is a process with many different features (section 4.9). To conclude, some special aspects of the world economy's growth process are dealt with (section 4.10).

4.1 Economic growth: the historical record

The world economy is not static, but dynamic in character. In the course of time, various changes take place. In the last 200 years, a sizable increase in per capita income of the early industrialized countries can be observed (Figure 4.1). However, the two world wars, the European hyperinflation in the 1920s and the Great Depression halted the increase in economic welfare.

A decisive question for growth processes is whether economies are open or closed. Historically, there seems to be a relation between the openness of an economy and economic welfare. In the countries that were industrialized earliest, gross national product has risen with growing openness. The two world wars of the 20th century reduced the openness; they represent a period of decline and stagnation. This also holds for the 1920s and early

1930s, whereas after 1945 a continuous upward movement begins.

A rich source of historical data on economic growth in a long-run economic perspective is specified in Maddison (2001). For instance, growth in China and Europe is compared for two millennia. The book also looks at the impact of Europe on the world economy in the second millennium and in the second half of the last century.

4.2 Global economic growth and cyclical movements

Cyclical fluctuations

In the world economy, as well as in a national economy, long-term growth processes are characterized by cyclical movements. In Figure 4.2, a growth trend with cycles is shown for the industrialized nations, i.e. the OECD countries. Real gross national product

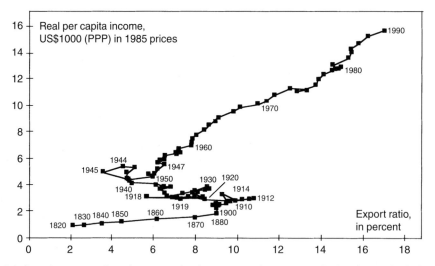

Figure 4.1 Development of real per capita income and export ratio in the early industrialized countries,[a] 1820–1990

[a] Australia, Austria, Belgium, Canada, Denmark, Finland, France, Germany, Italy, Japan, Netherlands, Norway, Sweden, Switzerland, United Kingdom, United States.
Source for data: Maddison (1992); own calculations.

oscillates around a trend. The recessions of 1974/1975, 1982/1983 and 1992/1993 in the industrialized countries are clearly visible. Economic growth is thus not constant over time, but varies with the ups and downs of economic activity.

Cyclical movements are not necessarily synchronized in the world economy. One region of the world may be in a recession while other regions are in an upswing. In this case, different regional factors are responsible for the cyclical movements, such as home-made and specific problems in one region, a weakening of impulses of growth in one area of the world or structural issues specific to one region only. The cyclical situation in a big country spills over to other economies (international business-cycle interlink). Thus, the US accounting for 30 percent of world GDP has a strong impact on other areas including Europe. If a worldwide disturbance (like the oil crisis) occurs, the world business cycle evolves in a rather synchronous way, resulting in a uniform world business cycle.

The processes of economic growth are accompanied by crises and other disturbances. The disintegration of the world economy in the 1930s, for example, went together with a breakdown of the world economy characterized by a significantly negative growth rate (see the Kindleberger spiral in Figure 1.3).

Crises

Whereas periods of growing integration in the world economy, like the two decades after the Second World War, went along with high growth rates, the oil crisis of the 1970s partially devalued the existing stock of capital that was contingent on low energy prices. This lowered the marginal productivity of capital, with the consequence that growth collapsed. At the same time, the export revenues of the OPEC countries increased. With higher purchasing power, this increase led to a redirection of trade flows, to trade balance surpluses, to the accumulation of financial assets and to a redirection of financial flows (petro-dollar recycling). Other disturbances had their effects on the growth process as well, like the Korean War which led to a boom with strong price rises, and the Vietnam War, where the strong expansion of the money supply in the United States ended in the inflation of the Bretton Woods system's anchor currency and, finally, in the collapse of this system. The debt crisis of the 1980s cut the Latin American countries off from real capital inflows. In real terms, a temporary transfer of capital in favor of the industrialized countries took place ('capital flowed up the hill'). The collapse of the centrally planned economies is another aspect of the subject of growth processes in the world economy. In 1997 the Asian countries experienced a financial crisis with negative growth rates, high current account deficits, currency devaluations and serious adjustment problems.

Some impulses of growth

Technological breakthroughs like the first industrial revolution in Great Britain in the 18th century represent an impulse for world economic growth. This also holds for the settlement and the industrialization of new areas such as North America. Moreover, changes in a country's economic policy can influence growth processes worldwide through the redirection of investment flows.

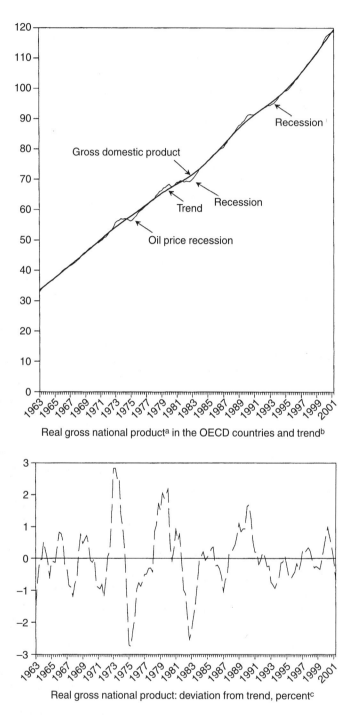

Figure 4.2 Growth and business cycle in the OECD countries

[a] Index 1995 = 100.

[b] Hodrick/Prescott filter (smoothing factor 1600).

[c] Deviation from a Hodrick/Prescott Filter (HP 1600).

Source for data: OECD, *Main Economic Indicators*, current volumes.

Kondratieff cycles

Basic innovations can be interpreted as stimulating long-run growth cycles lasting for half a century. Such basic innovations change the technological structure of an economy comprehensively. While it may be somewhat arbitrary to pin down the time span of such basic innovation waves, five Kondratieff cycles can be distinguished:

1 Kondratieff (1800–1850): steam engine
2 Kondratieff (1850–1900): steel railroads
3 Kondratieff (1900–1950): electro-technology, chemistry
4 Kondratieff (1950–1990): automobile, petro-chemistry
5 Kondratieff (1990–2020): information technology and biotechnology

It is a question whether a sixth Kondratieff is about to start with biotechnology.

4.3 The driving forces of growth

World production function

Following at first a global view, i.e. of the world economy as a whole, a possible approach to the analysis of growth processes in the world economy is a world production function

$$Y = F(L, K, T, R, \ldots)$$

where the world national product Y depends on the production factors labor (L), capital (K), technological knowledge (T), resources (R) and other production factors. Therefrom, the growth equation

$$\hat{Y} = G(\hat{L}, \hat{K}, \hat{T}, \hat{R}, \ldots)$$

can be derived; according to this the growth rate of the world product is a function of the growth rates of labor, capital stock, technological knowledge, natural resources and other production factors. As a rule, we refer to an increase (or decrease) of per capita output ($y = Y/L$) when analyzing world economic growth, as it is a measure for people's provision with goods and thus a rudimentary measure for welfare.

Such a formulation of a world production function is certainly interesting for historical analyses, where the importance of particular growth factors like capital accumulation, population growth, technological progress or changes of the natural resources supply can be investigated. The world production function and the growth equation represent a general framework for an economic analysis and can also be the basis for econometric studies. In the ideal case, however, a formulation like this would require us to be able to empirically measure with sufficient accuracy the inputs of a world production function, like the world's capital stock, the world's labor supply and its technological knowledge. This is impossible at the moment. We thus have to content ourselves either with applying the production factors and the growth equation to the world as a whole in a rather general interpretation, or to refer to the growth processes of particular regions of the world where outputs and inputs can be measured accurately. In both cases, it is worthwhile to further investigate the role of the particular determinants of growth.

Growth through capital accumulation

A first approach to explaining growth refers to capital accumulation in the context of neoclassical growth theory (Solow 1956).

Capital accumulation does not concern a static look at the allocation of capital in one period, i.e. a flow equilibrium (as in Chapter 3), but the accumulation of capital over time. In such an intertemporal context, we distinguish between a long-term equilibrium and the time path to the equilibrium. In a long-term equilibrium (steady state) all variables grow at the same rate and the ratios between these variables remain constant. A special case is the stationary state where the equilibrium growth rates of all variables equal zero. The time path indicates how an economy moves from the initial situation to the long-run equilibrium.

Pure capital accumulation without population growth or technological progress is the simplest case of growth. The world accumulates capital and a higher capital stock means more output, i.e. growth. The process of accumulating capital continues until the marginal productivity of capital and the discount rate (of utility, δ) are equal. Using a per capita version of the production function $y = f(k)$ with k being the capital intensity we have as an optimality condition for capital accumulation $f_k = \delta$ (Figure 4.3). As long as $f_k > \delta$, capital is accumulated; when $f_k = \delta$ (point G),

capital accumulation comes to a halt (stationary state).

According to this concept, the world moves downwards along the negatively sloped marginal productivity-of-capital curve. The growth rate of gross national income, however, falls with increasing capital formation (increasing k) because each additional unit of capital has a lower marginal productivity. In the long-term equilibrium (point G), the growth rate is then zero because no further capital is built up.

Let the discount rate now approach zero, i.e., $\delta \to 0$. Then, the marginal rate of capital productivity also approaches zero. Point G approaches the horizontal axis.[1]

Real capital and human capital

Besides real capital (K), human capital (H) can also be regarded as a production factor of its own, comprising the skills, the capabilities and the knowledge of workers. All these characteristics are influenced by formal education or by 'learning on the job'. Furthermore, a traditional factor 'labor' (L: simple labor) is regarded as input. The production function, e.g. of the Cobb–Douglas type, then takes the form $Y = K^{a}H^{\beta}K^{1-\alpha-\beta}$ instead of $Y = K^{a}L^{1-\alpha}$. Obviously, the weight of the traditional factors, labor and capital, measured by the elasticities of production α and $(1 - \alpha)$, changes. Under the assumption of perfect competition, the factors' elasticity of production corresponds to their shares of national income. With the share of labor in national income being $1 - \alpha = 0.7$, the production elasticity of labor is estimated by that value in the traditional Cobb–Douglas function (and the share of capital at $\alpha = 0.3$). By taking human capital into account, the share of traditional labor is reduced, whereas the importance of capital formation (including human capital)

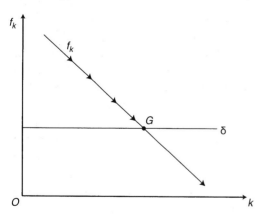

Figure 4.3 Optimal accumulation of capital

increases. The formation of human capital in the form of education requires abstaining from consumption, i.e. saving, like the formation of real capital. Saving thus becomes increasingly important. If we correspondingly define a broad notion of capital Z: (K, H) that comprises real and human capital, this factor is attributed a weight of $\alpha + \beta$.[2] Empirical studies show that this elasticity of production $\alpha + \beta$ is 0.7 or higher and that traditional labor's elasticity of production lies at 0.3 and lower (Mankiw 1995). Income differences between economies can thus be explained not only by differences in the provision with physical capital, but also by different qualities of human capital, especially a different impact of education systems (years of schooling, universities).

Population growth

Taking population growth into account as well and assuming a discount rate near zero, a long-term equilibrium would be reached when the marginal productivity of capital (f_k) and the growth rate of the labor supply (n) are just equal, i.e. $f_k = n$ (point G in Figure 4.4). Each additional worker is equipped with additional capital. This follows from the neoclassical growth model and is called the 'golden rule of capital accumulation'. It ensures the highest per capita income possible in long-term equilibrium. This golden rule is not valid, however, if a positive discount rate is explicitly assumed.[3] With a higher capital stock per worker, it would indeed be possible to achieve a higher domestic product, but due to the positive discount rate, the economy is not willing to wait for it. With a positive discount rate, less capital is accumulated (point G' in Figure 4.4). The rule for optimal allocation is $f_k = \delta + n$. Here we have an analogy to renewable resources where it would be possible to achieve a maximum extraction quan-

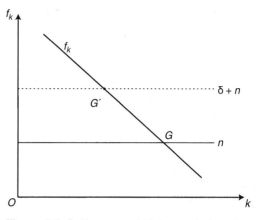

Figure 4.4 Optimum capital accumulation, time preference and population growth

tity ('maximum yield') at a discount rate of zero, but owing to a positive discount rate, the resource stock that is being held is smaller. Analogously, less capital is accumulated (Blanchard and Fischer 1989, p. 45; Siebert 1983, Chapter 5).

The optimum time path for consumption and capital

The position of the long-term equilibrium and the adjustment path leading to the equilibrium can be represented in a c–k diagram. The long-term equilibrium is defined by per capita consumption (c) and the capital stock per capita (k) no longer changing. This means $\dot{c} = 0$ and $\dot{k} = 0$ where a dot indicates the change of a variable over time. Per capita consumption does not change any more when the condition $f_k(k) = \delta + n$ is satisfied (where δ and n are constant).[4] From this condition follows that in the c–k space, the $\dot{c}$ curve is a vertical line since $f_k(k)$ is determined by $\delta + n$ (Figure 4.5). From the system's equation of motion $\dot{k} = f(k) - c - nk$, it follows for $\dot{k} = 0$ that $c = f(k) - nk$, meaning that with k increasing, c first rises on the $\dot{k} = 0$ curve (if $f_k > n$), but then decreases again due to falling marginal productivity ($f_k < n$). At a positive discount rate $\delta > 0$, point G' will result in the world economy in long-term equilibrium. Note that for $\delta \to 0$, point G would be reached (maximum yield). The positive discount rate implies a lower capital formation. Note that Figure 4.5 also holds for renewable resources where c is resource withdrawal from nature and $f(k)$ represents a production function of a natural resource stock k (i.e. a regeneration function of a forest or a fish population) with $f_k > 0$ below a natural equilibrium k^* and $f_k < 0$ above k^*.

If technological progress is present and if labor input is measured in efficiency units $\tilde{A} = a(t)A$, a figure analogous to Figure 4.4 results in the simple Solow-type model, where n has to be replaced by the term $n + x\varepsilon \approx n + \kappa$ (where ε is the rate of technological progress and $x = -cu''/u'$). In this case as well, a positive discount rate causes the accumulation of capital to come to a stop earlier. In Figure 4.4, new technological knowledge moves the marginal productivity of capital curve upward, shifting points G and G' to the right. Technological progress thus prevents a 'walking down the marginal productivity of capital curve'.

Technological progress

As a rule, the growth rate decreases with a growing capital stock per capita, owing to decreasing marginal productivity. Every additional unit of capital has a smaller output effect. If we look at an economy where only the accumulation of real capital plays a role as a growth factor, capital formation comes to a standstill in the long run; a stationary state is reached. This holds, for example, with a per capita production function $y = k^{\alpha}$ with $\alpha < 1$.

Endogenous growth in technological knowledge

Marginal productivity does not necessarily fall if the production function shows increasing returns to scale. This is Romer's (1986; see also Grossman and Helpman 1991a) concept of knowledge capital (Z). With capital formation per worker in an enterprise (k), knowledge capital $Z = Z(k)$ develops as well, and this capital can also be used in other enterprises, i.e. capital accumulation in one firm has positive effects in other enterprises. For the marginal productivity of capital, we then have $f_k(k, Z)$; that is, the marginal

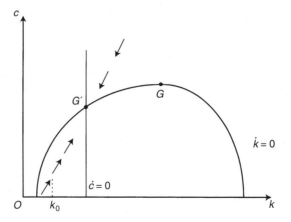

Figure 4.5 Long-term equilibrium

productivity of capital is positively affected by knowledge capital. Assuming $Z(k) = k^\gamma$, the production function takes the form $y = k^a Z(k) = k^{a+\gamma}$. Here, the traditional production function shows constant returns to scale for labor and capital and thus a decreasing marginal productivity of capital intensity k^a ($\alpha < 1$). The production function as a whole, however, has increasing returns to scale. This is related to technological knowledge being not a private commodity with rivalry in its use, but a public commodity, e.g. software that can be used in various places without the occurrence of rivalry. If the effect discussed here is strong enough and if $\alpha + \gamma$ approaches 1, decreasing marginal productivities of capital disappear completely.

What drives the determinants of growth?

To explain growth processes, it is important to know what drives the determinants of growth. Thus, capital accumulation depends on the savings and on the expected return on investment. A country having a low time preference rate will tend to have higher savings. High rates of return are an incentive to invest and to build up a capital stock. Institutional arrangements such as a pay-as-you-go system or a capital-funded system influence the volume of savings. Technological progress depends on investments into research and development. High expected profits from research and development are an incentive to invest and to innovate. In the Romer model (1986), for example, the profit expectations in the high-technology industry drive the expenditures for research and development. The development of the growth determinants has thus to be explained endogenously.

The historical shift from physical capital to intangible capital

Historically, different growth factors were the driving force in the growth process; the importance of growth factors has shifted considerably over time. Looking at the US as an example (David 1999), working capital was the source of growth in labor productivity at the beginning of the 19th century; fixed (physical) capital took the leading role in a process of capital deepening in the later part of the 19th century. In the 20th century, intangible capital (knowledge capital) with investments in education and training became the dominant growth factor.

4.4 Capital importers and exporters

Let us now study open economies that do not have to rely on their own savings for their investments, but can import capital. Similarly, other countries may export capital. In order to determine whether a country is a capital importer or exporter, the interaction between the marginal productivity (f_k), the discount rate (δ), and the world market interest rate (r) has to be discussed.

Efficiency gains through capital movements

If the marginal productivity of capital and the discount rate in a country are higher than the world market interest rate, i.e. $f_k = \delta > r$, it is worthwhile to import capital from the world market for capital (Figure 4.6a). If, however, the discount rate is lower than the interest rate in the world market for capital, it is worthwhile to export capital (Figure 4.6b). The capital importer gets an advantage (in the case of $\delta > r$) by passing from autarky to free capital mobility: with capital from the world market, they can produce more in their home

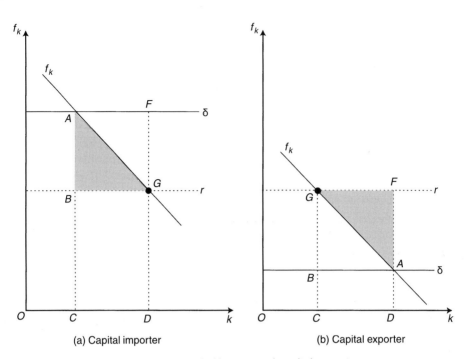

Figure 4.6 Long-term equilibrium with capital import and capital export

country (point *G* instead of point *A*). The importer pays interest on the imported capital amounting to the rectangle *CBGD* and additionally produces the area *CAGD*. The part of the production that additionally remains for the importer is the triangle *BAG*. This is the advantage from importing capital.

The capital exporter also has an advantage by passing from autarky to free capital mobility. They produce less than in autarky, but receive a higher income from interest. The exporter gains the area *GFA* in Figure 4.6b.

Figure 4.6 exhibits an equilibrium in only the short run. In the long run, the current account has to be balanced for the two equilibrium solutions *G*, so there is an intertemporal budget restriction to be respected. To balance its current account in the future, the debtor country thus has to fulfill its interest obligations by exporting goods to the creditor country. For the capital-importing country,

gross domestic product exceeds gross national product which can be interpreted as gross residents' product. In long-term equilibrium, it cannot use its whole production for consumption, but has to set some part aside for paying interest and acquittance.

Capital movements and the time path of consumption

In Figure 4.7, the long-term equilibrium of a capital-importing country is represented in the *c–k* diagram. *G* characterizes the long-term equilibrium without capital import and thus in autarky. Starting from the capital endowment of the original situation k_0, this equilibrium is reached through own savings. This takes time. Compared to the autarky situation, a capital-importing country can reach the consumption level *G'* faster by importing capital instead of saving on its own

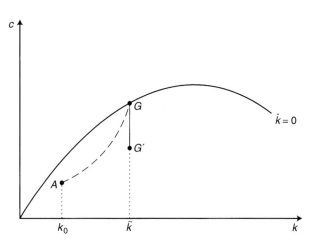

Figure 4.7 Growth path of a capital-importing country

(*G*). But in the long-term equilibrium, this country has to pay *GG'* for debt service and debt acquittance. Its long-term consumption level is lower; through own savings it could have reached a higher consumption level (point *G*), but waiting for it would have been longer, meaning a loss of utility. The mirror image is the capital-exporting country that reaches a higher consumption level (Maurer 1998).

The two-country case is represented in Figure 4.8. It is assumed that the productivity of the capital stock per capita f_k is lower in the home country, e.g. owing to its lower level of technology (lower part of the diagram). At a capital stock per capita of k_0, the marginal productivity of capital in the home country is higher than in the foreign country which is assumed to have a capital stock per capita of $\tilde{k}^*$. Thus, the home country imports capital. In the long-term equilibrium, the home country pays interest and acquittance (distance *GG'*), implying that in the long run it can consume only less than it produces. The foreign country provides capital to the home country, receiving capital income for it in the long run (distance *S*S*'*). For simplicity it has been

assumed that in the original situation, the foreign country was in a steady state already (point *S**).

Possible scenarios of capital accumulation

If all countries in the world have the same discount rate and if one country has the highest capital productivity, capital will be accumulated first in this country. The country with the highest capital productivity grows fastest at first, causing marginal capital productivity to fall gradually so that eventually capital accumulation becomes attractive for the other countries as well.

Let us now look at a situation where initially all countries have the same marginal productivity of capital, but one country has a lower discount rate. This country will be more inclined to abstain from consumption. This results in a consumption level that is lower at first, but also in faster capital accumulation owing to higher savings. Because of this, it can consume more later on: its consumption increases faster in time. The other countries, on the other hand, have a high discount rate and are thus more impatient. They start with

79

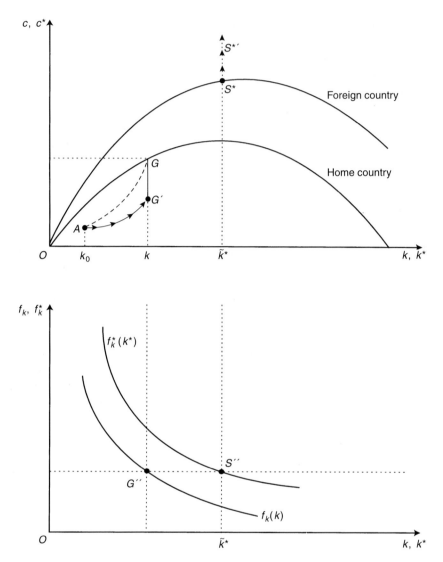

Figure 4.8 Growth path of capital importer and capital exporter

a higher consumption level, but they build less capital, and their consumption increases more slowly in time.

If all countries have different discount rates, the country with the lowest discount rate determines up to which point capital is accumulated in the world economy.[5] The country with the lowest discount rate provides capital until its discount rate and the real interest rate are equal, then its consumption stays constant. For the other countries, $\delta > r$ holds, and consumption decreases in the course of time. In a simplifying model context, the patient country finally accumulates all the capital of the world.

Taking different discount rates, different population growth rates and different rates of technological progress into consideration, the implications for the capital market become very complex. Under *ceteris paribus* assumptions, the country with the low discount rate remains the world's net creditor, and this result should not change if, owing to population growth, the debtor country needs more capital and has a high national discount rate. A country with strong technological progress can also indebt itself to the country with the low discount rate. The technological progress may be strong enough to finance the interest service in favor of the creditor country.

4.5 How important is the openness of economies?

Economic growth is related to the openness of economies. Figure 4.9 shows the growth rate of the early industrialized countries for the period 1870–1990 and the openness, measured as the rate of increase of the export ratio, i.e. of the share of exports in GDP. Except for the two world wars and the inter-war period, the export ratio increases, and the growth rate of the gross domestic product per capita rises. Exports are beneficial to economic growth.

There is a variety of mechanisms through which growth occurs in an open economy. The first to be mentioned here are traditional gains from foreign trade with final products, generating a higher gross domestic product. In the course of economic development, countries manage to gain comparative price advantages through the formation of real and human capital. The advantages of endowment change; and these advantages can be influenced by policy ('acquired comparative advantage'). At the same time, some comparative advantages migrate away from industrialized nations to the developing countries, e.g. because production no longer pays off owing to increasing factor costs (like labor costs or regulation). Gains of specialization add to the welfare gains; especially, economies of scale (learning effects) are of

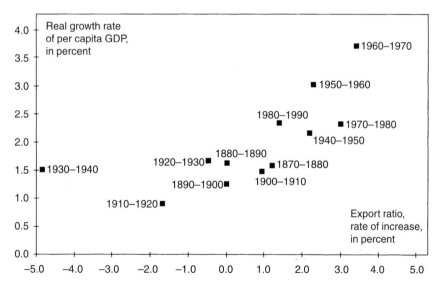

Figure 4.9 Real per capita growth and foreign trade in the early industrialized countries,[a] 1870–1990

[a] Countries: see Figure 4.1.
Source for data: Maddison (1992); own calculations.

relevance. A wider variety of products is made possible. The hypothesis of the product cycle also explains why production moves away from industrialized countries (via a diffusion of knowledge from the innovator to the imitators) and eventually finds its locations worldwide. The intensification of competition that is related to foreign trade (with the consequence of falling costs and new technological knowledge discovered) results in higher growth as well.

If trade with capital goods is also taken into account, additional effects result. Debt allows the import of capital goods so that the capital stock can be accumulated faster; the economy moves on a higher growth path towards the long-term equilibrium. Competition in the production of capital goods is intensified so that efficiency gains can be expected. The sectoral resource allocation between research and development on the one side and production on the other are improved through trade with capital goods, leading to a higher long-term growth path with income gains. In the long-term equilibrium, a higher per capita production is reached. Finally, the international diffusion of technological knowledge, like the trade in patents and the flow of ideas, is a channel through which the growth process can be influenced favorably in open economies.

4.6 Localization factors

Economic activities are not uniformly distributed in space (Krugman 1991). One reason is that space itself is not homogeneous, but structured by resource deposits, agricultural areas, natural highways and harbors, settlement possibilities and other factors. Beside these basic locational advantages, advantages of agglomeration play an important role as factors that constitute spatial

structure. These concern positive external effects between economic activities, referring to technological as well as pecuniary external effects. This comprises spatially limited diffusion processes related to new technological knowledge (spillover, spatially bound knowledge capital), informal or formal information networks delimited in space and 'proximity advantages', e.g. between enterprises and politics. A case in point is the labor market. If a region has a qualified labor supply at its disposal (historical examples: the Swiss Jura for the watch industry, Baden-Württemberg in Germany for precision engineering), it is easier for the enterprises to rely on a pool of qualified workers. If a region is occupied by enterprises that demand similar qualifications, such a region is attractive for qualified workers simply because they do not depend on just one company. They have the option of switching to other companies, and thus their risk of becoming jobless is smaller.

Transport costs are another factor that has structuring effects on space. They determine the size of the market. The decline of transport costs increases the size of the market. The reduction of virtual distance in the internet improves the size of networks.

Once a certain structure is given, like the existence of a city with a homogeneous area around it, it can be shown that rings of economic activity develop around the city as a function of transport costs (Thünen 1826); other things equal, businesses with high transport costs will settle near the city (Alonso 1964).

Furthermore, the historical development of the spatial structure is path dependent. The spatial structure given in a specific moment of time is the base for economic decisions that for their part have spatial effects in the future. Thus, the future spatial development is in some way shaped by the original structure. Old locations have the advantage that various investments have already been made there, comprising real capital of the companies, durable consumption goods of the households (real estate), infrastructural capital (roads, harbors, universities). The costs related to these are partly 'sunk costs'; production stays at the old location, even if these costs can no longer be covered.

In contrast, a new location does not have the sunk-cost advantage. It has to compete with an old location that can neglect the sunk costs in locational competition. As the capital stock of a region is, in a disaggregated view, defined by a variety of capital goods, the decision about choices of location for the individual capital good is dispersed on the time axis. As a consequence, decisions about the location of capital goods that are currently installed at an old location and need replacement have to be made again and again. If a capital good stays at an old location, chances improve for another capital good at that place to be renewed there as well.

However, sunk costs cannot justify a location permanently. At some time, the marginal productivity of investments may decline so much or the locational quality elsewhere may improve so strongly that a change of location becomes worthwhile, despite sunk costs.

During the process of economic development, self-amplifying factors may occur that lead to the development of growth poles, especially if a region can attract resources owing to advantages of location and agglomeration (polarization). The growth process in the world economy is then seen as taking place in a large set of regional growth clusters. During the further development, such growth poles then radiate out to other regions and pull them along. Here, the question arises of whether a process of convergence will come about or whether economic development is finally accompanied by divergence (see below).

On a more aggregated scale of the world economy, the concept of the center (or centers) and periphery plays a role. Over the last century, the two centers of Europe and North America have been distinguished. In the 20th century, a third center or growth pole in Asia, with Japan, the four or six 'tigers' and China, has appeared beside the two centers of North America and Europe.

4.7 Empirical evidence: capital formation

The variety of the approaches to explaining economic growth presented here has produced a considerable literature striving for empirical scrutiny. Let us look at the importance of capital formation as a growth factor.

Economies with a high marginal productivity of capital should, other things being equal, be characterized by a strong capital formation. Capital is also needed if the population increases, to equip the additional workforce with machines. Moreover, strong technological progress will lead to high investment activity. We can expect a high investment activity to be linked to high growth rates because the capital stock is an important ingredient of the growth process. The higher the investment rate, the stronger is the growth rate. The thesis that the average growth rate is positively related to the investment rate is empirically corroborated (Figure 4.10). It is remarkable that the four tigers, with investment rates of significantly above 25 percent (Singapore 37.7 percent) have had annual growth rates of over 6 percent.

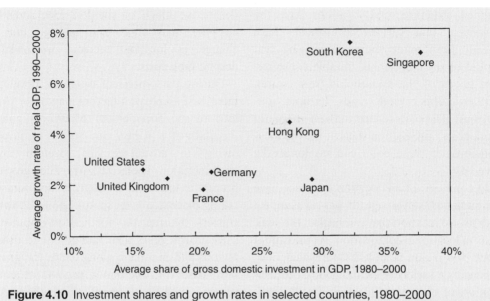

Figure 4.10 Investment shares and growth rates in selected countries, 1980–2000

Source for data: IMF, *International Financial Statistics*, CD-ROM, 2001; World Bank, *World Development Indicators*, 2001.

4.8 Catching-up processes in the world economy: convergence or divergence?

The convergence hypothesis

The marginal productivity of capital falls with growing capital accumulation. Consequently, the contribution of a unit of capital to growth decreases as well. We thus have to expect the growth rate to fall with capital accumulation. This argument can also be pointed in another direction: as poor countries have a small capital stock, they should – all other things being equal – have a higher marginal productivity of capital and thus a higher growth rate than rich countries with better capital equipment. The hypothesis thus is: 'Poor countries grow faster'. Differences in income are then (at least partly) leveled out in the course of time.

In the extreme case, we should – with a fully integrated world market for capital and without differences in risk – expect that there cannot be any differences in the marginal

product of capital. In the simplest of models with perfectly mobile capital and identical production technology everywhere, the international capital mobility would have to lead to an almost immediate equalization of growth rates. This cannot be observed empirically, however. One reason is that there is no perfect capital mobility. In reality, the international capital mobility performs a balancing function only at peaks, as the discussion of the Feldstein–Horioka (1980) result in Chapter 3 has shown. In addition, there are other factors that are specific for a certain country and explain differences in economic growth; these factors particularly comprise the institutional set-up and the growth of technological knowledge.

In the very long run, differences in marginal productivity should be impossible even under imperfect capital mobility if we assume identical production technologies and institutions. In this case, there would be absolute convergence, i.e. output per worker would, in the long-run equilibrium (steady state), be equal in all countries. In the simple neoclassical model of the Solow type, though, absolute convergence is only reached if the exogenous data for the long-run equilibrium, like population growth (n) (if it is exogenously given), the savings rate and human capital are identical. Regarding different long-term equilibria, we have to make corrections for these differing exogenous conditions.[6] This is why we speak of conditional convergence, where the different exogenous conditions of different countries are taken into account. Then, neither do countries reach the same long-term equilibrium nor are the per capita incomes equalized between countries.

Some formulae of convergence

To get an impression of the time required for convergence, we take a look at two economies with constant growth rates g (home country) and g^* (foreign country) of per capita income. Note that this represents a simplification because on a growth path to a long-run equilibrium the rates would change. Assuming that Home has a lower initial per capita income than Foreign, i.e. $y_0 < y_0^*$, the convergence rate $\hat{\alpha}$ satisfies $\hat{\alpha} = \hat{y} - \hat{y}^* = g - g^*$. If Home grows at a rate of $g = 5$ percent and Foreign at $g^* = 2$ percent, the income difference is leveled out at a rate of about 3 percent per year.

The duration of the absolute convergence (t) is calculated by setting the per capita incomes of the two countries in t equal, so that

$$y_t = y_t^* \Leftrightarrow y_0 e^{gt} = y_0^* e^{g^*t}$$

with

$$t = \frac{\ln(y_0/y_0^*)}{g^* - g} = \frac{\ln(y_0) - \ln(y_0^*)}{g^* - g}$$

With a growth difference $g - g^*$ of 3 percentage points and an income level of one third in the original situation (e.g. $y_0 = 100$ and $y_0^* = 300$), it takes nearly 37 years until both countries have the same per capita income. For the half-life of the income difference,

$$t_{\text{half}} = \frac{0.5 \ln(y_0/y_0^*)}{g^* - g}$$

holds.[7] With a growth difference of 3 percentage points and an income level of one third in the original situation, it takes 18.5 years until the income differential (more precisely: the income relation expressed in logs) is halved. For this formulation, absolute convergence and half-life depend on the original situation (Table 4.1).

Applying these considerations to East Germany, we have to expect a long-term adjustment process. In 2001, the East German region (including West Berlin) has attained 65 percent of West Germany's per capita (of the population) level of production. If an adjustment to 80 percent of the West German level is set as a target and if the East German growth rate exceeded West Germany's growth rate by 3 percentage points, the level of 80 percent would be attained in 2008. With a growth rate differential of 2 percent, we would have to wait until 2011.[8] Unfortunately, East Germany has not been growing at a higher rate than West Germany in the last three years, but at a lower rate.

Convergence between regions

Thus far, the analysis has been simplified in the sense that the growth rates of two countries are assumed to be fixed. In the adjustment period of the neoclassical model, the growth rate changes, however, when approaching the steady state. Strictly speaking,

Table 4.1 Time required for convergence

Percentage points of lead in growth (%)	Half-life[a]: difference of per capita incomes halved in . . . years			Absolute convergence[b] in . . . years		
	Starting from an original level of					
	30%	40%	50%	30%	40%	50%
1	60.2	45.8	34.7	120.4	91.6	69.3
2	30.1	22.9	17.3	60.2	45.8	34.7
3	20.1	15.3	11.6	40.1	30.5	23.1
4	15.0	11.5	8.7	30.1	22.9	17.3
5	12.0	9.2	6.9	24.1	18.3	13.9
6	10.0	7.6	5.8	20.1	15.3	11.6

[a] Calculated according to the formula:

$$t_{half} = \frac{0.5 \ln(y_0/y_0^*)}{g^* - g}.$$

[b] Calculated according to the formula: $t = \ln(y_0/y_0^*)/(g^* - g)$.

convergence addresses the question whether the actual per capita income is converging against the per capita income in the long-term equilibrium $\tilde{y}$. In this formulation, the average growth rate per year over a period spanning from the initial period 0 to the steady-state period T is given by the growth rate x in the long-term equilibrium and the 'distance' of the per capita income in the steady state $\tilde{y}$ from the original situation y_0 (Barro and Sala-i-Martin 1995: 81).[9]

$$\hat{y} = \frac{1}{T} \ln\left[\frac{y(T)}{y_0}\right] = x + \frac{1}{T}(1 - e^{-\beta T})\ln\left[\frac{\tilde{y}}{y_0}\right]$$

The further the per capita income in the initial situation is away from the income in the steady state, the higher is the average growth rate over the period from 0 to T. β is the rate of convergence. At a constant rate of convergence β, the expression $(1/T)(1 - e^{-\beta T})$ approaches zero if T approaches infinity. The growth rate is then dominated by the steady-state rate (x).[10]

The Barro rule

Barro and Sala-i-Martin (1992) have applied these considerations to the regions of the US for the period from 1880 until 1988. Their result was that the differences between the regions were leveled out at a rate of 2 percent per year. This is the so-called Barro rule. At a rate of convergence of 2 percent, it takes about 35 years until the difference of per capita incomes between regions is halved. As the regions of the US surveyed by Barro are relatively similar, we can assume that they approach the same long-term equilibrium (steady state) in the long run. These results suggest that catch-up processes exist, but that these processes require considerable time.

Convergence of early industrialized countries

For the period from 1870 until 1979, Maddison (1982) concludes that early industrialized countries with a high per capita income had smaller growth rates of per capita income whereas economies with a lower per capita income showed a higher growth rate. The regression[11] yields (*L*: number of workers, standard error in parentheses):

$$\log\left(\frac{Y_{1979}}{L_{1979}}\right) - \log\left(\frac{Y_{1870}}{L_{1870}}\right) = 8.46 - \underset{(0.09)}{1.00}\log\left(\frac{Y_{1870}}{L_{1870}}\right),$$

$$R^2 = 0.88$$

The slope of −1 means that for every percent that a country's per capita income was below the average in 1870, the cumulated growth rate in the period 1870–1979 was higher by 1 percent. According to this result we thus observe a long-term convergence, in fact an absolute convergence. A critical objection to this is that the country selection is biased in the sense that all the examined countries have a high per capita income today as well. If instead countries are examined that do not have a high per capita income today, but did in 1870 (thus additionally taking into account, among others, Argentina, Portugal and Spain), and if Japan is excluded from the observation as a one-off case, we can at best speak of a convergence that is only weak.

Convergence in the OECD countries

If we take the OECD countries – and thus the industrialized countries – into account, a negative relation between the level of the growth rate and the per capita income results as well, but the differences for the period from 1870 to 1993 are leveled out at a rate of only 1 percent compared to 2 percent in the Barro estimates for regions of a country (Figure 4.11). Inside an economy, the catch-up processes are thus, as a rule, stronger than they are between countries. Since the Second World War, the European economies and Japan have grown significantly more strongly than that of the US. In 1990, the income differences per capita of 1950 had been reduced by well over a half (Obstfeld and Rogoff 1996, p. 455).

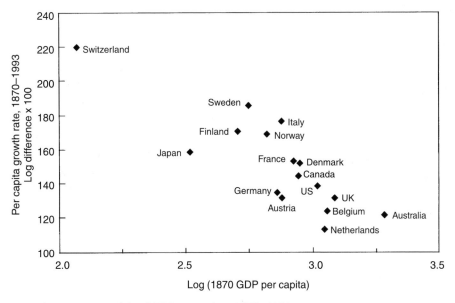

Figure 4.11 Convergence of the OECD countries, 1870–1993

Source for data: De Long (1988) and Maddison (1982); own calculations.

Convergence in the European Union

For the countries of the European Union, convergence of per capita incomes with a convergence rate of 1.4 percent for the period 1960–1995 can be observed (Figure 4.12). As countries in a regional integration like the European Union have an intermediate position between regions of an economy and the nation states like OECD countries, the catch-up processes in regional integrations (like the EU) are not as swift as between the regions of a country (2 percent), but faster than between the OECD countries (1 percent). Thus, it seems that the Barro rule differs with respect to the level of disaggregation and the level of institutional integration. Regions with a common institutional framework of a nation have a high rate of convergence. Autonomous countries have a much lower convergence. Countries belonging to a regional integration like the EU are in between.

Divergence between industrialized countries and developing countries

Convergence does not occur any more, however, if the number of countries is greatly increased. In a study of 98 countries, a moderately positive regression between growth rate and development level results (Barro and Sala-i-Martin 1992). Countries with a higher income level grow (moderately) stronger. Divergence prevails; accordingly, industrialized countries and developing countries grow apart. For the developing countries as a whole, again convergence cannot be found. This image presumably changes if some countries like the African countries south of the Sahara (and possibly some Latin American countries) are excluded. A possible explanation for the fact that convergence cannot be observed in these cases is that the parameters of technology and of resource endowment are very different. Economic policy plays an

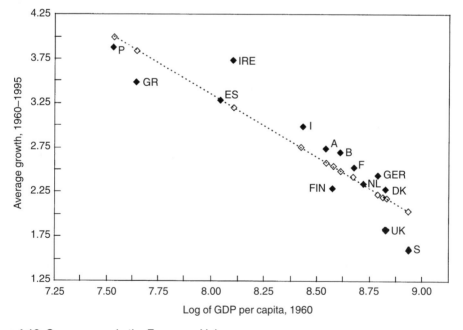

Figure 4.12 Convergence in the European Union

Source for data: IMF, *International Financial Statistics*, CD-ROM, 1998; Gundlach (1998).

important role as well, as in the misorientation of Latin America in the four decades until 1990. The countries are then characterized by different long-term equilibria.

Absolute and conditional convergence

Conditional convergence refers to the fact that not all factors of economic growth are identical between countries and regions, but that differences in initial factor endowments exist that are permanent. For instance, cultural differences could be such a factor. Then, the country or region in question cannot reach the same steady state as other areas. The steady state is conditional upon the endowment difference. If, however, the initial differences in factor endowments can be overcome by accumulation in the course of time, the same steady state can be reached; we speak of absolute convergence.

Convergence clubs

Empirical analyses suggest that convergence can be more easily shown for a subset of countries and for a subset of regions of a country (Bode 1998). Some countries or some regions diverge; if these are excluded from the analysis of a set of countries or regions, the convergence process is stronger.

Sigma convergence

So far, the discussion about convergence has been based on the catching-up rate of the per capita income. This is called 'Beta convergence'. Sigma convergence, on the other hand, refers to the coefficient of variation of the per capita income expressed in logs. We have Sigma convergence if the per capita income coefficient of variation for a group of regions (or countries) decreases. Beta convergence and Sigma convergence are different measures. Beta convergence is geared to the growth rates of the per capita income over a period; Sigma convergence refers to the variance of the per capita incomes at two points in time. The two measures thus do not lead to identical statements about convergence processes: regions with a low per capita income can grow so strongly (high Beta convergence) that at the end of a period of comparison the variance of the per capita income is higher than at the beginning (Sigma divergence).

4.9 Growth as a process

Growth is a dynamic process where the accumulation of factors of production plays a major role, i.e. the accumulation of physical capital, of human capital and of technological knowledge. Accumulation means that there is a ratchet effect in economic growth with the process possibly occurring in a stepwise fashion. Growth is a continuous process which, if disturbed, will tend to resume. There is an immense diversity of historical experiences (David 1999), a wide diversity of outcome. Here are some aspects of the growth process.

A Schumpeterian process

Unlike in the model concept of a steady state, things do not grow in equal proportion; rather, there is some imbalance and an increase in diversity which keeps the process going. The process does not go smoothly, there is boom and bust, up and down, and there is a tremendous structural change in which existing sectors disappear and new sectors come into existence. In a Schumpeterian (1934) process of creative destruction existing capital becomes obsolete. The economy and society undergo profound changes, growth transforms society.

Growth leaders and countries that fall back

The analysis of catching-up and convergence processes says something about how fast economies close in on the countries with the highest level of wealth or the highest growth rate. But studies about catch-up processes do not answer the question how an economy manages to take the leading role in the growth process of the world economy (like the US relative to the UK in the last two centuries) and to reach a very high level of production per head. Apparently, a country has, in this case, the possibility to activate growth factors in some special manner.

The opposite image is that countries fall back, either absolutely or relatively. It is by no means a given fact that growth processes of economies go on and on. There can be stagnation and decline. Some examples are the centrally planned economies in the 1970s and 1980s until the systems finally collapsed, but also Sweden during the last 20 to 25 years, the UK after 1945, or Argentina which figured among the 10 richest countries of the world at the end of the 19th century.

The new frontier

In the stagnation thesis of Alvin Hansen as illustrated by his student Higgins (1959), the lack of a new frontier is the major reason for stagnation. In Hansen's view, extending to the west in US history was such a new frontier opening up new investment opportunities, and his fear was the lack of such a frontier in the future. Technological breakthroughs and the integration of the world economy with an increase in the size of the market may represent such a new frontier.

Path dependence

Initial conditions, like the capital stock per worker given in the initial situation (k_0) which determines output per head and thus the starting point for the growth process, can play a more important role than in the neoclassical model. Even in the neoclassical model some aspects of endowment may not be overcome in the growth process and economies may reach a different long-run equilibrium and, consequently, may move on a different growth path. But the initial level may have even greater importance. Thus, the technological knowledge available at a certain moment of time determines the direction in which the technology will develop. Localization factors are another important example. In this sense, growth processes are path-dependent. Added to this, the determinants of an initial constellation can interact. If a combination of factors is what matters in the initial situation, economic policy may have to start at several points simultaneously to reach a more favorable growth path. In that sense of path dependence, history matters.

Thresholds and the poverty trap

A different case of path dependence is that thresholds exist which must be overcome for growth to take place. Countries can find themselves in a trap of weak growth from which they cannot find their way out. These aspects are relevant, for instance, for growth processes in developing countries. Here, the path dependence of economic development plays a special role; a big push may be necessary to get out of a trap (Chapter 9).

Open societies

The organization of societies is an important aspect determining the growth process.

Whether societies are closed or open in the sense of Popper (1945) is of major relevance for the growth process. An open society allows choice and individual freedom. This implies decentralization and subsidiarity. It also implies competition as the principal element of organizing a society. Competition can be interpreted as a discovery process (Hayek 1968) helping to find new techno-logical, economic and institutional solutions. The alternative to competition is a corpora-tivistic approach where corporations like trade unions and employers' associations play a decisive role in decision making. As a rule, this means that insiders have an import-ant weight in decision making, that the status quo is protected and that new avenues, espe-cially if unknown and uncertain, are not pursued.

Self-enforcing institutional weakness

In Asia, the industrialized countries of Europe that fall back were (before the Asian crisis in 1997/1998) ironically named NDCs, or newly declining countries, following the newly industrializing countries (NICs). Some of the industrialized countries, most promin-ently the major countries in continental Europe, France, Germany and Italy, have become rigid in their institutional structures; they seem to be unable to modernize their incentive systems, and of the conflicting aims of equity and efficiency they have chosen equity. This leads to an Olson-type inflex-ibility (Olson 1982). Internal institutional constraints make these countries incapable of reforming the social insurance systems or their regulatory framework of the labor mar-ket. Institutionally, they have started a silent erosion of their competitiveness.

Aging societies

In many countries, such as in Germany, in Japan and – not to the same extent – in the US, a population has to be expected in the next decades that will be older on average. At the same time, the changing age structure is related to a decrease in population. All this causes a change in the demand structure (e.g. lower demand for housing, higher demand for leisure services and medical supply), a lower supply of labor and changed demands on the old-age insurance systems. These and other changes have feedback effects on the growth processes.

4.10 Particular topics of economic growth

Resource shortage

The stock of natural resources (Z) changes over time, satisfying

$$\overset{\circ}{Z} = -R + g(Z)$$

where $\overset{\circ}{Z}$ denotes the change of the resource stock in a period, R represents the resource extractions from nature in a period and $g(Z)$ is a natural growth function for renewable resources. In the case of non-renewable resources, this function is dropped, and the resource stock (Z) declines according to the equation $\overset{\circ}{Z} = -R$ in every period.

Starting with a production function that contains natural resources as a production factor, the decisive question is whether the natural resource can be substituted. If this is not the case, nothing can be produced with-out natural resources, so that $Q = F(L, K, R = 0) = 0$. If substitution is possible, the non-renewable natural resource is substituted by other factors, and the production does not come to a standstill when the natural resource cannot be utilized any more.

Sustainable development

The question of substitutability also comes up in the discussion about sustainable development. Taking substitutability into account, the preservation of a given stock of resources is not required in a concept of sustainable development. It is then sufficient to pass a stock of production factors on to the future generation, with natural resources eventually being replaced by real (and human) capital.

Notes

1 Note that $\delta = 0$ violates the transversality condition; therefore $\delta > 0$ is a necessary condition for a solution to the maximization problem.

2 The production function then becomes $Y = Z^{\alpha+\beta}L^{1-\alpha-\beta}$.

3 When maximizing the present value of the utility

$$U = \int_0^\infty u(c_t)e^{-\delta t}\,\mathrm{d}t$$

under the restrictions

$$f(k_t) = c_t + \dot{k}_t + nk_t$$

and

$$k_0 > 0 \text{ given},$$

maximizing the Hamilton function

$$H_t = u(c_t) + \lambda_t[f(k_t) - nk_t - c_t]$$

yields

$$\frac{\partial H_t}{\partial c_t} = u'(c_t) - \lambda_t = 0$$

$$\dot{\lambda}_t = \delta\lambda_t - \frac{\partial H_t}{\partial k_t} = \delta\lambda_t - \lambda_t f_k + \lambda_t n$$

A dot over a variable indicates the derivative with respect to time. Differentiating the first marginal condition with respect to time and

substituting the result into the second one yields, with $\lambda_t = u'(c_t)$ and $\dot{\lambda} = u''(c_t)\dot{c}$,

$$\left[-\frac{c_t u''(c_t)}{u'(c_t)}\right]\hat{c} = \delta + n - f_k(k_t)$$

In a growth equilibrium without technical progress, the rate of change in consumption is zero. Consequently, $f_k(k) = \delta + n$ holds. With technical progress, consumption in equilibrium grows with the progress rate κ.

4 For the equation of motion for consumption see the preceding note.

5 See Blanchard and Fischer (1989, p. 69), in analogy to the closed economy.

6 The empirical analysis shows that factors like population growth and the investment ratios of real and human capital can make a significant contribution to the explanation of country-specific growth rates (Barro and Sala-i-Martin 1995, p. 382).

7 More precisely, the logarithm of the income relation y_0/y_0^* is halved.

8 According to the formula

$$t = \frac{\ln(y_0) - \ln(\alpha y_0^*)}{g^* - g} = \frac{\ln(y_0) - \ln(y_0^*) - \ln \alpha}{g^* - g}$$

See Siebert (1995).

9 By rewriting this equation, $\ln(y_t) = (1 - e^{-\beta t})\ln \tilde{y} + e^{-\beta t}\ln(y_0)$ results. The half-life is defined by y_t reaching precisely a medium value between the original level y_0 and the steady-state level $\tilde{y}$. This is the case if $e^{-\beta t} = 0.5$. Solving for t, we obtain $\beta = (1 - \alpha)(x + n + \pi)$ for the half-life which is, in this formulation, independent of the original level. At a rate of convergence of 2 percent (3 percent), it takes 34 (23) years to halve the income difference. The half-life can also be calculated according to the formula $(1 - 0.02)^x = 0.5$.

10 At a constant savings rate (Solow model), $\beta = (1 - \alpha)(x + n + \pi)$ holds. If we insert $\alpha = 0.75$ for the elasticity of production to labor, $x = 0.02$ for the long-term growth rate, $n = 0.01$ for the population growth and $d = 0.05$ for the rate of wear and tear of capital, a value of 2 percent per year results for b.

11 The regression is taken from De Long (1988).

Monetary and Financial Markets

••

In Part II, we introduce money, different currencies and financial markets into the international division of labor. We analyze how economic processes are affected. If money were a veil it would have no impact on the real sphere of the economy. Since money is more than a veil, the real economy is affected by such phenomena as inflation and hyperinflation, exchange rate fluctuations and changing trends as well as financial and currency crises. An important issue is how financial and currency crises come into existence and how they can be prevented.

Chapter 5

Global money and currency markets

••

What you will understand after reading this chapter

In national economies as well as in the world economy, money plays an important role, as a unit of measurement, as a medium of exchange and as a store of value. Money reduces the costs of transactions. Its invention, i.e. the transition from an exchange economy to a money economy, must be interpreted as an important innovation to lower the costs of transaction. In the following, we start with a thought experiment assuming that there is a world money market with only one currency (section 5.1). As a result, some simple conditions can be derived for an equilibrium on the global money market. But in reality this standardized money does not exist and thus the prices of currencies, the exchange rates, play an important role. The exchange rate can follow purchasing power parity (section 5.2), but it may also be determined by interest rate parity (section 5.3) and it may overshoot in the short and the medium run (section 5.4). Expectations play a major role (section 5.5). Some empirical evidence on purchasing power parity is presented (section 5.6). Finally, the role of the three major currencies of the world is discussed (section 5.7).

5.1 Global monetary equilibrium and national monetary policy

A thought experiment: world market equilibrium for a uniform currency

If there were a single currency for the world economy, an equilibrium of the world money market would require excess demand to be effectively zero for this currency, which we shall assume is the dollar:

$$E^\$ = L^\$(i, Y, P, \ldots) - M^\$(\cdot) = 0 \qquad (5.1)$$

where E is excess demand for money, L nominal demand for money and M nominal money supply. If there were a disequilibrium, the factors influencing money demand and money supply, e.g. the interest rate (i) and world domestic product (Y), would have to change until an equilibrium is reached. Another factor is the price level. An excess money supply can be removed if the world price level (P) were to increase; then the given money supply would be devalued in real terms. Thus, the price level can be seen as a positive function of the money supply, i.e., $P = f(M)$.

As an example consider the increase in the money supply of Argentina in the four decades since 1970 (Figure 5.1). It shows that the increase in the inflation rate corresponds to an increase in the money supply.

Money as a means of transaction and as a store of value should be stable. Central banks therefore steer the money supply in a way such that the increase in the price level does not surpass a target, for instance 2 percent in the case of the ECB. In order to be non-inflationary, an increase in the money supply should not exceed the increase in the production potential. In contrast to this approach of steering the money supply, a central bank may use inflation targeting or practice a more informal approach of monetary policy.

The equilibrium on the global monetary market with two currencies

Of course, there is no single global currency. But we can imagine two countries that couple their currencies so firmly that the legally different currencies are perfect substitutes.

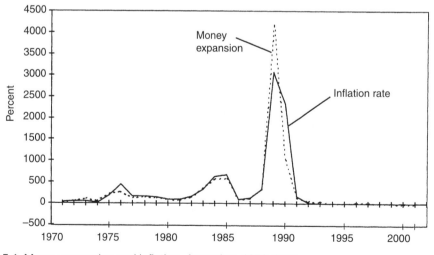

Figure 5.1 Money expansion and inflation, Argentina, 1970–2001

Source for data: IMF, *International Financial Statistics*, June 2001.

During the time of the gold standard, national currencies almost came close to this scenario. To keep the argument simple, let us assume the exchange rate between two national currencies to be equal to one, so that the two countries' quantities of money $\tilde{M}$ and $\tilde{M}^*$ can be added up to the total quantity of money in the world $\tilde{M}^W$, i.e. $\tilde{M} + \tilde{M}^* = \tilde{M}^W$. The quantity of money in the world is given exogenously and is shown in Figure 5.2 by the straight line WW'. A single point of this straight line shows how the quantity of money in the world is allocated to the two countries.

The equilibrium allocation of the quantity of money in the world is determined by the demand for money in the two countries. Assume that the nominal demand for money is determined by transaction purposes only, i.e. it is governed by nominal national income ($L = kp_1 Y$ for the domestic country and $L^* = kp_2^* Y^*$ the foreign country; see Ethier 1995). This is in accordance with the Cambridge

equation. For simplicity let us assume that the coefficients of transaction k, k^* are equal in the two countries. Real national incomes in the domestic country (Y) and in the foreign country (Y^*) are considered to be exogenously given. Moreover, it is assumed that the domestic and the foreign country are both completely specialized in the production of their export goods. Then, the equilibrium of the money market in the domestic country is given by $\tilde{M} = kp_1 Y$. For the foreign country it is $\tilde{M}^* = kp_2^* Y^*$.

Dividing the conditions for the national equilibria by one another, the equilibrium allocation of both quantities of money between the two countries is given by:

$$\frac{\tilde{M}^*}{\tilde{M}} = \frac{kp_2^* Y^*}{kp_1 Y} = \frac{Y^*}{pY} \tag{5.2}$$

In the monetary equilibrium, the ratio between the two quantities of money ($\tilde{M}^*/\tilde{M}$) is determined by the ratio of the national incomes and the relative price $p = p_1/p_2^*$.

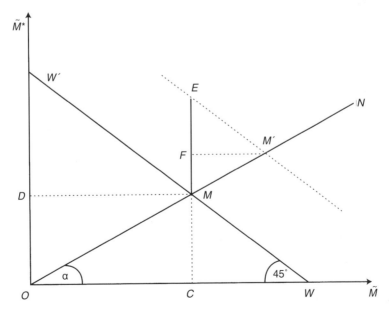

Figure 5.2 Equilibrium of the quantity of money in the world with two currencies

National income is determined on the supply side in the real sphere of the economy. The relative price is established in the equilibrium on the global product market, i.e. in the real sphere. In Figure 5.2, the equilibrium ratio of the quantities of money is given by the angle α of the straight line *ON*, where tan α = Y^*/pY.

The equilibrium on the global monetary market and the real economic equilibrium

In the world market equilibrium, the transaction demand for money has to be equal to the world money supply (equation 5.3). All variables in the demand-for-money equation 5.3 are determined in the real sphere of the economy, except for the domestic price level (p_1). Consequently, the domestic price level is proportional to the quantity of money in the world, $\tilde{M}^W$. As the quantity of money expands, the domestic price level has to rise as well. According to the quantity theory of money, the expansion of the quantity of money influences the price level.

$$k(p_1Y + p_2^*Y^*) = kp_1(Y + Y^*/p) = \tilde{M} + \tilde{M}^* = \tilde{M}^W$$
$$(5.3)$$

Under the assumption of two currencies with a fixed exchange rate, the increase in the price level is not limited to the domestic country. The price level in the foreign country increases as well. The money market equilibrium (point *M* in Figure 5.1) is coupled to the real economic equilibrium. If, for example, the foreign country raises its quantity of money (by the distance *ME*), then the world money market line is shifted outward. In point *E*, foreigners keep a larger quantity of money than they need for their transactions. They get rid of this excess money by demanding goods from the home country. The home country has a surplus in its balance

of trade; thus its quantity of money is increased. Therefore, the domestic price level has to rise. The foreign country has a balance of payments deficit; its money surplus is reduced. At the end of the adjustment process, the same real economic equilibrium (point *M'*) is reached for both currencies, but the price level of both countries has increased.

This simple formulation makes it clear that a national monetary policy that expands the money supply beyond the production potential leads to an increase of the price level, i.e. to inflation. Under the conditions of the model, inflation also occurs in the country in which monetary policy has not changed the money supply.

5.2 The exchange rate and purchasing power parity

The exchange rate

What has been vaguely described so far as the ratio between two currencies is the exchange rate. The exchange rate *e* is defined as the ratio of a unit of one currency per unit of another currency. Using the euro (€) and the dollar ($) as an example, the dimension is €/$. It indicates how many euros have to be given up in order to obtain one unit of US$.

From the very simple scenario of a fixed exchange rate in the previous section, we can derive an obvious conclusion: whenever two national currencies have a fixed exchange rate, a stable price level in both countries can only exist if the real money supply stays in line with real economic conditions. Under static conditions, the relative money supply is determined by the relative price of national outputs and by the ratio of national incomes. In a growing economy, the relevant point of reference for the increase in the money supply, which is equivalent with price level stability, is the growth of the production potential.

In the following, the exchange rate is no longer regarded as fixed but as flexible. In trade equilibrium, the law of one price is valid

$$p_1 = p_1^* e \text{ with the dimensions } €/Q_1 = (\$/Q_1) \cdot (€/\$)$$

where Q_1 is the quantity unit of commodity 1. From this, the exchange rate results as

$$e = p_1/p_1^* \text{ as well as } \hat{e} = \hat{p}_1 - \hat{p}_1^* \qquad (5.4)$$

where ^ indicates the rate of change. Equation 5.4 is the purchasing power parity condition, with p_1 and p_1^* being interpreted as price levels of the two economies. A currency like the euro depreciates, which means that e rises, if the price level increases more in Europe than in the US; it appreciates, which means that e decreases, if the price level increases less in Europe than in the US.

Consider now the case of complete specialization of both countries, for instance if the home country (Europe) specializes in good 1 and the foreign country (USA) specializes in good 2. Then the exchange rate can be defined as the relative price for two currencies where p_1 and p_1^* can again be interpreted as the price level in the two countries. But besides the prices for goods 1 and 2, the relative price p also has to be taken into consideration; it is once again defined by the world market equilibrium. Hence, the exchange rate is now defined as:

$$e\left[\frac{€}{\$}\right] = \frac{p_1\left[\frac{€}{Q_1}\right]}{p_2^*\left[\frac{\$}{Q_2}\right] \cdot p\left[\frac{Q_2}{Q_1}\right]} \qquad (5.5)$$

According to the concept of purchasing power parity, fluctuations of the exchange rate can be explained by the variation of the ratio of the two currencies. Equation 5.5 is

shown graphically in Figure 5.3b. The tangent of α is given by $1/p$. Thus, the exchange rate is given by purchasing power parity.

Monetary equilibrium with flexible exchange rates

Let us now look at the monetary equilibrium with flexible exchange rates. If both sides of the money market equilibrium condition of the foreign country are multiplied by the exchange rate, we get $e\tilde{M}^* = kep_2^*Y^*$. Dividing the conditions for the national equilibria by each other, we obtain

$$e\frac{\tilde{M}^*}{\tilde{M}} = \frac{kep_2^*Y^*}{kp_1Y} = \frac{Y^*}{pY} \qquad (5.6)$$

Equation 5.6 describes the monetary equilibrium of the domestic and the foreign country with explicit consideration of the two currencies (i.e. of the exchange rate). With a given relative price p, with given national incomes in the domestic and the foreign country, and with a given money supply in the two countries, there is only one exchange rate e at which the money supply of both countries is equal to the demand for money: the product of the exchange rate and the relative money supplies is constant, Y^*/pY.

In Figure 5.3a, monetary equilibrium is shown with two currencies and a flexible exchange rate. The horizontal axis depicts the money supply of the two countries as a ratio. The distance OG denotes the exogenously given relative money supply between the foreign and the home country ($\tilde{M}^*/\tilde{M}$); the vertical line GM shows the relative supply. The curve through MM' indicates the relative money demand. Equation 5.6 can also be written as a hyperbolic equation $L^*/L = \tilde{M}^*/\tilde{M} = a/e$ with the constant $a = Y^*/pY$. The monetary equilibrium M is marked by the point of intersection of the two curves.

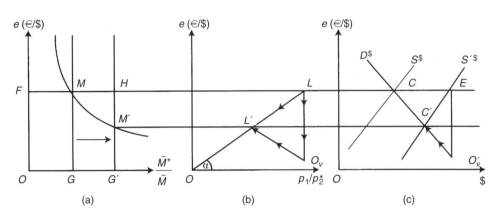

Figure 5.3 Monetary equilibrium, purchasing power parity and the foreign currency market

The equilibrium in the real economy is described in Figure 5.3b. According to equation 5.5, there is a unique relation between the exchange rate and the ratio of nominal prices p_1/p_2^* for a given relative price which is determined in the exchange equilibrium, i.e. $e = p_1/p_2^*p$. This relation is determined by $\tan \alpha = 1/p$ or line OL in Figure 5.3b. It portrays purchasing power parity.

Assume, now, that the money supply $\tilde{M}^*$ rises in the foreign country (US). Then the foreign currency ($) is devalued and the long-term equilibrium moves from M to M'. The expansion of the money supply also results in an increase of the goods prices in the foreign country. In Figure 5.3b, the economy moves from point L to point L'. Thus, we have two changes: the price level in the foreign country rises and its currency depreciates. The currency of the home country appreciates and by this the domestic (European) price level is insulated against the expansion of the money supply in the foreign country.[1]

The foreign currency market and the balance of payments

Monetary equilibrium and purchasing power parity are also related to the foreign currency market and to the balance-of-payments

position of a country. The foreign currency market explains the demand for and the supply of the foreign currency ($) as a function of the exchange rate (Figure 5.3c). It is assumed here that the supply curve of the foreign currency has a positive slope and does not bend backwards. Excess demand for the foreign currency $E^\$$ is defined by the difference between demand for US dollars and the supply thereof.

$$E^\$(e) = D^\$(e) - S^\$(e) \qquad (5.7)$$

Demand for and supply of US dollars can easily be explained if we consider commodity exchange only. Then US dollars are demanded by European importers (IM^{EU}); and US dollars are supplied by Americans who want to import from Europe (IM^{US}). Thus, excess demand in the foreign currency market is equivalent to a balance-of-trade disequilibrium with

$$D^\$(e) - S^\$(e) = IM^{EU} - IM^{US} = IM^{EU} - X^{EU} \;(5.8)$$

if it is assumed that the world consists of two countries only and that US imports are identical to EU exports ($IM^{US} = X^{EU}$).

Assume now that the US money supply is expanded. At a given exchange rate OF, this disturbs monetary equilibrium M in Figure 5.3a. It also leads to an excess supply of foreign currency (US dollar), *CE* in Figure 5.3. This is equivalent to a trade deficit for the US. Americans swap excess money (which they do not want to hold) for European goods. This process takes time. The US dollar depreciates and the price level in the US rises until the excess money supply disappears (point *M'* in Figure 5.3a). The purchasing power parity reaches its new equilibrium (point *L'* in Figure 5.3b), the foreign exchange market clears (point *C'* in Figure 5.3c) and the deficit in the trade account disappears.

Purchasing power parity: a first glance

Our analytical considerations have shown that an expansion of the money supply does not only affect the price level but it may also lead to a depreciation of the currency. Figure 5.4 shows that the inflation rate was more or less accompanied by a depreciation of the Argentinian peso. As can be seen from Figure 5.1, an expansion in the money supply of Argentina went along with an increase in the price level. Whenever the money supply increased, the price level went up and the peso was devalued. This corresponds to equation 5.4. We will look at other examples of excessive increases in the money supply in Chapter 9. Purchasing power parity will be reviewed in more detail in section 5.6.

5.3 Interest rate parity and portfolio equilibrium

A portfolio equilibrium with respect to domestic and foreign financial assets (such as bonds) exists when the expected rate of return on assets in the home country is equal to the expected rate of return on assets in the foreign country.[2] The rate of return on financial investment in the home country is given by the domestic interest rate, whereas the rate of return on investment in the foreign country is defined by the foreign interest rate plus the expected appreciation gains (interest rate parity),

$$1 + i = (1 + i^*)e^e/e_0 \qquad (5.9)$$

where e^e is the expected exchange rate at some

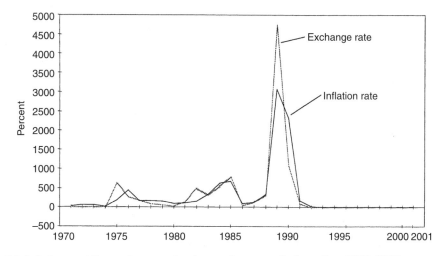

Figure 5.4 Inflation and the exchange rate change (in percent), Argentina 1970–2001

Source for data: IMF, *International Financial Statistics*, June 2001, *Country Report* (2001).

future date and e_0 is the spot rate. This is also written as

$$i = i^* + \hat{e}^e \qquad (5.10)$$

Here $\hat{e}^e$ indicates the expected rate of change of the exchange rate, i.e. the expected devaluation ($\hat{e}^e > 0$) or appreciation ($\hat{e}^e < 0$). The expected rate of change of the exchange rate is defined as ($e^e - e_0)/e_0$. The interest rate refers to short-term or long-term financial assets.

If the domestic currency is expected to be devalued within the next year ($\hat{e}^e > 0$), then investing in the foreign country has the advantage that the money invested is worth more at the end of the investment period. If, for example, a devaluation by 2 percent of the domestic currency is expected, then for the portfolio equilibrium a domestic interest rate of 5 percent is compatible with a foreign interest rate of 3 percent. Therefore, in the portfolio equilibrium the foreign interest rate can be correspondingly lower than the domestic interest rate. If, in contrast, an appreciation ($\hat{e}^e < 0$) of the domestic currency is expected to take place, then the investment in the foreign country suffers a loss in value. The foreign interest rate has to be correspondingly higher.

5.4 Exchange rate overshooting

The exchange rate has to adjust, i.e. a currency has to depreciate or appreciate, when at a given exchange rate excess supply or excess demand exists in the foreign exchange market. If the disequilibrium in the foreign currency market is due to an excessive money supply; that is, if the money supply has increased significantly more than it should relative to the growth of the productive potential, there are several ways in which the imbalance can be reduced. One is by goods

arbitrage in the sense of purchasing power parity, as described above.

A disequilibrium can also be eliminated by capital flows, especially by restructuring a given portfolio (Dornbusch 1976). In this case, an overshooting of the exchange rate may occur if the prices of goods are sticky in the short run. Consider a monetary expansion in the foreign country. This implies that people in the foreign country hold more money than they want to. Their portfolio is not optimal. They react and adjust their portfolio. Instantaneously, they demand bonds and bond prices in the foreign country rise. The interest rate in the foreign country falls and demand shifts to the bonds of the domestic country. As a result, the demand for the domestic currency increases abruptly, there is an excess supply of foreign currency. Consequently, the foreign currency is immediately devalued as a result of the change in the money supply (point O_v in Figure 5.3b). Note that the interest rate parity implies the overshooting of the exchange rate. In equation 5.9, interpret e^e as the exchange rate expected in the long run equilibrium, i.e. from equation 5.6:

$$e^e = \frac{Y^*}{pY} \Big/ \frac{\tilde{M}^*}{\tilde{M}}$$

Since $i^* < i$, according to the interest rate parity of equation 5.9, we must have $e_0 < e^e$ which means that we have an overshooting of the exchange rate relative to a long-run equilibrium.

Only gradually does this devaluation have an impact on the flows of goods. Devaluation improves price competitiveness of the foreign country, which then develops an export surplus. Domestic importers have to obtain foreign currency which works against the devaluation of the foreign currency. The price level in the foreign country rises. Finally, purchasing power parity is reached again (movement from point O_v to point L'). Apparently, the exchange rate can deviate from purchasing power parity in the short run. It can overshoot temporarily.

Note that the eventual long-run equilibrium of the exchange rate according to purchasing power parity is not a sufficient intertemporal fix point to prevent overshooting. Even assuming that people know that the purchasing power parity holds in the long run, the time needed to reach the long-run equilibrium allows the short-term flows to deviate from the long-run equilibrium.

5.5 *The role of expectations*

Exchange rate change expectations

If the condition for the portfolio equilibrium is not fulfilled, the portfolio is adjusted, which implies capital flows. If, for instance, $i > i^* + \hat{e}^e$, then the rate of return on portfolio investment in the home country is higher than in the foreign country. For instance, a devaluation of the foreign currency may be anticipated, because a less favorable economic development is expected in the foreign country, or because of greater political instability or rising public debt with the expectation of policy uncertainty. This will be an incentive for adjusting the portfolio in favor of the domestic assets. Another possible reason for the anticipation of a devaluation might be an excessive increase in the money supply of the foreign country.

The interplay between interest rate parity and purchasing power parity

Purchasing power parity and interest rate parity interact. The interest rate parity $i = i^* + \hat{e}^e$ determines the capital flows, the purchasing power parity determines the exchange rate expectations, $\hat{e}^e = \hat{p}^e - \hat{p}^{e*}$. Combining both equations, price level expectations enter into interest rate parity, so that $i = i^* + \hat{p}^e - \hat{p}^{e*}$ holds (Figure 5.5). If people expect a stronger rise of the price level in the foreign country than in the home country, they expect a devaluation of the foreign currency. Of course, the anticipation of the exchange rate change is not determined by changes in the price level only, but also by a number of other factors, e.g. by political instability. But usually these factors also have a long-term effect on the price level.

An example for the interplay between the interest rate parity and the purchasing power parity was the European Exchange Rate Mechanism (ERM) in the European Monetary System (EMS) before EMU started. On the one hand, interest rate imparity sets into motion capital flows as soon as economic policy of a single country erred away from the stability target. The markets quickly required a premium on the national interest rates and eventually induced a devaluation of the national currency. Therefore, interest rate parity determined the pain of instability; it served as a control mechanism.

On the other hand, purchasing power parity shaped the exchange rate expectations, which entered into interest rate parity. If a larger price differential between countries developed, market participants expected that the exchange rate would have to be adjusted. Governments anticipated the consequences of a stability-averse policy which were made explicit by this mechanism, and consequently

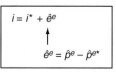

Figure 5.5 Interest rate parity and purchasing power parity

they had to aim at stability. An example of this controlling mechanism is the economic policy situation in France in 1983. The Mitterrand government had to completely reverse its economic policy approach which had led to budget and balance-of-payments deficits, a rising price level and a devaluation of the French franc.

Defending a pegged exchange rate by interest rate policy

A country that wants to defend its weak currency may have to take recourse to high interest rates in order to prevent portfolio capital from leaving the country. A case in point is the 500 percent interest rate that Sweden used in the days of financial crisis in September 1992 in order to prevent the outflow of short-term capital and in order to defend the Swedish krona. In early 2001, the interest rate in Turkey was raised to 5000 percent in order to prevent the devaluation of the Turkish lira. Another example is the high real interest rate of 30 percent of Brazil prior to the devaluation of the real, the national currency, in January 1999.

Applying interest rate parity, a high interest rate differential $i - i^*$ is needed to compensate devaluation expectations with respect to the domestic currency. Assuming a given expected depreciated exchange rate at a future date t, e_t, interest rate parity $i - i^* = (e_t - e_0)/e_0$ indicates how high i must be in order to prevent e_0 from rising. For example, if the expected exchange rate $e_t : 100$ and if the spot rate $e_0 : 5$ is to be defended and if the interest rate i^* is given as 6 percent, the domestic interest rate must be chosen as 25 percent in order to prevent a capital outflow, so that $25 - 6 = (100 - 5)/5$.

In August 1998, the Russian rouble was devalued (the exchange rate rouble/US dollar increased). There was an attempt to prevent the devaluation of the rouble by high nominal interest rates up to more than 100 percent in the spring of 1998. Such a high interest rate, however, did not prevent the rouble from being devalued (Figure 5.6).

In the case of South Korea, it seems that a high interest rate relative to the US has (together with other measures and an IMF stand-by credit) helped to keep the Korean won from depreciating further (Figure 5.7). The reason for the different outcome in Korea can be seen in better fundamentals relative to Russia.

Defending an exchange rate by a high interest rate poses quite a burden on an economy. Private investment including construction is suppressed, and this impedes economic growth. Therefore, such a policy can only be followed temporarily in order to establish confidence. A policy of high interest rates is not sustainable in the long run. Eventually, the exchange rate must be in line with the fundamentals.

5.6 Long-term purchasing power parity versus medium-term deviations: the empirical evidence

Every day, foreign currency transactions on the foreign exchange markets of the world amount to a volume of US$2 trillion. Compared to this, the world trade volume of an entire year amounts to only US$6 trillion (1999). The world trade volume of a single year is reached on the foreign currency markets in three days. There may be a lot of double counting and counter-transactions, for instance hedging, which have to be excluded to determine the net transactions. And yet, it is undisputed that capital flows can influence the exchange rate in a way quite

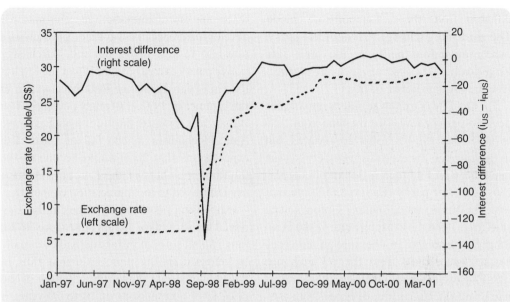

Figure 5.6 Russia: interest rate[a] and exchange rate with respect to the US, 1997–2001

[a] Russia: money market rate; United States: federal funds rate.
Source for data: IMF, *International Financial Statistics*, CD-ROM, May 2001.

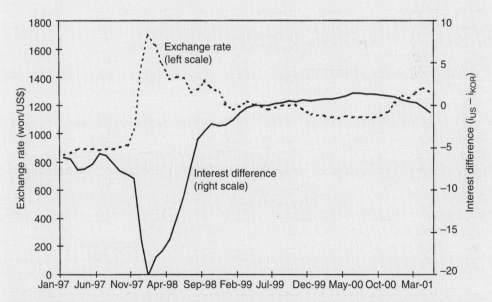

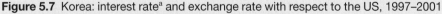

Figure 5.7 Korea: interest rate[a] and exchange rate with respect to the US, 1997–2001

[a] Korea: money market rate; United States: federal funds rate.
Source for data: IMF, *International Financial Statistics*, CD-ROM, May 2001.

different from the transactions of goods. Therefore, the exchange rate does not follow purchasing power parity in the short run. Empirically, we observe such divergences from purchasing power parity.

For the DM/$ exchange rate a remarkable deviation can be found for the time from 1980 to 1985 when the US dollar appreciated, but in the long run the exchange rate between the deutsche mark and the US dollar follows purchasing power parity (Figure 5.8). Note that with the European Monetary Union having started in 1999, the exchange rate DM/$ is no longer determined in the foreign currency market but derived from the €/$ exchange rate. The exchange rate between the deutsche mark and the Italian lira deviated from purchasing power parity in the European Exchange Rate Mechanism (Figure 5.9). But

when the discrepancy between the national developments became too large, the exchange rate had to give in. In the end, purchasing power parity came through. When the lira left the European Exchange Rate Mechanism in the summer of 1992, it strongly devalued. The Italian lira rejoined the European Exchange Rate Mechanism in the fall of 1996. The expectations that Italy would be one of the founding members of the European Monetary Union led to an appreciation of the lira.

Purchasing power parity reigns in the long run. This should be no surprise since in the long run all sorts of instability will eventually be reflected in the price level and thus in the exchange rate. Regarding changes of the price level over periods of 10 to 20 years, a correlation between changes of the exchange rate and differences between inflation rates

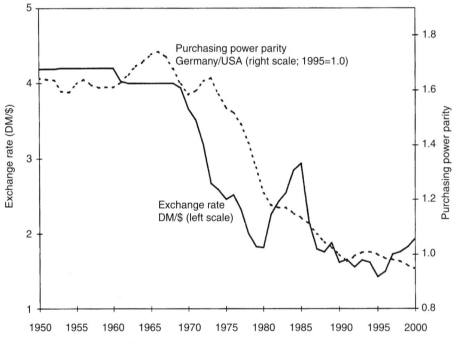

Figure 5.8 Exchange rate DM/$ and purchasing power parity[a]

[a] Consumer price index Germany to consumer price index US, 1995 = 1.0, annual averages.
Source for data: IMF, *International Financial Statistics*, CD-ROM, December 2001: Datastream.

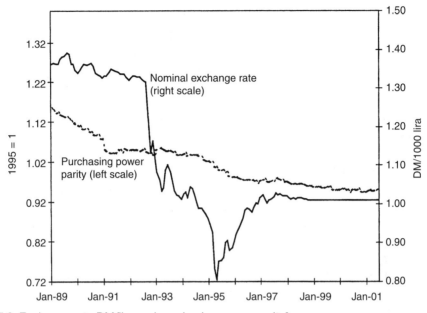

Figure 5.9 Exchange rate DM/lira and purchasing power parity[a]

[a] Purchasing power parity: consumer price index Germany over consumer price index Italy (1995 = 100).
Source for data: IMF, *International Financial Statistics*, CD-ROM, October 2000; Deutsche Bundesbank, *Monthly Reports*.

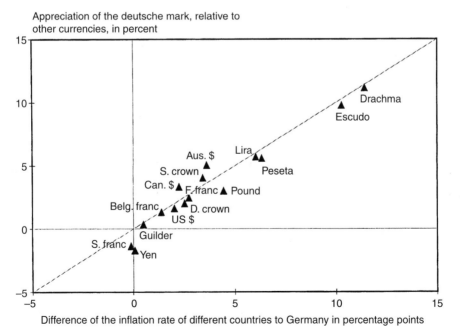

Figure 5.10 Inflation and exchange rate changes of some important currencies, 1974–1998[a]

[a] Geometric average of the period ranging from 1974 until 1998 (based on annual averages).
Source for data: IMF, *International Financial Statistics*, December 2000.

5.7 *The three major currencies of the world*

The values of the three major currencies of the world, the US dollar, the deutsche mark and the yen, in the last 50 years reflect fundamental changes in the three major economies. These include differences in the strength of economic growth, long-term shifts in comparative advantages and trade flows, switches in capital flows, as well as other phenomena such as synchronous or asynchronous business cycles between the countries and differences in stabilization policies, i.e. in monetary, fiscal and wage policies. Moreover, institutional arrangements for the exchange rate are of relevance.

In the 1950s, 1960s and 1970s, the catching-up process of Germany and Japan and the growth of their exports worked towards an appreciation of the deutsche mark and the yen. During the 1950s and 1960s, the exchange rates between the US dollar and the deutsche mark and the yen were revalued at intervals, but remained relatively stable due to the Bretton Woods system. From 1970, both currencies appreciated against the US dollar (Figure 5.11). In the 1970s, Japan was exposed more intensively to the oil crisis, so that the yen had to depreciate temporarily during the two oil crises. In the first part of the 1980s, the US dollar appreciated. After 1985, the deutsche mark and the yen gained value relative to the US dollar. In the late 1990s, the US dollar appreciated. After 1980, the deutsche mark depreciated against the yen.

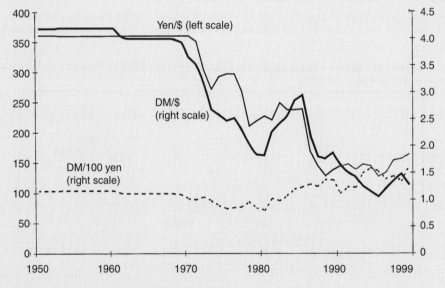

Figure 5.11 US dollar, deutsche mark and yen[a]

[a] Yearly averages.

Source for data: IMF, *International Financial Statistics*, CD-ROM, December 2000; Deutsche Bundesbank, *Balance of Payments Statistics*, April 2000.

becomes visible. In Figure 5.10, the appreciation of the deutsche mark (vertical axis) and the differences of the inflation rate between different countries and Germany from 1974 to 1998 are recorded. It is obvious that purchasing power parity is valid for this time period.

Purchasing power parity holds for the exchange rates in the long run of 10 or 20 years, but when a disturbance occurs the alignment to this long-term tendency takes time. Empirical studies show that divergences from a filtered trend are reduced only by a rate of 15 percent per year. The half-life, i.e. the time period in which the divergence halves on average, is three to five years (Rogoff 1996). At the same time, the short-run divergences are high and volatile.

Notes

1 There is a complete insulation of the home country, if p_2^* rises proportional to $\tilde{M}^*$ and inversely proportional to e, so that $\tilde{M}$ in the home country as well as p_1 remain unchanged.
2 This assumes that investors are risk neutral.

Chapter 6

Financial crises

· ·

What you will understand after reading this chapter

An optimal portfolio is a delicate equilibrium, in which expectations play an important role; if they lose touch with fundamentals, a bubble may develop (section 6.1). Historic examples of financial bubbles are discussed in section 6.2. Preconditions may lead to a bubble and some mechanisms reinforce it (section 6.3). The bursting of a bubble has implications on the real economy (section 6.4). The Japanese bubble represented a major financial crisis with a long-run impact (section 6.5). Financial exuberance in the US in the late 1990s exhibits aspects of a financial bubble (section 6.6). A specific form of a financial crisis are bank runs (section 6.7). Financial exuberance has implications for the anatomy of the business cycle (section 6.8).

6.1 An optimal portfolio

Portfolio equilibrium requires that the expected rates of return of different assets are equal. Assets may be all sorts of interest-bearing financial assets such as money market funds, bonds or dividend paying shares. Neglecting risk and considering a closed economy, the rate of return of holding money in interest-bearing form like money market funds, i.e. the interest rate i, should be equal to the rates of return on other financial assets in a portfolio equilibrium. For instance, the rate of return on bonds is the interest rate on bonds (i_B plus the rate of change in the bond price, $\hat{p}_B$). Similarly, the rate of return on shares is given by the dividend, d, relative to the share price and the rate of change in the share price, $\hat{p}_{SH}$. Besides financial assets, a portfolio may also include real estate where the rate of return is the change in the real estate price, $\hat{p}_{RS}$. Finally, storable commodities like natural resources also have a rate of return, namely the convenience yield (here neglected) plus the rate of change in the resource price, $\hat{p}_R$. The condition for an optimal portfolio is

$$i = i_B + \hat{p}_B = d + \hat{p}_{SH} = \hat{p}_{RS} = \hat{p}_R \qquad (6.1)$$

Price changes become relevant for portfolio decisions whenever stock variables are involved. This means that commodities, factors of production or financial assets are considered that are durable and have a longer life than a single period. In that case, an intertemporal decision has to be made as to when to sell, buy, hold or use the product or resource in question.

In an open economy, currency changes have to be taken into consideration as well. The optimal portfolio requires, for instance for shares, that the dividend plus the rate of change of the domestic share price is equal to the dividend plus the rate of change of foreign shares plus the currency gain

$$d + \hat{p}_{SH} = d^* + \hat{p}^*_{SH} + \hat{e}^e \qquad (6.2)$$

where d, d^* represent the domestic and foreign dividend; $\hat{p}_{SH}$, $\hat{p}^*_{SH}$ denote the rate of change in the price of domestic and foreign shares. In this chapter, we will study financial crises in which currency issues are not at the center and which are more or less contained to the individual country. Currency crises are discussed in Chapter 7.

A portfolio equilibrium very much depends on expectations. If people expect prices and currencies to behave according to a certain trend, their expectations will influence their market behavior, and this trading behavior reinforces the expected trend (self-fulfilling expectations). If expectations change abruptly, economic variables will adjust quickly to the new expectations unless the variables are sticky.

6.2 Case study: historic examples of bubbles

Historic famous bubbles have been the Mississippi Bubble in Paris in 1719–1720 and the related South Sea Bubble in London. Another well-documented bubble is the Dutch Tulipomania (Garber 1989, 1990). In the tulipomania bubble, the price of tulip bulbs rose increasingly during the years 1634–1637. Some special tulip bulbs reached a value equivalent to a house.

At the end, the prices collapsed. There also was a railroad mania in England in 1846–1847.[1]Real estate bubbles have occurred frequently; an example is the real estate booms in Florida and in California in the 1980s. In yet another example, after the two oil crises expectations changed in the early 1980s on the excess liquidity and on the prospects of syndicated bank loans to developing countries.

More prominent examples of a financial bubble are the late 1920s which led to the Great Depression and the Japanese Bubble of 1989 (see below). In the Great Depression stock prices collapsed from an index above 350 in 1929 to 70 in 1932 (Figure 6.1). Industrial production halved in the same time span, unemployment jumped from 1.8 percent in 1926 to 24.9 percent in 1933.

Consumer prices fell by 20 percent thus indicating a deflation. The Great Depression was a major shock. World trade declined and the depression spread to the European countries. The money supply, both in nominal and real terms, remained relatively constant in the second part of the 1920s; it even fell prior to 1929. Therefore, excess liquidity was not at the root of the problem.

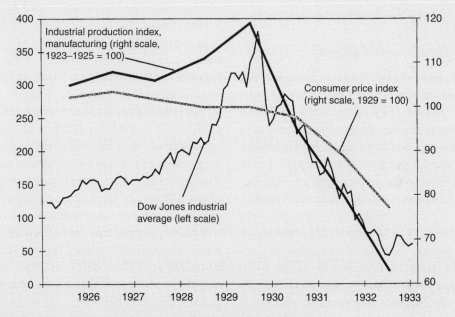

Figure 6.1 The stock market bubble and the Great Depression

Source for data: United States Department of Commerce, *Survey of Current Business*, various issues; Pierce (ed.), *The Dow Jones Averages 1885–1995*.

6.3 *Speculative bubbles: the important mechanisms*

Actual product prices, real estate prices and share prices can differ from medium-term or long-term fundamental values. At the root of such a divergence are expectations of rising goods, basic materials, real estate and share prices. These expectations are reinforced when the prices actually do increase (self-fulfilling expectations). If actual prices deviate more and more from a medium- or long-term fundamental value we speak of a speculative bubble. In this situation, self-fulfilling expectations move the price of a good away from the equilibrium level, which is determined by long-term fundamental factors.

Some preconditions for a bubble

There are several prerequisites for the appearance of a bubble. One is that the valuation of goods, real estate assets and other financial assets can change abruptly; the price increase does not stimulate supply sufficiently to counteract the price rise. A second is that, apart from price information of the spot market, agents form expectations regarding the future rate of change of an asset price and take their expectations into consideration when pricing the asset. This implies that the current value of the asset is linked to its expected future value. A third condition is that expectations are temporarily reinforced. For instance, in an open economy the anticipation of a revaluation of the (domestic) currency implies the import of short-term portfolio capital, so that the currency is actually revalued. Or if an increase in land prices is expected, suppliers of land hold back their supply, and land prices actually rise. Thus, the expectation is (at least temporarily) confirmed. Finally, if there were a day of settlement in the future that was already

known today, such a speculative bubble could not start because agents would rationally take the discounted value of the asset into account when deciding how to price the asset in the current period. Market participants would project the future equilibrium price backwards in a recursive process to the present day until the spot price would be somewhat in line with the long-run equilibrium. Such an intertemporal[2] fix point would control the expectations and link them to the real economy. Without such a fix point, it is advantageous for every single individual to follow the herd. For instance, assume that a currency appreciates. It will keep on appreciating as long as all participants expect it to do so and keep on buying the currency.

In order to start a bubble, there must be a stimulus in the initial situation. One such stimulus can be a change in expectations, for instance that oil prices will be rising owing to an increased actual scarcity or that additional gold will be found after the first nugget has been discovered. A specific stimulus may be an excessive expansion of the money supply. This may lead to an inflationary bubble in which the price level rises, eventually ending in a hyper-inflation. Alternatively, the excessive money supply may not affect the price index of traditional goods very much, but may show up predominantly in the real estate and share prices and thus start a real estate and stock market bubble. Credit expansion is usually a mechanism going hand in hand with money expansion and feeding the price spiral, for instance in the real estate sector. This was the case in the 1994 Mexican crisis as well as in the 1997 crisis in Thailand.

When the bubble bursts

At some time during the process, the speculative bubble will reach a point when people realize that the process is not sustainable. Then the expectations change. The economic agents sell their shares, real estate, natural resources, inducing prices to fall and making other market participants adjust their portfolios as well. Banks are reluctant to renew short-term credits when expectations change. For instance, with problems in the real economy of South Korea in 1997, Japanese banks, under pressure themselves, were no longer prepared to renew credits to Korean firms.

Some reinforcing mechanisms

There are several mechanisms which reinforce the collapse of a bubble:

Balance sheet mechanics

As soon as asset prices are falling, the asset side of bank balance sheets is affected (Mishkin 1998). Bonds and stocks lose value, and the asset side shrinks; eventually loans and advances to other banks or to customers change their risk status (Table 6.1). Banks may not have enough coverage for their credits with the remaining value of their assets; deposits may be withdrawn, and banks lacking refinancing may have to start restraining credits. A credit crunch is the result. An example are the magic numbers for stock market indices. Thus, a Nikkei index of 15,000 was considered necessary to be surpassed at the end of March 1998 in order for the Japanese banking system not to get into trouble. The balance sheet mechanism means a ripple effect working its way through the banking system. It is aggravated when the majority of the banks are affected by the same phenomenon.

Balance sheet mechanics operate within a country when problems of one bank spill over to other banks. It is also relevant between countries. An example in 1998 were the credits given by Japanese banks to Korean firms. When Korean firms defaulted, the asset side of Japanese banks was affected. In addition, exchange rate changes play a major role, for instance when bonds or stocks in foreign currency lose value owing to a depreciation of the foreign currency.

Threshold values and changes in expectations

For a number of reasons, expectations can change. A case in point are the critical parameters in software programs for portfolio investment, the 'stop-loss' points. Another case is when threshold values are surpassed and market participants start to ask questions about sustainability.

6.4 The impact of the bubble

A speculative bubble may be limited to the financial sector, but in most cases it has an

Table 6.1 Balance sheet of a commercial bank

Assets	Liabilities
Cash reserves	Deposits by banks
Loans and advances to banks	Customer deposits
Loans and advances to customers	Securitized liabilities
Bonds	Equity
Stocks	

impact on the real sphere of the economy as well. There are several mechanisms by which the real economy is affected.

Relative prices and relative demand change. Assume the real estate sector and the construction sector are over-expanding in the bubble. Too many factors of production are attracted to construction, leading to a distorted allocation of resources. When the real estate bubble bursts, the construction sector collapses. In other bubbles, too many resources may have been placed into specific production sectors, for instance the oil industry. When prices fall and when demand weakens, the resource allocation is not sustainable. The misallocations have to be corrected after the speculative bubble has burst.

The wealth effect for households reduces consumption demand. Consumers lose wealth, and they will adjust their spending, albeit not in a one-to-one relationship because the lower valuation of financial assets and houses does not directly translate into lower household incomes.

The balance sheet effect forces firms to use their cash flows to pay back debt instead of spending it for investment. Moreover, firms experience a lower aggregate demand.

The change in asset values leads to a change in the balance sheet of banks who become more cautious in giving new credits; this leads to a credit crunch affecting the financing possibilities of firms.

Cost-cutting strategies of firms include the shedding of labor, which increases the economic uncertainty for households and makes them more than cautious in their spending. Taken together, these effects imply a lower growth rate with higher unemployment and lower tax revenues.

6.5 Case study: the Japanese bubble

The development of the Japanese stock and real estate markets between 1986 and 1990 is an example of a speculative bubble. In the second part of the 1980s Japan expanded the money supply strongly (Figure 6.2); the interest rate was reduced (Figure 6.3). This was in response to a strong political US pressure to play the demand locomotive for the world economy; academics also asked Japan to expand aggregate demand. For instance, Bergsten wrote:

> Japan and Germany (and possibly the United Kingdom) need to adopt new expansionary measures on the order of 2–3 percent of their GNPs.
>
> (1986, p. 40)

and

> [Japan and Germany] must keep their domestic demand growing rapidly for some time. They must cooperate to achieve and then maintain a set of equilibrium exchange rates preferably through the adoption of target zones
>
> (1988, p. 191)

Krugman (1989) plays a similar tune with respect to Germany:

> A . . . problem is posed by the unwillingness of Germany to expand domestic demand
>
> (p. 104)

A similar theme of using the devaluation of the US dollar as a means to get Japan and Germany to expand domestic demand is addressed by Dornbusch (1987):

> A falling dollar would do much good abroad. It would force on America's reluctant trading partners the recognition that they must become the locomotives for the world economy or face deep recession themselves.

Owing to a strong revaluation of the yen, the strong expansion of the money supply in Japan during the 1980s did not lead to an increase in the cost of living (i.e. there was only a minor increase in the consumer price level, at least in the case of the traditional goods). The additional liquidity, however, found its way into the demand for shares and real estate, so that these prices rose. Then in 1989, the speculative bubble burst, the Nikkei stock index fell from almost 39,000 in December 1989 to 20,000 in January 1990 and moved further downward from then on. The prices for real estate went down dramatically as well (Figure 6.4). The banks entered a state of crisis because of reduced asset values in their balance sheets.

In the case of Japan, the economy was negatively affected by the bursting of the bubble.

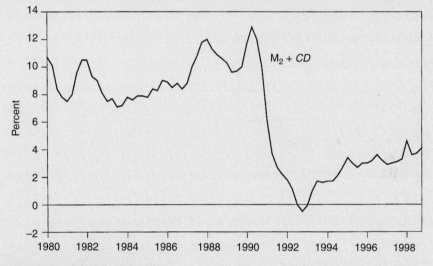

Figure 6.2 Money expansion in Japan[a]

[a] M2 + CD: quarterly data, seasonally adjusted; change over previous year for data

Source for data: Datastream, OECD.

The immediate result of the burst bubble was that financial capital was lost. Cumulative capital losses in the period 1990–1996 since the 1989–1990 peak amounted to 967 trillion yen which corresponds to Japan's GDP of two years (OECD 1998; Table 6.2). Households took more than 40 percent of the total losses.

The impact for the banking sector consists of a serious debt overhang. Since 1992, the Japanese economy has been nearly stagnant (with the exception of 1996); it slid into a severe recession in 1997/1998 (Figure 6.5).

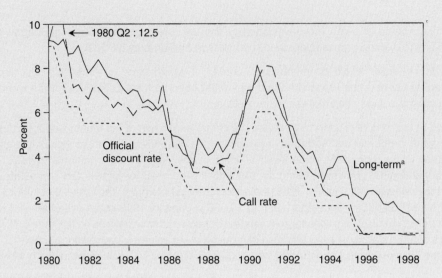

Figure 6.3 Interest rates in Japan

[a] Weighted average of government bond yields.

Source for data: Datastream, OECD

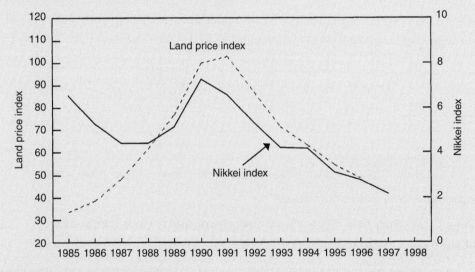

Figure 6.4 The Japanese bubble

Source for data: Statistics Bureau, Management and Coordination Agency, Government of Japan, *Statistical Yearbook of Japan 1993 and 1997*; Datastream

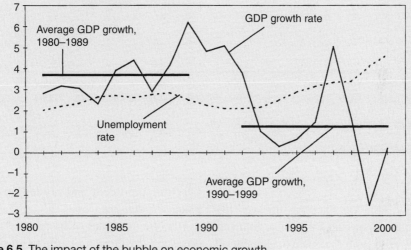

Table 6.2 Capital losses[a,b] in Japan, 1990–1996 (in trillion yen)

Non-financial corporations	–334.7
Financial institutions	–181.0
General government	–98.5
Households	–427.9
Total nation	–967.3

[a] Gross assets.
[b] Since the 1989–1990 peak.
Source: OECD (1998, Table 9).

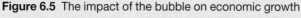

Figure 6.5 The impact of the bubble on economic growth

Source for data: OECD, *Main Economic Indicators 2000.*

6.6 Financial exuberance in the US

Case study

Share prices in the United States in the period from 1995 to 2001 developed similarly as in Japan in the period from 1985 to 1991. The S&P 500 rose from roughly 500 points to 1400 in a similar way to the Nikkei index (Figure 6.6). Thus, there is some similarity between the financial exuberance in the US (Shiller 2000) and the pre-bubble situation in Japan. There is also a similar increase in the share of investment of GDP during these two periods in the different countries. Nevertheless, there are differences. First, the United States did not experience a construction boom. Second, the interest rate was not lowered as much as in Japan. Third, the US economy exhibits quite a flexibility in its production capacity. This is due to the fact that all the sectors of the economy are exposed to the competitive forces of the market whereas in Japan some domestic sectors were protected by heavy regulation. Finally, the banking system is organized differently.

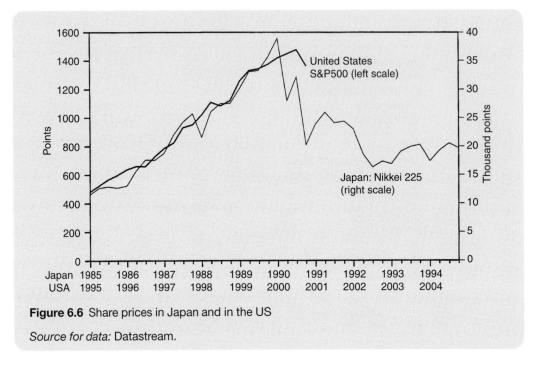

Figure 6.6 Share prices in Japan and in the US

Source for data: Datastream.

6.7 Bank runs

Bank runs are a specific form of a financial crisis. They arise from the mismanagement of a bank or an exogenous shock such as the loss of assets leading to an over-exposure of liabilities relative to assets. Customers lose confidence in the reputation of a bank. When a bank panic occurs, customers tend to withdraw their deposits as quickly as possible in the attempt not to lose their funds. The reserves, in currency, in deposits in central banks, or in other liquid forms that a bank holds as a safety cushion against withdrawals may not be sufficient to provide currency to the customers. Reserves can dwindle quickly. If only a single bank is affected, customers take their deposits to another bank. If the run spreads from one bank to others, customers shift from deposits into currency. Thus, the failure of a single bank can extend to other banks; it can lead to a systemic banking crisis affecting imprudent and prudent institutions alike.

Historic examples of bank runs and bank crises are the German banking crisis of 1931 and the US banking crisis in the Great Depression. In Germany, in May 1931, difficulties in an Austrian bank led to a loss of confidence in German banks and a withdrawal of foreign short-term money. Some banks had to be closed, the stock market was closed in July and a bank run occurred. In the Great Depression of the US, bank failures increased from 650 in 1929 to 4024 in 1933. A four-day bank holiday had to be declared in March 1933 and non-solvent banks were suspended. Another crisis, the US bank crisis of 1907, led to the Federal Reserve System. Regulation attempts to prevent bank failures by requiring adequate capital and by other prudential standards. In most countries, some safety nets exist such as risk pools of savings and loans and of private banks. In case of a bank crisis, the central bank can serve as a lender of last resort by providing sufficient liquidity to keep the banking system from failing.

6.8 *A new anatomy of the business cycle*

The business cycle of an economy, i.e. the ups and downs of economic activity over time, is influenced by many factors. A most fascinating question is how it comes to a turning point from an upswing to a downswing. Many hypotheses have been put forward why an economy eventually runs out of steam. Besides negative external shocks such as an oil price increase, a first endogenous phenomenon is that labor becomes scarce with rising production so that labor costs rise. This may be amplified by trade unions pushing for higher wages and thus causing a negative supply shock to an economy. If costs increase, profits may be squeezed and investment is reduced. A second phenomenon is over-investment; too much capital is accumulated so that overcapacity squeezes profits. A third endogenous phenomenon is that the money supply is expanded excessively and that eventually the central bank will have to put its foot on the brake and reduce the excessive increase in the money supply by raising the interest rate and thus squeezing profits. In this chapter, we have met yet another version of an endogenous cycle, namely financial exuberance. If the excessive increase in the money supply does feed a financial bubble in the stock market and the housing market, the bubble may burst at some time, for instance when the central bank no longer can provide the additional liquidity necessary to feed the bubble. Such a bubble goes hand in hand with over-investment in the real economy. In a way, it expands over-investment. When the bubble bursts, the rate of investment becomes negative. Financial exuberance thus aggravates the business cycle.

Notes

1 See 'Financial Crises' in *The New Palgrave* (1987).
2 In intertemporal models a transversality condition prevents the emergence of speculative bubbles.

Chapter 7

Currency crises

••

What you will understand after reading this chapter

In an open economy, foreign currencies and capital flows enter the picture. Portfolio capital in particular is highly mobile internationally. Consequently, the optimal portfolio with foreign currencies can be a very delicate equilibrium (section 7.1). For open economies with different currencies and with mobile portfolio capital, the nature and the mechanisms of financial crises change. The financial crisis is now a currency crisis (section 7.2). Speculative bubbles in exchange rates can be modeled as the actual exchange rate moving away from a fundamental rate. A divergence between the nominal and the real exchange rate, occurring simultaneously with a widening current account deficit, can be a signal that the onset of a currency crisis is nearing (section 7.4). Some recent currency crises are surveyed in section 7.5.

7.1 *Optimal portfolio with foreign currencies*

When different currencies are taken into account, a portfolio equilibrium requires that the rates of return of assets denominated in different currencies are identical. To simplify the exposition, we abstract from the riskiness of different assets. Currency holdings can be treated like a stock, and exchange rate changes are variations in stock prices. An optimal portfolio requires a rate of return parity

$$r = r^* + \hat{e}^e \tag{7.1}$$

where r denotes the domestic rate of return, r^* the foreign rate of return and $\hat{e}^e$ the expected rate of change in the exchange rate. As we know from equation 5.4, the nominal exchange rate e is defined as the domestic currency in terms of one unit of the foreign currency, i.e. from the European point of view $e[€/\$]$. Consequently, $\hat{e}^e > 0$ means that more euros have to be spent for one unit of $, i.e. a depreciation of the home currency (euro), and $\hat{e}^e < 0$ means an appreciation of the home currency (euro). Examples of the rate of return parity are equation 6.2 for shares and, of course, the interest rate parity (equation 5.10).

As in any portfolio equilibrium, expectations play a major role because it is expected depreciations and expected appreciations of a currency that enter the rate of return parity. If expectations change, the given portfolio is no longer optimal: it cannot hold. Adjustment can be instantaneous because portfolio capital is highly mobile. Thus, if a depreciation of the currency is expected, portfolio capital can exit immediately, implying that the exchange rate also changes instantaneously once expectations become different. Portfolio capital is said to have the memory of an elephant, the heart of a roe deer and the quick legs of an antelope. If a portfolio equilibrium is disturbed, capital flows will reverse.

The exchange rate can also deviate from the mid-term or long-term value. The value of a currency can change, for example, without the central bank changing the usual expansion of the money supply.

7.2 *Mechanisms in a currency crisis*

In Chapter 6, we discussed some mechanisms that lead to a financial bubble or reinforce it. When currencies enter the picture, additional mechanisms have to be considered.

The sustainability of the balance-of-payments position

A bubble will burst when it becomes apparent that a situation is not sustainable. An important restraint is the balance of payments, more specifically the current account. A bubble in a country will normally be associated with an inflow of short-term capital. This means that a current account deficit is financed by capital imports. The nominal exchange rate is supported by capital imports. Apparently, it is difficult to separate the bubble from a healthy environment in which a capital inflow finances capital accumulation. Then, a current account deficit is sustainable because capital accumulation will be the basis for increasing the production potential and for repaying debt and serving the interest payments in the future.

As soon as expectations change, the financial markets may no longer be willing to finance the current account deficit of a country. Capital inflows will dry up.

Running out of foreign currency reserves

As long as foreign currency reserves are sufficiently large to defend a currency, market participants will not attack the currency. As soon as reserves are exhausted, the value of the currency will fall very quickly. Moreover, when markets become aware of an increased risk that reserves will be depleted, they start to react. Losing reserves indicates that it becomes more difficult to finance a current account deficit. Consequently, the exchange rate has to give in and the currency depreciates.

Contagion

A change in expectations can be contagious in a psychological interpretation. A problem showing up in one country leads to the question whether a similar problem may develop elsewhere. This triggers uncertainty, a more cautious portfolio investment and less generous credits. Once a general mood has spread and once the herd is running, other countries are affected.

Deregulation of financial markets may make it easier for a bubble to arise. If a country's capital account is liberalized and if its banking system does not have the appropriate regulation, banks may have too easy access to foreign liquidity that then can be fed, for instance, into the real estate sector. This was one trigger of the financial crisis in Thailand in 1997. A similar phenomenon could be observed in Sweden in the crisis of 1992 (Lindbeck *et al.* 1994). Thus, there is an optimal mix of institutional reforms. A specific measure like liberalizing the capital account may not be first-best if not accompanied by appropriate other institutional changes such as reforms of the domestic banking sector (complementarity of institutional reforms).

7.3 *A model to explain a bubble*

In a speculative bubble of the exchange rate, the actual exchange rate moves away from a fundamental rate. Assume the exchange rate process is given by the following relationship:

$$e_t = x_t + \delta E(e_{t+1}) \tag{7.2}$$

where e_t is the exchange rate in period t under the assumption of rational expectations and δ is a discount factor. Iterating this process forward in time gives:

$$e_t = \sum_{i=1}^{\infty} \delta^i E_t(x_{t+i}) + \lim_{i \to \infty} \delta^i E_t(x_{t+i}) \tag{7.3}$$

This model can generate rational bubbles if $\lim_{i \to \infty} \delta^i E_t(x_{t+i}) \neq 0$, i.e. the so-called transversality condition does not hold. In this case, rational speculative bubbles are compatible both with a macroeconomic equilibrium and rational expectations. To see this, denote the fundamental exchange rate by

$$e_{F,j} = \sum_{i=1}^{\infty} \delta^i E_t(x_{t+i})$$

A speculative bubble then implies:

$$e_t = e_{F,t} + b_t = x_t + \delta E_t(s_{F,t+1} + b_{t+t}) \tag{7.4}$$

such that the bubble term is given by

$$E_t(b_{t+t}) = \delta^{-1} b_t \tag{7.5}$$

In the literature, three types of speculative bubbles are distinguished: The *never-ending* bubble with $b_{t+t} = \delta^{-1} b_t$. The *stochastic* bubble $b_{t+t} = \delta^{-1} b_t + \varepsilon$ where the stochastic term ε has an expected value of zero. Blanchard and Watson (1982) additionally analyze the case of a *bursting* bubble that has a certain probability to burst.

7.4 The nominal and the real exchange rate

What are potential clues that a situation is not sustainable?

- A negative current account balance may be a warning signal if capital imports are used for consumption purposes or for non-investive government spending (such as social policies).
- A negative current account is a warning signal if it is associated with a large budget deficit of the government.
- A negative current account is a warning signal if it is associated with an excessive increase in the domestic money supply.
- A negative current account is a warning signal if it is associated with a diverging development of the nominal and the real exchange rate where the currency experiences a real appreciation but remains relatively constant in nominal terms.

The real exchange rate

If the nominal exchange rate develops in a marked difference to the real exchange rate, while at the same time the imbalance in the current account increases, this can be an indication that a fundamental disequilibrium is developing, even if the foreign currency market temporarily clears. The nominal exchange rate is defined as the relative price of two monies, for instance the euro and the US dollar, $e = €/\$$; the nominal exchange rate clears the foreign currency market.

The real exchange rate corrects the nominal rate by the foreign and the domestic price levels. The real exchange rate is defined as

$$e_R = eP^*/P \qquad (7.6)$$

where P^*, P are the respective national price levels being used as correction factors of the nominal exchange rate. The real exchange rate indicates the real price of products of the foreign country, i.e. of a country's export goods in terms of its imports or import substitutes. The real exchange rate has the dimension

$$\frac{Q}{Q^*} = \frac{€}{\$} \cdot \frac{S}{Q^*} \Big/ \frac{€}{Q}$$

Therefore, it depicts the relation between the quantities of the domestic good (Q) and the quantities of the foreign good (Q^*), i.e. the ratio at which domestic goods can be exchanged for foreign goods. It tells us something about the purchasing power of the domestic good. Thus, the real exchange rate is a relative price. In the simple two-goods model, it has the inverse dimension of the terms of trade (Q^*/Q), i.e. we have

$$e_R = 1/p \qquad (7.7)$$

Whereas the nominal exchange rate clears the foreign exchange market, the real exchange rate brings the current account into equilibrium; it must also be consistent with the internal (macroeconomic) equilibrium in the real economy. For allocation decisions, for instance when a real distortion of the economy exists because not enough exports are produced and too many imports are consumed, it is the real exchange rate that has to do the job of bringing about a new equilibrium. Countries that want to remove a trade deficit have to carry out a real devaluation. Putting a higher real value on exports, domestic demand for export goods is reduced; domestic supply of exports is stimulated. The relationship between the real exchange rate and the current account is depicted in Figure 7.1. A high real exchange rate means that it is easy to export, and the country will have a surplus in the current account. With real appreciation (i.e. e_R falls), the surplus will be reduced and eventually a deficit arises [1] (see also Figures 2.20 and 2.21).

The idea behind the real exchange rate is to ask the question: How does the exchange rate move in real terms? A nominal devaluation of a currency may be neutralized in its effects on trade flows, when the price level in the country that devalues rises correspondingly. Therefore, a country devaluing its currency in nominal terms has to make sure that a nominal devaluation is not contradicted by a strong rise of its price level. This implies that monetary policy has to restrain a potential price increase.

What does a real appreciation mean?

A real appreciation ($\hat{e}_R > 0$) can mean two different things if we look at the exchange of goods. (i) A real appreciation can occur if the price level in the domestic country increases by more than that in the foreign country – because of rising labor costs or because of a failure of stabilization policy – and if the nominal exchange rate does not change accordingly. Then, the currency is overvalued in real terms (which has happened quite often in developing countries). The current account situation worsens, i.e. a deficit increases; the real appreciation indicates a need for structural adjustments. (ii) A real appreciation can also signal that an economy has gained a higher competitiveness in the exchange of goods. Owing to an improved supply in the home country or owing to a higher demand of the foreign country, the price at home increases by less than that abroad when the exchange rate is given. Then, the terms of trade improve; the real appreciation has its root in the greater competitiveness of a country. In that case, the curve in Figure 7.1 shifts to the left allowing a balance in the current account with a currency that has appreciated in real

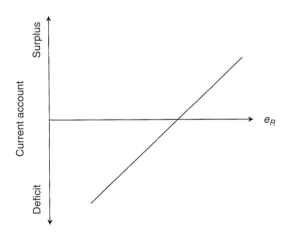

Figure 7.1 The real exchange rate and the current account

terms. Incidentally, the real appreciation reduces an export surplus.[2] Therefore, one has to look very closely at which of the two different things are meant when we talk about a real appreciation.

A real appreciation can also take place if capital flows in. Again, it can mean two different things. A currency is revalued in nominal terms, which implies a real appreciation if goods prices do not change. (i) The inflow of capital can be used to finance private consumption or government expenditure for consumption; it can go along with a bubble. The resulting nominal appreciation leads to a real appreciation (which means an overvaluation of the currency). The current account deficit that already goes with an overvaluation may not be sustainable. (ii) The capital inflow may be used for investment purposes. Then, the real appreciation can indicate a strengthened competitiveness (attractiveness of a location) for real capital. With the additional investment, the competitiveness for goods can be improved in the future. The curve in Figure 7.1 will shift to the left (in the future) when the new capital becomes productive, allowing a balanced current account with a currency that is appreciated in real terms.

As in the case of commodity exchange, the real revaluation can again imply two different things. As for any real price, the real exchange rate has to be judged against the background of an equilibrium or a disequilibrium in the economy, both with respect to an internal macroeconomic equilibrium and with respect to a balance or an imbalance in the current account.

If the real exchange rate appreciates and if the nominal exchange rate remains more or less stable and if at the same time a current account deficit develops, then the risk arises that the nominal exchange rate will have to give in.

Figure 7.2 exhibits the real exchange rate between the US dollar and the deutsche mark. The real exchange rate of the US dollar decreased in the first half of the 1980s, i.e. the US dollar appreciated in real terms. Between 1985 and 1995, the US dollar depreciated. From 1995 on, the US dollar has been appreciating. The real exchange rate of the deutsche mark increased in the period from 1973 till the mid-1980s; this means a real devaluation of the deutsche mark. Afterwards, the real exchange rate of the deutsche mark fell again, which corresponds to a real revaluation. Since 1995, the deutsche mark has been rising.

An alternative definition of the real exchange rate

The real exchange rate can alternatively be defined as

$$e_R = eP_T^*/P_{NT} \tag{7.8}$$

where eP_T^* is the price of tradables denominated in foreign currency and P_{NT} is the price of non-tradables in terms of the domestic currency, so that the dimension is:

$$\frac{Q_{NT}}{Q_T} = \frac{€}{\$} \cdot \frac{\$}{Q_T} \bigg/ \frac{€}{Q_{NT}}$$

A real appreciation ($e_R > 0$) means that the price of non-tradables increases more than that of tradables. The economy will have an incentive to produce more non-tradables, and a balance-of-payments surplus will be reduced.

The concept of an equilibrium real exchange rate

Since the real exchange rate is a relative price that brings exports and imports or tradables and non-tradables in line with a macroeconomic equilibrium, the concept of the equilibrium real exchange rate has some prominence in economics. From equation 7.7 we have

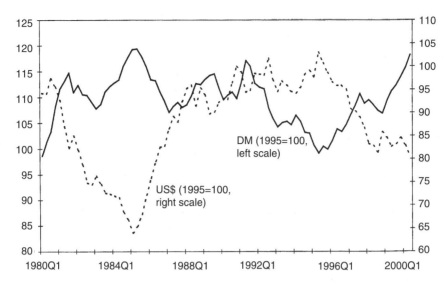

Figure 7.2 Real exchange rate[a] of the deutsche mark and the US dollar

[a] The real exchange rate is calculated as the reciprocal of the nominal effective exchange rate adjusted for relative movements in consumer prices of the home country and its partner (or competitor) countries (calculated by the IMF). The nominal effective exchange rate represents the ratio of an index (1995 = 100) of the quarterly average exchange rate of the currency in question to a weighted geometric average of exchange rates for the currencies of selected partner (or competitor) countries

Source for data: IMF, *International Financial Statistics*, CD-ROM, December 2000; own calculations.

$$\hat{e}_R = -\hat{p} \qquad (7.9)$$

The real exchange rate has to move in the opposite direction of the relative commodity price. If preferences shift or if relative supply conditions change, the real exchange rate must adjust so that a new macroeconomic equilibrium is reached. In terms of Figure 5.3b this means that tan α of ray *ON* changes.

This long-run relationship between the real exchange rate and the fundamentals overlaps with temporary phenomena, such as overshooting or bubbles. As a very simple relationship we have, from equations 5.6 and 7.6:

$$\hat{e}_R = \hat{e} + \hat{M}^* - \hat{M} + \hat{Y} - \hat{Y}^* \qquad (7.10)$$

Consider the case where the nominal exchange rate is fixed ($\hat{e} = 0$) and where the money supply in the home country ($\hat{M}$) expands by much more than the production potential ($\hat{Y}$) with the foreign country expanding its money supply according to its production potential ($\hat{M}^* = \hat{Y}^*$). Then, the price level of the home country will rise, and the home country will experience a real appreciation that will hurt its competitiveness. Such a development would not be consistent with an equilibrium. Instead, the nominal exchange rate would have to adjust and, with $\hat{e} = \hat{M} + \hat{Y}$, there would be no impact on the real exchange rate.

129

In theory, it is possible to precisely define the equilibrium real exchange rate (as the one establishing equilibrium in the balance of payments and in the macroeconomy). For policy purposes, it is extremely difficult to determine the equilibrium real exchange rate. This is especially so because it would have to be done *ex ante*. That is why concepts for exchange rate policy based on the idea of an equilibrium exchange rate (Williamson 1983) are not very promising (see below). However, if the nominal and the real exchange rate diverge for a longer period of time, it is very likely that some adjustment has to take place.

7.5 Some recent currency crises

The Czech devaluation

A divergence between the nominal and the real exchange rate developed in the case of the Czech crown (koruna). Czechoslovakia and (since 1993) the Czech Republic *de facto* pegged the crown to a basket of currencies (65 percent DM, 35 percent US$ since May 1993). Until 1997, the Czech National Bank was able to defend the nominal exchange rate. In real terms, the currency appreciated and the external value rose (Figure 7.3). This went along with an increasing current account deficit which was financed by capital inflows. The real appreciation hurt the competitiveness of the Czech economy. Eventually, a situation developed in which the nominal exchange rate could no longer be defended. The crown had to devalue.

The Mexican crisis

The Mexican peso more or less followed a crawling peg to the US dollar in the early 1990s. The rate of devaluation of the peso was lower than the inflation differential between the two countries, i.e. $\hat{e} > \hat{p}^* - \hat{p}$. With prices and nominal wages rising at a higher speed than in the US, Mexico did not succeed in effectively using the exchange rate as a nominal anchor. The Pacto agreement between the government, employers' associations and trade unions to limit wage and price increases did not work out. The slow nominal depreciation and the higher inflation differential implied a real appreciation of the peso which began in the late 1980s (Figure 7.4). Monetary policy was expansionary (see Chapter 10). Together with a real appreciation of the peso, a current account deficit developed that was financed by short-term capital inflow, attracted by high real interest rates and a booming stock market. Eventually, investors lost confidence, capital flows reversed, and Mexico lost US$122 billion in foreign currency reserves in 1994. The peso had to devalue and the current account deficit was almost eliminated afterwards.

Meanwhile, the nominal and real rate diverge again. It seems that the real appreciation does not lead to a balance-of-payments deficit. This may be owing to Mexico having joined NAFTA. The expansion of the money supply seems to be under control, there are no inflationary pressures and the governmental budget deficit is not excessive.

The Asian 'tigers' in financial crisis

In 1997, the Asian financial crisis broke out. Some of the Asian tigers, in the past greeted with the enthusiasm of international investors because of their high real growth rates, got into trouble in spite of sound macroeconomic fundamentals in the traditional interpretation: growth rates as well as savings and investment ratios were high, inflation was low, budget deficits did not give rise to concern, and export performance was strong. Large current account deficits were excused because of the booming economies.

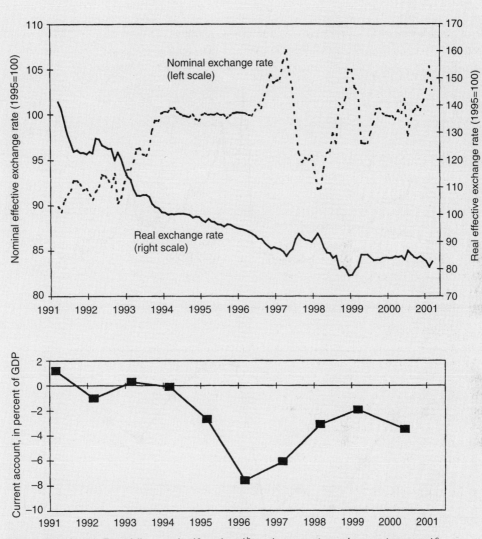

Figure 7.3 Czech Republic: nominal[a] and real[b] exchange rate and current account[c]

[a] 1995 = 100. [b] 1990 = 100. [c] In percent of GDP.

Source for data: IMF, *International Financial Statistics 2001*; *EBRD Transition Report*, various issues.

With hindsight, the countries were vulnerable to some extent for different reasons. In Thailand, for instance, where the crisis started, the relatively high capital inflows, i.e. the current account deficit, went hand in hand with a construction boom. Once the construction boom was no longer sustainable or was expected not to be sustainable, capital flows reversed. The liberalization of the domestic financial sector implied that prudential standards were not being implemented. This meant that a bubble could develop owing to credit expansion. Pegging the national currency to the US dollar contributed to an appreciation of the real exchange rate

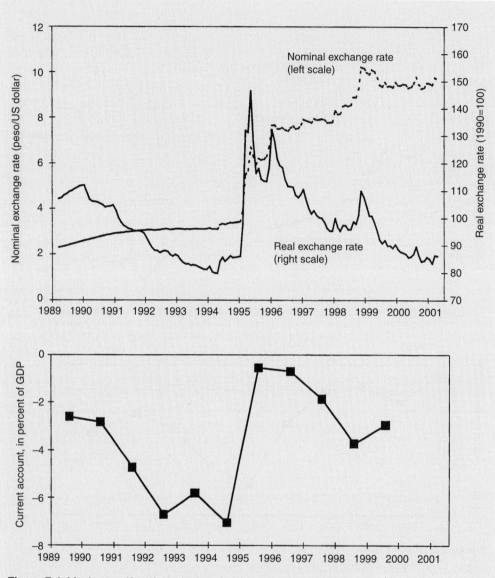

Figure 7.4 Mexico: real[a] and nominal exchange rate and current account[b]

[a] 1990– = –100.

[b] In percent of GDP

Source for data: IMF, *International Financial Statistics 2001*.

relative to the nominal exchange rate, which made it more difficult to reach a sustainable equilibrium even if the divergence was not too large. Finally, the Asian crisis showed that it is not sufficient to look just at budget deficits and public debt. A high indebtedness of the private sector, as in the case of South Korea, increased vulnerability.

South Korea

When the Asian crisis erupted, it was not expected that South Korea – number 11 in the world economy in terms of GDP prior to the financial crisis – could become part of the problem. The real exchange rate had only slightly moved away from the nominal exchange rate (Figure 7.5). The large current account deficit of 5 percent of GDP could be explained by the liberalization of current and capital account transactions in anticipation of South Korea's accession to the OECD. However, the deficit in the current account had increased in 1996, albeit not to high

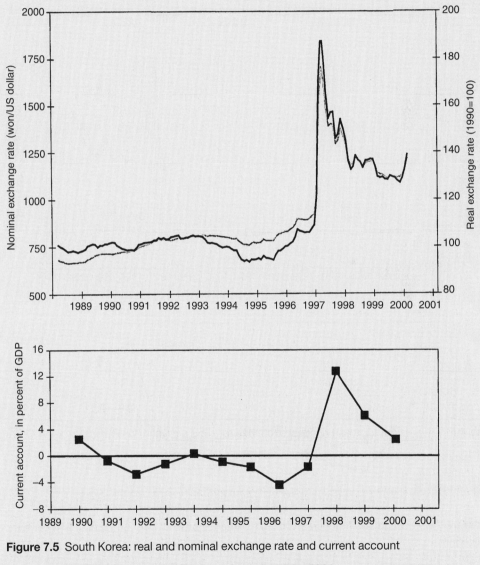

Figure 7.5 South Korea: real and nominal exchange rate and current account

Source for data: IMF, *International Financial Statistics*, June 2001.

levels in comparison to Latin American countries. Moreover, the private sector had accumulated high debt, including foreign debt in foreign currencies. This represented a liability for the country as a whole. The crisis erupted when it was reported that large conglomerates (*chaebols*) faced insolvency.

Thailand and Indonesia

The Asian crisis started when the peg of the Thai baht to the US dollar was abandoned on 2 July 1997. Within two weeks, the baht lost 15 percent of its external value. On 12 July, the

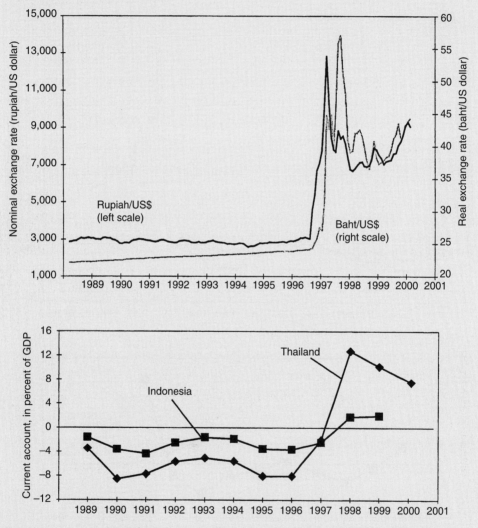

Figure 7.6 Thailand and Indonesia: nominal exchange rates of baht and rupiah and current account

Source for data: IMF, *International Financial Statistics*, June 2001; Bank of Thailand.

intervention band for the Philippine peso was widened. On 14 July, Malaysia could no longer defend the exchange rate of the ringgit; the Indonesian rupiah lost about 10 percent of its value in the second half of July. By the end of October, these currencies had lost between 25 percent (Malaysia, Philippines) and 35 percent (Indonesia, Thailand) of their values. At the peak of the currency crisis, the currencies had devalued to one fourth or one third of their pre-crisis values (Figure 7.6).

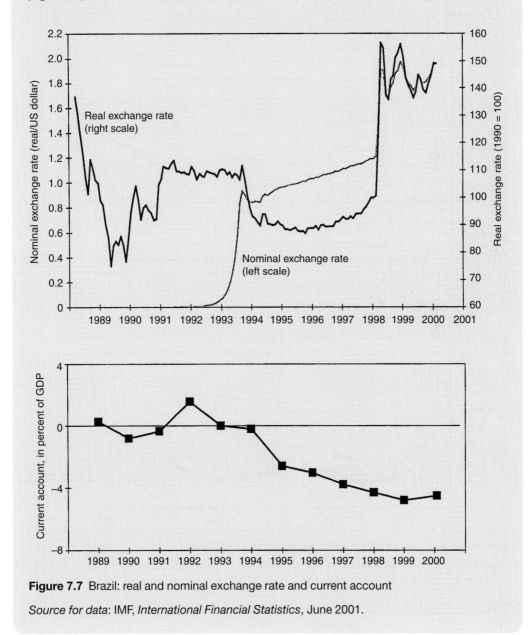

Figure 7.7 Brazil: real and nominal exchange rate and current account

Source for data: IMF, *International Financial Statistics*, June 2001.

Brazil

In January 1999, Brazil had to widen its exchange rate band in the crawling peg and then to float the real which was devalued until March by about 40 percent. There was quite a divergence between the nominal and the real exchange rate (Figure 7.7). Brazil used a high real

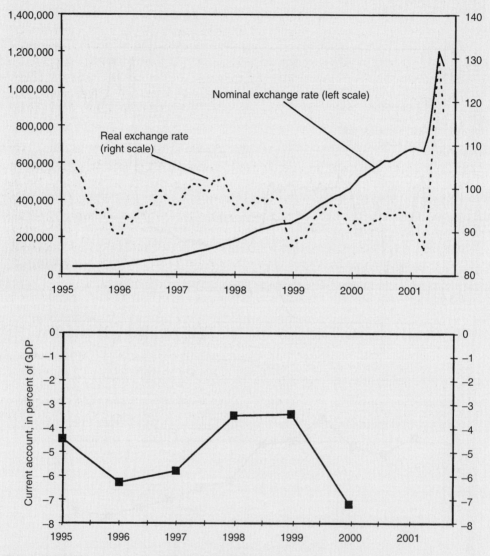

Figure 7.8 Turkey: real[a] and nominal exchange rate and current account[b]

[a] 1997 = 100.
[b] In percent of GDP.

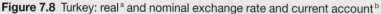

Source for data: IMF, *International Financial Statistics*, CD-ROM, May 2001.

interest rate of 30 percent to defend the nominal exchange rate; this, however, proved not to be sustainable. The current account became more and more negative in the 1990s; at the same time, the budget deficit was 8 percent of GDP. The Brazilian crisis is thus more in line with the typical Latin American pattern of a currency crisis.

The financial crisis in Turkey

The Turkish currency crisis of 2001, after a crisis in 1993, exhibits some of the typical crisis pattern. We observe a strong real appreciation of the Turkish lira and at the same time an increasing current account deficit; we also have a widening gap between the nominal rate and the real exchange rate. The nominal exchange rate depreciated throughout the late 1990s, but it never fully reflected the chronic inflation in Turkey that resulted in an inflation differential of 50 to 90 percent (annual inflation) relative to the US. Eventually, the discrepancy was too strong, and the Turkish lira had to devalue by more than 70 percent in the spring of 2001 (Figure 7.8).

Argentina

Yet another experience is the financial crisis of Argentina in 2001/2002. With the currency board, the nominal exchange rate was fixed to the US dollar and remained constant. But at the same time, there was a considerable real appreciation of the peso *vis-à-vis* the currencies of Argentina's trading partners in the nineties. This made life more difficult for Argentine exporters; imports became cheaper. This lead to a current account deficit. When expectations changed, especially after problems became apparent in the aftermath of the currency crises of 1997/98 elsewhere in the world and as a negative spillover of the Brazilian devaluation on Argentine trade, the current account deficit was no longer sustainable.

Notes

1 Assume the home country exports good 1 and the foreign country good 2. Then $e_R = e(p_2^*/p_2)$. Enlarging the right-hand side by p_1, we have $e_R = e(p_2^*/p_2 p)$. From $\hat{e}_R = [\hat{e} + \hat{p}_2^* - \hat{p}_2] - \hat{p}$. If purchasing power parity holds, $\hat{e}_R = -\hat{p}$. The current account CA is

$$CA\left(e\frac{p_2^*}{p_2}\right) = CA(e_R p)$$

Thus, the curve in Figure 7.1 shifts with a change in the relative price.

2 Appreciation also shows a better competitiveness, if (with unchanged productivity in the foreign country) productivity in tradable goods of the home country increases more than in nontradables (for this definition of the real exchange rate, see below).

Chapter 8

How to prevent a monetary–financial crisis

∙∙

What you will understand after reading this chapter

Monetary–financial crises appear in different forms (section 8.1). A stable money requires a set of conditions including the independence of a central bank (section 8.2). The solidity of the banking system is an important condition for financial stability (section 8.3). When a financial crisis arises, it is the role of the IMF to prevent it from spreading into a systemic crisis of the global economy (section 8.4). Some propose to impede and to control international capital flows (section 8.5). The Tobin tax has gained prominence (section 8.6). Finally, approaches to stabilizing the exchange rate are described (sections 8.7 and 8.8).

8.1 Different types of monetary-financial crises

In Chapters 5–7, we have analyzed different types of disturbances that can be traced to the existence of money.

- *Inflation* (including hyperinflation) occurs when the money supply expands at a quicker pace than the production potential.
- A *banking crisis* arises when customers withdraw their deposits and the balance sheet of an individual bank or a banking system gets into disarray.
- A *financial bubble* (asset price inflation) occurs when asset prices deviate considerably from a fundamental equilibrium.
- A *currency crisis* is a specific form of a financial crisis for a currency. It occurs when the exchange rate can no longer be maintained and has to adjust abruptly to a new equilibrium.

Sometimes only one of these different forms of monetary–financial crises is prevalent, but very often the different forms appear simultaneously. In the following, we distinguish these different forms of crises and discuss approaches to prevent them.

8.2 Providing a stable money

Inflation and hyperinflation can be prevented by correct institutional arrangements and an adequate monetary policy. The independence of the central bank is of utmost importance. A basic rule is that public budget deficits should not be financed by printing money. This condition has been violated in Latin American countries in the past. In industrial countries, the interrelations between politics and the central bank are more intricate. The central bank must be strong enough to resist political pressure for an easy money policy if such a policy is in conflict with price-level stability.

Sound fundamentals

Another important prerequisite is that a country has sound fundamentals. This relates to solidity in public finances, i.e. it is necessary that the government has a sustainable budget position. It also means that the balance-of-payments situation is sustainable. More generally, economic policy should be oriented towards stability. If structural issues are not solved, if short-termism dominates, then the fundamentals are not in order. Constitutional constraints for policy makers should ensure that long-run opportunity costs of budget deficits are not disregarded. Thus, a country needs rules by which excessive public deficits are prevented.

It may also be wise for a country to make sure that it is not vulnerable and that it has enough strength to withstand a blow from the outside and a less friendly environment including reduced credit access to the international capital markets.

Monetary strategies

With respect to monetary strategies, a rule-based monetary policy such as targeting the money supply or inflation targeting may be followed. Alternatively, monetary policy may be discretionary. A money supply target keeps the increase of the money supply in line with an economy's growth of the production potential. Inflation targeting aims at directly influencing the price level. Preventing asset price inflation is a new issue for monetary policy; this may be more difficult to achieve with targeting the consumer price level and easier to do with money supply targeting.

Price-level stability as an anchor

Usually, monetary policy is oriented towards a stable price level. Then, in accordance with purchasing power parity, the change of the exchange rate is simply determined by the inflation difference to the foreign country. Thus, an appreciation of the domestic currency takes place when the price level of the domestic country rises less than that of the foreign country. In this way, a country is able to uncouple itself from the inflation of the foreign country.

Exchange rate policy

Countries can only use the exchange rate as a nominal anchor if their governments are strong enough to stick to a strict stabilization policy or, to put it differently, if they succeed in controlling their budget situation and if trade unions effectively subscribe to price-level stability. If these conditions are not satisfied (as, for instance, in the Pacto agreement in Mexico prior to 1994), pegging the exchange rate will fail. Even a crawling peg cannot help if the inflation difference is larger than the rate of depreciation in the peg. Note that pegging exchange rates was one reason for the Asian crisis. A pegged exchange rate or a currency board will also come under pressure if there are no institutional constraints for provincial governments to engage in foreign-currency denominated debt (as in Argentina).

8.3   A solid banking system

The financial system of a country has to be constrained such that a crisis is unlikely to start or to be reinforced. This involves setting standards for commercial banks and other financial institutions including investment banks. The 1988 Basel I Accord of the Basel Committee on Core Principles for Effective Banking Supervision has established a capital adequacy framework for individual financial institutions. Internationally active banks have to back their claims on the non-bank private sector by an 8 percent capital endowment (in terms of shareholders' equity or retained earnings). The Basel II Accord attempts a more risk-sensitive framework in which different types of risks of claims are distinguished. Not all claims receive the same weight. The overall limit of 8 percent continues to hold. External ratings and standardized internal control mechanisms can be used to assess credit risks.

Some standards should also be applied to hedge funds. One approach is to require them to register in a country; if they then go offshore, this may signal to the customer that a higher risk is involved and that these funds are less likely to be bailed out. Credits given to hedge funds and derivatives should be adequately reflected in the risk evaluation of banks.

8.4   The role of the IMF

The purpose of the IMF, as specified in Article I of the IMF statutes, is 'to shorten the duration and lessen the degree of disequilibrium in the balances of payments' (section iv), to 'facilitate the expansion and balanced growth of international trade' (section ii) and to 'promote exchange stability' (section iii). Solving disequilibria in the balances of payments is a short-term task; promoting exchange rate stability is rather a long-term objective.

Short-term and long-term tasks

To define the short-term role of restoring a

balance-of-payments equilibrium and the long-term role of exchange rate stability was relatively easy during the time of the Bretton Woods system when the main objective of the IMF was to bridge foreign currency shortages in a world of relatively stable exchange rates and when trade in goods and services was the major driving force of balance-of-payments situations. The case for the IMF was when financing was needed because there was a temporary negative external shock that would eventually go away, but that was causing problems in the interim period. In the days of Bretton Woods, this was the traditional balance-of-payments crisis that arose from a widening trade deficit, due, for instance, to temporarily unfavorable terms of trade.

Today, with flexible exchange rates and with portfolio capital being the main determinant of short-term exchange rate movements, the task of the IMF is to deal with currency crises triggered by a sudden capital flow reversal, reflecting some fundamental disequilibrium in the economy, i.e. a situation that is not sustainable. In today's world, the short-term and long-term roles of the IMF are more intertwined. In a world with high portfolio capital mobility, currency runs can be a problem. Unfortunately, currency runs, which are a short-run phenomenon when they take place, have long-run causes.

The two roles of the IMF are potentially conflicting. The short-run approach requires the IMF to bridge-finance a liquidity gap by providing liquidity. In this interpretation, the IMF is a fire brigade stopping a potential currency run from arising from a (short-run) liquidity problem. This is the IMF's role *ex post*. The more long-run approach is to prevent a currency run from developing and from spreading into systemic risk for the world economy; in this interpretation, the IMF undertakes a precautionary policy. This is it's role *ex ante*.

The IMF facilities

Countries with balance-of-payments problems can use the IMF-reserve tranche which does not constitute a credit. In addition to this support, the IMF has several credit facilities. The credits are usually deposited in the country's central bank and are freely available for use.

The initially created Stand-by Arrangements serve to alleviate temporary balance-of-payments disequilibria and allow members to draw up to 100 percent of their quota during a prescribed period (usually 12 to 18 months, but up to three years) conditional on the borrower meeting specified performance requirements. The credit has to be repaid within 3¼ to 5 years.

The Extended Fund Facility, created in 1974, is aimed at structural deficits, i.e. at balance-of-payments difficulties requiring a longer period of adjustment. It involves larger amounts of financing than under Stand-by Arrangements. Repayment is within 4½ to 10 years.

In 1997, a new facility, the Supplemental Reserve Facility, was established, aiming at a large short-run financing need and at exceptional balance-of-payments difficulties as applied in the Mexican and Asian crises. It extends to a period of up to one year. This is in response to 'a sudden and disruptive loss of market confidence reflected in pressure on the capital account and the Members' reserves'. Repayment is expected within 1–1½ years; the interest rate starts 3 percentage points above the IMF lending rates; the rate increases over time.

A new facility, Contingent Credit Line, is supposed to shield member countries with solid economic policy against contagion. The IMF also provides low-interest to low-income countries through the Poverty Reduction and Growth Facility and supplies grants under the Initiative for the Heavily Indebted Poor Countries (HIPCs).

A bankruptcy procedure

If a crisis erupts, the IMF has to act like a bankruptcy court judge (Sachs 1994, 1997; Minton-Beddoes 1995): working capital has to be arranged, a moratorium has to be declared and existing debt has to be restructured. Fresh working capital must have priority over obligations to previous creditors.

There are, however, no procedural rules for a bankruptcy procedure for sovereign debtors. Thus, actually the moratorium is declared unilaterally by the country in trouble. In contrast, a new system of sovereign bankruptcy rules can be compared to Chapter 11 of the US bankruptcy code. In this case, the IMF would declare the moratorium; the IMF would also have a say in determining to what extent existing debt including bank credits would be rolled over into the future without interest payments or to what extent they would default. During such an instance, capital flight has to be prevented so that capital controls have to be put in place; such controls, however, are difficult to administer and have reputational effects negative for attracting fresh capital.

The moral hazard problem

By lending to national governments, the issue arises as to what extent the IMF sets the wrong incentives, so that governments and private lenders tend to rely on future IMF help and become negligent in their own efforts to prevent vulnerability. This problem of wrong incentives, also discussed under the heading of moral hazard, is a complex issue (Hayek 1973). Thus, wrong incentives and moral hazard do not necessarily mean an explicit calculus to take advantage of IMF support in the future in the form of opportunistic behavior. However, with crises often being homemade and being the result of a national institutional or a policy failure, potential IMF support may be in the minds of economic agents; more formally, with IMF support a side condition of decision-making changes, thus influencing behavior more or less implicitly. Countries or creditors may feel protected against low-probability/high-damage risk in the tails of the probability distribution. The impact of institutional arrangements on incentives and the real economy is difficult to prove, especially econometrically, because the effects show up in a long-run process, very often without much short-run movement in the data. In addition, there is the question what would have happened under different institutional arrangements ('Lucas critique'; see Lucas 1981). Nevertheless, there is no doubt that institutions matter and have an impact on economic behavior and processes.

The sums that the IMF has used in order to prevent financial crises have increased considerably since the 1960s and 1970s. During this time, credits amounted to roughly US$1 billion. In the early 1980s, the credit level reached US$3.5 billion. In the 1990s, IMF credits were in the US$15–20 billion range. In relation to the recipient country's GDP, IMF credits increased from below 2 percent to a range of 6–8 percent (Figure 8.1). Note that countries in crisis do not only receive IMF credits, but that other institutions such as the World Bank and Regional Development Banks provide credits as well (Table 8.1).

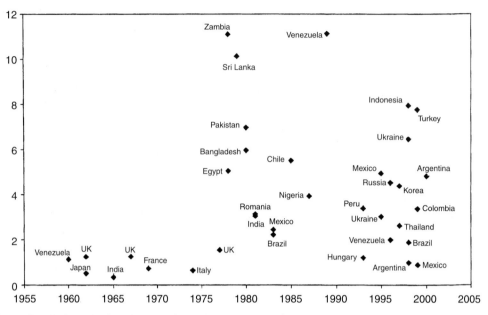

Figure 8.1 IMF credits[a] in percent of recipient country's GDP

[a]Year of approval or extension

Source for data: IMF, *International Financial Statistics*, monthly reports (various issues) and CD-ROM, 2001; for GDP data, also World Bank, *World Development Indicators*, CD-ROM, 2001; own calculations.

Table 8.1 Official creditors' long-term debt outstanding and disbursed in countries in crisis (in billion US dollars)

		IMF	World Bank	Regional development banks[a]	Bilateral credits	Total
Mexico	1995	15.8	13.8	4.8	20.4	54.8
Indonesia	1997	3.0	10.7	5.0	26.7	45.4
South Korea	1997	11.1	4.6	2.3	1.9	29.9
Thailand	1997	2.4	1.8	1.8	11.8	17.8
Brazil	1998	4.8	6.3	10.1	14.6	35.8
Russia	1998	19.3	6.3	0.2	62.1	87.9
Turkey	2001	12.5	n.a.	n.a.	n.a.	n.a.

[a] Includes loans from other multilateral and intergovernmental agencies, except the World Bank and IMF.
[b] Debt outstanding and disbursed as of August 2001.
Source for data: World Development Finance, CD-ROM, 2001; for Turkey: IMF, *International Financial Statistics*, CD-ROM, December 2001.

The size of operation of the IMF has come under scrutiny. The larger the size of operation, the more money the IMF takes in its hands, the weaker will be the willingness of private creditors (banks) to take over credit risk in the case of a crisis and the weaker is the incentive for governments to prevent the instances that lead to a stability problem.

A lender to troubled governments?

In a down-to-earth interpretation, the IMF lends to troubled governments. Unfortunately, in the real world a crisis may very well be homemade, i.e. it may be the result of a domestic institutional failure or of a national policy failure. As a matter of fact, all the financial crises of the 1990s have domestic causes with homemade failures or weaknesses becoming apparent under changing international conditions. Even more unfortunately, the shock may prove to be permanent instead of transitory. Thus, the IMF is very close to national policy failure. It should be careful not to become a funding agency for countries in self-made trouble, i.e. the troubled countries' global bank. Since the IMF itself is subject to political pressure, there is the risk of becoming an international correction agency for national government failure.

The IMF should not make up for national political mistakes and national institutional deficiencies. If it did, and sometimes it does, it would honor economic policy mistakes and it would thus be likely to induce new ones in the future, generating a *perpetuum mobile* in which the causes for the next crisis are laid down. A case in point is the IMF's role in Russia, where the IMF failed to implement conditionality and where for a long time it was trying to iron out internal problems without being able to change the fundamental economic situation.

Preventing a crisis

The IMF should be more aware of what can be done to prevent a crisis from developing. A currency crisis arises when market participants lose confidence in a currency, i.e. in the money of a country relative to other monies, and when they move out of it. An economic situation and the exchange rate are judged to be unsustainable; and what is unsustainable is vulnerable. The root of this evaluation is that a fundamental disequilibrium or an imbalance exists that has to be corrected. Possible causes for this are that

- the money supply has expanded excessively so that there is an oversupply of the national money and devaluation is unavoidable;
- financing a current account deficit for private or government consumption has driven up foreign debt, so that the intertemporal mechanics mandate some adjustment;
- financing long-term private investment by short-term foreign capital eventually runs into problems, especially if overcapacity and external shocks increase the risks of capital already invested.

In these and other cases, the currency crisis is rooted in a policy failure, especially in a deficiency of the institutional arrangements of the economy. This includes the misuse of monetary policy to finance public deficits, lacking independence of the central bank, unsustainable exchange rate binding, nonexistent rules to prevent public deficits and the accumulation of public debt. Insufficient strength of the financial sector owing to ineffective regulation that does not prevent an excessive short-term financing of private long-term investment is another aspect.

An improved early warning system

The IMF should improve its early warning system. More and better information should be provided to the markets so that markets will require higher risk premia from countries with a poor economic performance. The IMF should not be a silent supervisor who deliberates behind closed doors with the country where a problem is developing. This involves the risk that not enough is done to prevent the crisis. It is better to blow the whistle before the train crashes. It is also better to allow a small crisis if, in this way, you can prevent a large one. Of course, signaling more actively to the markets that a problem is developing is a very delicate task, and the IMF should not start the hurricane or strengthen it, but it also should not hold back information so that people are misdirected from searching for shelter.

The Asian crisis has shown that more information on the financial status of countries is needed, including more accurate data on foreign exchange reserves (are they swapped?). In addition to macroeconomic data, more information on short-term private debt is required, especially on short-term debt of the private enterprise sector. Data must include the maturity structure of debt and its composition in terms of different currencies. Information should also cover the financial sector, for instance in the form of the consolidated balance sheet of the financial sector as a whole and of the major financial institutions (*x* percent of the market volume). Moreover, a measure of reserves' adequacy for the banking sector should be developed, indicating the necessary reserves in relation to total short-term debt. The problem with the approach of defining capital adequacy is, of course, that in a crisis assets melt away. An important aspect of transparency is to what extent international banking rules, including prudent standards, have been adopted.

Data should be provided in a standardized form; they should get a stamp of approval from the IMF or other specialized international organizations like the Bank for International Settlements. This secures comparability of the data, and it enhances credibility of the data. If countries are reluctant to provide the necessary data, there should be definite costs of non-compliance, for instance by

their behavior and should bear the costs of their unsound economic policies and of the externalities of instability they cause for other countries as well as for the international community. In analogy to the 'polluter-pays principle' of environmental economics, a 'troublemaker-pays principle' should be a line of orientation. Such an approach attempts to internalize the social costs caused by countries behaving in a manner that generates instability and adds to the risk of a systemic crisis. The obligation to provide stability is assigned to the individual country. It should make sure that stability prevails at home and that the economic situation is sustainable. The alternative would be the 'victim-pays principle' which implies that the international community has to compensate the potential troublemaker for not causing trouble.

The IMF should be more conscious of the incentive and moral hazard aspects of its support policy. It should define more credibly its line of operation in the case of a crisis. It should move away from the discretionary decisions of its case-by-case approach favored by US pragmatism and bind itself by rules (favored by the Europeans). Preannouncing *ex-post* rules and sanctions serving to deal with a crisis would reduce systemic risk *ex ante*. This would also protect the IMF against implicit or explicit political influence, including the criticism that IMF lending is dominated by US foreign policy interests.

The IMF should change its policy and not implicitly defend a pegged exchange rate (Rubin 1999). It should be a specific rule that the IMF does not intervene and defend a pegged exchange rate when the money supply has increased excessively and when the nominal and the real rate have been drifting apart markedly for some time (a year or more) while the current account deficit has been worsening. On the contrary, this should be a signal that the IMF will not provide funds.

Credible rules for sovereign debtors

The IMF takes over an *ex-post* role, but this *ex-post* role has an *ex-ante* impact by forming expectations and influencing the behavior of sovereign debtors. The announcement effect of a clear *ex-post* rule will be to reduce systemic risk *ex-ante*, for instance by an improved early warning system. Countries should bear the costs of their unsound economic policies and of lingering problems early on. The costs should not jump upward in a discontinuous way (or to infinity) if a problem develops. The IMF should apply a sliding scale of the costs of a credit, for instance in terms of interest rates rising over time or with the size of the credit. By this, the country would have an incentive to avoid getting into a situation of illiquidity.

A penalty rate should be charged if additional credit is provided (Meltzer 1998). A penalty rate, which should be preannounced together with the modalities of the early warning system when IMF credits have not yet been provided, would be an important signal to markets. A penalty rate could partly reduce the borrower's moral hazard problem.

The IMF should specify the sanctions to be levied when standards are not respected. For instance, if standards relating to the banking system are ignored, countries should not have access to IMF loans (Calomiris 1998; Calomiris and Meltzer 1998). This can mean that an individual country would go without IMF support. The alternative is that non-qualifying countries would have to pay a higher interest rate on the IMF loans.

Letting private lenders take the risk

An important means of internalizing the social costs of instability is to involve the private sector in the case of a crisis. 'Bailing-in' the private sector requires an arrangement on how to handle private credits when private debtors and sovereign countries get into trouble. For equity capital, private creditors are bailed in automatically when stock prices fall. This holds irrespective of whether equity ownership is widely spread or concentrated on a few equity holders. For bonds and bank credits, sharing clauses, rules on collective representation and majorities required for the modifications of the terms of credit represent an institutional mechanism by which creditors could assume some of the risks (IMF 1999; Eichengreen 1999a). These rules would help to internalize the credit risks to the creditors, inducing them to be more cautious in giving credits. In contrast to the mostly used American-style bonds, British-style trustee deed bonds are more appropriate as they include such provisions. These provisions would also be instrumental in reducing aggressive litigation by dissident creditors. The clauses should not require a discretionary decision of the IMF to become active. Additionally, private creditors should develop their own international insurance schemes. Note, however, that this type of bonds and these arrangements mean that foreign capital would become more costly for the debtor countries because it would increase the risk for creditors, so that they would be more cautious in buying bonds and giving credits. The IMF should credibly pre-announce rules on the involvement of private lenders that the IMF wants to be respected if it is supposed to intervene. It can specify such rules as a precondition for lending support in the case of a crisis. Thus, the IMF could trigger standards written into an international agreement that have to be respected by sovereign states and private lenders when a liquidity crisis develops.

Lender of last resort?

The IMF cannot credibly play the role of a lender of last resort. There are three major differences between the IMF and the national lender of last resort. First, the lender of last resort lends to financial institutions, while the IMF lends to national governments when they run into trouble or threaten to default. Second, in the international context an insurance mechanism between banks, such as national insurance schemes in the case of bank failures, does not exist. Third, the national lender of last resort can print money and can thus credibly stop a crisis. For the IMF, this is not possible. On the contrary, the IMF has only a limited amount of resources. The usable IMF resources of about US$139 billion (August 2001)[2] would be a trickle if an extended crisis developed; for instance, if Japan or Euroland needed financial assistance or if a group of countries that are more important than the past problem countries became involved in a financial crisis. In addition, weak currencies are not usable for lending. Therefore, the IMF could even accentuate a currency problem if it ran out of funds. This would be a destabilizing function because of 'bets' of financial markets on IMF budget constraints.

If a systemic crisis for the world economy develops, the central banks will have to play the role of a lender of last resort. The institutional arrangement for such a scenario, however, cannot be put into writing. It has to be left open, whether and under what conditions central banks will step in. If the conditions were specified *ex ante* and if they became known, an uncontrollable moral hazard problem would develop where market participants and governments would play strategically against the central banks.

It seems that the IMF is only involved in

the pre-battleground of the lender of last resort, somewhat easing the task of the true lender of last resort, the central banks. Borrowing an expression from chess, in the lender-of-last-resort game the IMF is the pawn, the central banker is the king.

8.5   Controlling capital flows

Since exchange rate volatility and financial crises are linked to the mobility of portfolio capital, it has been proposed that the free movement of portfolio capital be limited in order to prevent financial crises. This discussion runs counter to the view prevailing until the Asian crisis broke out, namely that the gains from the international division of labor are seriously reduced if countries restrict the convertibility of currencies. This impedes both the exchange of goods and the efficient allocation of capital. Therefore, the condition of the convertibility of currencies seemed to be generally accepted. Especially due to the experience during the Great Depression, there has been much effort to establish convertibility and to liberalize capital flows since the Second World War.

In this discussion, different approaches have been proposed with respect to portfolio capital.

The level of intervention

On the national level, a set of different instruments are being discussed, including foreign exchange controls, different types of convertibility, different exchange rates for capital flows relative to commodity trade and the taxation of capital flows and other forms of capital controls. On the international level, the Tobin tax and approaches to stabilize the exchange rates are proposed.

The cons against capital controls

Sequencing of liberalization

It has now been accepted that there is a sequencing problem in liberalizing the banking sector and the capital account. If the capital account is liberalized and if, at the same time, the banking sector is not adequately regulated with respect to prudential standards, an over-expansion of credit may result. Sweden and Thailand are two examples. Owing to the complementarity in institutional reforms, the liberalization of the capital account should be accompanied by an appropriate regulation of the banking sector.

Preventing the loss of credibility

It is one thing to liberalize the capital account, it is another thing to undo a liberalization that has already been introduced. In the latter case, reputation is lost. Liberalization should be undertaken only when a country is strong enough to maintain it. Once liberalization has been introduced, care must be taken that it is not reversed.

Delineating capital flows from commodity exchange

A major issue is that all measures discussed here presuppose that capital flows can be clearly delineated from the exchange of goods and services. Experience shows that administrative capital controls can be circumvented in many ways, for instance by over-invoicing or under-invoicing of exports and imports.

The opportunity costs of capital controls

Another major issue in controlling portfolio capital is that controls are likely to limit the

Instruments available for controlling capital flows

Foreign exchange controls

There is a broad spectrum of controls, for instance requiring a license to obtain foreign currency, restraining convertibility or using other administrative controls. This includes making capital exports illegal.

Auctioning off the currency reserves

One way of introducing capital controls is to auction off the total supply of foreign currency reserves that a country receives in a year. However, a perfect auction system would only mimic the market so there would be no use in introducing it. A state-run auction system would intervene in defining privileged access or other aspects.

Multiple exchange rates

Another proposal is the privileged access to favorable exchange rates, for instance by splitting the exchange rates between different transactions, e.g. between goods considered to be important and less important or between trade of goods and capital movements as practiced in the system of import licenses and the exchange rate protectionism that was pursued in Latin America until the mid-1980s. Such an approach *de facto* implies multiple exchange rates.

Non-residents' and residents' convertibility

Restraints on the convertibility is another way of reducing the international mobility of portfolio capital. This relates to restricting a currency's convertibility for foreigners (non-residents' convertibility) and for residents (residents' convertibility). In order to attract capital, countries usually first introduce the convertibility of their currency for foreigners. This implies that foreign investors have the right to repatriate their profits and also their investment. Without this right, they will not provide capital. Convertibility for residents is often introduced at a later stage in the process of liberalization.

Limiting capital flight

Countries are very interested in attracting capital, but at the same time they want to reduce capital outflows, more specifically to prevent capital flight. It is difficult to define policy instruments that apply to one aspect of capital flows only. Policy instruments that may limit the outflow of capital such as capital export restraints simultaneously reduce the incentive to invest in a country. Capital outflow restraints define the expectations of potential foreign investors. Limiting exit always reduces the incentives for entry.

Reserve requirements for portfolio capital

In order to make incoming capital less volatile, a non-remunerated reserve requirement has been proposed for incoming capital so that no interest is paid during a certain time period, for instance a year. Chile has used this approach in the 1990s, requiring initially a non-interest-bearing 30 percent deposit for the first year. This approach was given up in 1998 when Chile had problems attracting foreign capital. Such a deposit limits the inflow of capital (including short-run capital) but it does not prevent capital that at a given moment has been invested in a country from leaving quickly.

attractiveness for real capital that countries need for their development. Therefore, countries hurt themselves by introducing capital controls.

Assigning the correct risk premia

A promising approach is to assign the correct risk premia. This includes an effective banking regulation and an efficient supervision of the financial sector.

Stability-oriented policy

If a country wants to reap the long-term benefit of capital inflows, it must establish a reputation so that capital is attracted and so that capital has no incentive to leave the country. This requires that a stability-oriented policy be followed that is convincing for the international financial markets.

The pecking order of capital flows

It is important to distinguish different types of capital flows, namely foreign direct investment, equity capital, bonds and bank loans. Foreign direct investment tends to be a more long-run-oriented form of capital flow; equity capital is generally also intended for the longer run, but shares can be sold instantaneously; the same holds for bonds. Bank loans may be for the long run or the short run. There is a pecking order of capital flows in the sense that some forms of capital flows have advantages relative to others. Thus, foreign direct investment is an appropriate form for developing countries, one reason being that this type of capital flows allows to solve the problem of asymmetric information. The other forms of capital flows are more adequate for developed countries.

8.6 An international Tobin tax

Tax base and impact on the arbitrage condition

In order to reduce the volatility of the flow of capital, a Tobin tax on the movement of capital has been proposed (Tobin 1978). The intention is to raise the costs of short-term capital movements. This is supposed to reduce the amount of short-run capital flows. The argument is that if less capital is moved, the exchange will be less volatile.

Consider a tax z per unit of a currency transaction and neglect changes in the exchange rate. Then, without a tax, interest parity is $i = i$. With a tax on capital flowing in and flowing out, i.e. a tax levied in the sending as well as in the receiving country, and neglecting the tax on interest earned, interest parity for an amount x is:

$$x(1 + it) = x(1 + i^*t) - 2zx \qquad (8.1)$$

or

$$it = i^*t - 2z \qquad (8.2)$$

(where t is the time period of portfolio investment like a day or a week as a fraction of the year, i.e. 30/365 for a monthly investment). This can be written as

$$i = i^* - 2z/t \qquad (8.3)$$

where the second term on the right-hand side indicates that portfolio investment becomes less attractive the shorter the time period. Assume the interest rate in the home country is 5 percent. Then with a Tobin tax of 1 percent, the foreign country would require an interest rate of 7 percent if portfolio capital would remain there for a year ($5 = 7 - 2 \cdot 1$). For half a year, the interest rate would have to be 9 percent ($5 = 9 - 2 \cdot 2$), for a month (1/12) 24 percent and for a day 735 percent ($5 = 735 - 2 \cdot 365$).

Cons against the Tobin tax

There are quite a few serious arguments against a Tobin tax. First, exports and imports are financed by short-term credits; a Tobin tax would thus make trade more expensive and would prevent countries from reaping the benefits from trade; it would thus hurt developing countries. Second, foreign direct investment and equity flows are linked to portfolio capital; a Tobin tax would prevent countries from enjoying the benefits of attracting capital (often including technology) as a factor of production. Third, not all capital flows are speculative; quite a large part even of portfolio flows are related to hedging and using arbitrage gains. Again, the international division of labor would be restraint with negative impacts. Fourth, in the real world, it would be impossible to put the Tobin tax solely on the 'bad' or unwanted portfolio flows and to exempt the good flows, for instance to finance trade or foreign direct investment. Fifth, while a Tobin tax may reduce the inflow of capital somewhat, it does not prevent a massive outflow of capital when a crisis breaks out. Such a sudden outflow, however, is at the root of a currency crisis. Thus, the Tobin tax will not prevent currency crises. Sixth, the Tobin tax requires an international agreement with a uniform tax rate for all countries. It is unrealistic that such an agreement can be reached. It is also open whether the tax is applied to outflowing or inflowing capital and which country receives the tax revenue. If the Tobin tax is applied unilaterally by one country, the tax will negatively affect the necessary real inflow of capital. For instance, Chile had to give up its deposit tax for short-term bank credits remaining for less than a year in 1999 when the inflow of capital dried up. Finally, the Tobin tax would necessitate an immense amount of controls; in the real world, it is extremely difficult to delineate trade flows from portfolio flows; market participants will find many ways around these regulations, for instance by over-invoicing or under-invoicing.

Further reading

Harcourt, G. (2001). Turn to the Tobin Alternative. *The Guardian* (www.guardian.co.uk/archive/article/0,4273,4262953).

Tobin, J. (1978). A Proposal for International Monetary Reform. *Eastern Economic Journal*, 4: 153–159.

8.7 Stabilizing exchange rates: approaches for individual countries

The wish for stable exchange rates

Regarding money as an important innovation, which diminishes transaction costs, the volatility of exchange rates reduces the intended reduction of the transaction costs. Volatility of the exchange rate can mean two things: first, exchange rate movements can deviate in the short run (up to one year) from a long-term trend or a somehow defined frame of reference. Second, the exchange rate can follow a trend for some years and then follow a different trend, changing from appreciation to depreciation. Both types of volatility cause transaction costs. Unexpected short-term deviations from a longer trend may be hedged to some extent. A trend reversal has the consequence that trade flows and direct investment flows have to adapt to the new currency relations. This means that product specialization, factor allocation and the sectoral structure have to adjust. The transaction costs arising from volatility are the reason why there are always efforts aiming at stable exchange rates.

We distinguish between approaches that

individual countries can follow and institutional arrangements that several countries or, in the extreme, the world economy can strive for.

Exchange-rate-oriented monetary policy

Individual countries can pursue an exchange-rate-oriented monetary policy, which means they choose the exchange rate as a nominal anchor. They tie their domestic currency to another currency. That implies that monetary policy has to influence the domestic price level in such a way that the exchange rate remains stable. Following the equation of purchasing power parity, $\hat{e} = \hat{p} - \hat{p}^*$, the policy aims at an exchange rate change $\hat{e} = 0$. If the currency of the foreign country is used as an anchor, then the rate of change of the foreign country's price level is regarded as the point of reference, i.e. $\hat{p} = \hat{p}^*$. The domestic price level follows the foreign price level. In the pre-euro era, Austria, Belgium and the Netherlands were examples of an exchange-rate-oriented monetary policy holding their currencies in a constant ratio to the deutsche mark.

Such an exchange-rate-oriented monetary policy is normally only carried out by smaller countries. Larger economies prefer to determine their price levels themselves. If larger economies pursue an exchange-rate-oriented monetary policy, at least one country has to provide a stable currency as a nominal anchor (anchor currency).

The credibility of a nominal anchor

Especially the experience of developing countries shows that very often an exchange rate taken as the nominal anchor cannot be sustained, because a credible stabilization policy is given up after a couple of years. This gives rise to the issue of how credible nominal anchors are (see Chapters 9 and 10).

Currency board

The currency board is a special form of an exchange-rate-oriented monetary policy. In such an approach, the domestic currency has to be covered completely by foreign currency reserves. The central bank binds itself in the way that it provides domestic money only to the extent that foreign monetary reserves are available. To give credibility to such a policy, the foreign currency can be authorized as legal tender. Then, the domestic currency has to be as stable as the foreign currency, or it is driven out of the market. Argentina had to give up the policy of a currency board in 2001; Estonia also has pursued such an approach since 1992.

The approach of the currency board can only be chosen by some countries, usually small ones. These economies follow another country in their monetary policy. They use the other currency as an anchor, because they cannot provide an anchor themselves. Thus they import the stability of the anchor currency. An important condition is that the markets of these countries, including the labor market, are very flexible. The country must be able to digest external shocks by price adjustments. This condition is especially relevant if the countries are very sensitive to external shocks. For instance, a currency is difficult to sustain if a country is a resource exporter and if resource prices are volatile.

Crawling peg

Another approach is the crawling peg. This approach is followed when over a longer period of time it is expected that the inflation rate in the domestic country will be higher than that in the foreign country. Through the crawling peg, the exchange rate is brought in line with the inflation rate, normally with a preannounced rate of change of the exchange rate. A crawling peg has to be chosen if it is expected that a stringent stabilization policy which would be necessary for a constant exchange rate cannot be kept up.

8.8 Stabilizing exchange rates: multilateral approaches

Anchor currency

In the case of an exchange-rate-oriented policy, a (theoretical) problem is that not all of the n countries can choose the exchange rate as a nominal anchor. Formally, this can also be described as the problem of the $n - 1$ exchange rates. For n countries with n currencies, every single country has $n - 1$ exchange rates. At least one of the currencies (of the nth country) must take the role of the 'numeraire'. As a result, one currency has to be the anchor in a system of fixed exchange rates. In the system of Bretton Woods, the dollar used to be the anchor; in the European Exchange Rate System, it was the deutsche mark. Normally, a currency of a large country which has proved to be stable in the long run develops as the anchor currency. Which currency is finally accepted by other countries remains to be determined by the markets.

Reference zones

With the introduction of reference zones or target zones, the exchange rate is allowed to fluctuate within a band. The exchange rate should only deviate from the (real) equilibrium exchange rate within a limited range. Coordination of monetary and stabilization policies has to ensure that the limits of the range of fluctuations are not surpassed. As long as monetary policy and the other fields of economic policy of the countries involved do not contradict the credibility of the band, the exchange rate can be kept in the target zone. But as soon as the markets doubt the credibility of the band, such a system has a destabilizing effect.

If in such a system the limit of the band is reached, the central banks have to intervene. Such a situation is shown in Figure 8.2, in which the supply of the foreign currency ($) increases; for example, because of an excessively rising money supply in the foreign country. The supply curve of the foreign currency shifts to the right. This means that without an intervention, the foreign currency will be devalued and the euro will be revalued (point E). Such a devaluation of the foreign currency can be avoided if the central banks intervene by demanding additional foreign money to the extent of line AB in exchange for domestic money.

Two problems arise with such an approach of reference zones:

1 Who has to intervene at the limits? If the European Central Bank supplies euros and has to buy the foreign currency, this means that the money supply of the European Central Bank is *de facto* steered by a foreign central bank. If the foreign central bank expands its money supply and the foreign currency is threatened with devaluation, then the European Central Bank would have to supply euros accordingly. But, in the end, this would imply that the European Central Bank would be heteronomous in its monetary policy. The way

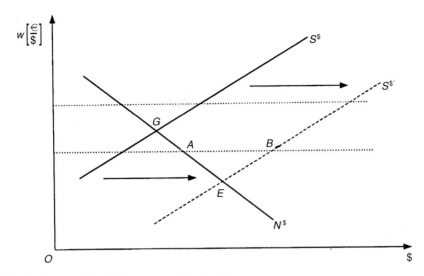

Figure 8.2 Exchange rate within a range of fluctuations

out of this dilemma is that the intervention has to be undertaken by the central bank whose currency is under pressure.

2 How to determine the reference standard of the real equilibrium exchange rate? On the one hand, an equilibrium exchange rate has in theory to be established *ex ante*. In this respect, a model has to be available that includes all relevant definitions of the equilibrium exchange rate and also identifies the factors that could change the expectations of market participants. On the other hand, a political agreement of the sovereign states has to be achieved in order to determine the equilibrium exchange rate.

The European Exchange Rate Mechanism

The European Exchange Rate Mechanism can be interpreted as a system of reference zones. It was a distinct combination of interest rate parity, which determined the capital flows, and of purchasing power parity, which defined the expectations for the exchange rate. In their monetary policies, but also in their fiscal policies, all participating countries were eager to keep their currencies stable and to prevent devaluations. The additional risk premium for a less stable price level represented a burden for the countries and, therefore, national policy attempted to minimize that risk. This system managed to keep the exchange rates stable during 1987–1992 (Figure 8.3). In this case, the intervention mechanism was very helpful.

However, it proved that real economic changes have to lead to an adjustment of the exchange rates when they do not affect all countries in the same way and when changes are adequately strong. These changes are called 'asymmetric shocks'. German reunification was such a shock. Real interest rates in Germany rose because of investment opportunities in Eastern Germany and because of a higher national debt. For that reason, the exchange rates had to be adjusted. In due course, Italy and the UK left the European Exchange Rate Mechanism in 1992. For the UK, a too high entry rate had been chosen in 1990, so that the British currency was overvalued. For the remaining currencies, the band of ±2.25 percent was raised

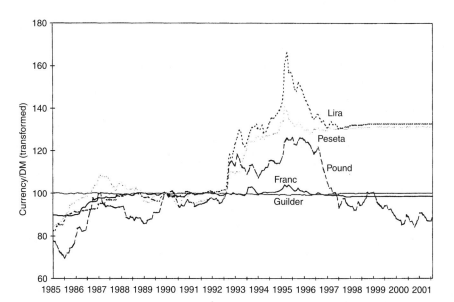

Figure 8.3 Exchange rates in the EMS[a]

[a] January 1990 = 100.
Source for data: Deutsche Bundesbank, monthly reports; own calculations.

to ±15 percent in 1992. The lira and the peseta stayed at their devalued level. With the monetary union in place, only those EU countries outside the euro area, the so-called pre-ins, participate in the ERS-II, except the UK.

Exchange rate zones can induce speculation by making it less costly. The costs of speculation are relatively low as soon as the limit of the band is reached. If a speculator can expect realignments, i.e. an adjustment of the target rates, then this implies a high expected return on investment. If the realignment does not take place, possible losses are limited. If, for example, a devaluation is imminent (by a shift of the supply curve for the foreign currency to the right in Figure 8.2), investors can speculate on an adjustment of the exchange rate. Accordingly, they will buy deutsche marks and finance this by a credit in foreign currency, which is to be repaid later in a weaker currency. Or they will

sell foreign currency now at a future date that they themselves will buy in the future at a lower price (selling short). Once the realignment has taken place, they will make a profit. If there were no realignment, investors would not have any losses (except for the interest costs). As demand for deutsche marks is increased by speculation, any intervention of the central bank to defend the old rate is made more difficult.

Coordination of national monetary policies

According to a proposition of McKinnon (1982), the exchange rates could be stabilized by a coordination of national monetary policies. The world quantity of money should increase according to the quantity rule of money. If a currency gets under pressure to depreciate, then monetary expansion of this country has to be reduced, whereas a currency with a tendency for a revaluation would

The Bretton Woods system

In 1944, 44 countries met in Bretton Woods, New Hampshire, USA, to reach an agreement on the post-war international monetary system. Like the GATT, which was established in 1948, the exchange rate system of Bretton Woods was created in order to establish a stable environment during the period of reconstruction after the Second World War. While the GATT aimed at a rulebased system for trade, Bretton Woods attempted to establish stable exchange rates. The system came into force in 1946. The anchor currency was the US dollar. The central banks (not the private banks) could change their dollar reserves into gold at the US central bank, at fixed exchange rates. In order to join the International Monetary Fund, each country had to establish a parity to the US dollar (or to gold). The governments had to keep the exchange rates of their currencies within a margin of +1 percent. Only in the event of fundamental imbalances were exchange rate adjustments allowed to leave that fixed margin: international agreement was required for this. Temporary deficits in the balance of payments were to be balanced by loans from the International Monetary Fund.

The system collapsed in 1971 when the United States unilaterally discontinued the gold parity. As a result of the Vietnam War, the United States was no longer willing to maintain the necessary price-level stability of the anchor currency. Because of its economic policy problems, the US carried out an excessive short-term monetary expansion, implying a devaluation of the US dollar. Consequently, the Bretton Woods system lost its nominal anchor and was replaced by floating exchange rates in 1973.

need a more generous monetary expansion. It has to be kept in mind that such a system would first of all stabilize the exchange rates but there would be the risk of fluctuating national price levels. Further on, it would be necessary that the sovereign states agree on a reasonable monetary expansion. But it would be insufficient to exclusively coordinate monetary policies since expectations on interest rates and exchange rates play a role as well. Stabilization policy, including fiscal policy, is of great importance, if monetary stability is to be established.

How to prevent volatility of exchange rates?

After the Second World War, countries attempted to liberalize their capital account in order to reap the benefits of capital mobility. Recently, the pendulum has threatened to swing in the opposite direction owing to the volatility of nominal exchange rates. Again and again, currency turbulences have led to calls for more stability in the international monetary system. There is no doubt that nominal exchange rates are considerably influenced by capital flows, that they can overshoot and thus distort trade flows. It is also true that speculative bubbles can occur. But it has to be taken into account that it is not nominal but real exchange rates that have an influence on trade flows. Very often, changes of the exchange rate are the result of a mixture of political and economic policy changes, especially in stabilization policy and in monetary policy. Then exchange rate changes are a barometer of fundamental trends. Also real economic changes can cause a different exchange rate: in the long run, there is no way to counteract fundamentals by using exchange rate measures.

Economic policy proposals aimed at limiting the volatility of exchange rates have to be judged skeptically:

The gold standard

The gold standard was established in the 19th century. In 1821, the obligation was introduced for the Bank of England to redeem bank notes into gold coins. In the Bank Charter Act of 1844, the obligation of redeeming was guaranteed by cover clauses. Later on, other countries joined the gold standard, like Germany (1871), Japan (1897) and the US (1879).

The redeemability of the bank notes into gold meant that the central banks had to exchange the money in circulation for gold at any time at a legally fixed ratio. As a result, gold became a means of international payments and constant exchange rates existed. Because of the fixed ratios mark/Q_G and \$/Q_G, the ratio mark/\$ was also fixed (Q_G: unit of gold). The decisive task for the central banks was to keep the official parity between gold and the domestic currency. Therefore, it was important to keep sufficient gold reserves. This was guaranteed if the balance of payments was in equilibrium.

Figure 8.2, which has already been discussed above, can also be used to explain the effects of a gold currency in the 19th century. Instead of euros consider marks. Suppose, for instance, that the US dollar had a lower value, e.g. because of a rising supply of US dollars shifting the supply curve to the right. Starting from an equilibrium point *G* with flexible exchange rates, a new equilibrium *E* would be reached by the devaluation of the US dollar.

But this is different in the case of a gold currency. If the dollar is sufficiently devalued, the market participants will be able to buy more US dollars, because for one mark they get a relatively larger amount of US dollars. With this amount of dollars they buy gold in the US, transport it to Germany and change it into marks. By this, the exchange rate e cannot sink under the so-called 'lower gold point'. Then it would be worth exporting gold from the US, i.e. dollars would be supplied. In Figure 8.2, the gold export from the US is marked by *AB* (this means capital export of the foreign country). The lower gold point, which depends on the costs of transportation, insurance and interest payments, indicates the lowest possible exchange rate. The upper gold point has a corresponding effect: if the exchange rate increases, i.e. if the mark is devalued, from a certain threshold onwards it is worth changing dollars into marks; it is now worth buying gold with the marks purchased in Germany and transferring it to the US (upper gold point).

If the appropriate institutional rules for a gold currency are chosen, the exchange rate will find its equilibrium between the upper and the lower gold point. Thus, the exchange rate is stable.

- Reference zones (Williamson 1983) will not be feasible, unless the conditions for stability are fulfilled in all individual countries.
- To return to a system similar to the one of Bretton Woods does not take into account the globalization of financial markets.
- To throw sand in the wheels of the international financial markets, i.e. to impose a tax (Tobin tax; see Tobin 1978) on short-term portfolio movements, works against the objective of reducing the costs of transactions for the allocation of real capital.

Stable exchange rates can be obtained by a commitment of all countries to establish a credible currency system and to pursue a policy dominated by the stability of the price level. One possible solution could be that all countries accept a stability-guaranteeing system. From the historic point of view, the gold standard was such a system. The countries gave up their national stabilization policies. They accepted fluctuations in the output of production and in employment in order to realize exchange rate stability. Today, such an approach is not practicable worldwide. On the one hand, there is no anchor; gold can hardly serve as an anchor, since the gold-producing countries would gain enormous rents. On the other hand, the willingness to submit to such an international system is not given. Small countries can solve the problem of too high a volatility by an exchange-rate-oriented monetary policy or by a currency board. For bigger countries, this option is politically not acceptable. Furthermore, one strong country would have to provide the anchor.

National stabilization policy as a contribution to the currency stabilization in the world

Too often – if not always – the triggers for exchange rate volatility are political ones reflecting economic policy conditions, above all failed stabilization policy, fiscal disorder and misguided monetary policy. Exchange rate movements thus represent a barometer of fundamental disturbances.

In the face of the difficulties of the systems shown above, it is a realistic assessment of the possibilities for the stabilization of exchange rates to emphasize national responsibility.

The scenario is as follows. Each country aims at monetary stability at home. It basically expands its money supply according to the growth of the national production potential. Then, the price level remains stable in each country. Consequently, the exchange rates do not change as far as monetary policy is affected. However, stability orientation of monetary policy alone is insufficient to keep exchange rates stable. Fiscal policy and the whole economic policy, including wage setting, also have to be oriented towards stability.

Thus, a solution can only consist in each individual country's keeping its own house in order and maintaining a stable domestic price level. Then, exchange rates will generally remain stable. This approach should be complemented by some minimum agreement on prudential rules for the financial sector in order to shield the overall system against instability and contagion.

Notes

1 It now seems to be agreed in the literature that conditionality on fiscal policy and on structural reforms was too tight, for instance in Korea. It is still being debated whether conditionality on monetary policy to keep the interest rate high in order to avoid further devaluation of the won was justified (Ito 1999; Radelet and Sachs 1999).
2 Net uncommitted usable resources are of $98 billion; balances available under the General Agreement to Borrow and the New Arrangement to Borrow: $44 billion.

Part III

Regional Dimensions of the World Economy

• •

Apart from a global view of world economic structures and processes, economic phenomena within regions of the global economy are of interest. This is especially true for the integration of developing countries into the international division of labor. Quite a few of these newly industrialized countries have successfully managed to adapt to the global economy, but some countries still remain in poverty (Chapter 9). The transformation of the formerly centrally planned economies and their integration into the international division of labor is another important world economic theme (Chapter 10). Regional integrations in the world economy are an interesting trend (Chapter 11) with the European Union being the most advanced form of integration (Chapter 12).

Chapter 9

Developing countries

· ·

What you will understand after reading this chapter

Developing countries are commonly considered to be caught in a poverty trap from which they cannot escape (sections 9.1 and 9.2). A closer look can lead to a more differentiated view. For example, we have to distinguish between underdeveloped countries, newly industrializing countries and newly industrialized countries (section 9.3). Nearly all the countries have improved in absolute terms in the last 25 years (section 9.4). Import substitution and export diversification are discussed as the main development strategies (section 9.5). An important condition for a successful development is an adequate institutional infrastructure (section 9.6). Its lack is one of the reasons for the debt crisis of the 1980s (section 9.7). Macroeconomic instability is a severe economic problem of most developing countries (section 9.8). Finally, the approaches of expenditure reduction and expenditure switching are discussed (section 9.9).

9.1 Characteristics of developing countries

An economy is regarded as underdeveloped when it is characterized by a very low income level or high poverty. Characteristics are malnutrition, diseases, high infant mortality, low life expectancy, and an inefficient supply of public goods in, for example, the public health sector, schools and universities. Further characteristics are illiteracy, few opportunities to earn a sufficient income, and insufficient living and housing conditions. In comparison to other countries in the world, the developing countries only reach a low income level (Table 9.1). In some of these countries, people live on US$1–2 a day.

On the production side of gross national product, a developing country is characterized by a primary sector (agriculture, exploitation of natural resources) contributing a relatively high proportion of total national income and of employment. Agriculture has a relatively low productivity and is often economically discriminated against in favor of other sectors like manufacturing. Very often, agricultural production is concentrated on just a few products (single-crop farming). Far too often, the natural resource sector represents an export enclave, i.e. it is not intensively linked with the rest of the economy, and therefore does not exert noticeable economic spillover effects. The high value-added stages in the chain of vertical production are

Table 9.1 The 10 poorest countries in the world (gross national product per capita in US dollars, 1999)

Countries	At current nominal exchange rates	Gross national product per capita
		At purchasing power parity
Ethiopia	100	599[b]
Burundi	120	553[b]
Sierra Leone	130	414[a]
Malawi	190	581[a]
Niger	190	727[b]
Chad	200	816[b]
Eritrea	200	1,012[b]
Angola	220	632[a]
Nepal	220	1,219[b]
Mozambique	230	797[b]
For comparison:		
Portugal	10,600	15,147[a]
Germany	25,350	22,404[a]
United States of America	30,600	30,600[a]
Japan	32,230	24,041[a]
Switzerland	38,350	27,486[a]
World	4,890	6,490

[a] Extrapolated.
[b] Regression.
Source for data: World Bank, *World Development Report 2000/2001*, Table 1.

lacking. The manufacturing sector accounts for only a small share of national income and of employment. The tertiary sector, especially domestic commerce, binds many employees.

In developing countries, real income, which is on average much lower than in other countries, is unevenly distributed. This means that the Lorenz curve of income distribution strongly deviates from the 45° line. Most of the population is characterized by a low income per capita. There is no middle class, so that there is a big gap between rich and poor. This implies that an important condition for political stability is missing. However, the relationship between the level of development and an uneven income distribution is not altogether clear. Based on the same development level, there is more dissimilarity in Africa (south of the Sahara) and in Latin America than in Asia. Any analysis is also made difficult by statistical problems, since measuring the distribution of personal income is one of the most unreliable fields in development economics. There is hidden unemployment, which is marked by many employees having a marginal productivity close to zero. Their work could be abandoned without a noticeable reduction of production.

The expenditures of the majority of the population are directed towards the necessities of life. Because of low incomes, it is argued that savings are nearly impossible (this, however, is not quite correct since quite a few low-income countries have high savings rates). Groups with a high income often have a traditionally high propensity to consume, so their savings are quite small. They spend their income on conspicuous durable consumer goods without productive capacity. Very often the desire to be an entrepreneur is missing. If there are savings at all, they frequently flow into capital exports.

All in all, the underdeveloped countries are characterized by a dual economy: on the one hand, there are export enclaves of the raw material sector and, on the other hand, a few industrial products are produced which have quite good profit potential but cannot stimulate the rest of the economy sufficiently. Too often the underdeveloped country remains a subsistence economy.

9.2 Reasons for underdevelopment

Several factors have to be considered as possible reasons for underdevelopment.

Excessive population growth

Even if the gross national product rises strongly, the growth of income per capita can be quite low or even negative, if the population grows fast. This is shown in Figure 9.1 (Nelson 1956). Assume that there is a positive growth rate of gross domestic product ($\hat{Y}$), because some savings, i.e. some capital formation, is possible once a threshold income per capita is surpassed. However, the expansion rate of the population ($\hat{B}$) increases with a rising income per head; it later stays constant (or even decreases in 'old' economies). Above all, this development of the population is explained by a reduction of the mortality rate in the case of an increasing prosperity at a given birth rate. Above an income level y_0, the mortality rate falls very quickly, thus the population rises strongly, because of a higher life expectancy and especially a far lower infant mortality as a result of better medical conditions. Eventually, with a higher income per capita the birth rate falls, inducing the population to be stable (or even to shrink). Below an income per capita y_0, the population decreases.

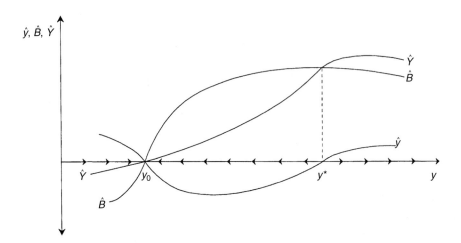

Figure 9.1 The development trap

From the definition of income per capita, $y = Y/B$, it follows for the rate of change of income per capita that $\hat{y} = \hat{Y} - \hat{B}$. As long as the population is growing faster than domestic product, income per head decreases ($\hat{Y} < \hat{B}$, i.e. $\hat{y} < 0$). But when gross domestic product increases more than the population ($\hat{Y} > \hat{B}$, i.e. $\hat{y} > 0$), income per capita rises. Income per capita y_0 is a steady-state equilibrium on a low level. Below y_0, there is a tendency of a rising income per capita, because the population rises less than national product. The economy moves to the point y_0. Above y_0, at first the population grows more than domestic product. This is the reason why the economy tends to go back to the point y_0. Only when the level y^* is exceeded does income per capita rise, because then national product rises more than the population. Between y_0 and y^* the economy always moves back to y_0. The country persists on a low level and is captured in a trap of underdevelopment. It requires a push, normally a positive external shock, to get out of the situation. The economy has to move beyond the threshold y^*.

Missing institutions

In many developing countries, there are no institutions that make sure that necessary long-term concerns, i.e. long-term opportunity costs, are taken into consideration. As a result, politicians are very often satisfied with short-term and populistic solutions, which lead to long-term costs for the country. As an example, there are no adequate rules to prevent a budget deficit of the state.

Because of the lack of efficient tax systems and because of too small a tax base – above all the trade of international goods is taxed by a system of export and import duties – the state finances itself partly by the central bank and monetizes the public debt. As a consequence, inflation appears, occasionally turning into a hyper-inflation. This means that the state is actually levying an inflation tax. The domestic currency loses its value, and owing to the anticipation of a devaluation capital flight occurs. One of the reasons why the government cannot be forced to balance its budget deficit is that the central bank is not independent.

Lack of capital formation

Low savings result in a small capital stock which implies that production is quite low. Usually, new physical capital embodies new technological knowledge. Thus, weak capital formation means that hardly any new technological knowledge can be realized. Little capital formation, i.e. only little abstinence from consumption, also means that human capital is not built up sufficiently, for example, by training on the job. Impediments to capital formation are also due to a low income per head. If a government tries to finance its expenses by an inflation tax, the high inflation will work against savings, because people flee into unproductive inflation-proof uses of their income.

No entrepreneurship

Developing countries often lack entrepreneurship, for several reasons. One is that the role of the entrepreneur is not highly valued in a society and that value orientation does not assign a special importance to achievement. Another reason is that the country has no entrepreneurial tradition, for instance because of its educational system.

National debt

Some developing countries, especially in Latin America, have accumulated a high foreign debt (V) on the international financial markets for several reasons, mainly because of high budget deficits of the state. This requires high interest payments (rV) and leads to a negative balance of services. Ignoring other positions of the balance of services and transfer payments, the financing restriction for an open economy is given by

$$S - I + (T - G) = Z^H - rV - \dot{V}$$

where Z^H is the trade balance and $-\dot{V}$ is the reduction of foreign debt or the increase in foreign assets. For highly indebted countries, the trade balance minus the interest payments is negative, with low domestic savings and an often prevalent budget deficit of the government. This means that indebtedness rises ($\dot{V} > 0$). It is hard for such an economy to reduce consumption in order to balance the public budget, to achieve positive net financial investment and a positive trade balance in the end.

Vicious circle

A multitude of factors can keep developing countries on a basic level. Strong growth of the population, a low savings rate, a small stock of real capital (including infrastructure capital) and of human capital lead to a small output, which itself does not allow a sufficient formation of capital (Figure 9.2). High inflation rates and high foreign debt accelerate this vicious circle, which has to be broken through for economic development to take off. Instead of 'vicious circle' or 'cumulating effects', this phenomenon is also called a 'low-level equilibrium'. Such a low-level equilibrium can be characterized as hysteresis. It is path-dependent in the sense that once such a situation is reached it is extremely difficult to get out of it. Similar considerations define the so-called economics of thresholds ('*économie des seuils*') which has to be overcome before economic development can take place.

Different endowment conditions

Yet another aspect is that the countries of the world are characterized by different conditions for economic growth. Some of these conditions are determined by nature, like access to the oceans (coastal country versus

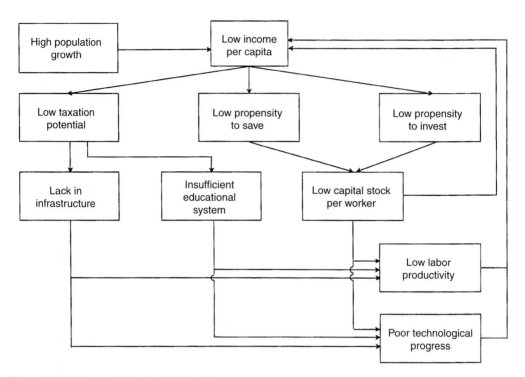

Figure 9.2 Vicious circle of underdevelopment

landlocked country, tropical conditions, etc.), others are synthetic (acquired comparative advantage). These conditions can lead to different growth rates.

9.3 Developing countries – newly industrializing countries – new industrialized countries: a broad spectrum

The picture described above has been related to those countries where the developing process has not yet started ('underdeveloped' countries). A number of African economies south of the Sahara and a few South Asian countries (including e.g. Bangladesh) belong to this category. But it would be wrong to put all countries which are normally called 'underdeveloped countries' in this category. In the industrializing countries, sufficient growth processes have already started, e.g. in

most Latin American countries and in South-East Asia. Capital formation is surprisingly high with investment and savings shares amounting to more than 30 percent of GDP, quite in contrast to the widespread belief that poor countries cannot save. For some economies the term 'newly industrialized countries' is becoming more accepted – such as, for example, Argentina, Brazil, Chile, Mexico, Korea, Hong Kong, Singapore and Taiwan. In the statistics of the World Bank, these countries are ranked in the middle-, upper- or even high-income groups (Table 9.2). Meanwhile some of them (e.g. Mexico, South Korea) have been admitted to the OECD. These countries have succeeded in a broad increase of their industrial exports, and manufactured goods constitute a considerable part of their exports. The industrializing countries and the newly industrialized

Table 9.2 The newly industrialized countries, 1999

	Gross national product per head in US dollars		Share of industry-exports in total exports (in percent)[a]
	At current nominal exchange rates	At purchasing power parity	
Countries in the upper range of the middle-income group			
Mexico	4,400	7,719	85
Brazil	4,420	6,317	55
Chile	4,740	8,370	17
Argentina	7,600	11,324	35
High-income countries			
Korea, Republic of	8,490	14,637	91
Hong Kong	23,520	20,939	95
Singapore	29,610	27,024	86
World	4,890	6,490	79

[a] The shares of industrial production in the exports refer to 1998.
Source for data: World Bank, *World Development Report 2000/2001*, Tables 1 and 20.

countries are on the way to another stage of economic development. Some of the economic policy problems to be discussed below have already been solved by these countries.

9.4 Which countries failed, which succeeded?

It is heavily debated by the NGOs whether third world countries have benefited from the international division of labor. It is postulated that the economic situation has worsened for third world countries. In order to shed some light on that question, two different criteria can be used. First, whether GDP per capita has increased in absolute terms and, second, whether the relative position to the US has improved.

There are several problems with this approach: in order to make a comparison in time and between countries, a common measuring rod has to be applied. This may be constant US dollars where, for international comparisons, market exchange rates are used. Or purchasing power parity rates can be applied. Both data sets are provided by the World Bank. We here use purchasing power parity data because they are more appropriate for comparisons of standards of living. Another problem is that changes in the standard of living are not only linked to the international division of labor but are influenced by quite a set of factors including purely internal conditions of a country.

Looking at the period 1975–1998, all countries for which data are available have improved their situation in absolute terms except the Democratic Republic of Congo (Figure 9.3a and b where the 1998 position is always indicated by a circle). This also holds for countries like Bangladesh, Ghana, Nicaragua and the Sudan.

Relative to the US, Chile, China, India and even Bangladesh have gained. Argentina, Brazil and Mexico have lost in the position relative to the United States. Nicaragua has lost even more in its relative position. Ghana and Sudan also have less favorable relative positions. The latter three countries have all been affected by war and internal turmoil.

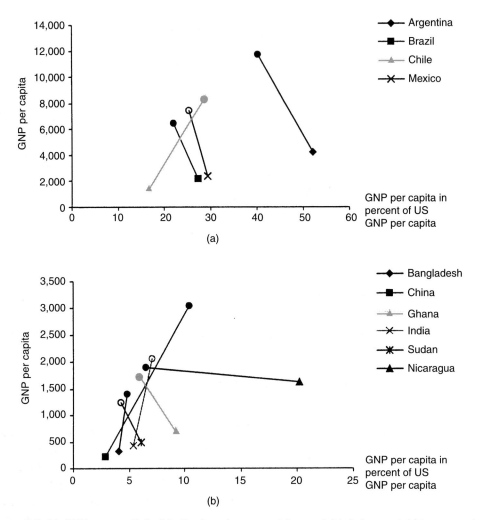

Figure 9.3 (a) GNP per capita[a] of Latin American countries and (b) Asian and African countries, absolutely and relatively to the US, 1975 and 1998

[a] Purchasing power parity.
Source for data: World Bank, World Development Indicators 2000.

Depicting the average annual rate of increase of the absolute GNP level per capita on the vertical axis and the change of the relative position to the US in terms of percentage points on the horizontal axis between 1975 and 1998, the countries can be arranged in two quadrants with the winners in both accounts in the right quadrant and the losers in the relative position in the left quadrant (Figure 9.4).

China, Chile, Indonesia, Sri Lanka, India, Pakistan and Bangladesh gain on both accounts. Countries like Argentina, Nicaragua, Brazil, Sudan, Ghana, Burundi, Zambia and Mexico, while gaining in absolute terms, lose in their relative position.

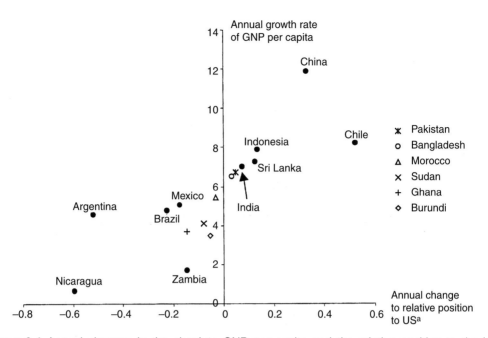

Figure 9.4 Annual changes in the absolute GNP per capita and the relative position to the US between 1975 and 1998

[a] In terms of percentage points
Source for data: World Bank, *World Development Indicators 2000*.

9.5 Development strategies

Concerning strategies of economic development we have to distinguish between import substitution and export diversification.

Import substitution

During the four decades from 1950 to 1990 the development policy of Latin America was characterized by a lack of confidence in the international division of labor as an important source of economic growth. Latin American development policy followed the strategy of import substitution. The starting point of this strategy was the thesis of decreasing terms of trade, which was developed by Prebisch (1950) and Singer (1950). This policy was directed at replacing imports by domestic goods. The domestic sectors were supported in their development and shielded against foreign suppliers. A basis for the industry was supposed to be built up by the protection of young industries (infant industry argument). In this respect it is significant that traditional trade relations had been interrupted by the Second World War. Unlike the European countries, Latin America did not place its hope on a closer integration of the world economy.

Typical instruments of such a policy were protectionist instruments like import licenses or import duties, which increased with the vertical level of processing and thus protected the domestic producers of finished goods. This development strategy, which was predominant in the 1950s and 1960s, at first seemed to be successful in Latin America, but from the mid-1960s onwards, the problems became visible. Above all, the industrial sector developed very poorly. One reason was that the policy of import substitution was associated with considerable distortions. Intermediate goods became more expensive because of import protection, and this reduced the competitiveness of the export sector. Import protection had the same effects as taxation. The price structure was distorted in favor of the domestic import substitutes so that this sector expanded too much and attracted too many resources. Because of the protection from international competition, the domestic producers did not feel the necessary pressure to cut costs and to innovate. The system of import licenses opened the doors for corruption. In the end, the strategy of import substitution caused serious misallocation and created more market failure – and also political failure – than had existed initially.

Export diversification

While the strategy of import substitution is rather inward-oriented, the strategy of export diversification, which was pursued by some Asian countries, can be seen as an outward-oriented development strategy. The objective was and still is to expose the export sectors to international competition and not to distort the allocation between the export sector and the sector of the import substitutes. Detrimental effects of import protection for exports were at first compensated by special export promotions. Owing to high domestic savings this was not harmful to a balanced budget for the state. In short, it tried to enhance domestic production by intensive competition and by this to develop a sustainable economic basis. The predominant philosophy was that the world markets would offer interesting opportunities to the domestic producers. The exchange rate policy could prevent

massive overvaluations. There is no proof for undervalued currencies over a longer period of time; the real exchange rate was mainly left to the markets. There have been almost no bureaucratic restrictions for currency-related questions in the commercial area.

Particularly the Asian economies followed the policy of export diversification, which has proved to be very successful. The exports were an enormous stimulus for the process of industrialization and economic development. They provided the countries with high gains from trade and made considerable real growth rates possible.

9.6 Institutional infrastructure

An essential requirement for a positive economic development is a reliable institutional framework, providing a good basis for decisions in the private sector. Many economic decisions have a long-term impact. This is valid for real capital investments, for the tapping of natural resources, for the decisions to start up businesses, and also for human capital investments. Therefore, stability of the institutional set-up is required. One important institutional condition is the right of ownership, i.e. the acceptance of private property rights. Another crucial prerequisite is a stable tax system, preventing taxes from being changed frequently and irregularly thus creating uncertainty for private investors.

Above all, it has to be guaranteed that the state must not balance the budget by printing money, i.e. by making the central bank increase monetary expansion and widen the supply of money. Monetization of the budget deficit is only possible because in many countries the central bank is not independent from political influence. For that reason, another important aspect is the independence of the central bank and the explicitly formulated prohibition of financing budget deficits by monetary policy. The institutional framework of the monetary system has to be credible. In the extreme case of a currency board (e.g. in Argentina), this credibility is in fact imported, since the domestic currency has to be completely covered by foreign currencies (US dollar and euro).

9.7 The debt crisis

Especially for the countries of Latin America, the 1980s were marked by the debt crisis. For example, the volume of foreign debt in Argentina reached 93 percent of its gross domestic product (Figure 9.5). Net foreign debt in relation to exports of the 17 most indebted countries was at 384 percent, in comparison to the 200 percent which is considered to be acceptable by some (Cline 1995). Interest payments have been one important reason for a negative current account. New

credits had to be raised so that countries were able to pay interest. The new credits were used to finance the budget deficits of the state rather than to create a new capital stock.

When the financial markets realize that a country is not able to fulfill its interest and repayment commitments, then the markets lose the willingness to provide the country with credits, i.e. capital. As usually happens when a devaluation is expected, capital flight takes place. The prices of bonds of highly indebted countries fall. Normally, bank syndicates and international organizations have to provide a fresh starting position for new capital. Creditors lose a considerable amount of their claims by accepting a write-off on their debt (Brady Plan).

The debt crisis of the 1980s has now been overcome, if it is interpreted as a crisis of insolvency of the middle-income countries. But it is still relevant for the indebted countries. Argentina and Brazil, for example, still

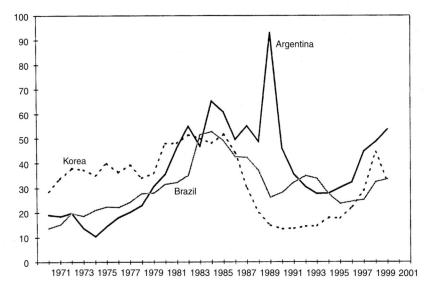

Figure 9.5 Debt of Argentina, Brazil and South Korea, 1970–1999 (in percent of gross national product)

Source for data: For 1970–1992: World Bank, *World Development Indicators*; for 1993–1999: World Bank, *Global Development Finance (Country Tables)*, 2001.

have to use more than 50 percent of their export revenues to pay the interest on their net foreign debts, foreign debt reaching roughly 400 percent of the export revenues (see Table 9.3). In 2001, Argentina got under severe pressure owing to its foreign debt.

Some Asian countries like Korea and some transformation countries like the Czech Republic are in a far better position. However, other Asian countries like Thailand and Indonesia have now reached similar and even higher magnitudes of debt relative to GDP compared to those of some Latin American countries (Figure 9.6).

Table 9.3 Foreign debt of selected countries, 1998

| | Foreign debt in percent | | |
	Of gross national product	*Of exports*	*Debt service in percent of exports*
Argentina	52	463	58
Bolivia	59	448	30
Brazil	29	395	74
Chile	50	192	22
Mexico	39	124	21
Indonesia	169	275	33
Thailand	79	131	19
Czech Republic	45	75	15
Hungary	64	111	27
Poland	28	110	10

Source for data: World Bank, *World Development Indicators*, CD-ROM, 2000; World Bank, *World Development Report 2000/2001.*

Figure 9.6 Debt of Thailand and Indonesia, 1970–1999 (in percent of gross national product)

Source for data: For 1970–1992: World Bank, *World Development Indicators*; for 1993–1999: World Bank, *Global Development Finance (Country Tables)*, 2001.

9.8 *Macroeconomic instability and Latin American countries*

Case studies

Macroeconomic instability is a special problem for the newly industrializing countries in Latin America, for example with exorbitantly high inflation rates of 2,314 percent in 1990 for Argentina or 2,938 percent in the same year for Brazil. The inflation rate is correlated with an unusually high expansion of the money supply (Table 9.4). Besides inflation another major problem is the volatility of the inflation rate. Most of the time, high public deficits and current account deficits occur simultaneously. This can be explained by insufficient institutional conditions for macroeconomic stability.

Table 9.4 Macroeconomic instability, 1985–2000

	Expansion of the money supply[a]	Inflation rate	Budget deficit[b]	Current account balance[b]
Argentina				
1985–1990	181.1	192.9	–2.1	–1.2
1991–1995	19.5	9.9	–0.5	–2.5
1996–2000	1.0	–0.2	–2.0	–3.9
Brazil				
1985–1990	201.5	204.5	–12.7	–0.3
1991–1995	219.9	223.7	–4.9[c]	–0.3
1996–2000	14.3	5.2	–4.0	–4.1
Mexico				
1985–1990	52.3	52.8	–8.5	–0.7
1991–1995	8.8	15.1	1.4	–5.0
1996–2000	19.2	14.6	–1.1	–2.3[d]

[a] Expansion of the money supply and inflation rate in percent.
[b] Budget deficit and current account balance in percent of GDP.
[c] 1991–1994.
[d] 1996–1999.
Source for data: IMF, *International Financial Statistics*, June 2001; IMF, *Country Reports on Brazil* (2000) and Argentina (2001).

Money expansion and inflation

The correlation between the expansion of the money supply and inflation can clearly be seen for Argentina (see Figure 5.1) and Brazil (Figure 9.7). Argentina managed to get the expansion of the money supply under control in the 1990s and to keep the price level stable by economic policy reforms, i.e. by the transition to a currency board.

Usually, inflation has an effect on the exchange rate, although the impact might be delayed temporarily. This results from the purchasing power parity $\hat{w} = \hat{P} - \hat{P}^*$. For instance, the peak of the inflation rate in Argentina in 1989 and 1990 is related to a visible devaluation of the peso (Figure 5.4 in Chapter 5).

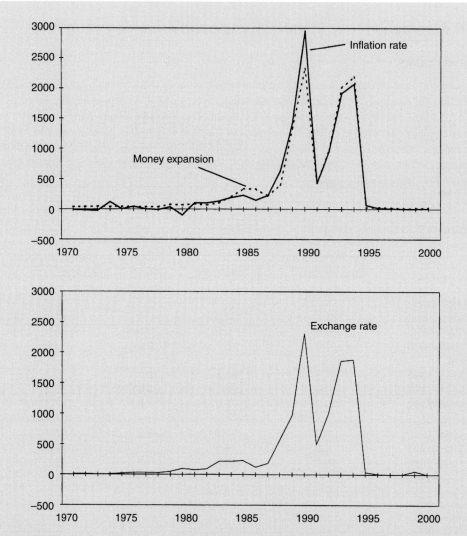

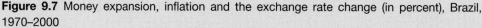

Figure 9.7 Money expansion, inflation and the exchange rate change (in percent), Brazil, 1970–2000

Source for data: IMF, *International Financial Statistics*, June 2001, IMF, *Country Report* (2000).

Brazil seems to be a somewhat different story. At the beginning of the 1980s a strong devaluation took place, but the money supply and the price level did not change significantly. This is the effect of the beginning of the debt crisis. At relatively constant product prices, a nominal devaluation induces a real revaluation, which is necessary to improve the current account. The other phases of devaluation were marked by monetary reforms. In the mid-1980s the cruzeiro was replaced by the cruzado. Its exchange rate was regularly devalued in the framework of a crawling peg. The cause of the monetary reform was an internal imbalance with a budget deficit of 11 percent. At the beginning of the 1990s the cruzeiro was introduced once again and was devalued by floating. Now, the cause was an external imbalance accompanied by a drop of foreign capital inflows. Finally, with a new monetary reform in 1993 the real was introduced. The Brazilian financial crisis of 1999, in which the real was devalued by 64 percent, shows up in Figure 9.7 with a tiny peak only because this devaluation of the real was low relative to the Brazilian long-run experience.

In Mexico (Figure 9.8) there is also a connection between the expansion of the money supply and the inflation rate but it is not as visible as in the case of Brazil. Thus, during the debt crisis in the beginning of the 1980s, the increase in the inflation rate was stronger, while at the same time – as in Brazil – a strong devaluation took place. A drop in the inflow of foreign capital was visible in the mid-1980s and in connection with the peso crisis at the end of 1994. The strong

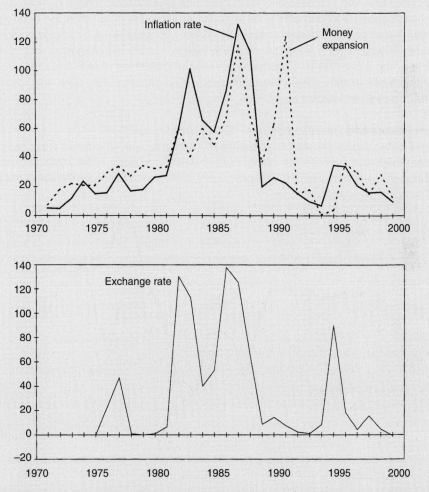

Figure 9.8 Money expansion, inflation and the exchange rate change (in percent), Mexico, 1970–2000

Source for data: IMF, *International Financial Statistics*, June 2001.

expansion of the money supply in the early 1990s surprisingly had at first neither an effect on the price level nor on the exchange rate. This might be the temporary result of the policy of an active crawling peg, attempting to stabilize the expectations on the foreign exchange markets. But if for a period of time the rate of change of the price index is higher than in the reference country (i.e. the US) as in 1983 and 1984 and in the period from 1988 to 1994, there has to be a realignment of the nominal exchange rate (compare also with Figure 7.4). In 1994, the peso crisis occurred and the peso was strongly devalued.

Chile pursued different exchange rate policies. During 1980–1981, a policy of fixed exchange rates was pursued. This was combined with a real revaluation. This approach could no longer be carried out after the outbreak of the debt crisis. After a period of flexible exchange rates, Chile moved on to a passive crawling peg with an exchange rate band, in which since 1989 real economic realignments were regarded as more important than the fight against inflation. The parity of the peso was regularly adjusted to a basket of currencies, in between interventions were used to keep the exchange rate in a band. In comparison to a constant exchange rate, a crawling peg has the advantage of preventing abrupt adjustments if it is applied correctly. In 1999, Chile gave up its policy of an exchange rate band and committed itself to a 2–4 percent inflation target.

Budget deficits and the exchange rate

Changes of the exchange rate are a reaction to internal as well as external imbalances. For instance, there was a remarkable public budget deficit in Mexico in the 1980s (Figure 9.9). Combined with an expansion of the money supply, this was the cause for the rise of the price

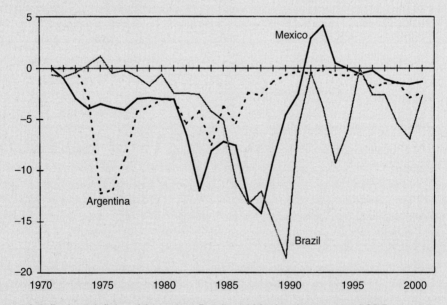

Figure 9.9 Budget deficits of Argentina, Brazil and Mexico, in percent of GDP

Source for data: IMF, *International Financial Statistics*, June 2001; IMF, *Country Reports on Argentina* (2001) *and Brazil* (2000).

level and the devaluation of the peso. Although the budget deficit had been reduced until the beginning of the 1990s, the current account deficit increased after huge short-term inflows of portfolio investment. The collapse occurred in December of 1994, when the capital flow turned around and the peso had to be devalued. At the same time, an international support program became necessary. During the 1980s, Brazil also had a significant budget deficit with up to 20 percent of its GDP. An increase of the budget deficit became visible in Argentina particularly in the first half of the 1980s. These budget deficits signal that credible stabilization policies were not carried out.

The experience of the Latin American countries shows that a stabilization policy with the exchange rate as a nominal anchor could rarely be kept up, if public budget deficits cannot be avoided. Then the confidence in the stability of a currency gets lost. Something similar can be seen when economic policy is dominated by income distribution considerations (or policies). A lack of flexibility of the labor market as well as wages that do not correspond to labor productivity, make a stabilization policy far more difficult in the long run.

Instability and the real exchange rate

Fixing the nominal exchange rate does not imply a constant real exchange rate. Very often the domestic inflation rate is higher than the foreign one. Then, a real revaluation takes place. P rises stronger than P^*. The real exchange rate $e_R = eP^*/P$ falls. This is also valid for the crawling peg if the devaluation rate does not fully compensate the difference between the two inflation rates. A real appreciation can turn out to be even stronger if high net capital inflows occur. The real appreciation has allocative effects. Furthermore, it is linked to deficits in the current account. If the currency is overvalued in real terms an adjustment is unavoidable. Then, a real depreciation has to take place. Normally this means a nominal devaluation; the fixed exchange rate is given up. As an alternative, the price for imports or for non-tradables has to rise.

Although the newly industrialized countries of Latin America have been successful in establishing macroeconomic stability for some time, the question is whether this stability will last or whether a new crisis will occur, thus making new stabilization efforts necessary. Because of political constraints, too often there are deviations from the stabilization programs. This happens because institutional changes are insufficient to keep the expansion of the money supply at a low level in order to assure a constant money value. The volatility will remain the Damocles sword of Latin America.

9.9   The real exchange rate once more: expenditure reduction and expenditure switching

A crucial role for development processes is played by the real exchange rate (e_R). As we know from Chapter 7, the real exchange rate differs from the nominal exchange rate in that the nominal exchange rate is weighted by a ratio of goods prices. If the ratio refers to the prices of foreign and domestic goods, the real exchange rate, i.e. $e_R = eP^*/P$, provides information on the production incentives for domestic goods relative to foreign goods. If the ratio refers to the prices of tradables and of non-tradables, i.e. $e_R = eP_T^*/P_{NT}$, the information signal is on incentives for the production of tradables relative to non-tradables.

The real exchange rate is an important variable that influences both the equilibrium

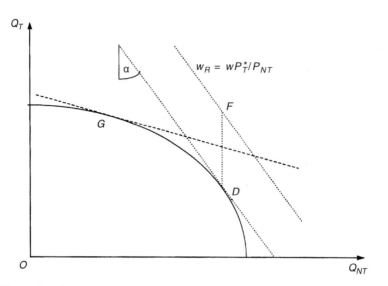

Figure 9.10 The real exchange rate

of the balance of payments and the internal equilibrium of the goods market. The real exchange rate is a determinant of absorption and of production.

Developing countries, which all too often have a current account deficit, have to reduce this deficit. Such a situation can be seen in Figure 9.10. The real relative price eP_T^*/P_{NT}, i.e. the real exchange rate (Q_{NT}/Q_T) is given by the tangent of the angle α. The country's production point is D and the consumption point is F. The country absorbs more than would be feasible according to its production conditions. There is a trade deficit between demand and supply of the tradable DF. If the deficit is to be reduced, there are two possible ways. First, absorption can be reduced (expenditure reduction, movement from F to D). For instance, government demand can be reduced. Higher taxation can cut down private consumption (then, with given relative prices and a homothetic utility function, the point of consumption is on a line OF). Second, the country could carry out a real devaluation, i.e. the real exchange rate has to increase in order to reduce the deficit of the current account (expenditure switching, movement from D to G along the transformation curve). This implies that the price of the tradable good denominated in national currency rises relative to the non-tradable good. This implies that the sectoral structure has to change. After a real depreciation, it is more profitable to expand the production of the tradable good, and the production of the non-tradable good decreases. Owing to the change of relative prices there is a reallocation of resources towards the tradable good (export and import substitutes). The trade account is balanced in point G. The production of the non-tradable good has decreased and the production of the tradable good has risen.

A real devaluation can be brought about by a nominal devaluation; but it can also take place when the price for the non-tradable goods falls in the home country while prices for tradables remain constant.

Chapter 10

The transformation countries

....

What you will understand after reading this chapter

At the end of the 1980s and the beginning of the 1990s, a radical change took place in the world economy. The countries of Central and Eastern Europe gave up central planning and switched over to a market economy approach. They had to rebuild their economic systems and adapt their economies to the new conditions. Together with the new economic concept, the political decision structures and the institutional set-up changed (section 10.1). Initially, a collapse of output occurred (section 10.2). Especially the sequence of reform steps was the subject of intense discussions (sections 10.3 and 10.4). A lot of economic problems such as privatization, tightening budget constraints and inflation had to be solved (section 10.5). The international economic aspects of transformation are of particular interest (section 10.6). More than 30 formerly centrally planned economies are in a process of reform at the moment. East Germany is a special case of the transformation process (section 10.7). Already at the end of the 1970s, China had begun to decentralize and to reorganize its economic system, though without changing its political structures (section 10.8). The Soviet Union dissolved into a number of countries, among them Russia, Ukraine, Belarus, Uzbekistan and other nations (section 10.9).

10.1 Rebuilding a centrally planned economy

In the process of rebuilding a centrally planned economy into a market economy, there are three main areas of reform which can be distinguished: the creation of a new institutional framework, macroeconomic stabilization and the real adjustment of the firms and sectors on the microeconomic level (Figure 10.1).

The institutional framework

The rules and incentives of the centrally planned economies have to be replaced by institutional arrangements that allow market transactions, let firms decide on their production and their investments autonomously and let households determine their consumption, savings and labor supply on their own. A legal framework is imperative, particularly the law of contract and the law of enterprises. A decentralization of economic decisions is not possible without reliable property rights. Property rights are responsible for long-term effects being taken into account in economic calculations. But property rights are also a crucial incentive for individuals to do business. Above all, property rights establish an area of decisions in which the individuals can move without being influenced by government. Thus, one essential element of the framework of a market economy is from which responsibilities the government withdraws; that is, which responsibilities the government leaves to the private sector. Finally, a two-tier banking system, in which the responsibilities of monetary policy and intermediation are separated, can be regarded as an important aspect of the institutional framework.

Macroeconomic stabilization

During the transition from a centrally planned economy to a market economy, macroeconomic instabilities arise. The existing excess

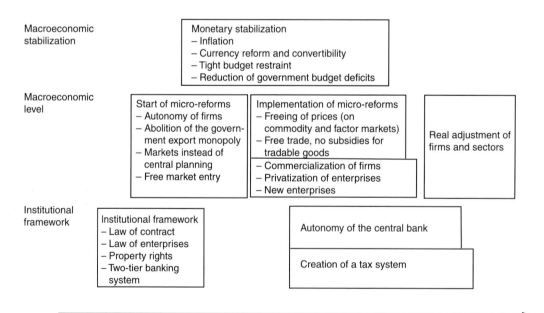

Figure 10.1 Areas and sequence of reforms

supply of money causes inflation, which is hard to keep under control. As a result, there are negative effects on the real sphere of the economy during the transformation process. Therefore, one objective has to be a stable money. Usually, this can only be achieved by a currency reform, when a new currency with a new name is introduced or when a massive currency cut is carried out. Moreover, the newly independent successor states of the Soviet Union and Yugoslavia have had to introduce their own new currencies.

But a currency reform remains unsuccessful unless the necessary institutional design for the monetary sector is introduced. One important step is to guarantee the independence of the central bank. It must be prohibited, in particular, that the central bank finances government budget deficits with its monetary policy. Finally, macroeconomic stabilization cannot succeed and an increase in efficiency for the whole economy cannot be obtained unless the state budget deficit is reduced and a tight budget restriction for the government is introduced. Exchange rate policy must take the purchasing power parity into account. For that reason the nominal rates must move in line with the inflation differences. A higher domestic inflation rate than abroad means a real appreciation, possibly causing a deficit in the balance of payment.

Real adjustment of firms

The institutional framework and macroeconomic stability are necessary requirements for the transformation process, but, at the core, the transformation must take place on the microeconomic level inside the enterprises. Micro-reforms include the introduction of markets with price liberalization, the conversion of state enterprises into separate legal entities (commercialization) and their privatization. The real adjustment process must then take place inside the privatized firms. The transition to a market economy means a 'shock' for the firms: some of their products cannot be sold any more, prices of the production factors are now based on scarcity, factor allocation does not correspond to the new market prices, the capital stock of the enterprises is largely obsolete. The existing firms have to find new products, change the factor allocation and build new capital. Even more important for the real adjustment process on the microeconomic level is the setting up of new firms.

10.2 The J-curve of transformation

The transformation of a centrally planned economy involves a collapse of national output. A crucial reason for this breakdown is that the capital stock of the transformation country that was adapted to the old conditions of a centrally planned economy became obsolete to a large extent due to the new scarcity relations. Therefore the reform countries have to rebuild their capital stock. This process takes time and, moreover, involves adjustment costs. Additionally, the existing human capital has to be integrated into the new factor allocation. Another aspect of the economic breakdown is the institutional vacuum at the beginning of the transformation process, which implies uncertainty over the rules that will hold in the future.

The Visegrad countries (Poland, Hungary and the then still united Czech and Slovak Republics), where the reforms started around 1989, had to face a breakdown of roughly 20 percent of their gross domestic products (Figure 10.2). While the breakdown took place at a similar pace, the Czech Republic,

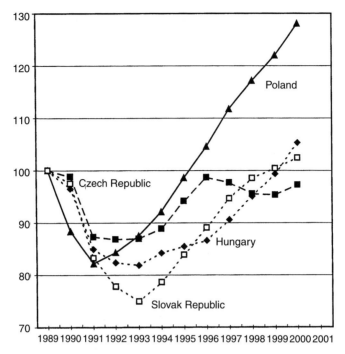

Figure 10.2 The J-curves in Central Europe (gross domestic product in real terms)[a]

[a] 1989 = 100.

Source for data: EBRD, *Transition Report, 2000*; 1999: preliminary estimates; 2000: EBRD projection.

Hungary and the Slovak Republic have needed more time to recover than Poland.

In Russia, where the reforms started around 1991 rather than 1989, the gross domestic product halved (Figure 10.3); the decrease in Lithuania was even stronger. There was also a massive breakdown in East Germany, where the industrial production fell to one third of the former level (section 10.7).

10.3 The sequence of reform steps

There are different opinions on strategies of transformation. It is fair to point out that American economists emphasized the importance of macroeconomic stabilization, taking the experience with stabilization policy in Latin America as a frame of reference. German economists, on the other hand, put more emphasis on the development of the institutional framework. For them, the process is characterized by the Erhard reforms of West Germany in 1948.

A time pattern of the most important reform steps in the three main areas of institutional framework, macroeconomic stabilization and real adaptation is shown in Figure 10.1.

At the beginning of reforms, the creation of an institutional framework is required. This is a prerequisite for the reforms on the microeconomic level and the real adjustment. Having created this framework, the reforms on the microeconomic level can start. Central planning is replaced by market allocation.

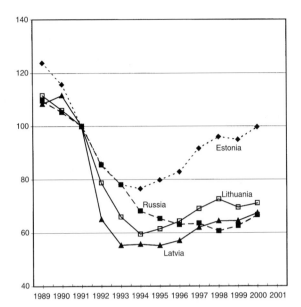

Figure 10.3 The J-curve in Russia and the Baltic States (gross domestic product in real terms)[a]

[a] 1991 = 100.

Source for data: EBRD, *Transition Report, 2000*; 1999: preliminary estimates; 2000: EBRD projection.

The export monopoly of the state is abolished, firms decide autonomously.

In a second step these micro-reforms are implemented. The prices on the commodity markets are liberalized. Additionally, scarcity prices on the factor markets are established. The wage structure has to be adapted to the new situation. After commercialization of enterprises, privatization has to start.

Approximately at the beginning of the micro-reforms, monetary stabilization must be tackled. This includes a currency reform and an (at least partial) independence of the central bank with the appropriate institutional arrangement. In this phase, it is important to tighten the budget constraint. Centrally planned economies were characterized by 'soft budget constraints' for state enterprises and for the state itself (Kornai 1980). Enterprises received cheap credits and direct subsidies from the national budget. This practice has to be given up. The newly developing banking system cannot support the old enterprises by favoring them with special rates of interest any longer, because this implies a higher interest burden for the new firms, and this in turn means an international competitive disadvantage for the economy as a whole. As the government should not be allowed to cover its deficits with the help of the central bank any longer, a tax system must be developed that allows government expenditures to be financed by taxes. In this context, the question arises to what extent the state is able to cushion the social problems (old-age insurance, healthcare, unemployment) that are partly caused by transformation.

Finally, the economy has to adjust in real terms. This means that the factor allocation within the firms must be changed (see above).

The set of goods that is produced and the sectoral structure have to adjust.

In principle, it is reasonable to carry out as many reform steps as possible in a short period of time. There is a bundle of essentials that has to be introduced at once. For example, there is good reason to believe that after the creation of an institutional framework, the decontrol of prices, the opening of commodity markets to foreign countries, the privatization of enterprises and monetary stabilization must be put into effect more or less simultaneously. This must be quickly followed by the autonomy of the central bank. With regard to the tax system, one will have to start with a rudimentary tax system (customs duties, sales taxes) that will gradually be rebuilt towards a value-added tax and income tax system. It can also be discussed whether some steps can be postponed; for example, the residents' convertibility of the domestic currency. But the problem is that the reform loses credibility.

10.4 Big bang or gradual adjustment?

The different elements of the reform can be realized in one big step ('big bang') or gradually (Figure 10.4). It has been intensively discussed in the literature whether the 'big bang' or rather the gradual approach promises to be more successful. Psychological aspects and political economy arguments speak well in favor of the 'big bang' approach. After the collapse of a centrally planned economy, people are prepared to try a new approach and to make sacrifices for it. For example, real wages (we use producer wages for lack of data on consumer wages) in Poland (1990) and in the Czech Republic (1991) fell by more than 30 percent within one year (Table 10.1). The quicker the necessary and painful steps of adjustment are carried out, the quicker the country will get out of the 'vale of tears'. The Poles have expressed this philosophy with the motto: 'You cannot cross a gorge with two leaps'. When the countries of Central Europe introduced the new

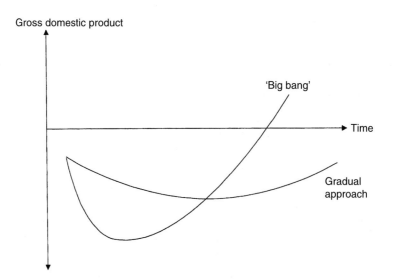

Figure 10.4 'Big bang' versus gradual adjustment

Table 10.1 Important economic variables in the transformation process

	1990	1991	1992	1993	1994	1995	1996	1997	1998	1999[a]	2000[b]
Real GDP growth (percent)											
Czech Republic	−1.2	−11.6	−0.5	0.1	2.2	5.9	4.8	−1.0	−2.2	−0.2	2.0
Hungary	−3.5	−11.9	−3.1	−0.6	2.9	1.5	1.3	4.6	4.9	4.5	6.0
Poland	−11.6	−7.0	2.6	3.8	5.2	7.0	6.1	6.9	4.8	4.1	5.0
Slovak Republic	−2.5	−14.6	−6.5	−3.7	4.9	6.7	6.2	6.2	4.1	1.9	2.0
Russia	−4.0	−5.0	−14.5	−8.7	−12.7	−4.1	−3.5	0.8	−4.6	3.2	6.5
Consumer price inflation (percent)											
Czech Republic	10.8	56.6	11.1	20.8	10.0	9.1	8.8	8.5	10.7	2.1	3.9
Hungary	28.9	35.0	23.0	22.5	18.8	28.2	23.6	18.3	14.3	10.1	9.5
Poland	585.6	70.3	43.0	35.3	32.2	27.8	19.9	14.9	11.8	7.3	9.9
Slovak Republic	10.8	61.2	10.0	23.2	13.4	9.9	5.8	6.1	6.7	10.6	11.9
Russia	5.6	92.7	1,526.0	875.0	311.4	197.7	47.8	14.7	27.6	86.1	20.7
Change of real producer wages in manufacturing (percent)											
Czech Republic[c]	0.1[c]	−31.5	8.7	13.4	9.9	8.7	11.9	8.4	5.6	6.3	n.a.
Hungary	0.7	−5.3	12.1	12.5	7.7	−3.8	−0.6	3.6	7.4	8.5	n.a.
Poland	−34.8	15.8	3.1	2.7	10.1	5.4	14.5	12.1	8.4	5.8	n.a.
Slovak Republic	−1.2	−31.1	10.5	4.4	6.3	6.0	9.8	7.5	6.1	−3.9	n.a.
Russia	n.a.	n.a.	−41.4	−6.1	−17.5	−31.3	9.6	−13.7	7.7	−9.2	n.a.
Budget deficit (in percent of GDP)											
Czech Republic	−0.2	−1.9	−3.1	0.5	−1.1	−1.4	−0.9	−1.7	−2.0	−3.3	−4.2
Hungary	0.0	−3.0	−7.2	−6.6	−8.4	−6.7	−5.0	−6.6	−5.6	−5.6	−3.6
Poland	3.1	−2.1	−4.9	−2.4	−2.2	−3.1	−3.3	−3.1	−3.2	−3.3	−3.0
Slovak Republic	0.1	−2.0	−11.9	−.06	−1.5	0.4	−1.3	−5.2	−5.0	−3.6	−3.3
Russia	n.a.	n.a.	−18.9	−7.3	−10.4	−6.0	−8.9	−7.6	−8.0	−1.0	2.0
Current account deficit											
Czech Republic	−1.1	1.2	−1.0	1.3	−1.9	−2.6	−7.4	−6.1	−2.4	−2.0	−3.5
Hungary	0.4	0.8	0.9	−9.0	−9.4	−5.6	−3.7	−2.1	−4.9	−4.2	−3.4
Poland	1.0	−2.6	1.1	−0.7	0.7	4.5	−1.0	−3.2	−4.4	−7.6	−7.1
Slovak Republic	n.a.	n.a.	n.a.	−4.7	4.6	2.1	−10.6	−9.6	−9.7	−5.5	−3.3
Russia	n.a.	n.a.	n.a.	n.a.	2.1	1.4	1.7	0.1	0.8	13.6	17.2

[a] Preliminary.
[b] Projections.
[c] 1990: former Czechoslovakia; n.a. = not available.
Source for data: EBRD, *Transition Report*, various issues; own calculations from EBRD data.

economic system, they simultaneously changed their political system and introduced democracy. This is another important argument in favor of the 'big bang' approach: there is a narrow window for reform. If the fundamental social consensus for reform loses momentum, the government can be replaced; then, the consistency of the reform approach can be lost.

As an alternative, a gradual approach was discussed in the early literature on the transformation. The argument in favor of the gradual approach was that the transformation process would turn out to be less hard if the steps of reform were stretched over a longer period of time. But this requires a deep breath for the transformation, particularly a prolonged willingness of people to stand the necessary reform steps. If the willingness to reform is lost in the course of time, the transformation process can come to a halt. The growth rates of Poland (more than 4 percent in the period 1993–2000) and the comparatively lower budget deficits in Poland of around 3 percent after 1992, compared to Hungary (deficits of more than 5 percent in the period 1993–1995), seem to confirm the advantages of the 'big bang' (Table 10.1; Figure 10.2). This is all the more valid in comparison with the many successor states of the Soviet Union, like Russia, where the reforms were tackled only hesitantly and where the collapse of production was nevertheless sizable. The experience of the Czech Republic with the financial crisis in 1997 suggests that a 'big bang' may lose the support of the voter.

10.5 Some central issues of economic policy

Privatization

An important step in the transformation process is the privatization of the state-run enterprises. In this context, different procedures were used. In the Czech Republic, the problem was solved by means of coupon privatization: citizens received coupons which allowed them to buy company shares at an auction. The relative price between shares and coupons was found on the market, i.e. at the auctions. In Russia, coupons were used as well, but insiders of the enterprises got preferential treatment. Employees were entitled to keep up to 51 percent of the shares of their enterprise out of the coupon auctions

that were otherwise open to the public. In addition, they could acquire shares under preferential conditions. The consequence was predominantly an insider privatization. In fact, the managers appropriated the right of disposal for the enterprises. Meanwhile, external investors increasingly succeeded in acquiring larger share packages in connection with capital increases, via stock markets or directly from the employees. Coupons were also used in most other transformation countries. In East Germany, the trustee approach was applied: the enterprises were sold to investors by a government agency (Treuhandanstalt). The same holds for Hungary and Estonia.

Privatization has probably reached the most advanced level in the Czech Republic, where 80 percent of the gross domestic product originates from the private enterprise sector. Poland (65 percent) and Hungary (80 percent) are at a similar level. For Russia, the privatization ratio is also given as 70 percent; for China the figure is 62 percent if the municipal enterprises are considered as private enterprises (Table 10.2). The level of privatization, measured by the production share of the private sector, does not correspond to the high share of government spending in GDP, as the state draws resources from the private sector by means of taxes.

The tightening of the budget restraint

Transformation countries are often characterized by high budget deficits. After 1992, the deficits amounted to significantly more than 5 percent of GDP in Hungary until 1999; they reached or surpassed 8 percent in Russia (Figure 10.5). Changing present expenditure structures is difficult. The government cannot give the remaining state-run enterprises cheap credits through the banks any longer, or only to a limited extent. The state does not succeed

Table 10.2 Privatization of production and government expenditure of the state in distribution in percent of GDP, 1999

	Private production[a]	*Government expenditure*[a]
China	33 (62)[b]	n.a.
Czech Republic	80	42.0
Hungary	80	44.8
Poland	65	44.7
Russia	70	36.0
Slovak Republic	75	43.3
Ukraine	55	37.1

[a] Percentage share in GDP.
[b] In parenthesis: including municipal enterprises; n.a. = not available.
Source for data: EBRD, *Transition Report*, 2000; National Bureau of Statistics; People's Republic of China, *China Statistical Yearbook, 1999*; International Finance Corporation, *China's Emerging Private Enterprises*, 2000.

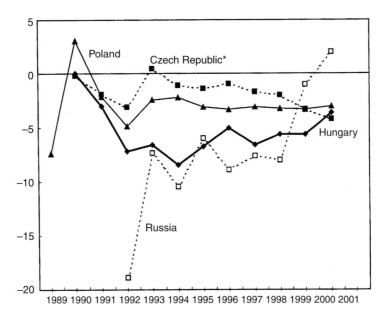

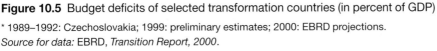

Figure 10.5 Budget deficits of selected transformation countries (in percent of GDP)

* 1989–1992: Czechoslovakia; 1999: preliminary estimates; 2000: EBRD projections.
Source for data: EBRD, *Transition Report, 2000*.

in tightening the budget restriction for state enterprises. The social cushioning of the transformation process requires additional expenditures, especially if the reorganization process is delayed and the new tax system has not yet been developed. The budget deficits increase government borrowing and restrict the maneuvering space of the state owing to interest payments. Moreover, budget deficits force the interest rates up and in this way crowd out private investment. Besides, high budget deficits reduce the credibility of monetary policy. People prepare themselves for higher inflation and a devaluation of the domestic currency. High budget deficits must therefore be interpreted as a warning signal of vulnerability.

The tightening of the budget restrictions for enterprises can turn out to be difficult if, *inter alia*, the enterprises give credits to each other – as in Russia – and fall into arrears with their payments. In 1998, the payments in arrears were estimated at 300 percent of the money supply M_2 or at 37 percent of GDP.

Current account deficits

In Hungary, the budget deficit coincides with the current account deficit (twin deficits). The current account deficits of Hungary after 1992 in relation to its gross domestic product were large (Figure 10.6). In the Czech Republic and the Slovak Republic, large current account deficits have been recorded since 1996 (Table 10.1). A profligate financial policy seems to be the reason for the high current account deficit in Hungary, whereas in the

Czech Republic the situation has probably been caused by relatively high real wage increases in connection with rather low productivity gains and a constant nominal exchange rate. The Czech Republic turned to a flexible exchange rate in 1997 and took measures to dampen the domestic demand.

Inflation

The transformation process is often linked to a high rate of inflation, not least due to the lack of an institutional framework for the monetary system and a loose monetary policy (Russia 1992–1994). Monetary stability proves to be a necessary condition for the transformation process. Empirical studies of the transformation countries come to the conclusion that the annual rate of inflation must be lower than 50 percent if a growth process is to begin (Fischer *et al.* 1996). In Central Europe and in the Baltic States, the gross national product decreased up to the

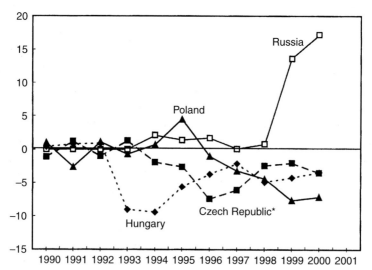

Figure 10.6 Current account deficits of selected transformation countries (in percent of GDP)

* 1990–1992: Czechoslovakia; 1999: preliminary estimates; 2000: EBRD projections.
Source for data: EBRD, *Transition Report, 2000.*

year when the stabilization was started. Two years later the growth rates became positive.

10.6 Foreign trade aspects of transformation

Opening up to foreign trade

The opening up to foreign trade is of great importance for the reform countries because trade signals the world prices to those countries. This reduces distortions and sets the right incentives to allocate resources for the production of goods efficiently.

Efficiency gains from foreign trade

The opening up to foreign trade involves efficiency gains from international exchange. The domestic enterprises are exposed to international competition. Relative prices of the reform countries are brought into line with those of the world economy. Inefficient enterprises come under pressure from imports. We can see a dramatic new orientation in the foreign trade of the reform countries. For example, the reform countries that are currently negotiating to become new members of the European Union exported roughly 65 percent of their exports into the EU in 1999 (compare Table 12.4). The reform countries resemble the EU members not only in trade volume, but also in the product structure of trade. With the gains from trade, higher growth rates become possible.

Capital inflow

The opening up to foreign trade improves the prospects for attracting foreign capital that can give significant new growth momentum. Thanks to their liberal foreign trade policies, Poland, the Czech Republic and Hungary have attracted considerable foreign direct investment, comparable to that of Latin America and Asia. The share of foreign direct investments in total gross investment, for example, amounted to 20 percent in Hungary and significantly more than 10 percent in Poland in 1992–1996 (Table 3.3). China has also been successful in attracting foreign direct investment. Without the special economic zones in the south of the country that were vested with foreign trade privileges and without the considerable sums of foreign investment capital that were attracted by those zones, China's economic rise during the last 20 years would have been completely unthinkable. For years, China has by far been the most important location for new foreign direct investments in developing countries and was the number two worldwide from 1992 until 1997, after the US.

Exchange rate policy

In the sense of the purchasing power parity ($\hat{e} = \hat{P} - \hat{P}*$), the nominal exchange rates must reflect the differences in the inflation rates. For example, Russia had to strongly devalue the rouble; at first, the devaluation of the rouble approximately followed, though with a certain delay, the rate of inflation. Note the inverted scale. Then the rate of devaluation exceeded the rate of inflation, i.e. a real devaluation took place (Figure 10.7). Poland (Figure 10.8) and the Czech Republic (Figure 7.3) also underwent massive nominal devaluations early in the transformation process. The excessive money supply in Poland was significantly larger than in the Czech Republic, therefore the devaluation had to be stronger as well. In the Czech Republic, the macroeconomic imbalance and foreign debt were relatively low at the start of the transformation process and the country pursued a

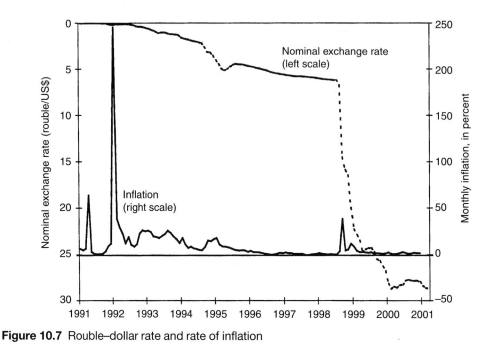

Figure 10.7 Rouble–dollar rate and rate of inflation

Source for data: *Russian Economic Trends* (1998); IMF, *International Financial Statistics*, CD-ROM, May 2001.

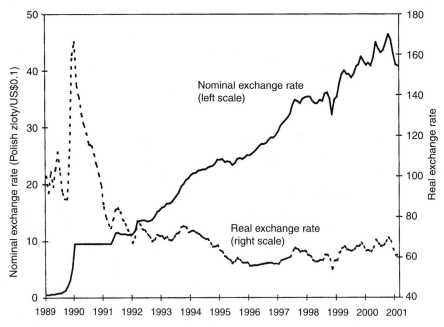

Figure 10.8 Polish zloty: nominal[a] and real[b] exchange rate *vis-à-vis* the US$

[a] Zloty/US$0.1. [b] January 1989 = 100.
Source for data: IMF, *International Financial Statistics*, CD-ROM, May 2001; own calculations.

consistently restrictive fiscal policy after its independence in 1993. Moreover, a wage restraint was prevalent at first, and capital inflow from abroad increased quickly. Thus, the nominal exchange rate could be kept stable in relation to a basket of currencies for a long time. Owing to a growing current account deficit, however, the Czech crown had to be devalued in 1997; the fixed currency anchor was then abandoned.

In Poland, the nominal exchange rate was further adjusted even after the initial devaluation. Since the autumn of 1991, an active crawling peg linked to a basket of currencies has existed, meaning that the domestic currency has been devalued by a pre-announced margin each month. After an initial quick stabilization success, the rate of inflation was maintained at a high level, compared to the Czech Republic. Hungary devalued at the beginning of the reforms and in discretionary steps afterwards.

In Russia, several early attempts to stabilize the exchange rate failed. The high rates of inflation in 1991 and 1992, which were due to a budget deficit that got out of control and to an expansionary monetary policy, led to massive devaluations of the rouble. In the middle of 1995, an exchange rate corridor, though with significant ranges of fluctuation, was introduced. In 1996, the government went on to a gradual, pre-announced adjustment of the corridor. As the range of fluctuation was decreased by a certain percentage at the same time, the exchange rate policy increasingly resembles an active crawling peg. In August 1998, this policy was more or less abandoned.

The reform states practice a crawling peg, with the continuous devaluation falling short of the current inflation rate by a predetermined percentage. The currencies are thus nominally overvalued. In this way, price increases are dampened. As the domestic currency usually undergoes a drastic nominal devaluation at the beginning of a stabilization program, it is undervalued in real terms at first. In the course of time, this undervaluation changes into an overvaluation.

Real exchange rate

A possible option for an exchange rate policy is to choose the nominal exchange rate as an anchor. Following this strategy, the leeway for price divergence is narrowed and the inflation expectations are stabilized. These goals can – partly – be achieved by means of a crawling peg as well. But if the inflation difference relative to the anchor currency decreases only slowly under a crawling peg, the consequence is a real revaluation. The real exchange rate $w_R = wP*/P$ falls due to a strongly increasing domestic price level; this means a real appreciation. The less monetary policy is oriented towards stabilization, the higher will be the real revaluation. This also holds for fiscal policy. The inflow of capital involves a (nominal and) real revaluation. This is completely harmless if the international competitiveness improves and if thereby the equilibrium exchange rate rises.

The strong nominal devaluations in Poland (1990) and Czechoslovakia (1991) first went hand in hand with a real devaluation that was also necessary to restructure expenditures in favor of tradable goods (expenditure switching). But later on, a real revaluation can be noticed (Figures 10.8 and 7.3). In Poland, the devaluation within the framework of the crawling peg was not sufficiently large to counteract the real revaluation; the rate of inflation was not compensated by nominal devaluation. The Czech Republic, on the other hand, had a lower real revaluation, with a nearly constant nominal exchange rate for quite some time. This was not sustainable. We have to take into account that a real revaluation counteracts positive net exports. It dampens price increases and therefore partly keeps inflationary tendencies under control.

Eventually, the nominal exchange rate policy cannot be judged from the point of view of monetary stability alone. In addition, it must be guaranteed that the resulting real exchange rate allows a current account that can be maintained in the long run and that is compatible with a national economic equilibrium between absorption and production. If an imbalance occurs here, the real exchange rate must be corrected. In this context, a nominal devaluation is a possible lever to achieve a real devaluation.

Case study: the transformation of East Germany

East Germany is a special case in the transformation process. Two of the three big reform steps in the transformation process – the creation of an institutional infrastructure, macroeconomic stabilization and the economic adjustment in real terms – were realized practically overnight: by joining the Federal Republic, the constitution and all other legal arrangements of West Germany were taken over. At the same time, the currency union guaranteed monetary stability. The real economic adaptation is therefore at the core of the transformation process in East Germany.

But East Germany is also a special case because transformation overlaps with integration, i.e. German reunification. Owing to this, the exchange rate was not available as a buffer in the transformation process, and the enterprises did not only have to cope with the inefficiency of the centrally planned economy, but also had to accept a strong revaluation of the East German mark (by approximately 400 percent). The population pressed for similar living conditions and a quick wage alignment. In this way, a wide gap opened up between wages and productivity. This involved high unemployment and, moreover, hampered investment. East Germany is also a special case in the sense that, quite differently from the usual transformation process, significant transfers were made. They amounted to 5 percent of the gross domestic product of Germany as a whole, per year ('big bang with a big brother').

East Germany experienced a dramatic collapse of production. Gross industrial production, with all reservations regarding the comparability of data, fell to less than one third of its former level. The low level of industrial production after 1990, as drawn in Figure 10.9, is partly due to a lack of comparable data. After 1990, net production is shown; prior to 1990, gross production (including intermediate inputs and depreciation) is shown. Moreover, East German 'industrial production' included huge amounts of additional contributions such as fringe benefits, which are no longer counted. Starting with 1992, an increase in net industrial production can be observed. Gross domestic product fell to approximately two thirds. Employment decreased from 10 million by almost 5 million if the political measures concerning the labor market (for example, up to 2 million short-time workers at times) are not considered (Siebert 1995).

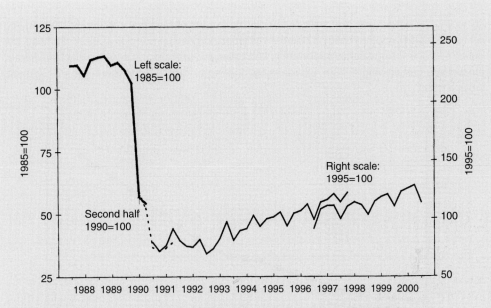

Figure 10.9 The J-curve in East Germany, industrial production 1988–2001[a]

[a] Quarterly data; since 1997 new classification of economic branches (WZ93)

Source for data: Statistisches Bundesamt, Produzierendes Gewerbe, various issues; Statistisches Amt der DDR, Statistisches Jahrbuch.

East Germany (including West Berlin) reached approximately 72 percent of the West German labor productivity level in 2000, after approximately 30 percent in the new Länder (without West Berlin) in 1991. The gross wage and salary sum per employee (including West Berlin) reached approximately 81 percent in 2000. The process of replacing and building up the capital stock is under way. An export basis is still being built up. If the results concerning catching-up processes are analogously applied, we have to conclude that a complete alignment will still take some time (see Chapter 4).

Case study: the experience in China

In contrast to the reform countries of Central Europe and Russia, China does not show a J-curve of transformation (Figure 10.10). Gross domestic product has continuously risen with real growth rates of approximately 10 percent per year since the beginning of the reforms at the end of the 1970s. Some reasons have been given for this development: on the one hand, property rights for land were introduced in the rural areas. These rights, even though valid for only 50 years, but including transfer and bequest permissions, constituted strong production incentives. The free economic zones guaranteed sufficient leeway for the private sector (including the enterprises that were put under the control of the local authorities). The private sector generated approximately 62 percent of gross domestic product in 1999. In this way, the public sector is losing relative importance. Moreover, the economic policy approach is characterized by a certain pragmatism, expressed by the motto: 'You have to touch the stones if you cross a river'.

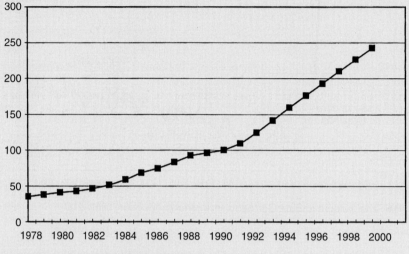

Figure 10.10 Growth of real GDP in China[a]

[a] 1990 = 100

Souce for data: IMF, *International Financial Statistics*, CD-ROM, May 2001.

Another reason for the fact that China did not have to go through a transformation crisis is that China, still being a developing country at the beginning of the reforms, had only a relatively small capital stock and a weakly developed industrial sector at its disposal. Therefore it was possible to realize substantial efficiency gains by liberalizing economic activity only in the countryside and without a reform of the state-run industrial enterprises in the cities.

10.9 Case study: The disintegration of the Soviet Union

The transformation crisis becomes particularly apparent in most of the successor states of the Soviet Union. The former Soviet Union, a union of 15 'republics', dissolved at the end of 1991 (Gros and Steinherr 1995). It dissolved into a number of now autonomous states, as the communist party lost its power. The political center was not accepted any longer; it disappeared. The individual states declared themselves independent and pushed through their own laws instead of the rules of the Soviet Union that were in place at that time. But this presupposed that each country created its own new institutional set-up. This held especially true for tax revenue and public spending, but new social security systems and a separate currency also had to be created. The rouble zone dissolved in 1992 when the countries began to introduce their own currencies, starting with the Estonian crown. The collapse of the Soviet Union and of the rouble zone also involved an almost total collapse of the system of payments between the successor states, and thus the trade relations suffered significantly. As the successor states showed particular patterns of specialization within the former Soviet Union but maintained only minor trade relations with the rest of the world, they were severely hit by the breakdown of trade flows among themselves. The necessity to adapt their production structure to the changed scarcity conditions and to divert their trade to the world markets is therefore even bigger for the successor states of the Soviet Union than for other transformation countries.

Up to now, many successor states have not succeeded in coping with these problems. They have not yet passed the bottom of the transformation crisis. But the example of Estonia proves that the problems are not insoluble. Owing to a policy that was consistently oriented to free-enterprise principles, Estonia managed to limit the initial fall in output as well as to stabilize the economy quickly and to follow a growth path.

Chapter 11

Regional integration in the world economy

••

What you will understand after reading this chapter

With regional integration countries aim at intensifying the international division of labor, albeit within regional borders. We first report the experience with different forms of regional integration (section 11.1). An important aspect is the impact of regional integration on regional and world welfare, i.e. whether regional integration is trade-creating or trade-diverting (section 11.2). A fundamental question is whether regional integration facilitates or impedes the development of a multilateral order (section 11.3).

11.1 Regional integration

Types of regional integration

Regional integration is characterized by a lowering of transaction costs between member states relative to non-members. In fact, it is a mutual preferential treatment between countries in international trade. Thus, regional integration deviates from the principle of non-discrimination because of different rules being in force with regard to non-members. The WTO rule of non-discrimination has a waiver for regional integrations (see Chapter 16). Depending on the extent of economic integration, different types of regional integration have to be distinguished.

Preferential trade agreements (PTAs) are the least strict form of regional integration. For certain goods tariffs are reduced among the members of a preferential area (sometimes even unilaterally). There is no equal treatment of non-members according to the most-favored-nation clause. Within preferential areas there is neither a general reduction of internal tariffs nor a common external tariff. Examples of this type of economic integration are the ACP treaty (70 participating countries in Africa, the Caribbean and the Pacific areas – also known as the Lomé Convention) with the European Union as well as the preferential system of the Commonwealth.

Free-trade areas (FTAs) abolish internal tariffs, but there is no common external tariff. Each member maintains its own external tariff against non-FTA members. To prevent opportunities of arbitrage in conflict with the FTA agreements, rules of origin and strict controls of the origin of goods are of great importance. Examples are EFTA (European Free Trade Association, founded in 1960 by Austria, Denmark, Norway, Portugal, Sweden, Switzerland and the United Kingdom, with Finland becoming a member in 1961), NAFTA (North American Free Trade Agreement) and CEFTA (Central European Free Trade Area) of countries in Middle and Eastern Europe.

Customs unions abolish internal tariffs like free-trade areas, but additionally there is a common external tariff as well as a common external trade policy with respect to third countries. Examples are the European Economic Community, founded in 1957, which changed into the European Community (EC, from 1967) and then the European Union (EU, from 1993).

Common economic areas, as established by the EU of 12 and by five EFTA countries (Austria, Finland, Iceland, Norway and Sweden) in 1994, are characterized by the use of common rules and common technical standards. The European Economic Area now consists of all 15 member countries of the EU as well as three of the four current EFTA countries (Iceland, Norway and Liechtenstein); in 1992, Switzerland, the fourth remaining EFTA country, decided by plebiscite not to participate in the European Economic Area.

A common market is characterized by the complete abolition of all barriers, not only with respect to the free trade of goods, but also the free exchange of services and the free movement of capital and labor. Additionally, it is aimed at a common competition (or antitrust) policy and common rules for procurement as well as a subsidy code.

A monetary union performs a common monetary policy, and an *economic union* strives for harmonization of other elements of economic policy including the institutional framework of the market economies, for instance in common competition policy and subsidy control.

Finally, in a *political union* common institutional mechanisms (constitution) are created in the area of political decision making (i.e. the right to vote, a common parliament) with some political power being allocated to a central level, especially the power to tax.

Existing groups of regional integration

Since the establishment of the GATT in 1948, nearly 150 regional trade agreements have been notified by GATT/WTO. Of these agreements, around 80 are currently in force.

Europe

The European Union (EU) with its now 15 member states has developed from the European Economic Community, which was founded in 1957 by Belgium, France, Germany, Italy, Luxembourg and the Netherlands. The realization of the four freedoms allows the free movement of goods and services, of capital and labor. With the northern enlargement, Denmark, Ireland and the United Kingdom joined in 1973. With the southern enlargement in the 1980s, Greece (1981) and Portugal and Spain (1986) became members. With another enlargement the neutral states Austria, Sweden and Finland joined in 1995. Within the next few years an eastern enlargement by the new market economies of Central and Eastern Europe is expected to take place (see Chapter 12). The European Monetary Union started in 1999.

The European Free Trade Association (EFTA) was founded in 1960 by Austria, Denmark, Norway, Portugal, Sweden, Switzerland and the United Kingdom in order to secure free trade in industrial goods. Since then Denmark and the United Kingdom (1973), Portugal (1986), and Austria, Finland and Sweden (1995) have left the EFTA, which now consists of Iceland, Liechtenstein, Norway and Switzerland.

The Central European Free Trade Area (CEFTA) between the Czech and Slovak Republics, Hungary and Poland, the so-called Visegrad states, came into force in 1993. They were joined by Slovenia in 1996 and by Romania in 1997. The aim is to reduce tariffs and barriers to trade and to increase intra-regional trade which collapsed with the breakdown of the COMECON in 1990. At the same time, CEFTA is a waiting room for EU membership. By the end of 1998 all members of CEFTA had applied for EU membership.

The Americas

The North American Free Trade Agreement (NAFTA) between the US, Canada and Mexico started in 1994. Its aim is to remove tariffs and substantially reduce non-tariff barriers over a period of 10–15 years. By liberalizing the trade of goods and services, facilitating foreign investment and establishing an effective dispute settlement mechanism, NAFTA is expected to become an important area of regional integration in the world. Additional agreements have been concluded upon environmental standards, intellectual property and labor standards.

In contrast to the European Union, NAFTA is not a customs union with a common external tariff; it is a free-trade area. NAFTA does not intend to introduce a common market with the free movement of people. Moreover, NAFTA does not have an executive arm; the NAFTA commission plays only a mediating role in resolving conflicts. Finally, there is no transfer of resources.

At the moment there is a discussion about widening NAFTA by the accession of new members in Central and South America (e.g.

Chile) as well as plans for further free-trade agreements with African and Asian countries. The NAFTA countries are members of APEC (see below).

A Trans-Atlantic Free Trade Area (TAFTA) is proposed to integrate the European Union and NAFTA. But instead of a free-trade area it may be attempted to first create a common economic area, in which production standards creating non-tariff barriers would lose their significance, e.g. by mutual recognition of standards. In a Trans-Atlantic Free Trade Area, the development of basic elements of a common competition policy seems to be necessary; moreover, the agricultural sector should be included.

In 1960, Mexico and most of the South American countries formed a free-trade area called the Latin American Free Trade Association (LAFTA). As a result of the reduction of tariffs and non-tariff barriers, intra-trade between the LAFTA countries was growing until the end of the 1970s. But, as the barriers to trade with the outside world remained in place, the competitiveness of their economies diminished. In 1980, 11 of its members changed the LAFTA into the Latin American Integration Association (LAIA), which has not so far been successful in liberalizing trade. In 1991, Argentina, Brazil, Paraguay and Uruguay created the MERCOSUR (Mercádo Común del Sur), which is a customs union, additionally linked with Chile and Bolivia by a free-trade agreement. Within this free-trade area, internal tariffs have been abolished, but Chile has a lower external tariff with respect to third countries than do the members of MERCOSUR.

The Caribbean Community (CARICOM, comprising Antigua and Barbuda, Bahamas, Barbados, Belize, Dominica, Grenada, Guyana, Jamaica, Montserrat, St. Christopher and Nevis, St. Lucia, St. Vincent and the Grenadines, and Trinidad and Tobago) is a free-trade area and has mostly succeeded in eliminating all barriers to intra-regional trade.

In the long run, the creation of a so-called Free Trade Area of the Americas (FTAA), which would require an integration of both NAFTA and MERCOSUR and other Latin American countries, is aimed at reducing barriers to trade in the western hemisphere. Negotiations for an FTAA are scheduled to be concluded by 2005.

Asia

There are two reasons why regional integration is not particularly important in Asia: one is that some countries are large; the other is that economies have been open to the world market anyhow.

The Association for South-East Asian Nations (ASEAN), consisting of the seven countries Brunei, Indonesia, Malaysia, the Philippines, Singapore, Thailand and Vietnam, was founded in 1967. ASEAN is mostly oriented towards economic cooperation. Recently, plans have been discussed to establish an Asian Free Trade Area (AFTA).

In 1989, the Asia–Pacific Economic Cooperation (APEC) was founded in order to encourage free trade among its member states, now comprising Japan, China, Australia, New Zealand, South Korea and Taiwan as well as some other fast-growing economies of South-East Asia, the NAFTA members and Chile. In accordance with the WTO principles, APEC wants to reduce barriers to the trade of goods and services, but there is no desire to establish a common external tariff (open regionalism).

Between Australia and New Zealand, the Australia New Zealand Closer Economic Relations Trade Agreement (ANZCERTA or

CER for short) came into force in 1983, and induced the unrestricted free trade of goods. Additionally, both states strive for a liberalization of the trade in services as well as a harmonization of regulations and business law.

11.2 Elementary theory of integration

Usually, static and dynamic effects of regional integration are distinguished. In a static (or comparative-static) framework, it is analyzed how the allocation of resources, of production, of sectoral structure and of welfare change when some countries form a customs union and others remain outside. Dynamic effects arise when the impact of integration on economic growth is considered.

Trade-creating and trade-diverting effects

According to Viner (1950), the static effects can be trade creation and trade diversion. Assume country *A* forms a customs union with country *B*, excluding country *C*. We analyze both effects first from the point of view of country *A* (the home country), then from the point of view of countries *A* and *B*

together, and finally from the point of view of all countries (the world). We will use the partial analysis of a market diagram rather than a general equilibrium analysis.

When analyzing trade creation (and trade diversion), we have to specify for which country trade is created (and for which it is diverted). From the point of view of the home country, a simple case of trade creation is realized when, despite import tariffs, the home country *A* had obtained imports from country B before the customs union came into being. By abolishing internal tariffs trade is created. This is shown in Figure 11.1a, depicting the curves of demand (*DD*) and supply (*SS*) of the home country. Before the customs union was established, the home country had imported quantity *MQ*, afterwards it imports *M'Q'*. Supposing that the total revenue (*c*) generated by tariffs before the trade union was transferred to the households, the households of the home country will have a net gain from the customs union equal to the amount of the triangles *a* and *b*.

The case is different when a third country with a horizontal supply curve *C* is more favorable for the home country than that of country *B*, i.e. *B* > *C*. Prior to the customs union, country *C* is competitive even though

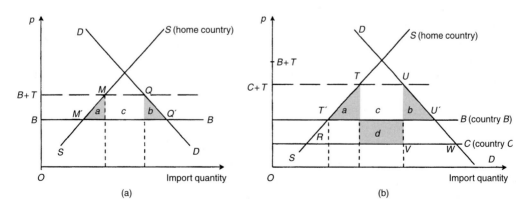

Figure 11.1 Trade-creating and trade-diverting effects of a customs union

the home country imposes a tariff, whereas country B is not competitive when a tariff (T) is introduced. $B + T$ lies above $C + T$. It should be noticed that the initial import tariff in Figure 11.1b is supposed to be higher than in Figure 11.1a. In the initial situation, the home country imports TU from country C. After the formation of the customs union country C still has to pay the tariff (in this case the initial tariff), but for country B the tariff has been abolished. As a result of the customs union, country B now supplies the imports $T'U'$, whereas country C loses its price competitiveness.

What is the effect on the welfare of the home country? On the one hand, there is additional trade with country B which induces a gain in consumer surplus of $a + b$. The previous revenue from tariffs c has become a consumer surplus for the households. On the other hand, the country now loses revenue from tariffs d of the previous imports that have been transferred – as assumed above – by the government to the households. If the area d exceeds $a + b$, the net welfare effect for the home country is negative. The negative effect of trade diversion exceeds the positive effect of trade creation. Then the home country loses. Consequently, in a partial analysis, the result of integration can be a loss of welfare for a member country of a customs union. It is important to notice that in this partial analysis the home country would experience even stronger gains from introducing free trade globally instead of joining a regionally restricted customs union. In comparison with a customs union, the additional gain from global free trade would consist of additional consumer surplus as indicated by the area $RT'U'W$.

In order to find out whether the total effects of a customs union are positive for the union members as a whole, it would be neces-sary to calculate the trade-creating and trade-diverting effects for all member states and net them out.

A third country loses when the revenues generated by its exports, induced by a shrinking demand in the members of the customs union, are smaller after the formation of the customs union. Its terms of trade deteriorate and the consumer surplus shrinks. Remember that welfare is measured in terms of consumer surplus, which means that other criteria, e.g. the change in unemployment, are not relevant in this respect.

Finally, it is necessary to consider whether the welfare of the world as a whole – all the member states of the customs union and the third country – has been increased by the formation of the customs union. To assess the total effect for the world as a whole, the trade-creating and trade-diverting effects for the customs union as well as for the third country have to be calculated and netted out.

Dynamic effects

Apart from a comparative-static change of trade flows of a customs union in the partial equilibrium models, there are additional effects in a richer analysis. These impacts are in fact equal to the advantages of foreign trade (see Chapter 13). These effects are, *inter alia*, the exploitation of economies of scale and increased specialization, intensified intra-industry trade and – in a more general sense – a higher mobility of both capital and labor. In addition there are dynamic effects stemming from an improved competitiveness of firms, from innovation, from the accumulation of capital and from higher growth. These gains in efficiency also have positive effects on third countries because a higher GDP implies an increased import demand. For regional integrations of developing countries enhancing industrialization has been given as an argument. Empirical studies have emphasized the relative importance of dynamic effects in comparison with comparative-static effects.

11.3 Block formation as a step towards a multilateral order?

Regional integrations may eventually lead to a multilateral order and may thus be a way to reach a maximum of welfare in the world economy in the long run. Or they may lead to separation and thus reduce the chances of increasing welfare. This is a central issue for trade policy. Clearly, regional integrations violate the WTO rule of non-discrimination (and the most-favored-nation principle); this is a kind of discrimination against non-members. Nevertheless, there is a waiver for regional integrations.

Consider the three largest trading blocs in the world, the European Union, NAFTA and Japan, which had a combined share in world merchandise trade of about 67 percent in 1999 (Table 11.1). Note that these data do not net out intra-EU and intra-NAFTA trade. When intra-regional trade is excluded, the share in world trade is 31.2 percent. In Europe, an internal market is clearly established; eastern enlargement is in the making. In America, politicians aim at strengthening NAFTA by integrating the countries of Latin America. In Asia, it remains to be seen whether the Pacific area with Japan (and China?) might develop into a region similar to an internal market, with low barriers to trade.

Figure 11.2 illustrates some possible time paths depicting the development of welfare in respect of multilateral trade liberalization and regional integration (Bhagwati 1992). In the initial position, a utility level U^0 is given. Different paths are portrayed.

Path I characterizes the development of welfare in a scenario of multilateral rounds of liberalization. At the end of this process, a situation of free trade providing a utility level U^* is realized. Paths II and III show the effect of regional integration having both a trade-diverting and a trade-creating effect. When the trade-diverting effect prevails, then utility is falling to a level U^1 (point A) and remains at this level (path II). When the trade-creating effect is stronger, then welfare is rising to U^2 (point B). If only short-term effects had to be

Table 11.1 EU, NAFTA and Japan, 1999

	EU	NAFTA	Japan
Population (million)	375	401	127
GDP (billion US$)	8,458	9,796	4,395
GDP per capita (US$)	22,555	24,429	34,606
Gross merchandise exports in percent of world merchandise exports (including intra-regional exports)	39.8	19.6	7.7
Net merchandise exports in percent of world merchandise exports (excluding intra-regional exports) [a,b]	14.5	9.0	–
Net merchandise exports in percent of GDP	9.4	5.0	10.9

[a] 63.5 percent of total EU trade is intra-EU trade.
[b] 54.1 percent of total NAFTA trade is intra-NAFTA trade.
Source for data: IMF, *International Financial Statistics*, CD-ROM, May 2001; World Bank, *World Development Report, 2000/2001*; WTO, *International Trade Statistics*, 2000; own calculations.

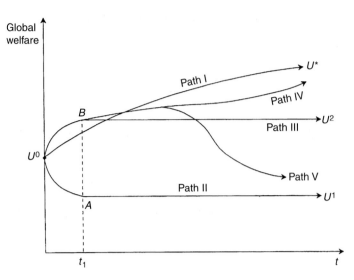

Figure 11.2 Regional integration and free trade

taken into account, then the world economy would stay on this level (path III). But there are also dynamic effects which raise welfare. Especially when regional blocs open up to new members and expand liberalization according to the most-favored-nation principle to third countries, and, vice versa, when third countries themselves grant such 'concessions', then regional integration is moving towards the utility level of free trade (path IV).

Does a multilateral approach to liberalization represent a faster and more secure track towards free trade than a regional approach (Bhagwati 1992; Frankel 1997)? The advantage of the regional approach is that barriers to trade are more or less totally abolished within a partial area of the world. In addition, the member states are enabled to conclude an agreement much more easily. For that reason, regional integration might be realized faster. Further barriers can be dismantled in the long run, when the regional integration opens itself to additional members. This is especially the case when regional

integration can be extended multilaterally by the use of the most-favored-nation rule.

The advantage of the multilateral approach consists in creating a set of rules that are legally binding nearly all over the world. GATT Article XXIV, which departs from the most-favored-nation principle by explicitly allowing free-trade areas and customs unions, in principle gives rise to the risk of destroying the multilateral order by the formation of regional trading blocs. Regionalism might be combined with protectionism which would impede utility from rising to U^*, the level of free trade. Then the path could lead away from U^*; and even U^2 might not be reached in the case of retaliation against third countries (path V). Thus, the risk of disintegration of the world economy exists. For instance, the world economy could be subdivided into the triad Europe, North America and Japan. Up to now, however, regional integration has not led to important forms of separation. In Latin America, attempts towards regional integration have not proved to be powerful, with the exception of MERCOSUR. In East

Table 11.2 Share of intra-regional trade (exports plus imports) as percentage of each region's total trade, 1948–1999

	1948	1958	1968	1979	1993	1996	1999
Western Europe[a]	42	53	63	66	70	68	68
North America[b]	27	32	37	30	33	36 (44)[d]	32 (46)[d]
Asia	39	41	37	41	50	52	51
World[c]	33	41	47	46	50	52	51

[a] Share of intra-European trade in total Western European trade.
[b] Canada and the USA.
[c] Weighted average.
[d] Including Mexico.
Source for data: WTO *Annual Report*, 1995, 1997; WTO, *International Trade Statistics*, 2000.

Asia, APEC has the goal of market integration with no tendency towards protectionism. European integration has proved to be open to new members, and despite some protectionist measures trade-diverting effects unfavorable to the rest of the world have been, judging with a grain of salt, overcompensated by its growth. The European Union has been open to the accession of new members in the northern, southern and neutral enlargements. The importance of intra-regional trade has been rising steadily during the last 40 years (Table 11.2). The internal coherence of NAFTA is different from that of the European Union. Although a common trade policy is still lacking *de jure*, the North American Free Trade Area would definitely strengthen the position of the United States in the event of a conflict between the two blocs.

It is certainly not evident whether the regional or the multilateral approach leads to the highest possible welfare of free trade. Indeed, the danger of an escalating trade war between the regional blocs is still a matter of importance. Therefore, it is necessary to find mechanisms which allow a multilateralization of regional integration.

Chapter 12

The European Union

···

What you will understand after reading this chapter

In the European Union, nation states have given up sovereignty in a number of policy areas and subjected themselves to joint decision making with other nations. The core of European integration is the Single Market and its four freedoms (section 12.1). With respect to the role of government, fiscal federalism is at the heart of European integration (section 12.2). The decision structure in the policy area is quite complex (section 12.3). Decision making in an enlarged union raises difficult questions to be solved (section 12.4). Monetary union is a major step in the process of European integration (section 12.5). The rigidity of the national labor markets contrasts with the requirement of more flexibility in the monetary union (section 12.6). Eastern enlargement and its impact will be a policy issue for the next few years (section 12.7).

12.1 The four freedoms and the Single Market

As an economic union, the European Union aims at establishing a common market by harmonizing important aspects of the institutional framework of the national economies. But European integration goes beyond establishing a common market in the strict sense. A set of economic policy areas is no longer in the hands of the nation states but is either shifted to the European level or requires some type of joint decision making of national governments. Joint decisions go together with different decision procedures (Commission, Council) and may require different majorities.

The EU began with the Community of Six in 1957 and the alternative of the EFTA, continued with the northern enlargement in 1973 (Denmark, Ireland and the UK), the southern enlargement in the 1980s (Greece 1981, Spain and Portugal 1986) and the addition of the neutral states in 1995 (Austria, Finland and Sweden). Now, the European Union of 15 will be enlarged to a Union of 27, including 10 Middle and Eastern European nations.

Free movement of goods

The common market requires the dismantling of all obstacles to the free movement of goods. Barriers to trade include not only tariffs and quantitative restrictions but also national regulations. It has proved to be impossible to harmonize all legal rules of the different countries. Therefore, in the *Cassis-de-Dijon* case of 1979, the country-of-origin principle was established by the European Court of Justice. The *Cassis-de-Dijon*, a fruit liqueur, was widely in use in France. It was not allowed, however, to be marketed in Germany. The German regulation, the

monopoly law on spirits (*Branntweinmono-polgesetz*) of 1922 required fruit liqueurs to have an alcohol content of at least 32 percent and thus the alcohol content of 17 percent in the *Cassis-de-Dijon* was '*verboten*'. The sense of such a law is a different question. The European Court of Justice ruled that a product legally brought to the market in one country of the European Union also has to be accepted by other countries. This verdict then allowed the export of beer from Belgium that was not brewed in accordance with the German beer purity regulations of 1516, and it allowed pasta to be exported that was not made from Italian buckwheat. According to this principle, the different regulations are *de facto* mutually recognized and coexist even if domestic producers are treated less favorably than foreign producers (discrimination against nationals). Only in the cases when products are hazardous and damaging to health, to safety or to the environment does the principle not apply (Article 30 of the EU Treaty).

Free movement of persons

Workers have the right to work anywhere in the European Union (right of free movement). Individuals have the right to establish businesses everywhere in the European Union (right of establishment). Discrimination based on nationality is to be abolished.

Free movement of services

Services offered in one member country can also be supplied in the other member countries. Thus, the *Cassis-de-Dijon* verdict of the European Court of Justice not only holds for goods, but also applies to services, for instance to banking and to insurance. The country-of-origin rules are mutually recognized. This principle has proven to be a can opener for national regulations. The free movement of services is especially linked to the right of establishment.

Free movement of capital

Until the late 1980s, capital flows were still controlled in some countries. With monetary union in the making, national controls of capital movements could no longer be justified. Consequently, they had to be given up.

Trade policy

Since the European Union is also a customs union, it has a common external tariff which now is at 2.7 percent for all trade in industrial products. Other trade policy instruments are applied uniformly. The EU has a Common Commercial Policy *vis-à-vis* non-members, for instance the United States or in the WTO.

Competition policy

In a single market, competition policy (anti-trust policy) has to apply to the market as a whole. Competition policy has to prevent cartels and to ensure that dominant positions within the common market do not arise. Thus, the abuse of market power in the EU and the creation of new dominating positions (monopolies) by mergers have to be controlled on the European level, where the Commission has taken a lead position.

Subsidy control

Competition in the single market should not be distorted by national subsidies. The Commission controls national subsidies and has established a respected power in this domain.

Agricultural policy

Agriculture receives special treatment. It is shielded from the market by Common Agricultural Policy (CAP) which defines reference prices. Agricultural prices in the EU are shielded from the world market by import tariffs. Inside the European Union, agricultural prices are guaranteed by market interventions. Agricultural policy is undertaken on the European level and absorbs nearly half of the EU budget. In the last years, direct subsidies have been substituted by income transfers; it is therefore debated that agricultural policy can be nationalized.

Indirect taxation

Different rates for indirect taxes including value-added taxes may create unnecessary distortions in the common market. Minimum rates have been set.

Monetary policy

With monetary union, monetary policy has been centralized for the EU-12 countries (section 12.5).

EU finances

The budget of the European Union is financed by import duties and contributions of the member states. Contributions by member states consist partly of the value-added tax resource; 1 percent of national returns of the value-added tax are transferred to the EU budget. The other EU revenue is the GNP resource, calculated as a proportion of national GNPs. It is intended to shift EU financing more to the GNP resource in the future. There is a cap on the tax base of the value-added tax resource of 50 percent of

GNP. Therefore, contributions are *de facto* related to GNP. The EU has no right to tax or to incur debt. The EU budget accounts for 1.27 percent of GDP of the member states.

EU expenditures

EU expenditures amounted to 96 billion euros in 2001. Of this, 46 percent was spent on agricultural policy, 34 percent on structural and regional funds.

Degree of centralization

The short survey in Table 12.1 indicates some areas of potential centralization.

12.2 Fiscal federalism and the subsidiarity principle

The economist's answer to the issue of the optimal degree of decentralization or centralization is the subsidiarity principle. According to this concept, an economic activity should be assigned to the lowest organizational level that can efficiently deal with that activity. The reasoning behind this principle is that a more decentralized unit has better information on preferences and on the structure of problems. Higher levels of an organization tend to have less information, distortions in collecting information are likely. The lower level can deal better with local or regional issues; it can respond more flexibly.

For the organizational set-up of states and other political units, fiscal federalism can be interpreted as an expression of the subsidiarity principle. According to the approach of fiscal federalism, the central governmental level should be in charge of public goods with a spatial dimension, extending over the whole political area. Lower levels should be responsible for those public goods that are spatially less extended. Note that the spatial dimension of public goods is also discussed under the heading of the spatial extent of technological externalities or spillover effects. Assigning public goods of different spatial dimensions to different levels of governments implies that the revenue side has to follow the expenditure side (fiscal equivalence; see Olson 1969).

For the EU, this means that economic problems of a European dimension such as trade policy should be dealt with at the European level, problems with a national

Table 12.1 Degree of centralization

Centralization	Trade policy
	Competition policy
	Control of state subsidies
	Monetary policy
Shared responsibility between the EU and nation states	Environment
	Consumer protection
	Trans-frontier movement of labor
	Energy
	Transport
Decentralization	Wage and income policy
	Social security systems
	Health
	Education

dimension should be decided at the national level, and regional problems should be under the responsibility of the regional authorities.

12.3 Decision making in the European Union

Giving up some national sovereignty

The European Union is not a confederation with an intra-state pattern of rules and it also is not an association of completely sovereign nation states. European integration relies on the method of intergovernmental cooperation where most of the decisions are taken in the European Council by reaching agreements between the heads of state or between the ministers of specific portfolios (Siebert 2002).

Its basis is the treaty as a multilateral arrangement by which sovereign nation states give up some sovereignty in favor of joint decision making on the European level. The European Treaty has developed in different stages from the Treaty of Rome to the Treaties of Maastricht and Amsterdam. It has been ratified by the national parliaments or by referenda in some countries; the Treaty of Nice is still to be ratified. In the European Treaty presently in force, member states have agreed to respect the decisions of the European Council and abide by them. This holds for decisions with simple and qualified majority. In other areas where unanimity is required each member state has a veto. In addition, a vital interest procedure has been practiced in the past when a qualified majority applied. Whenever a national government declared an issue as one of vital national interest, the member state was not out-voted.

The Community has been empowered by the individual member states through the treaty. Their power is to establish secondary law. New law can only be created in the context of the treaty, if it is according to the stipulations of the treaty. The treaty can only be changed in the same way that it was originally concluded, namely by negotiation and ratification by the individual member states. Thus, the member states are the masters of the treaty.

The EU treaty is not a constitution. If the EU had a constitution, the fundamental decisions would not be made by the Council but by the sovereign; that is, by the people or by a parliament representing the people. Lacking one of the decisive elements of a constitution, namely the European people as a sovereign, the EU is also not a state.

Types of legal rules

Community law, adopted by the Council – or in the case of co-decision procedure by Parliament and Council – can only be established in those areas which have been defined for joint decisions. Where unanimity is required, the power to legislate still rests with the individual member state. Article 308 of the EU treaty is a general clause for the Commission to become active; however, this does not imply that the Community has the right to go beyond the creation of secondary law.

Community law may take different forms. Regulations are directly applied; there is no need for national measures to implement them. Directives bind member states with respect to the objectives to be achieved. It is up to the national authorities to choose the appropriate means to implement the directives. Decisions are addressed to any or all member states and are binding. Informal procedures and rules of the game play an important role in the decision making of the European Union.

Institutions of the European Union

The system of governance of the European Union is a multi-level system. Decisions are taken in a complex web of decision-making bodies.

Council of the European Union

The Council of the European Union is the central decision-making body. It is made up of the member states and meets in more than 20 different forms: for instance, as heads of states (The Council) or as ministers for a specific portfolio (Council of Ministers; e.g. Foreign Affairs, Economy and Finance, Agriculture, Transport, etc.).

The European Commission

The Commission is the administrative arm of the European Union. Its main function is to implement policies, to launch initiatives and to be the arbiter between member states as the guardian of the treaty. The Commission has the right to propose new laws; it can create derived or secondary law according to Article 308. The Commission has a legislative monopoly. A set of decisions of the European Council presupposes recommendations by the Commission. Changes of the treaty require approval by national parliaments. The commission also represents the Union in international negotiations.

The European Parliament

The European Parliament participates in the different forms of approval, joint decision and hearing. The approval of parliament is needed in declarations of fundamental violations of the treaty. The proceedings of joint decisions according to Article 251 apply to proposals of the Commission to which parliament submits a statement. On the basis of this statement, the proposals of the commission become enacted by the Council. If the parliament alters the Commission's proposals in joint decisions, rules specify how to proceed. The Parliament does not have the right of initiative.

The European Court of Justice

The European Court of Justice is concerned with the interpretation of EC law. The Court also provides the judicial safeguards necessary to ensure that the law is respected. The types of actions include actions brought before the court by a member state against another member state and by the Commission against a member state.

Different types of majorities

For decisions of the Council, there are three different types of majority according to Article 205:

- If not stated otherwise, the majority of votes of the member states is needed. This is eight out of 15 member states in the EU-15 and 14 out of 27 in the enlarged Union.

- For a qualified majority in the EU-15, 62 of 87 votes (71.26 per cent) are needed. This holds for decisions which are taken by the European Council with respect to proposals of the European Commission. In all other cases, it is additionally required that 62 votes represent the approval of at least 10 member states (Article 205). The blocking majority is 26 votes. The Treaty of Nice changes these numbers for the case of enlargement: the EU of 27 will have 345 votes. Then a qualified majority, now at 68 of 87 votes or 71.26 percent, requires 258 votes (or 74.79 percent) and the majority of members. The blocking minority is 88 votes. If not all candidates have joined the European Union when the new weighting becomes effective by 1 January 2005, the threshold for the qualified majority will be moved up from a value below the actual level of 71.26 percent to a maximum of 73.40 percent. In this case, the blocking minority will be 91 votes and qualified majority will be 255 votes (73.91 percent) instead of 258 votes.

- Unanimity is required in the most important policy areas. Besides, in the case of qualified majority there seems to be a consensus, whenever a vital interest of a member state is involved, not to take votes and to continue negotiation.

Policy areas and majorities

Simple majority is required very seldom. It is used, for example, in the Governing Council of the European Central Bank. Qualified majority is required in such areas as agriculture and trade policy in a narrow sense (on the operative level). Basic decisions require unanimity. The most important areas where unanimity is required are: admitting new members (Article 49), indirect taxation (Article 93), direct taxation (Article 95), the budget of the European Union (Article 269) and fundamental rules (Articles 94, 95). Unanimity is also required in international treaties in trade policy (Article 133), cultural policy (Article 151), industrial policy (Article 157), social cohesion policy (Articles 157, 161), research and development policy (Article 166) and environmental protection (Article 175). Asylum policy, while respecting international agreements, is under national authority and has required unanimity so far. As of 2004, the procedure of codecision with qualified majority will apply if agreed upon unanimously by the heads of state. Of course, the unanimity principle in the area of taxation is at the heart of the question of national sovereignty and political union. Table 12.2 exhibits some policy areas and the

Table 12.2 Required majorities

Policy area	Required majority
European Central Bank Council	Simple majority
Agriculture	Qualified majority
Internal market	
Environment	
Transport	
Trade policy in the narrow sense	
Harmonizing the legal framework	Unanimity
Indirect taxation	
Direct taxation	
Regional and social funds	
Admittance of new members	
Entering into international agreements including trade policy	
In the wider sense	
Culture	

required majority in a very simplified presentation.

Allocation of votes

The allocation of votes has changed through the Nice Treaty that has to be ratified until the end of 2002 (Table 12.3).

12.4 Decision making and Enlargement

Voting according to the Nice Treaty

Enlargement implies that it will become more difficult to make decisions. In an enlarged European Union, the veto power that each country has due to the principle of unanimity becomes a powerful hindrance, eventually

Table 12.3 Allocation of votes in the EU

	Population[a] (in million)	Votes (Pre-Nice)	Votes (Post-Nice)
Germany (DE)	82.2	10	29
United Kingdom (UK)	59.6	10	29
France (FR)	59.2	10	29
Italy (IT)	57.7	10	29
Spain (ES)	39.4	8	27
The Netherlands (NL)	15.9	5	13
Greece (GR)	10.5	5	12
Belgium (BE)	10.2	5	12
Portugal (PT)	10.0	5	12
Sweden (SE)	8.9	4	10
Austria (AT)	8.1	4	10
Denmark (DK)	5.3	3	7
Finland (FI)	5.2	3	7
Ireland (IE)	3.8	3	7
Luxembourg (LU)	0.4	2	4
Poland (PL)	38.6		27
Romania (RO)	22.5		14
Czech Republic (CZ)	10.3[b]		12
Hungary (HU)	10.1		12
Bulgaria (BG)	8.2		10
Slovak Republic (SK)	5.4		7
Lithuania (LI)	3.7		7
Latvia (LV)	2.4		4
Slovenia (SI)	2.0		4
Estonia (EE)	1.4		4
Cyprus (CY)	0.7		4
Malta (MT)	0.4		3
Total votes	482.1	87	345

[a] December 2000.
[b] July 1999.

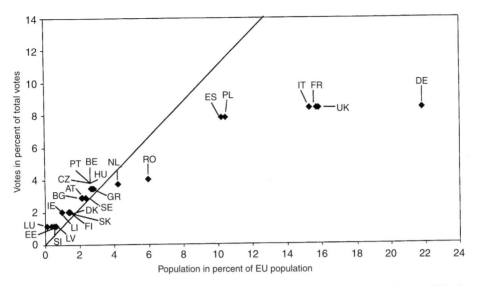

Figure 12.1 EU: population shares and shares of votes in the council after the Treaty of Nice[a]

[a] For abbreviations see Table 12.3.
Source for data: Eurostat, *Yearbook 2001*; Official Journal of the European Communities, *Treaty of Nice*, 2001/ C80/01.

meaning that no decision can be taken at all.

For a qualified majority, things will also get more complicated. The votes have not been allocated proportional to the population (Figure 12.1). The medium-sized countries (from Slovenia to Romania) have received an overproportionally larger share of the votes than the larger countries. Germany, with 82 million people, has only marginally more votes than Spain and Poland with half the population size. In the case of Germany, there is also a distortion relative to the three other larger countries. In order to mitigate that problem, a member state can request that a qualified majority also must represent the majority of the population, specified as 62 percent of the population. However, such a demand may have the bad odor of disturbing the friendly atmosphere and may appear extraordinary. In contrast it is self-evident in a democratic setting that a qualified majority must represent the majority of the population.

Another reason why it will become more difficult to reach decisions is that the threshold for a qualified majority has been raised from 71.26 to 74.40 percent while at the same time the number of members has been increased. This means that the system moves more towards unanimity. A further reason is that coalitions blocking a decision become more likely. Baldwin *et al.* (2001) argue that the Council's ability to act will be massively slowed. They use passage probability of a proposal being defined as the number of winning coalitions to all possible coalitions. Their result is that passage probability will be reduced considerably by the new voting allocation.

Above all, with respect to the important aspect of changing intergovernmental cooperation, Nice has not changed this institutional arrangement. This means that the democratic deficit has not been reduced; it continues to exist and has even been aggravated in an enlarged union. A correction of the Nice weighting of votes in the future seems to be extremely difficult especially after the new members have entered. Nice has tied down vote allocation. It has failed to grasp the opportunity to give integration an additional push.

In search of a constitution-like arrangement

A rough picture would imagine an improved democratic legitimacy of the European level as follows: more decision power is given to the European parliament. This implies that national parliaments cede some of their competencies. The European parliament can be conceived as a two-chamber system. For the first chamber representatives would be elected, for instance, by a majority rule for each election district; a second chamber would represent the member states. The electoral districts for the election of the members of the first chamber should be delineated such that each district represents a similar percentage of the population. The second chamber should represent the member states, ideally by electing the representatives of the member states directly (as in the US Senate). The Commission represents the European government. A constitution-like system of rules would define the competencies of the European parliament, its two chambers, the Commission, the member states and the regional level in the member states.

To describe the future road in this way exhibits all the problems that an enlarged Europe faces.

With respect to the basic concepts, different historical experiences in the countries of Europe exist. This means that the concepts are diverging widely and that even words have different meanings. For a German, a federal state (*Bundesstaat*) implies the sharing of responsibilities and also some control of central power by the regions. In the UK, the term itself seems to have a negative connotation and is associated with an agglomeration of power at the center and a loss of individual freedom. In France, the concept of *L'Etat* is not seen as a combination of somewhat autonomous regions and a central layer of government but as a hierarchical order with centralization.

Talking of a constitution-like arrangement is difficult to understand in the United Kingdom where a written constitution does not exist and does not need to exist. But even with an explicit constitutional approach in the German or French interpretation, a democratic state and therefore a constitution presupposes that there is a people as the sovereign. But a European people does not (or does not yet) exist. Moreover, a European public opinion does not exist either. Thus, the role of a European parliament must necessarily be limited in scope. Consequently, giving up national sovereignty must also be limited.[1] The concept of a European people is immediately relevant when burden sharing for a common cause is at issue. In a political sense, solidarity seems to be defined mainly within the national boundaries. From this it follows that the preparedness to give up some national sovereignty will be a function a European people evolving; in other words, of national identities becoming weaker.

At the core of this debate is taxation. Ceding national sovereignty would imply shifting the power to tax, the power to spend and the power of the budget to the European level. This would mean that a European institution such as the European parliament would be authorized to decide the type of tax, the tax base and the tax rate for the individual taxpayer; it would also be able to decide that a tax collected in country A can be spent in country B, either explicitly or implicitly. For instance, tax revenues could be used for infrastructure or to finance a Europe-wide tax-transfer mechanism that has as its strategic variable the level of personal income.

From historical experience we know that the principle 'no taxation without representation' is the basis of democracy. In a European Union it is doubtful whether citizens will be prepared to accept a system in which a European institution has the power to tax and the power to spend the tax revenues if this institution lacks a democratic legitimacy; that is, if it cannot be held responsible by the voter. This is the crucial point in the future development of Europe.

Variable geometry

The European Treaty allows member states to form special clubs that intensify their cooperation in specific areas such as border controls (Schengen countries) or monetary union. Countries may move at different speeds of integration. According to this approach, the dynamics of integration is provided by a subset of the member countries. Member countries may be given the right to opt out. Opting out, that is granting an exception, may be a dangerous strategy for a union because it leads to a greater heterogeneity in the institutional arrangements. An opting-out clause can be granted only in most unusual circumstances when the union cannot otherwise be held together. The EU is a single undertaking, and the net benefits come in a package.

Different speeds and variable geometry cannot, however, relate to the essentials of a union. They must refer to additional steps that one may consider as desirable but not strictly necessary. A variable geometry also cannot solve the core issue of a democratic void; it is simply not conceivable that a European Club as a subset of member countries

develops a separated constitutional arrangement diverging from the other members, including for instance parliamentary voting and taxation. Thus, the strategy of multiple speeds can only be applied in the context of intergovernmental decision making. It is not suitable for a more intense form of integration. Variable geometry or separate speed can only be an intermediate step of integration.

12.5 Monetary union

Introducing the euro is a project of historical importance. As a common currency, the euro is intended to bring the peoples of Europe closer together. From this point of view, monetary union is politically motivated. In addition, monetary union abolishes the cost of exchanging currencies. The transaction costs for the trade of goods, the exchange of services, the movement of people and the flow of capital – for the four freedoms – will be reduced; the Single Market will be completed from the monetary side. Thus, the process of European integration will receive a new impetus.

Institutional design

Monetary union means that monetary policy will be shifted to the European level. The institutional set-up can be explained as follows. In the European System of Central Banks, decisions on monetary policy are made by the European Central Bank (ECB). The decision-making bodies of the ECB are the Governing Council, the Executive Board and the General Council (Figure 12.2).

The Governing Council comprises all the governors of the national central banks of the member states of the monetary union and the six members of the Executive Board. Each member of the Governing Board has

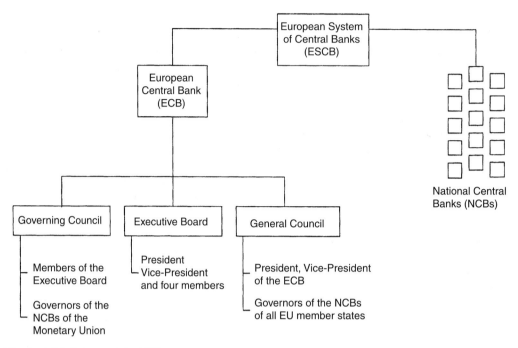

Figure 12.2 Set-up of the ECB

one vote, giving the governor of a central bank of a small country the same weight as that of a large country. The governors of the National Central Banks are appointed by the national governments for a minimum of five years; the appointment is renewable. The main task of the Governing Council is to formulate monetary policy and take decisions on the strategy as well on the monetary policy instruments such as the key interest rates.

The Executive Board comprises the President, the Vice-President and four other members. They are appointed by a common accord, i.e. by unanimity, of the governments of the member states at the level of the heads of state or government, on a recommendation from the European Council after it has consulted the European Parliament and the Governing Council of the ECB. The members of the Executive Board are appointed for a non-renewable term of eight years.

This gives them personal autonomy. The main responsibility of the Executive Board is to implement monetary policy in accordance with the guidelines laid down by the Governing Council of the ECB.

The General Council comprises the President and the Vice-President and the governors of all the National Central Banks of the European Union, including those EU countries which are not members of monetary union. Its task is to deal with issues related to the preparation of countries for EMU membership.

Formally, the ECB is part of the European System of Central Banks which also consists of the EU National Central Banks. The National Central Banks of those countries that do not participate in the euro area nevertheless are members of the European System of Central Banks, albeit with a special status. They do not vote on issues of the monetary union.

The task of the ECB

Article 105 defines the main objective of the European System of Central Banks (ESCB): 'The primary objective of the ESCB shall be to maintain price-level stability'. Other targets such as supporting employment are only secondary and conditional with respect to the target of price-level stability. 'Without prejudice to the objective of price-level stability, the ESCB shall support the general economic policies in the Community with a view to contributing to the achievement of the objectives of the community as laid down in Article 2' (Article 105). Article 2 defines the task of the Community in general, namely

to promote . . . a harmonious and balanced development of economic activities, sustainable and non-inflationary growth respecting the environment, a high degree of convergence of economic performance, a high level of employment and of social protection, the raising of the standard of living and quality of life, and economic and social cohesion and solidarity among Member States.

The role of the ECB is to define monetary policy, i.e. to develop a strategy and to implement this strategy. The ECB has set the target of price level stability as a change of the price-level below 2 percent. It applies a two-pillar strategy with the first pillar referring to a reference value for the expansion of the money supply (monetary targeting) and the second pillar relating to the price level including the future price level. In addition to defining and implementing monetary policy, the ECB will also conduct foreign exchange rate operations, manage the official reserves, support the authorities supervising financial institutions and ensure the smooth operation of payment systems. It has legislative power; its regulations are binding.

The institutional set-up gives a large weight to the 12 votes of national central bankers (in 2001) relative to the six votes of the members of the Executive Council. This weight will tilt even more in favor of national central banks if new members are admitted. Then a new procedure has to be found, for instance by rotating the membership for some countries. This formal structure points to the fact that the position of the ECB in the European system is different from the Bundesbank's Central Council in the German system where the state central banks had only nine votes relative to the eight votes of the directorate. In the Open Market Committee of the Fed (Federal Reserve Board), only five governors of regional reserve banks are represented relative to seven Washington-based members. Practical questions are whether committees dominated by the National Central Banks will play an important role and whether the small number of the ECB employees (about 1000 in 2001) will be strong enough to stand up against the 60,000 employees of the National Central Banks. A more fundamental question is whether such a decentralized system will eventually lead to too strong a national influence on a European institution and to an unreliable monetary policy.

The European Central Bank is independent from other institutions in the EU (Article 108). Neither the ECB nor any member of its decision-making body may take instructions from national governments or the EU. The statute of the ECB can only be changed by a new treaty which would require unanimity.

Instruments

The main instruments in steering the interest rate and in controlling money expansion are open market operations under repurchase agreements (repo). In these reverse transactions the ECB provides liquidity with a weekly frequency and a maturity of two weeks. The banks pay the deposit rate. Liquidity is allocated by standard tenders in which banks indicate the amount of liquidity they wish to have; usually more liquidity is demanded than offered by the ECB so that the total quantity has to be allocated to the individual banks in proportion to their demand. Furthermore, overnight liquidity can be obtained by banks (standing facility). Finally, the ECB requires credit institutions to hold minimum reserves on accounts with the ECB.

Conflict between price-level stability and employment

There can be a conflict between the objective of a stable money and other objectives of economic policy such as reducing unemployment. One should not have the illusion that the Phillips curve postulating a trade-off between the rate of inflation and unemployment can be a basis for monetary policy and that an excessive increase in the money supply can stimulate employment in the medium run. People would anticipate the inflation rate and they would require higher nominal interest rates, the value of money would deteriorate and the ECB would lose its reputation. Eventually, the ECB would be forced to put on the brakes, and a 'stabilization recession' would be the result. An excessive expansion of the money supply may also lead to an asset price inflation without affecting the consumer price index as happened in Japan in the late 1980s. When the bubble bursts, the real sphere of the economy will be affected negatively.

Conflict with the European Council in exchange rate policy

The European Council, the central decision-making body of the EU (see above), has the right to conclude formal agreements on exchange rate systems with non-EU members (by unanimity) and it may (by qualified majority) formulate the general orientation for exchange rate policy (Article 111). As a rule, the European Council consists of the economics and finance ministers (ECOFIN). In the area of exchange rate policy, a conflict between the ECB and the Council can develop.

Incompatibility of exchange rate orientation and a stable money

Exchange rate decisions or orientations of the European Council can be incompatible with an independent central bank. If the ECB were forced to maintain a predetermined exchange rate *vis-à-vis* other currencies, this would mean an exchange-rate-oriented monetary policy. In this case, the central bank would not be free to determine its monetary policy. The exchange rate would be the nominal anchor instead of price-level stability. Hopefully, this conflict between policy makers and the central bank is softened by the requirement of Article 111 that exchange rate policy must be consistent with the objective of price-level stability.

Stable exchange rates?

Politicians occasionally give the impression that the euro will bring about stable currency relations in the world economy. There is ample evidence that the much-conjured international cooperation – G-7 meetings and accords – has not been able to secure stable exchange rates in the past. The proposals to strive for exchange rate targets have not proven feasible. Stable exchange rates in the world can only be established if monetary policy provides for a stable internal value of the currencies and if all other aspects of economic policy, and fiscal policy in particular, do not give rise to negative expectations about currency stability. For this reason, one can only warn against overloading the monetary policy of the European Central Bank with the objective of pursuing exchange rate targets for the euro against leading world currencies.

Strategic external value versus internal value of a currency

Some want to use the exchange rate of the euro against other currencies of the world – like the dollar or the Japanese yen – strategically in the interest of the European export industry by driving down its external value in order to stimulate European exports. This is a misleading idea. Disruptions and quarrels in the international division of labor, turmoil in the financial markets and reactions of other players in the world economy would ensue. What is more important, a lower external value of a currency can only be brought about if this currency is supplied more generously than other currencies. That is, the expansion of the aggregate money supply has to exceed by far the growth of the production potential (plus the tolerated inflation rate and a correction factor for the velocity of money). This, consequently, causes the internal value of the currency to fall. External value and internal value of a currency are two sides of the same coin.

Conflict with the European Council in economic and budget policy

The European Council is responsible for common economic and budget policy. It may coordinate these policies (Article 99); it also is responsible for the stability pact (Article 101). An informal group of EU-12 finance ministers has been created to coordinate economic and fiscal policies of EMU members. Here is another area of potential conflict with monetary policy.

Shielding the Central Bank from political pressure

Central banks are always exposed to political pressure. Political pressure on the European Central Bank may originate from countries facing severe economic problems. This holds particularly true for countries with excessive deficits and high indebtedness. Countries with high government debt are interested in low interest rates, a rather lax monetary policy and a slightly higher inflation rate than the one anticipated by financial markets, because all this would ease their budgetary situation, especially because debts would melt away in real terms. Such a policy becomes even more attractive when political maneuvering space in the future is restricted by a high interest burden. Political pressure on the European Central Bank will be further increased if the economy of a highly indebted state is taken by recession and if it faces severe financial difficulties. The issue is not that a country will deliberately follow a policy of excessive deficits in order to eventually force the European Central Bank to step in as lender of last resort. The problem is that a long-run process of accumulating debt may occur as a result of political weakness so that eventually the European Central Bank has no other option than to monetize the public debt by a lax monetary policy. Consequently, the criterion of a sustainable public budget within the monetary union is well-suited to shielding the central bank from political pressure.

Control of unreliable fiscal policy with the stability pact

Sustainability of the governmental financial condition is therefore an important precondition for a monetary union (Article 104). The overriding target is that governments remain solvent; usually, this is interpreted as requiring stationarity of the debt. This means that the debt/GDP ratio has to remain constant. In the EU treaty, this limit for debt in relation to GDP has been set at 60 percent. This restraint for debt is associated with a limit for an excessive deficit of 3 percent of GDP if nominal GDP growth is 5 percent. The intention is to limit political pressure on the European Central Bank. Such a constraint on fiscal policy becomes especially necessary if countries have institutional arrangements that are not conducive to solid governmental finances. A case in point is a constitutional weakness with respect to limiting governmental expenditures as in Italy.

The general rule of the stability pact is that a budget deficit surpassing 3 percent of GDP is considered excessive. There are exceptions: a real decrease of GDP on a yearly basis of at least 2 percent is viewed without any further argument as an exception. In the intermediate range of a fall of GDP between 0.75 and 2 percent, a set of discretionary decisions of the European Council will have to be made. The determination of an excessive budget deficit remains undecided if a member state, after being put into delay by a formal resolution, indeed takes appropriate measures. Whether measures taken are appropriate is also

decided by the European Council. It should also be noted that initially only a non-interest-bearing deposit is required. This will be converted into a fine after two years if the budget deficit remains excessive. These discretionary steps raise the question whether the stability pact will be effective. Moreover, there is a conflict of roles, since those who are responsible for the excessive budgetary deficit will also be the ones to define it and to vote on the fines. Note that if GDP falls by less than 0.75 percent an exception does not exist.

No-bail-out clause

According to Article 103 of the EU treaty, the EU is not liable for the financial difficulties of any member state with a budget deficit, nor are other member states liable for this state's difficulties. Nevertheless, the political pressure for transfers granted by the European Union or by member countries will become perceptible in the future. Thus, if transfers have to be made after all – in spite of liability being excluded – the donor of transfers, as well as the recipient, may develop an interest in keeping these transfers as low as possible, replacing them by a rather lax monetary policy.

Common monetary policy and national decision-making

Common monetary policy must be oriented towards price-level stability in the monetary union as a whole. Consequently, it cannot take into consideration specific national conditions. In a monetary union, the monetary 'suit' is no longer custom-tailored for each nation; the one size must fit all. Thus, if nations are in a different position in the business cycle, one being in a boom and another in a recession, if countries experience an asymmetric shock and if they get stuck in a self-inflicted crisis, they must cope with the same monetary policy. Nevertheless, monetary policy is still judged in national political decision-making processes, since a political union does not come into existence simultaneously with a monetary union. Thus, a potential for conflicts inevitably arises between a common monetary policy and national economic interests. Quite a bit of political discipline is required from a country in crisis to accept a monetary policy that is oriented towards European price-level stability. If, however, the country in crisis could have its way in getting an easy monetary policy adopted, inflation in Europe would result.

By entrusting an independent European Central Bank with the authority to steer the money supply, i.e. to set the interest rates and determine other monetary policy instruments, the EU treaty has taken monetary affairs out of the hands of politics altogether; it has depoliticized the process of money creation.

It is an imperative requirement for the monetary union to establish a long-lasting consensus on the very essence of the European Monetary Union, namely on the depoliticization of the common currency. Thus, policy makers have to respect the decisions of the European Central Bank, above all, in situations where these decisions are unfavorable for a single country or its government – for instance, in times preceding an important governmental election or when a country is facing unfavorable economic conditions.

On the issue of an optimal macroeconomic policy mix

On the macroeconomic level, the issue arises to what extent macroeconomic policies should be coordinated. This question is especially relevant since monetary policy now has been Europeanized whereas the other areas of macroeconomic policy are still at the national level. One approach is to limit negative spillovers between the different macroeconomic policy areas. Thus, the stability pact is intended to control excessive fiscal deficits and in this way to protect the ECB and the euro against free-rider behavior of individual nation states. A rule that real wage increases in the different countries should not exceed productivity growth would help to prevent a negative spillover in the sense that national unemployment is not aggravated. Other attempts of coordination represent a form of atmospheric coordination including mutual information. This means that national policy makers are informed on what is intended elsewhere and start from a common frame of reference. Partly, coordination will have to rely on moral suasion; for instance, if a country with high growth rates benefits from the low interest rates of the ECB and is not willing to reduce its governmental absorption. Finally, most of the coordination philosophy is based on extremely simple and naive Keynesian ideas of controlling and fine-tuning aggregate demand over the cycle; inside and outside lags are neglected. The political process seems to be unable to smooth government expenditures over the cycle. While additional spending in a recession is grabbed wholeheartedly by the political process, reducing demand in a boom is unlikely to take place.

12.6 Monetary union and the labor market

In a monetary union, exchange rates are no longer available as a mechanism of adjustment. This has implications for the labor market. There are two lines of argument which describe specific requirements for the labor market and for wage policy in the monetary union: one relates to diverging labor productivities, the other to the role of wages as a substitute for the exchange rate.

Diverging labor productivities

The differences in labor productivity per head of total employment in the countries of Euroland (EU-11) are quite impressive. Let us define labor productivity as the nominal GDP in euro per head of total employment. Germany is set equal to 100. In 2000, France (108 percent) and Belgium (106 percent) reached a higher level than Germany; Ireland is close to 100 percent. A group of countries was in the 90–100 percent range. Spain (74 percent), Portugal (39 percent) and Greece are quite apart from the others. Using the actual

exchange rate for the British pound, the UK is at 91 percent (Figure 12.3).

In a monetary union, trading costs are reduced and market segmentations disappear. As a stylized fact, Jevons's law of one price will prevail. This equilibrium condition for the goods market translates into an equilibrium condition of the labor market. Diverging national labor productivities in the currency union are consistent with full employment only if national labor productivities are not exceeded by national labor costs. This means that labor costs have to be differentiated in the monetary union in line with productivity differences.

Wages as a shock absorber

In a monetary union, wages have to take over the role of exchange rate adjustments which can no longer be used as an equilibrating

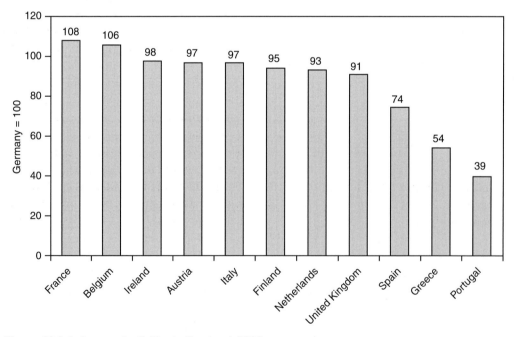

Figure 12.3 Labor productivities in Euroland, 2000

Source for data: Eurostat, *New Chronosdatenbank*, CD-ROM, 2000.

mechanism if economic development between countries diverges. An important case of diverging development is when a shock affects countries asymmetrically; that is, when a member country is struck by a negative exogenous shock more intensively than other countries in the currency union. Prior to the monetary union, the country could have devalued its currency to regain competitiveness. Within a monetary union, a member country fully experiences the asymmetric shock: in the case of a negative disturbance, production falls, the utilization of the production potential decreases and unemployment rises. The economy now has to adjust by using mechanisms other than the exchange rate.

Moreover, the exchange rate can no longer be used in other instances: when some countries have weaker growth than others, when the business cycle in the European Union is out of synchronization, when homemade problems evolve in some countries, when some countries respond more flexibly to a shock that is symmetric to the European Union as a whole and when the unemployment rates diverge strongly between countries.

Three substitution mechanisms for the exchange rate

A first mechanism of adjustment which can be taken into account as a substitute for a depreciation of the currency is the migration of labor. If workers leave a country that has been struck by a crisis and move to more prospering countries, unemployment decreases in the crisis area. The per capita income of the country in question will rise again. Nevertheless, this is a 'passive' cure. Moreover, under European conditions, one can assume that this form of adjustment will

not be accepted by the countries from which people emigrate nor from countries to which workers would have to migrate. The willingness to absorb workers from abroad will generally be low. Moreover, language barriers and cultural diversity will limit the mobility of people. Even though the free movement of labor is one of the four freedoms of the internal market, it seems realistic that labor migration will play a minor role as an equilibrating instrument in the divergent structural development in Europe. Unlike the United States, where labor mobility is generally high and where migration between regions as a reaction to an economic shock plays a central role (Blanchard and Katz 1992), labor mobility in Europe cannot be expected to be a sufficient substitute for exchange rate changes.

If labor migration is ruled out as an alternative to exchange rate adjustment, relative prices will have to do the job. In the case of a negative shock, a real depreciation will bring about improved competitiveness. This means that the relative price of non-tradables must fall, in order to stimulate the production of tradables. In bringing about this change in relative prices, wages (i.e. the price of the immobile production factor) will have to bear most of the burden of adjustment. Under static conditions, a decline in national wages makes a country regain its competitiveness. Under conditions of a growing economy, which is more realistic, wages should not rise as much as before. The decline in wages, or their reduced increase, stimulates the economy in the same way a devaluation would. There is one difference, however: a devaluation re-establishes competitiveness for all goods, a fall in wages favors labor-intensive production and thus re-establishes the competitiveness of jobs.

If wages do not react flexibly, differences in unemployment between the countries of the currency union are likely to develop. Then transfers are the only remaining mechanism to help nations adjust to a crisis (see below).

Thus, a cascade of equilibrating mechanisms exists which can be used to replace an exchange rate adjustment. First, the migration of labor can take the place of a devaluation of the home currency. If this is not possible, prices of the immobile production factor, predominantly wages, can adjust. Alternatively, if this also is not possible, financial transfers have to take over the shock-absorbing role of a devaluation.

Implications for wage policy

Since labor productivities diverge considerably between the countries of the European Monetary Union and can be expected to diverge in the future, labor costs will have to be differentiated between the member states of the monetary union since national labor costs must be borne by national productivities. Otherwise, unemployment will increase. Moreover, we know from empirical studies that convergence of productivities takes a long time.

Future wage policy in the individual countries should orient itself at the national labor productivities. Wage harmonization in the European Monetary Union should not be targeted. People must understand that the level of national wages must reflect the differences in national labor productivities.

Institutionally, wage formation should not be Europeanized, even if people now compare their wage in a single currency and thus money illusion will no longer segment wage-bargaining behavior of unions. Political demands of 'the same wage for the same type of work' that are likely to be articulated are not well founded with diverging differences in labor productivity. Europeanizing wage

formation would definitely increase the unemployment rate in the European countries. What is needed is a decentralization of wage formation, shifting wage formation from the economy-wide or sector level to the regional and to the firm's level. Wage formation, especially in the major countries of the continent, should follow more closely the market process.

Employment being a national responsibility, employment policy must be national as well. To organize employment policy on the European level and use national contributions to the EU budget or tax revenues for this purpose, would allow the governments of the member states to shift responsibility to the European level and to use the EU as a scapegoat, thus hurting the European cause if unemployment actually rises. National contributions and tax revenues would be used in favor of the countries that perform poorly. Countries which reduce unemployment would pay the contributions. Such an approach would represent the wrong incentives.

Implications for social union

Labor costs also include the contributions to the social systems paid by the firms. These labor costs, too, have to be borne by the national productivities. The divergence in labor productivities makes clear that the costs of social security systems in the different countries must also be different. This means that social security benefits cannot be harmonized. With such a divergence of national productivities, a social union cannot be realized and the Europeanization of social policy should be avoided. The territorial principle of social insurance in Europe, according to which benefits can only be obtained from the system to which contributions have been paid, is quite appropriate. But even if labor productivities were identical, the social security systems have developed differently over time. What is more important, countries have chosen different levels of public insurance relying for instance on a larger role of private insurance. Differences in the systems do not preclude that the issue of portability of claims in order to allow the mobility of people is to be solved.

Monetary union and transfers

Large economic regional units are usually characterized by some type of transfer mechanism. Transfers replace the exchange-rate adjustment mechanism when labor is not sufficiently mobile and when wages are not sufficiently divergent and flexible between countries. Taking as an example the US – an area with a common currency – transfers are made between different regions via the allocation of revenue between federal and state authorities and via the social security system. Additionally, the assignment of competences for expenditure and taxation to the various regional administrative bodies – the different hierarchical levels of the state – plays an important role in regional adjustment processes. In principle, a political union will be accompanied by higher transfers. As a rule, competences for expenditure and taxation will be assigned in a way that financial transfers between the different regions only have to net out major discrepancies in revenue. One must therefore be aware that the monetary union will necessarily be associated with a strong political demand for an additional transfer mechanism and for more tax revenue competences at the central level unless labor markets become more flexible.

12.7 *Eastern enlargement*

Adding ten new members from Middle and Eastern Europe to the existing 15 member states represents a major change of the European Union. There are three adjustment mechanisms: trade, capital flows and migration of people.

Changes in trade and capital flows

One would think that a major area of change is in trade. This, however, is not the case (Table 12.4). On average, the EU candidate countries export 65 percent of their exports to the EU as existing EU members do. This is a result of the Europe Agreements that were concluded in the early 1990s. Thus, from the trade perspective, the accession countries are already *de facto* EU members. Trade between these countries and the EU is not only inter-sectoral trade, but also already to a large extent intra-sectoral trade, albeit with some vertical structure. Trade of the EU with the new members will only increase in proportion to income convergence and other determinants of commodity exchange that apply in a general way to other countries as well. There will be no spectacular changes in trade.

There will also be no radical change with respect to capital flows. The potential new members have experienced a sizable capital inflow in their transition period. For instance, in Hungary foreign direct investment accounted for 50 percent of gross investment in 1995 (or 10 percent of GDP). For the Czech Republic foreign direct investment made up between 8 and 36 percent of gross investment or between 2 and 10 percent of GDP in the period 1995–1999. For Poland the figures are in a range between 14 and 18 percent and 3 and 5 percent respectively. It can be argued that foreign direct investment

Table 12.4 Candidate countries, 2000

	Bulgaria	Czech Republic	Estonia	Hungary	Latvia	Lithuania	Poland	Romania	Slovakia	Slovenia
GDP per capita in current prices and exchange rates in percent of EU average	7	23	16	21	11	13	18	7	16	44
GDP per capita in purchasing power in percent of EU average	24	58	37	52	29	29	39	27	48	72
Unemployment rate	17.8	8.7	13.2	6.5	14.4	14.7	16.7	8.4	18.9	7.2
EU share of total exports of each country[a]	52.6	69.2	72.7	76.2	62.5	50.1	70.5	65.5	59.4	66.0
Share of EU inward FDI as percent of gross investment[b]	4.4	4.9	10.9	4.3	5.9	8.6	4.0	5.0	2.7	1.0

[a] 1999.
[b] 1998.

Source: Siebert (2002), Table A1.

will tend to increase since the political risk premium will be reduced once these countries are members of the EU. However, the most profitable investment projects have already been undertaken in the first phase of the transformation process. Consequently, the level of foreign direct investment flows is unlikely to change markedly. We do not have to expect a major change in capital flows from the point of view of the EU. EU foreign investment in Middle and Eastern Europe was only 7.5 percent of total EU foreign direct investment (in the period 1993–1998).

Mass migration unlikely

Migration of people depends – among other factors – on actual and expected income differences and on opportunities for employment (and therefore on unemployment). Income differences between the accession countries and the EU are still high. Poland reaches 39 percent of the EU per capita level of GDP when purchasing power parity is used (data for 2000). For Hungary the relative level is at 52 percent, for the Czech Republic at 58 percent and for Slovenia 72 percent. In contrast, Romania reaches only 27 percent and Bulgaria 24 percent of the EU level. When GDP per capita is compared in current prices and nominal exchange rates, the Czech Republic is at 23 per cent, Hungary at 21 per cent and Poland at 18 percent of the EU average.

Some regions in some of the accession countries reach income levels that are not too far away from the EU average or are even higher. Thus, the region of Prague is at 115 percent of the EU level, Bratislava at 99 percent and the region Közep Magyarorszag in Hungary at 72 percent. For people in these areas, on average outmigration is unlikely to pay.

It is, however, not actual income differences and actual differences in unemployment rates that drive migration but expected income and employment gaps. In migration decisions the future stream of income is compared to the costs; the present value of the additional income in future periods net of migration costs must be positive. Therefore, expectations on future income play an important role. If people expect that the income gap will be leveling-in over time they tend to stay at home. In a model with uncertainty, for instance with a Brownian motion on future income, the option value of waiting is a relevant variable (Siebert 1993). If the option value of waiting is positive, people will stay at home. We know from many empirical studies that convergence takes a long time; nevertheless the expectation of convergence implies a positive option value.

Looking at the German experience and the Mediterranean countries, immigration surprisingly occurred in the late 1960s and early 1970s, way before the enlargement in the 1980s. Immigration from Greece, Spain and Portugal reached its maximum in 1970 with two persons per 1000 of the German population. As a matter of fact, there was negative immigration from these countries in the period after southern enlargement. Moreover, southern enlargement may not be a relevant analogue, anyhow, because historically people have not migrated from the south to the north, except for the tribes of the Angles and the Saxons from northern Germany, whereas migration from the East to the West was more normal.

Again, in the German case, there was a strong immigration in the late 1980s and early 1990s, but it is surprising that net immigration to Germany from the seven major Middle and East European countries (Bulgaria, the Czech Republic, Hungary, Poland,

Romania, Slovakia and Slovenia) has been less than 20,000 per year since 1995; this is about one person per 4000 of the German population. In 1993, a year of recession, net immigration from these countries was negative, in 1994 it was slightly negative. Admittedly, a free movement of people did not exist during that period but determined people are likely to develop an infinite imagination to overcome legal hurdles.

Looking at the analytical considerations and the empirical experience the tentative conclusion is that we will not see a major wave of immigration from the new EU members except in the event of a political shock. A larger migration from these countries can, however, not be ruled out if a massive disturbance occurs; for instance, if a major political risk arises from Russia. Migration from the very low-income countries like Romania and Bulgaria will be more important. These countries, however, will be admitted to the EU at a later stage. Commuters in the border regions of Austria and Eastern Germany may reach sizable numbers.

Agricultural policy

Eastern enlargement accentuates the problems of the Common Agricultural Policy (CAP). In agricultural production the European Union reaches high levels of self-sufficiency of above 100 percent in important areas: for instance, 132 percent for sugar, 112

percent for wheat, 105 percent for meat as well as for butter, milk and cheese. The CAP can simply no longer be financed if it is applied to the new EU members in the existing form. These countries do have a high production potential for agricultural products. This will be stimulated by price supports and export subsidies.

Structural funds have to be redesigned

In regional policy, regions of the EU are actually subsidized with 33 billion euros in the structural funds accounting for 34 percent of the EU budget (2001). The transfers are intended for areas where GDP per capita is below 75 percent of the EU average. If regional funds are continued in their existing form, additional financial means will be needed. Changes in the structural funds have to be made before Eastern enlargement because afterwards the new members in Middle and Eastern Europe will have a blocking minority.

Notes

1 This also relates to the second-best solution with respect to unanimity, the introduction of the 'unanimity-minus-one rule'. In this model, unanimity is deemed to exist in spite of the veto of one member state. It reflects the idea that no single member state should be in a position to veto a unanimity-based decision.

Part IV

National Economic Policy versus a World Economic Order

• •

Again and again, conflicts arise between national interests and the welfare of the world as a whole, i.e. of all countries together, with regard to the international division of labor. National interests may be rather short-term or even be linked to the advantage of particular groups in one country only, opposed to long-term benefits for that country or the world as a whole. Thus, the conflict between protectionism and free trade comes to life again and again (Chapter 13). With locational competition between countries, the mobility of capital has opened up a new dimension of international interdependence where countries are competing for the mobile production factors of capital and technology (Chapter 14). The utilization of the environment, a subject that will become more important in the future, is another field where national interests and worldwide concerns also can collide (Chapter 15). To prevent the strategic behavior of states, the countries have to commit themselves to a set of rules for the international division of labor that excludes non-cooperative behavior as far as possible. Such an international order includes rules for the exchange of goods, for factor migration and for utilizing the environment (Chapter 16).

Chapter 13

National protectionism versus worldwide free trade

••

What you will understand after reading this chapter

For a variety of reasons, the international division of labor has been tampered with through trade policy measures. Historic periods of protectionism were followed by epochs of free trade and vice versa (section 13.1). The most important trade policy instruments are surveyed in section 13.2. A whole arsenal of arguments for taking trade policy measures have been put forward. A number of arguments have a defensive orientation (section 13.3), others are rather aggressive (section 13.4), and yet other arguments concern retaliation (section 13.5) and the creation of equal conditions for competition (section 13.6). These arguments are critically reviewed. The reasons for a free international division of labor are summarized (section 13.7). Finally, the most prominent globalization fears are discussed (section 13.8).

13.1 Periods of protectionism and free trade

In the international division of labor, periods of liberalization and of protectionism have alternated in economic history. The beginning of the 19th century, with the Napoleonic Continental Blockade against Great Britain, was protectionist. In 1815, the British Corn Laws took effect. Intensely discussed in the literature, these laws aimed at ensuring self-sufficiency in agricultural goods in case of another conflict. The remaining part of the first half of the century was then marked by the intention of reducing trade barriers; the Corn Laws were abolished in 1846. A phase of liberalization began. Until the First World War broke out in 1914, there was a time of free trade, especially in the exchange between Great Britain and its colonies and its former colonies; important capital flows went into the newly independent states and the colonies. But the continental countries also reduced their trade barriers, e.g. in the German Tariff Union (1834). This phase of liberalization was accompanied by largely stable currency conditions in the framework of the gold standard.

With the First World War, the phase of integration in the world economy came to an end. The hyper-inflation that hit Germany and other European countries in 1923 and the Great Depression starting in 1929 seriously disrupted the world economy. Tariffs and other trade barriers increased; the 1930s saw devaluation races in which states tried to stimulate their exports by devaluing their currencies and thus improving their employment possibilities ('beggar-thy-neighbour policy').

After the Second World War, a framework for the world economy was created with the GATT (General Agreement on Tariffs and Trade) in 1948. Based on this framework, the international division of labor could develop beneficially, without trade barriers. Until 1971, the currency system of Bretton Woods succeeded in keeping foreign currency rates relatively stable. The World Bank and the International Monetary Fund, international organizations that aimed at a stronger integration of all countries into the world economy, were created (see Chapter 16).

A snapshot of this development is given in Figure 13.1. From 1900 on, the US tariff rate declined until the First World War, then it went up again until the 1930s. From then on, it was continuously reduced. World trade has risen continuously in the last 50 years.

13.2 Trade policy instruments

We briefly survey the most important policy instruments and their effects.

Import duties

A tariff on the imported good 2 makes this good more expensive. The incentive to produce becomes stronger for the domestic producers, whereas, owing to the higher price, the domestic consumers demand less. The domestically produced quantity of the import substitute increases, the imported quantity declines. Let $\tilde{p}_2 = p_2(1 + t)$ denote the domestic price after the introduction of the tariff (where t is the tariff rate). With a tariff, the relative price $\tilde{p} = p_1/\tilde{p}_2 = p_1/[p_2(1 + t)]$ falls. The production point moves from P to P' (Figure 13.2). This price ratio also determines the consumption point, C'. We assume that the tariff revenues are redistributed to the households as a lump-sum payment, shifting the budget line to the right. On the world market, the home country (as a small country) continues trading at the world market price ratio, p. For giving away $P'D$ in exports, it receives

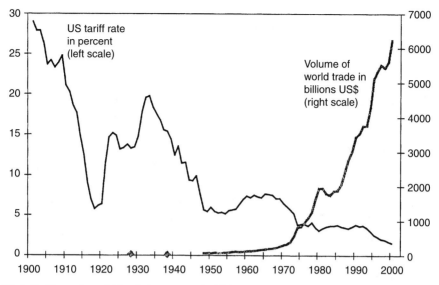

Figure 13.1 Tariffs and world trade in economic history

Source for data: For the US tariff rate (calculated as US tariff revenue in relation to the value of US imports): S.P. Magee et al. (1989, Chapter 13); Department of the Treasury of the United States Government; *Monthly Treasury Statement of Receipts and Outlays, 1990–1997*; *Monthly Bulletin 1998–2000*; World trade: world exports (fob), International Monetary Fund, IFS, CD-ROM, 2001.

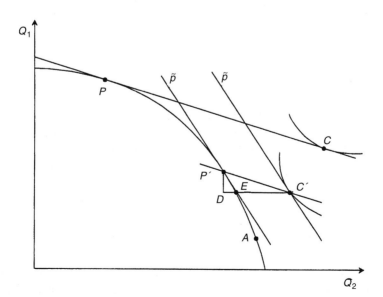

Figure 13.2 Effects of a tariff on imports

DC′ in imports. The domestic price ratio is *DE/DP′*. The tariff rate is *EC′/DE*; *EC′* is the government's tariff revenues.

The tariff on imports protects the domestic import substitutes sector, but the opportunity costs are considerable:

1 The export sector (producing good 1) shrinks as the import substitutes sector attracts production factors. Protecting one sector thus weakens the other sector. In a dynamic economy, import protection hampers the development of export opportunities. For instance, by protecting agriculture and coal-mining, more modern sectors, like engineering or the semiconductor industry, are penalized. If we enlarge the model to comprise monetary effects as well, this also follows from a tariff-induced revaluation of the domestic currency, as the protection against imports reduces the demand for foreign currency.

2 If the production of import substitutes is concentrated in a particular region of a country, protection against imports hampers the development prospects of this region or of other regions in a number of ways. One example is that protected sectors tend to pay high wages, impairing the development of new enterprises and also of the export business in that region. Furthermore, the incentives to increase efficiency are weaker, and finally – leaving the allocation model – the protection against imports leads to a reduced demand for foreign money and thus to a revaluation of the domestic currency, causing a negative effect for the export business in other regions.

3 Consumers reach a lower welfare level in the consumption point *C′* (instead of *C*).

Subsidies

Besides a tariff on imports, the protection of the domestic (or import-substituting) sector can also be realized through a subsidy. If, as an example, a production subsidy (*s*) is paid for the (domestically produced) import substitute, the producers face a change in the price ratio, as the producer price ($\tilde{p}_2^P$) for the domestically produced import substitute rises. The domestic producers' incentive to produce becomes stronger. The relative price that producers face, $\tilde{p}^P = p_1/\tilde{p}_2 = p_1/[p_2(1 + s)]$, declines. The production point is thus relocated from *P* to *P′* (Figure 13.3).

In contrast to a tariff on imports, consumers still face the world market price despite the subsidy: there is no market segmentation, and – if the country is small – they trade according to the world market price line that has to be drawn through point *P′*, as it was for the tariff. The difference, however, is that a subsidy for an import substitute leads to a split between the consumer price (*DC′/P′D*) and the producer price (*DE/P′D*) in the home country. The size of the trade triangle is determined by *C′*, the point of tangency between the indifference curve and the world-market price line. Subsidizing the import substitute makes this trade triangle shrink, and the country incurs a welfare loss. The point of consumption, *C′*, is situated on a lower indifference curve than *C*, and the trade triangle *P′C′D* is smaller than that without the subsidy (not shown in Figure 13.1, but with points *P* and *C*).

If we now take into consideration that the subsidy has to be financed, further effects arise; for instance, if sector 1 is taxed to finance the subsidy. With taxation of sector 1, the price ratio would yet again change in favor of sector 2. The production point then wanders down the transformation curve, starting from *P′*. In production as well as in allocating factors, taxes may distort the allocation and cause efficiency losses. The

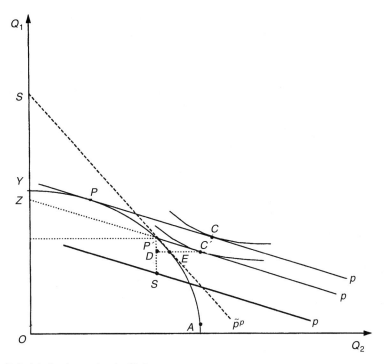

Figure 13.3 Subsidy for import substitutes

production point moves into the interior of the transformation area (point *S*), and the country incurs further welfare losses. The difference between a subsidy and a tariff on imports is that a production point *S* would represent a less favorable economic situation compared to *P'*. The world market price line ($\bar{p}$) then runs through point *S*.

Quotas

The domestic sector can also be protected by the use of quotas. Assume that the import quantity should not exceed *DF*. In this case, the permitted trade triangle is limited to *PDF* (Figure 13.4). If we move this permitted trade triangle along the transformation curve, the curve *FF'F''* describes the trade points allowed. A quota can be chosen to yield just the same result as a particular tariff on

imports, and vice versa. Under certain conditions a tariff and a quota are thus equivalent. We might choose a tariff rate so that the import quantity *DC'* in Figure 13.2 corresponds to the quota *DF* in Figure 13.4. This equivalence of effects occurs only if the government sells the import quotas (import licenses) in an auction and redistributes the revenues (which correspond to the tariff revenues *EC'* in Figure 13.2) to the households.

If the quotas (licenses) are distributed otherwise, different effects will occur. For instance, let *DC'* in Figure 13.2 represent the quota. If the import licenses are distributed according to the 'grandfather clause' (who imported in the past?), the first-come-first-served mode (who submits the application form first?) or political viewpoints, as happens from time to time in developing countries (who has a good friend?), then the

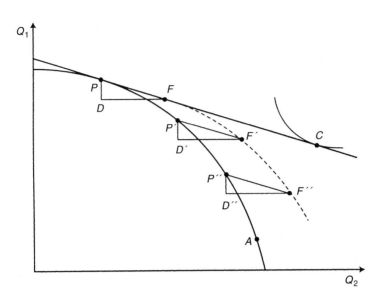

Figure 13.4 Quota

households cannot reach the consumption point C'. These distribution modes make it impossible to redistribute the revenue from the licenses uniformly to the households, and the households' budget line does not move outward by EC' as in Figure 13.2.

Voluntary export restraints

With an agreement on restraints for exports, governments agree on a maximum import quantity (from the point of view of the importing country) or a maximum export quantity (seen from the exporting country). Exporting countries enter export restraints under the threat of facing even harder entry barriers for their exports. An importing country could basically auction a quota among the exporters of a foreign country; as a rule, however, the distribution of the allowed export quantity among the exporters is left to the exporting country. This means that the exporting country receives the rent of the agreed quota, leaving the home country with an additional welfare loss compared to a self-

managed import quota. If the foreign government leaves these rents to its home companies, these have higher profits. As a rule, quotas cause foreign firms to export products of higher quality (upgrading). This can lead to further competitive distortions in the importing country. An example is the voluntary agreement on export limitations for cars between the European Union and Japan in effect until the end of 1999. This agreement was initially intended to protect firms in the lower product segment, but the upgrading of Japanese car exports brought increased competition in the upper segments of the European car market. According to new WTO rules, voluntary export restraints are no longer allowed.

Variable levy

This type of tariff lifts a low world market price to a guaranteed reference price at home. The lower the world market price, the higher is the levy. This system, for instance, was practiced in the framework of the European

Union's agricultural policy until after the Uruguay Round variable levies have been transformed into import tariffs (except for cereals).

13.3 Arguments for trade policy interventions: protection of domestic production

Trade policy interventions are justified with a variety of arguments. The motives can be either defensive or aggressive. They can be geared to an economy as a whole (or an economic region) or to single sectors. They can refer to national instruments or to international rules. We will first examine the arguments that deal with the protection of domestic production, especially of import substitutes.

Autarky

Under the label of 'autarky', political and also military arguments have been put forward. During the second half of the 19th and the first half of the 20th century for instance, this motive served to justify the protection of German agriculture as well as the special position of German hard coal and of the steel sector. Today, the autarky argument reappears in the somewhat refined form of supply risk, i.e. of being cut off from imports. However, in the modern world economy, the sources of supply for import goods are dispersed worldwide so that single-sided dependencies hardly exist. The risk of being cut off from deliveries is thus reduced. The globalization of the markets counteracts the dependency of countries *vis-à-vis* exclusive suppliers. Furthermore, a high-cost self-sufficiency has considerable disadvantages for those domestic export sectors that use these goods as inputs for their production. Suppose

that a country isolates itself from the import of, say, semiconductor products, to protect its domestic semiconductor producers. This will hamper its own export sectors (like the machine-building industry) that use semiconductors intensively in their products. And finally: even if we assume for a moment that reducing the supply risk was a goal of economic policy, this does not necessarily imply the protection of domestic producers; this goal can be better attained by piling up stocks. Autarky thus entails considerable welfare losses.

Protection of established industries

Another assertion is that existing domestic sectors have to be protected against foreign suppliers. In general, the starting point is a loss in competitiveness for a domestic sector producing import substitutes; the relative prices for the domestic producers become less favorable. In this situation, policy makers try to hold on to the production and employment of the domestic sector.

Stretching structural change

The argument of protecting certain sectors also appears in the form of stretching structural change. The assertion is that old industries like coal and steel should be helped to adapt to a new situation, but experience shows that subsidies tend to become irremovable over time.

Protecting infant industries

Some countries are not yet fully integrated into the international division of labor; they are still at the beginning of a development process. In these countries, the argument goes, import duties and other trade barriers should protect newly founded industries, so-called infant industries, until they become competitive. This process comprises making use of falling average costs by accumulating production know-how over time and by exploiting future economies of scale in production. Various measures can be applied: tariffs, quotas or preferential access to the domestic market for capital.

The basic intention is a temporary protection against imports until the domestic sector has reached a sufficiently strong position on the world markets. However, experience shows that such a protection tends to become entrenched in the course of time, contrary to its intended temporary character. This is confirmed by Latin America's experience in the four decades 1950–1990 with its import substitution policy that aimed at replacing the imports with domestic production. As this policy neutralized competition, cost control and incentives to find new economic and technical solutions were non-existent. The centrally planned economies also tried to make use of economies of scale by concentrating their production facilities at a small number of locations and isolating themselves from the international division of labor. They even tried to implement a division of labor from the top by making the specialization of the national economies a political decision. This method has proved a failure as well.

13.4 Arguments for political trade interventions: the maximization of profits from external trade

A different type of argument focuses on strategically maximizing a country's gains from trade. International trade causes gains; the idea is to redirect these gains into a certain country's pockets. In this case, the opportunity costs of the trade intervention do not arise in the country itself but elsewhere. Optimal tariffs and strategic trade policy belong to this category.

Optimal tariff

In contrast to a small country, a large country can influence the prices on the world market. As its market position is influential, it does not have to take prices as given by the world market.

Influence on the terms of trade

If a large country demands less of its import good (good 2) as a result of the tariff (making its offer curve shift to the left) there will be an excess supply at the previous price, and the price p_2 has to fall. The relative price $p = p_1/p_2$ rises, meaning that the terms of trade for the tariff-imposing country improve. With better terms of trade, domestic welfare improves, as the home country receives more import goods for its exports. The gradient of the straight line OS in Figure 13.5 represents the world market price ratio, p; the line runs steeper as p rises. Through its trade policy, the country shifts the equilibrium solution from point S to point S'.

Tariff rate and welfare

Figure 13.6 shows the effects of a tariff on national welfare, depending on the tariff rate. It is assumed that the foreign country does not react to an increase in the tariff. At a tariff rate of zero we have free trade, and the country reaches a real income OF that serves as a welfare indicator. A large country can increase its welfare by raising the tariff rate. OC is the optimal tariff, with a welfare level OB. Further tariff increases make the welfare fall because the quantity effect – the

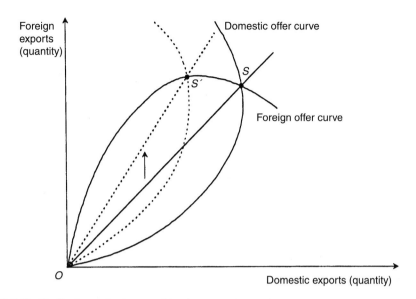

Figure 13.5 Tariff effects on the terms of trade

limitation of trade – now overcompensates the positive terms-of-trade effect on welfare. If the tariff is raised sufficiently (*OD*), the autarky situation results: the welfare level *OA* in this situation is lower than with free trade.

According to the assumptions, a positive terms-of-trade effect does not occur if the country is small. A rising tariff makes the trade triangle shrink; welfare decreases (along the *FA'* curve in Figure 13.6).

Tariff and opportunity costs: the large country case

At first sight, the argument concerning the optimal tariff appears striking. A country is able to increase its welfare by measures of trade intervention, but opportunity costs arise as well.

1 First of all, a position of market influence for our large country has to be assumed. Monopolistic positions, however, are often not defensible in the long run as processes of substitution take effect on the demand

side. OPEC is a good example for this effect. Even if the short-term import demand for a product may be inelastic, the long-term demand will become more elastic. In particular, markets that are contestable in the long run make it impossible for a country to pursue an optimal tariff strategy.

2 A tariff, whether on imports or exports, always entails long-run inefficiencies. What is optimal in a static model may prove absolutely wrong under the dynamic conditions of real life. The tariff-protected companies flag, and eventually their competitive advantage disappears. The rents, i.e. non-functional incomes, are no incentive for efficiency, and rent-seeking develops (see below).

3 The home country's welfare gains may prove elusive if the outside world reacts to the domestic tariff by imposing a tariff of its own: this makes the foreign trade curve shift as well, to the right. With such a retortion tariff, the former equilibrium situation *S* before tariffs (Figure 13.7) develops into

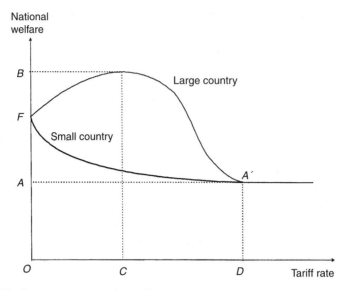

Figure 13.6 Tariff effects on a country's welfare

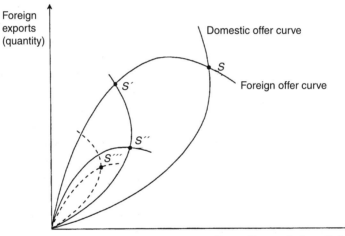

Figure 13.7 Tariff war

the new equilibrium S'' instead of S' (single-side tariff imposition by the home country). This non-cooperative behavior makes world trade shrink. The lens of potential trade gains becomes smaller (Figure 13.7). The form of the two countries' trade curves determines where this tariff war will finally end. In general, both countries lose.

Strategic trade policy

The basic model

In an approach similar to the argument concerning infant industries, strategic trade policy also has the goal of improving the domestic sector's position in foreign trade. This is based on the idea that the government can help a domestic company to reach a monopolistic position on the world market or a stronger position in an oligopoly. In the models of strategic trade policy (Brander and Spencer 1985), this can be attained by export subsidies (or subsidies for research and development) paid by the state, giving the domestic firm – at least in the model – an earlier start and helping it to reach a monopolistic position. The profits linked to this activity flow into the home country (rent creation). If another supplier is already present on the foreign market, the government may strengthen the domestic company's market position, e.g. by paying export subsidies. This gives the domestic firm the Stackelberg leadership in a duopoly, and profits are shifted from the foreign country into the home country (rent shifting).

Criticism

The approach described above is based on extremely simple models, like the one of Brander and Spencer (1985) where two duopolists from two different countries produce for the market of a third country, i.e. the world market. It has to be doubted whether models of such simplicity can yield sufficiently well-founded recommendations for economic policy.

1 The simple model is not robust with regard to the modeling of competition in a duopoly. In a model with Cournot quantity competition, an export subsidy is recommended for economic policy. If, on the other hand, the duopoly is modeled as a Bertrand price competition, even the export sector has to be taxed to shift rents to the home country.

2 Worldwide monopolies and worldwide oligopolies are rare. As a rule, markets are contestable; this contestability has been intensified by globalization. It is extremely difficult to find examples of oligopolistic structures on the world markets. The automobile industry is characterized by a worldwide dispersion, the market for semiconductors is competitive simply due to the short lifespan of its products. A duopolistic structure can be found in the market for large passenger airliners, with two suppliers (Airbus and Boeing).

3 Similarly to the optimal tariff argument, the models of strategic trade policy assume that the foreign government does not react, but reality looks different (compare the disputes of the US vs. Japan and of the US vs. the European Union). When governments retaliate with subsidies for their own companies, strategic trade policy results in welfare losses for all countries.

4 With respect to the concepts of 'rent creation' and 'rent shifting' we need to add the further concept of 'rent seeking'. Let us assume an environment where the government actively tries to shape the conditions for its export industries, according to each sector's specificities. In this context, companies invest a good deal of energy and considerable resources to get favorable conditions for their export sector. They will thus become active in the political arena instead of concentrating on the entrepreneurial task of pushing through new factor combinations and on creating new products. This binds resources, which cannot be used in production. A large share of the rent, or even the rent as a whole, is thus lost in the process of rent-seeking. An efficiency loss is inevitable.

5 Most of the models are partial (and naive), as they finance the governmental subsidies 'out of nothing' (as a lump-sum tax taken from the households). The negative effects that arise from financing the subsidies

through distorting taxes are not considered in this partial equilibrium framework.

6 If the state wants to help companies into a Stackelberg leadership position in the context of strategic trade policy models, it needs to know which products will thrive on the world markets of the future. Governmental offices and parliaments do not have this information. The information provided by industries about expected technological developments is biased by these industries' vested interests. Strategic trade policy thus lacks the necessary information base that is assumed in the models. Competition as a method of discovery in the sense of Hayek (1968) is given up.

13.5 Arguments for political interventions in trade: retortion as a necessary answer?

Anti-dumping

A frequently repeated argument is that a country cannot rest passive if another country's firms offer their products below production costs or below the domestic price on the world market but that it has to answer with anti-dumping measures such as quotas or import tariffs. It cannot be denied that an explicit dumping represents a distortion to the international division of labor; consequently, it is prohibited according to Article VI of GATT. It is equally true, however, that in many anti-dumping cases, protectionist goals gain the upper hand. Anti-dumping then, can easily develop into a protectionist division (Messerlin 1989).

Sliding into a non-cooperative trap

Unfortunately, retaliation entails the danger that a trade war develops. This would bring a less favorable welfare situation for both countries. It is therefore important to find, in the framework of the WTO, rules for the international division of labor that limit strategic behavior of particular economies. This also holds for anti-dumping measures, which must not be instruments of protectionism. Free trade is always advantageous for a country, as is shown in the following.

13.6 Arguments for interventions in trade: creating a level playing field

Industry and trade unions of the industrialized countries demand a worldwide equalization of conditions under which firms (and labor) compete (a level playing field), focusing often on equal social and environmental standards. As an example, demands are voiced that employees in newly industrializing countries should have the same social conditions as their counterparts in the industrialized countries.

As far as they are members of the International Labor Organization (ILO), the countries of the world have already laid down minimum standards for working conditions, like the ban on child labor. Most countries have also agreed to have free trade unions. To level out further social standards and to extend the industrialized countries' social standards to developing countries and newly industrializing countries would be amiss, however. Just as wages in China cannot be raised to the German level, a rich industrialized nation does not have the right to impose its social standards on a newly industrializing country. The decision as to how much social security a country wants to allow itself must be left to that country, as the purpose of the international division of labor is precisely to exploit the differences in factor endowment conditions. If everything were

The free-trade-for-one theorem

Free trade is beneficial for a (small open) country even if the other country or the rest of the world behaves in a protectionist way (free-trade-for-one theorem). For example, the foreign country can put an import duty on its import good (good 1), i.e. the home country's export good. This decreases the foreign demand for good 1. The world market price p_1 of good 1 falls and the terms of trade $p = p_1/p_2$ of the home country deteriorate. This would also be valid if the foreign country puts an export duty on its export good (good 2); this would make this good's price rise on the world market. As a small country, the home country has no possibility of reacting and the world market price line is relevant. This line runs steeper and the home country shifts its production from point P to point P' (Figure 13.8). Owing to the protectionist policy of the foreign country – e.g. if the foreign country applies its optimal tariff – the home country suffers a welfare loss as the new consumption point C' represents a lower welfare level than point C of the free-trade situation. But the home country is still left with an advantage from trade, as long as the consumption point C' is situated above the welfare level of the autarky point, A.

However, the theorem of the advantage of free trade for one must not deceive the fact that a single-sided activity of a particular country influences the distribution of gains from trade between the countries. If a country is large, it can seek to influence the terms of trade on its own by imposing a tariff. This may cause conflicts that finally lead all countries into a prisoners' dilemma of trade policy that they cannot get out of on their own.

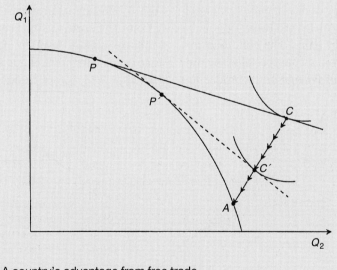

Figure 13.8 A country's advantage from free trade

harmonized, there would be no need for an international division of labor. This reasoning holds analogously for environmental standards.

13.7 Arguments for a free international division of labor

The arguments in favor of a free international division of labor are not only arguments against protectionism. More powerful are the arguments in favor of free trade.

Welfare gains for the world

The world as a whole gains from free international trade. This follows from the fact that free trade overcomes national restrictions: the more restrictions are overcome, the more leeway for economic decisions results, and this causes efficiency gains. If the production of one good remains constant, the possible production quantity of the other good rises. This argument can best be understood if we start from free trade and if then additional national restraints are introduced. This limits the choice set. Free trade takes away such restraints.

Figure 13.9 shows two situations: A is characterized by trade-restricting measures, while F represents free trade. In the initial situation, A, the price lines p and $p*$ intersect, indicating unexploited arbitrage opportunities and efficiency gains. The condition $p < p*$ means that Home can specialize in producing good 1 and Foreign in the production of good 2 if the trade barriers are lifted. In point F, the price ratios in the two countries are equal. The total worldwide production rises (shift from point O′ to O″) and the production of at least one good is higher now.

Welfare gains for a particular country: allocation-driven gains

Regarding welfare gains for a particular country, we distinguish between allocation-driven gains (or static gains) and dynamic gains.

Increased utility

Imports allow consumption at a lower price than in autarky. External trade permits specialization in producing the good for which a country has a comparative advantage. By shifting its production from point A to point P (Figure 13.10), a country can reach a higher welfare level in point C, as the households have more goods at their disposal than they had before trade. External trade

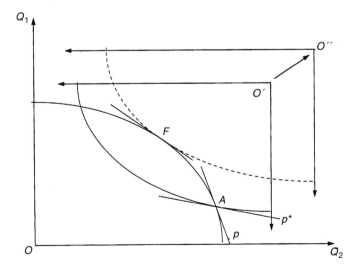

Figure 13.9 Welfare gains for the world

enlarges the consumption space: whereas the consumption space was limited by the transformation curve before trade was opened, it is now – with free trade – determined by the world market price line (budget line) running through point *P*. The production value, which is at the same time the gross domestic product, as measured in units of the import good, rises from *OD* to *OE*. An alternative representation with the simple market diagram of supply and demand shows that the households receive a higher consumer surplus by imports.

In detail, the welfare effect can be split into three effects. First, the quantity or volume effect represents the country's ability to buy more imports at given prices. The new price ratio on the world market is represented by a price line that would, other things being equal, run through point *A* (this line is not shown in Figure 13.10). Second, the price effect stems from lower opportunity costs and from terms of trade that are more favorable than those in autarky. Finally, we have a specialization effect. The combination of the quantity effect and the effect on the relative price can be called the 'trade effect'; its origin

lies in the possibility of trading at a free-trade price ratio that differs from the ratio in autarky. The specialization effect results from adjusting production to the new price ratio, i.e. by moving along the transformation curve.

The effect on factor incomes

Owing to the rise in the gross domestic product, the overall real income of the production factors increases. However, the real income of a particular factor (here: labor) may decrease if the country (partially) specializes in producing goods whose production is characterized by an intensive use of the other production factors (not labor).

The variety effect

If we consider preferences for different varieties of a product, external trade enlarges consumers' consumption possibilities. On the production side, the variety of inputs allows for higher efficiency owing to a more specialized intermediate import use.

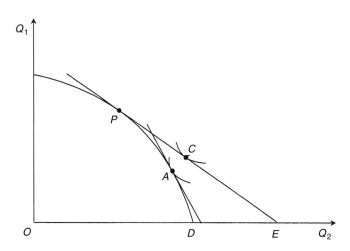

Figure 13.10 The welfare effect of external trade

The scale effect

Average costs fall with rising output. Factor and resource input per unit of output decrease.

The profit effect

In models with imperfect competition – i.e. with a product price above marginal cost – a rise in output means that the value of the additional production exceeds its production costs. Firms have higher profits; national welfare rises. However, trade can make markets contestable; this reduces market segmentation.

Dynamic welfare gains

In the long run, the dynamic effects of free trade can be considered to be more important than the effects that can be expected in a comparative-static context.

The competition effect

Free external trade ensures intensified competition between suppliers. The domestic producers have to face up to the foreign supply. This triggers a tendency to cut cost. Competition controls cost and ensures efficiency. It also forces economic actors to find new economic solutions and to discover new products. In the sense of Hayek (1968), competition is thus a method of discovery. External trade disposes of national monopolies; free trade is the best competition policy.

The innovation effect

External trade stimulates technological progress, as the strengthened international competition induces a search for cheaper production possibilities and for new products.

The accumulation effect

Trade is also an incentive for accumulating a larger factor stock (Baldwin *et al.* 1997). This accumulation effect holds for physical capital (including infrastructure capital) and human capital. For instance, the import of capital goods allows a larger stock of capital. The innovation effect is another form of the accumulation effect because a larger knowledge is accumulated, enabling producers to use the given production factors more effectively.

Whoever is still not satisfied with all these effects may take a look at the experience of those regions of the world that isolated themselves from international competition: Latin America in the four decades until 1990 and the centrally planned economies until the end of the 1980s.

13.8 On the most prominent globalization fears

Globalization has given rise to many concerns and fears among important groups of societies. These concerns are forcefully and sometimes militantly expressed by the NGOs. In the following, we will look at some of these concerns in more detail.

An overriding concern is that welfare is not enhanced, but seriously impaired. One line of argument is that developing countries will lose by the international division of labor. This argument is not valid for countries such as China and India that have gained in the absolute level of GDP per capita in purchasing power parity as well as in relative terms to the United States (see Chapter 9). Most countries in Asia and to a lesser extent in Latin America have improved their economic position. They have succeeded in building up an industrial sector and exporting industrial products. The (non-oil-exporting) developing countries have nearly doubled their share in world exports from 17 percent in 1970 to 30 percent in 2000. The transition economies in Middle and Eastern Europe have gained as well.

It is true that for national welfare to increase some conditions must be satisfied; political stability and non-disruption of the private sector by government are important conditions. Another one is that countries can adjust to permanent demand-and-supply shifts in the world economy. These conditions are not fulfilled in some of the sub-Saharan countries where a reliable institutional framework is lacking. Owing to path dependency, nations may be locked in their economic situation in vicious circles with no carryover from export enclaves in a dual economy.

Developing countries can also benefit from the inflow of foreign direct investment and foreign technology. Again, conditions must be met for these benefits to arise.

Some voice concern that industrial countries will lose in welfare. This is inconsistent with the fear that the developing countries will incur a loss; both the industrialized countries and the developing countries cannot lose simultaneously. On the contrary, all nations can gain through trade because trade is a positive-sum game. The developing countries experience an improvement in their terms of trade by specializing in the production of those commodities in which they have a comparative advantage. The industrialized countries have better terms of trade for their export products.

Another concern is that jobs will be destroyed in the industrialized countries. It is true that in our model of intersectoral trade real wages in the industrialized countries come under pressure when labor-rich countries enter the international division of labor. However, wages for human capital will rise in the industrial countries. Wages also will rise because of the benefit from trade. Moreover, the model assumes that all countries produce with identical technology and that labor is homogenous. But labor is much more productive in the industrial countries owing to higher human capital and to being equipped with a better technology and with more physical capital. Finally, labor in the non-tradable sector is protected against international competition.

It is feared that countries face additional constraints through trade and lose maneuvering space. This is wrong because trade dispenses with the restraint that not more commodities can be used for final consumption than can be produced according to the production possibility frontier. In that sense, trade increases the choice set of an economy. However, this does not mean that with trade there are no restraints whatsoever. Each country has to respect a budget constraint, i.e. it cannot import more in terms of value than it exports in any given period unless it can pay its imports through accumulated currency reserves, by drawing on its accumulated assets or by going into debt. Thus, the balance of payments has to respected. Beside the budget restraint, countries must be prepared for competition. Their internal economic and political processes must be such that they can compete.

Yet another aspect is the deterioration of environmental quality. If countries produce more for the international division of labor, they also produce more pollutants and harm their environment, the argument goes. This must not necessarily be the case. Scarcity prices for emissions can be introduced (see Chapters 15 and 16).

Chapter 14

Locational competition

••

What you will understand after reading this chapter

Countries compete for the mobile factors of production on a global basis (section 14.1). The essential channel of locational competition is the mobility of capital (section 14.2). The economic instruments used are the supply of public goods and taxation (section 14.3). Locational competition has a major impact on the position of the immobile factor labor and restricts the maneuvering space of national economic policy (sections 14.4 and 14.5). Furthermore, it can be interpreted as institutional competition; that is, competition between different institutional set-ups (section 14.6). It is quite controversial, in how far locational competition will lead to a race to the bottom (section 14.7). Locational competition controls excessive government power, the Leviathan (section 14.8). In particular, the smaller countries of the world economy are accustomed to locational competition (section 14.9).

14.1 On the concept of locational competition

Locational competition is geographic competition, competition between places, between cities, between regions and between countries. It takes place at three different level. First, firms compete in the world product markets. Second, countries compete in the world market for capital, for technological knowledge, for high-skilled mobile labor, and to some extent (for instance in historical cases), for residents. Third, there is a complex and intricate system of interrelations between the immobile production factors of countries, especially labor, by which these immobile factors also compete on a worldwide scale (Figure 14.1).

Firms aim for higher profits by selling their products in markets of other countries. They enhance their competitiveness by producing goods in high demand, by developing new products or by providing goods at lower costs.

Governments attempt to maximize the utility of their residents, i.e. the income of the immobile factors of production. In a scenario without factor mobility, national governments can induce an increase in the supply of factors of production such as (i) capital through savings, (ii) human capital through education, training and learning-on-the-job and (iii) technological knowledge through invention and innovation. In a scenario with factor mobility, countries can augment the income of the immobile factors of production by attracting mobile capital and mobile technological knowledge as well as inducing mobile factors not to leave the country. This improves the factor endowment of the country which in turn increases the productivity of the immobile factors. Besides firms and governments, workers strive to maximize their utility by searching for jobs with a higher income and with more secure employment. At first sight, they compete on the national labor markets. But the demand for labor is a

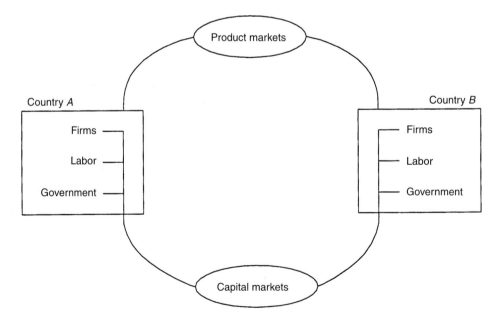

Figure 14.1 Levels of locational competition

derived demand, being linked to demand for the goods that workers produce. Thus, national labor markets are linked through global product markets, albeit through intricate mechanisms.

These three levels of international competition – firms, governments and workers – are interdependent. Whether a firm is competitive or not depends, among other things, on the framework that is provided by the government. Whether it is worth investing in a country or not depends on all conditions that influence firms. Whether the reward of labor is high or low depends on the capital endowment of workers in a country. The higher the capital stock the higher the marginal productivity of labor. Additionally, the marginal productivity of labor is influenced by technological knowledge. Finally, because of the fact that the demand for labor is derived from the demand for goods, the position of workers depends on the competitiveness of their firms.

Our concept of locational competition is thus a broad concept combining each of the three interdepending levels of competition (for another view see Krugman 1994). The traditional theory of trade is more focused on analyzing just one element, i.e. competition between firms on the world product market, of that broad concept of locational competition, including the implications of the Heckscher–Ohlin theorem for the income of factors of production. In contrast to this traditional approach, locational competition means that the immobile factors of production in a country compete for the mobile factors of production of the world. The issue is to what extent countries are able to keep mobile factors of production at home or whether they can attract mobile factors of production from abroad. In such a Tiebout (1956) context, countries provide public goods and semi-public or meritorious goods,

e.g. infrastructure capital, internal and external security, quality of the educational system and cultural amenities, thereby attracting mobile factors of production such as high-quality labor, capital and technology. These goods, however, have to be financed by taxes, fees and prices. Countries have to find the optimum mix between the supply of public, semi-public and meritorious goods and the opportunity costs of financing them. An ample supply of these goods may not be too desirable if it requires too high taxes. Conversely, very low taxes may not be attractive after all if the supply of public goods is extremely poor.

14.2 Channels of locational competition

Locational competition operates through different channels. In this paradigm, the main channel of interdependence between countries is the mobility of factors of production, especially the mobility of physical capital and of new technological knowledge. Additionally, the exchange of commodities leads to locational competition. A special kind of interdependence results from the mobility of portfolio capital. In extreme situations, people start to migrate. Finally, communication processes can lead to international demonstration effects.

The mobility of physical capital

Mobile capital can be relocated if conditions for investment change. It is necessary to distinguish physical and portfolio capital. Physical capital is completely mobile *ex ante* when capital is not yet embodied in machines; thus the mobility of physical capital mainly refers to new capital, i.e. to investment (or to clay in a putty–clay model). But even physical capital in place can be turned into funds *ex post* when depreciation allowances for physical capital are earned in the market and not reinvested in the same machinery, but reallocated to other uses. Then sunk costs no longer play a role. Thus, even *ex post*, the movement of new capital is a powerful force of interdependence between countries. This also holds if it is taken into account that real capital movements only represent a mechanism netting out excess demand or supply of national capital markets with national investment and national savings being in equilibrium most of the time. Empirical studies suggest that the importance of the global capital markets is increasing and that the segmentation has been reduced (Chapter 3). Furthermore, capital movements of different periods are gaining weight if accumulated in the long term. Finally, we know the importance of marginal changes in economics that are able to begin new long-term processes. Therefore, there is no reason to neglect the importance of capital mobility.

The mobility of portfolio capital

Apart from physical capital, portfolio capital is another important channel of interdependence between countries. When the agents on the financial markets lose confidence in the monetary and economic policy of a country, they reverse capital flows and induce a depreciation which signals to the voters the poor evaluation of national economic policy by the markets. As a result, financial markets and competition between currencies act as a controlling mechanism for the soundness of a stabilization policy in an economy.

The exchange of commodities

It is not correct to relate locational competition to capital mobility alone. In principle,

capital movements represent a similar mechanism to the movement of goods. In this sense the movement of factors and the movement of goods can create similar effects. Suppose capital and technological knowledge are totally immobile internationally. Locational competition will still take place through the exchange of goods. Consider a country that is making production less attractive, for instance, by a sharper regulation of business activities or by substantial increases of capital taxes. Consequently, the competitiveness of its exporting firms will deteriorate, absolute and comparative advantage will be reduced, exports will decrease, and in the long run other countries in the same economic sector will gain a comparative advantage. As a result, the country with heavy regulation and high taxation will suffer from its politics. In the long run, it will be less attractive to accumulate capital in the exporting sectors and in the sector producing import substitutes (of course, it will also be less attractive to accumulate capital in the sector of non-tradables, but competitive pressure will be especially strong in the tradables sector). The country will have a reduced capital stock that is not due to capital leaving the country but to a slackening capital accumulation, especially in the area of tradable goods because investment in this area has become less attractive. It is true, however, that the impact of changes in commodity flows is less noticeable than the impact of capital flows.

Migration

The importance of migration and its potential impact became obvious in the breakdown of central planning in Eastern Europe at the end of the 1980s. The mobility of people was an enormous factor in locational competition between the economic systems. The socialist planned economies were weakened politically when people started to exit, specifically when 600 East German tourists broke through the Hungarian border at Sopran on 19 August 1989 and Hungary did nothing to hold them back. It is therefore reasonable to relate the collapse of the communist systems to the exit of people. As already pointed out by Tiebout (1956), the exit option of people has a controlling function for national governments. Besides such an extraordinary case, the exit of highly qualified labor can represent a severe loss to a country.

The demonstration effect

Finally, another channel of locational competition is a demonstration effect which must not be underestimated. By observing the performance and success of others, people are able to gain experience, or, as Mark Twain mentioned: 'There is nothing so annoying as a good example.' This demonstration effect was of crucial importance in the competition between East and West.

As the global integration of economies further increases the mobility of physical capital and technological knowledge, locational competition is intensifying as well. The globalization of markets implies that the concept of locational competition becomes more important.

14.3 Competition in taxes and public goods

Instruments of locational competition

In the concept of locational competition, the comparative advantage of firms and sectors of an economy is not only an advantage owing to natural conditions, but it is also an acquired comparative advantage which is influenced by political decisions. Whether a country is able to attract mobile factors or not, does not only depend on its natural resources, but also on the skills of its workers (the quality of human capital), the efficiency of its infrastructure and on its institutional set-up. All these factors can be influenced. At least in the long run, i.e. over 10, 20 or 30 years, these endowment conditions can be improved substantially by investment in education and training as well as in transport and communication systems and by changing the institutional arrangement (acquired comparative advantage).

Which are the instruments governments can use to attract mobile factors and induce them not to leave the country? On the one hand, a state can increase the attractiveness of a location by the supply of public goods. On the other hand, any government activity has to be financed and raises the tax burden. In this respect, it is necessary to weigh up the advantages of the supply of public goods and the burden of financing them; a generous supply of infrastructure does not increase the attractiveness of a location unless taxes on mobile factors are kept at a reasonable level. But a country that levies very low or even no taxes on economic activity can also be unattractive for mobile factors if the infrastructure is not sufficiently developed. Obviously, there is a conflict of targets that can be solved by comparing costs and benefits.

Apart from competition in taxation and in the supply of public goods (competition in infrastructure), there is also competition between institutional arrangements of countries. Indeed, a large part of locational competition is institutional competition in the regulatory framework that determines the way things are carried out in a society. These institutional rules can be formal aspects, such as the constitution, the independence of the central bank or the right to free collective bargaining, as well as informal aspects, such as non-codified, habitual behavior, e.g. to start collective bargaining in a pilot region and then to generalize it to the other regions and the economy as a whole (as in Germany).

The effects of taxes and infrastructure

Mobile capital has the option to leave a country when conditions become less favorable, e.g. in case of tax increases. Consider an investment decision of a firm that maximizes profits. A source-based tax, e.g. a corporate capital tax, is levied at a tax rate t per unit of capital. Profits[1] are maximized if the marginal productivity of capital (F_K) equals the sum of the real interest rate (r/p) and the tax (t/p) per unit of capital in real terms, i.e. $F_K = r/p + t/p$. In Figure 14.2, line RR is the real interest rate, given by the world capital market, which means that we are considering a small economy. Line PM is the marginal productivity of capital. OK is the country's capital stock that is built up before levying a tax. The rectangle

$ORHK$ denotes capital income, whereas the area $OPHK$ denotes national output. The triangle RPH indicates the income of labor. A tax levied on capital reduces the marginal productivity of capital: the net productivity curve of capital is shifted downward ($P'M'$). In the new equilibrium I, less capital is employed in the country. Capital LK leaves the country. Interpreting the area under the capital productivity curve as national output, the country experiences a reduction of gross domestic product of $LJHK$. Gross national product additionally includes capital income $LIHK$ from abroad. Gross national product is reduced by IJH.

Figure 14.2 depicts the isolated impact of taxation. Assume taxes are used to finance public goods such as infrastructure G. If an improved infrastructure raises the marginal productivity of capital, the productivity curve of capital is shifted upward, and there is a higher incentive to accumulate capital. Thus, there are two opposite effects: taxation reduces capital accumulation and induces capital to leave the country whereas

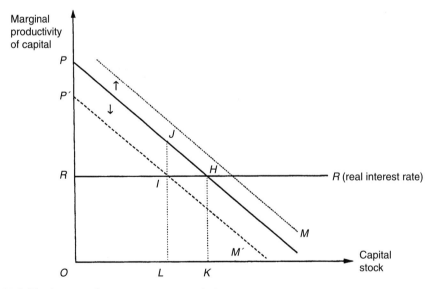

Figure 14.2 The impact of a source tax on capital

infrastructure attracts capital. Obviously there is some kind of trade-off between the two effects.

The optimal supply of infrastructure

It is necessary to find out which level of infrastructure and taxation is optimal. Figure 14.3 depicts the marginal benefit curve (*MB*) and the marginal cost curve (*MC*) of a public good like infrastructure *G*, which is financed by taxes. The positive effect of infrastructure, the marginal benefit, decreases when the provision of infrastructure is increased. However, the more infrastructure is provided, the higher are its marginal costs. The optimal quantity of infrastructure (*OA*) is determined by the point where both curves intersect, i.e. where marginal social benefits and marginal social costs of infrastructure are equal. *OZ* is the price of using one unit of infrastructure which is equal to its marginal costs at the optimum.

When explicitly taking infrastructure into account in the production function, i.e. *Q* =

$F(L, K, G)$, then, from the point of view of society, the supply of infrastructure is optimal if the marginal productivity of infrastructure F_G equals the marginal cost of infrastructure (in real terms) $C'(G)/p$:

$$F_G = C'(G)/p \tag{14.1}$$

In contrast to this view of society or the economy as a whole, firms view marginal benefits of an input provided by the government (or by someone else) as increasing their revenue, i.e. as marginal revenue; marginal costs of a unit of the input are given by the price firms have to pay for that input, for instance in the form of taxes. For firms, the optimal condition is that marginal profits are positive. In the case of benefit taxation, the beneficiaries of a public good and its payers are identical; there is no divergence between social and private costs and benefits.

Effects on the tax base

Consider now an open economy instead of a closed one, i.e. an economy with capital

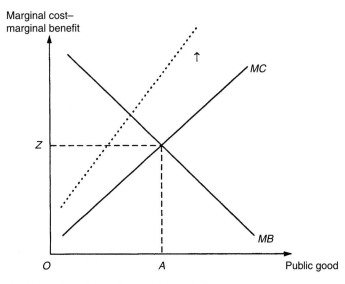

Figure 14.3 Marginal benefit and marginal cost of infrastructure

mobility instead of an economy without capital mobility. As a result, the marginal cost of supplying infrastructure also comprises the effect of capital leaving the country. Capital may leave a country if the price of infrastructure is more favorable in the foreign countries or if the price (taxes) to be paid for using the infrastructure in the home country does not correspond to the benefits for the firms. If capital leaves a country because of a tax[2], e.g. a corporate capital tax, the tax base is reduced. This has to be taken into account in the equation of the optimal amount of infrastructure as a loss in the objective function.[3] It means that the marginal cost curve of a public good shifts upward in comparison with the closed economy, because the opportunity costs of capital leaving the country have to be considered as additional costs (Figure 14.3). Let t be the tax rate per unit of capital and $dK/dt < 0$ the outflow of capital due to a tax-financed infrastructure. Let $\eta_{Kt} = (dK/dt)/(t/K)$ be the elasticity of capital with respect to the tax rate. Then the condition for the optimal supply of infrastructure is given by

$$F_G(G) = \frac{C'(G)}{p(1 + \eta_{Kt})} \qquad (14.2)$$

The marginal benefit (F_G) has to equal the revised marginal costs $[C'(G)/p(1 + \eta_{Kt})]$. If the capital stock declines with an increase in the tax rate, the revised marginal cost is *ceteris paribus* higher than in a closed economy (equation 14.1). If t is chosen too high, then $F_G(1 + \eta_{Kt}) < C'(G)/p$ and the cost of supplying infrastructure is too high. This is as an incentive for capital to leave. Consequently, the mobility of capital can change the cost–benefit calculation of governments.

With the introduction of capital mobility, another reason for the outflow of capital could be a better provision of infrastructure abroad at lower marginal costs owing to differing natural conditions, such as the existence of natural waterways. In such a case of better endowment owing to natural conditions, capital movements induce a more efficient global allocation.

The empirical evidence on the effects of capital mobility that we derived analytically is sketchy (Schulze and Ursprung 1999). Corporate taxes have been reduced in the European Union, but in most countries taxes on labor income have come down as well so that a redistribution of the tax burden from capital to labor cannot be observed.

Other policy areas

The necessity of comparing benefits and costs is relevant, not only for infrastructure, but in a similar way it also holds for other government activities. If, for example, the government finances basic research, then the marginal productivity curve of capital in Figure 14.2 moves upward. But since technological knowledge does not fall from heaven, it has to be produced somehow and the state has to find a method of financing it, e.g. by taxation. As a result of taxation, the marginal productivity curve moves downward again. It is obvious that there are positive marginal benefits of basic knowledge as well as marginal costs of its supply (Figure 14.3). The efficient supply of new basic knowledge is reached at the point where its marginal benefit just equals its marginal cost.

Environmental policy is another example of a government activity influencing the marginal productivity of capital. Consider an environmental tax on production processes. There are two effects. First, the marginal productivity curve of capital shifts downward (Figure 14.2). Second, even if the improvement of environmental quality induced by such a tax is not necessarily an advantage for mobile capital in the strict sense, there may be an indirect advantage by increasing the attractiveness of a location for a firm, e.g. through improved living conditions (environmental quality) for its employees. This shifts up the marginal productivity curve of capital.

14.4 The impact of locational competition on labor

Another important matter is the question of how the distribution of income is affected by capital mobility. This can also be shown in Figure 14.2. In the initial position (*H*) national investment is financed by internal savings. With the outflow of capital, savers and capital owners receive the same income as before the introduction of the capital tax. But now they earn income *ORIL* at home and income *LIHK* abroad. The income of the factor capital does not change: capital is able to avoid the capital tax entirely.

Labor income falls from *RPH* to *RP'I*, which is a substantially smaller triangle.[4] With the outflow of capital, labor as a production factor loses, its real income decreases.

This illustrates an important principle of taxation: mobile factors are able to avoid a tax put on them. In the long run, such a tax always hits the immobile factor, which means that a tax on internationally mobile capital always affects labor.

The bargaining position of trade unions aiming at a high income for their members and at secure employment are affected by capital mobility. Assume they succeed in pushing for a wage increase above productivity growth. In an open economy with capital mobility, capital will leave the country, and labor productivity will be reduced. Either wage income falls or, with the previous wage

remaining constant, more people will be unemployed. The opportunity costs for trade unions rise, and they must change their strategy except when social policies of the government accommodate the unemployed. Thus, the globalization of markets and the increased capital mobility have altered the relative bargaining position of trade unions.

Locational competition may also have an implication for the institutional set-up of wage bargaining because the bargaining equilibrium between employers' associations and trade unions is affected by the increased mobility of capital. Firms have an exit option, and this may lead employers' associations not to resist wage increases too strongly. Then, delegating the wage formation process to the social partners (as in the German concept of *Tarifautonomie*) will no longer yield positive results for the economy as a whole with respect to employment. This implies that locational competition requires the redefinition of the checks and balances of wage bargaining.

It is thus quite conceivable that locational competition has affected – among other factors such as deindustrialization or the reorganization of the work process – the position of trade unions in Europe. For instance, the German Trade Union Federation (DGB) lost about 4 million members in the period between 1991 and 2000, leaving 7.8 million members at the end of 2000.

14.5 A change in opportunity costs for national politics

Locational competition changes the cost–benefit calculus of national politics.[5] The exit option of capital redefines the opportunity costs of economic policy measures in the usual cost–benefit analysis. It has an impact on the constraint set, the maneuvering space, of the government. Locational competition reduces governmental power. The best example is the emigration of people from the centrally planned states of Central and Eastern Europe. Emigration affected the maneuvering space of decision makers so much that the political systems either collapsed or were compelled to adapt themselves entirely to the new situation.

Another example for the impact of locational competition on the maneuvering space of national governments is the controlling function of capital markets in the case of portfolio capital which can be reallocated at will. Consider stabilization policy (monetary policy, fiscal policy) and assume that a country expands its money supply in excess of the growth of the supply side. Then, purchasing power parity indicates that the national currency will be devalued and market participants will anticipate the devaluation. Thus, purchasing power parity affects exchange rate expectations. A similar effect also holds if public debt is increased and if therefore exchange rate expectations are affected. This mechanism (an interplay of purchasing power parity forming exchange rate expectations and interest rate parity determining portfolio adjustments) represents a check on governments' having a lax stability policy. This could be witnessed in 1983, when France had to reverse its economic policy, which had aimed at stimulating internal demand during the first two years of the Mitterrand presidency. The very fine controlling mechanism, an interplay of purchasing power parity and interest rate parity, of the European System of Exchange Rates (Chapter 8) implied that persistently high inflation, combined with an increasing current account deficit and rising foreign debt finally brought a devaluation of the French franc. This then required the change of policy.

14.6 Institutional competition

Locational competition also takes place as institutional competition, i.e. competition over regulations such as mechanisms of licensing or other regulations (Siebert and Koop 1993). For historic reasons, each state has developed its own institutional design, e.g. its legal system. These institutional rules can induce different effects on economic events, including for instance a slowing down of growth or an impediment to employment. For that reason, it is necessary to compare internationally the way things are (to be) handled within a country. Some regulations will persist in this competition, others will have to be adapted.

The best example for institutional competition still is the *Cassis-de-Dijon* verdict of the European Court of Justice (Chapter 12). This verdict started the recognition of the country-of-origin principle which automatically leads to institutional competition. Not only in Europe, but all over the world there is institutional competition taking place beyond the demonstration effect described above, in the sense that everybody poses the question of how others behave in a similar situation and whether others might accomplish the same tasks much more easily by doing things differently (benchmarking).

The alternative to the country-of-origin principle, according to which the country-of-origin rules are also applied to the importing country, is the country-of-destination principle. This means that the importing country defines the standard for an imported product. In the international exchange of goods, the country-of-destination principle would cause distinct impediments (Chapter 16). If every importing country were allowed to define its own product standards, this would represent numerous barriers to trade and especially a risk of protectionist abuse of product requirements. In order to prevent the rise of further barriers to trade, the rules of GATT and the WTO attempt to apply the country-of-origin principle.

14.7 Locational competition: a race to the bottom?

Some fear that locational competition leads to a race to the bottom in the supply of public goods, e.g. infrastructure, as capital mobility induces the marginal cost of the supply of public goods to rise. It is feared that individual countries might vie with each other in the creation of favorable conditions for private capital, e.g. by lowering taxes, which could cause the supply of public goods to fall to an inefficiently low level, possibly even to zero.

This is not true. First, if capital is leaving and if locational competition has an influence on the infrastructure that is supplied, the marginal benefit curve still defines a lower floor below which the supply of infrastructure cannot fall. This is due to the users of infrastructure, who – in spite of capital mobility – are willing to bear a higher tax rate in order to get the advantage of an improved infrastructure. It is therefore not correct to state that locational competition will lead to a zero supply of public goods.

Second, consider such goods as roads, ports and airports. They can be financed quite often by user charges and market prices. In this case no tax on the capital invested is necessary, so that the opportunity costs of providing infrastructure are not influenced by an outflow of capital. Indeed, by assuming an equivalence of the supply of infrastructure and user prices, the government cannot require revenues to be higher than the funds which are used for the supply of infrastructure.[6] Thus, there are a number of possibilities of how to secure an efficient supply of infrastructure even in the case of international competition. For example, benefit taxation could be introduced, which means that someone who takes advantage of a certain good has to pay the corresponding tax according to the equivalence principle. Additionally, it is possible to privatize parts of the previously publicly supplied infrastructure in order to set scarcity prices for infrastructure. A further variant is the interpretation of infrastructure as a club-good, which leads to the concept of fiscal equivalence (Olson 1969). In this respect, it is quite realistic to consider public goods as having different spatial spreadings. A theatre, for instance, is important only for the residents of a certain region. As a result – assume the costs of organization to be irrelevant – a specific form of organization is needed for each public good with a certain spatial spreading, which allows the supply of the public good as a club – good enabling the use of corresponding prices or user charges.

Even though there is only a weak correlation between taxes and the supply of public or merit goods in the sense of the equivalence principle, firms are still able to recognize positive effects from taxes as long as the advantages from the supply of a public good exceed the tax burden. For instance, this is true in the case of a good system of education. Firms are still ready to pay for public or merit goods such as social coherence or the cultural environment, which have no direct influence on the production function of a company. Therefore a race to the bottom does not necessarily take place.

14.8 Checking the Leviathan

Locational competition restricts the scope of action of the state: when the state is considered as an insurance against low incomes (Sinn 1997), possibly under the veil of ignorance concerning the individual's income (Rawls 1971), then the ability of the state to finance such an insurance by taxes on capital and companies is indeed limited by capital mobility. Accordingly, the social security contributions paid by the employers make labor more expensive, thus decreasing the return on capital. Since investors are able to elude payment by leaving the country, demand for labor diminishes and the revenues of the social insurance system are reduced. The opportunity costs of politics change.

But is this to be deplored? Locational competition – like competition on product markets – is a means to lower costs and to discover new solutions in the sense of Hayek (1968). Competition between states increases efficiency, rent-seeking of groups can be reduced (Lorz 1998). Locational competition can thus be seen as a device for taming the Hobbesian Leviathan (Sinn 1992b). This is especially relevant when people vote with their feet and leave their country as some residents of the centrally planned economies of Central and Eastern Europe did in the late 1980s. People in general leave their country only with the greatest reluctance, when they have lost all hope at their previous place of living. In this respect, the exit option controls governments. Thus, locational competition can be seen as an important political mechanism for freedom.

There are proposals to limit institutional competition, e.g. by international cooperation extending the right of a state to levy taxes on its citizens beyond national frontiers. This is quite understandable for fiscal reasons, and it may not be easy to draw the line where some tax coordination in a common market like the European Union may be justified. But on a worldwide scale, proposals

of limiting tax competition must not eliminate the exit option of people, which is a central human right of freedom. Any form of cooperation destroying the exit option would be a cooperation in favor of totalitarian systems, a cooperation against freedom. This would be in complete contradiction to an open society in the spirit of Popper (1945).

The terrorist attacks of 11 September 2001 have added a new dimension to the topic of locational competition. Terrorism is a threat to security, and people are understandingly looking for the state to establish security. International terrorism requires international cooperation. This reminds us that locational competition between nation states finds its limit when global public goods are in question. We will study this issue of a global system of rules in more detail in Chapter 16.

14.9 Locational competition between the regions of the world

Locational competition is also competition between political systems and economic philosophies. The diverging experience of different regions of the world with respect to policy approaches is quite impressive. Regions of the world that have faced locational competition head-on have had economic success in the past; regions that have shied away from locational competition have often fallen back.

Eastern Europe had a division of labor from above by managed trade where the exploitation of economies of scale was the leading doctrine. But in essence, Eastern Europe had not been exposed to competition from the world economy. Latin America was misled for nearly four decades up to the late 1980s by the economic doctrines of Prebisch (1950) and Singer (1950) and the policy of import substitution. This approach implied that the tradable sector of the economy was not exposed to world market prices. Eventually, Latin America lost its efficiency, but it changed its policy in the 1990s.

It is worth noting that these efficiency losses are long-run phenomena and that it takes some time for the erosion of efficiency and the slowdown of dynamics to eventually show up. This holds for Eastern Europe where the 1950s basically indicate a normal pattern of the catching-up process relative to the United States, but where eventually the grinding force of paralysis and inefficiency takes over. A similar story holds for Latin America where, with the passing of time, the restrictions imposed by the policy of import substitution eventually showed their fatal result.

The Pacific rim countries have followed the opposite route. They were outward oriented and they did not distort relative prices between export goods and import goods. Thus, their infant industries had to compete from the start with the world economy and find the markets for their products. This proved to be an incentive to make the national economy more efficient. A country or a region of the world not participating in this 'beauty contest' will eventually fall behind.

Some innovators in worldwide institutional competition are small countries like New Zealand and Chile. Owing to a high degree of openness, which is a distinct attribute of small economies, there is great pressure to adapt to institutional competition. New Zealand undertook a complete change of all aspects of economic policy in 1983. Incidentally, this had been induced by a Labour government. It seems as if New Zealand has solved many of the problems which arose in the past. Chile switched to a capital-funded national pension system during the 1980s. Two European examples of small economies

that have been successful in locational competition are Ireland and the Netherlands.

But even the big regions of the global economy have to face locational competition. The US has always been an open economy, which means that the US always had to adapt to the needs arising from locational competition. Continental countries in Europe, though open in most of their product market, have been slow to adjust in some areas, especially in the labor market.

Notes

1 Profits are defined as revenue, i.e. price (p) times quantity (Q), minus costs. Costs include capital cost (real interest rate as price of capital times capital input, rK) and labor cost (wage rate times labor input, wL). A company maximizes its profits taking into account taxes ($G = pQ - wL - rK - tK$), subject to the output constraint given by the production function ($Q = F(L, K)$). By differentiating the Lagrangian function $\mathcal{L} = pQ - wL - (r + t)K - \lambda[Q - F(LK)]$ with respect to Q, the optimum condition is: $p - \frac{1}{2} = 0$ which means that the shadow price $\frac{1}{2}$ equals the market price. By differentiating with respect to K we have: $F_K(\cdot) = (r + t)/p$.

2 Capital leaves a country if the net marginal productivity is reduced owing to a tax increase, i.e. if

$$\frac{d\{p \cdot F_K(K, L, G) - t\}}{dt} < 0$$

Because of the budget restraint of the state, $C(G) = t \cdot K$, there is an interrelation between the supply of infrastructure G and tax revenues tK: $G = C^{-1}(t \cdot K)$. The optimal tax rate in the case of capital mobility is characterized by profit maximization subject to tax revenues (tK) and the cost of capital (with r defining the interest rate in the world capital market, which is – for simplicity – supposed to be constant):

$$p \cdot F\{K(t), L, C^{-1}[t \cdot K(t)]\} - t \cdot K(t) - r \cdot K(t)$$

The resulting first-order condition is:

$$[p \cdot F_K - t - r]\frac{dK}{dt} + \frac{p \cdot F_G[K + t \cdot dK/dt]}{C'(G)} - K = 0$$

In the equilibrium of the capital market, the first term equals zero. This yields:

$$F_G = \frac{C'(G) \cdot K}{p \cdot [K + t \cdot dK/dt]}$$

Dividing the denominator and the numerator of the right-hand side of the equation by K, equation 14.2 results.

3 If capital moves out, income of the immobile factor labor will be reduced because labor productivity falls when workers are less well endowed with capital. Lower labor income also implies a lower tax base.

4 If the state redistributes its tax revenues $P'PJI$ among the households, then labor loses only IJH.

5 It is an interesting observation that institutional changes exert considerable influence on the allocation of power. A telling example is the transition from fixed to flexible exchange rates. With the use of flexible exchange rates, the balance of power between fiscal and monetary policy has shifted. Now monetary policy exerts a greater influence than fiscal policy (Siebert 2000, Chapter 18).

6 Additionally it has to be taken into account that the state has to balance its budget. There are tax revenues, but there is also expenditure on infrastructure. With falling average costs of infrastructure (owing to high fixed costs) this creates the problem that the budget might not be balanced with prices equaling marginal costs (Sinn 1997). Note, however, that the immobile factor (labor) also has an indirect advantage arising from the supply of infrastructure, namely if capital is attracted and if consequently labor is better equipped with capital and thus has a higher productivity.

Chapter 15

Using the national and global environment

••

What you will understand after reading this chapter

For the economist, the environment is a scarce good. Environmental systems have a spatial dimension. The environment can be a national or a global good (section 15.1). If the environmental endowment of countries differs, then the traditional theories on the international division of labor hold (section 15.2). For global goods, new institutional solutions should be found, in order to avoid non-cooperative behavior (section 15.3).

15.1 The economic paradigm of the environment

The environment is the set of the natural conditions of the human biosphere; it includes the quality of air, of rivers, lakes and the sea, of the soil and the quality of the living environment (e.g. biodiversity). From the point of view of an economist, the environment is a scarce good, but a good with its own specific features.

The environment as a scarce good

The environment has two competing functions for the economic system (Siebert 1998b): it is a public consumption good (arrow 1 in Figure 15.1) and it absorbs waste from consumption and production (arrows 2 and 3). These two roles are in conflict. Emissions from consumption and production are transformed into pollutants ambient in the environment by natural processes (diffusion) which influence the quality of the environment (damage function, arrows 6 and 7). In

addition, the environment supplies inputs for the production process (arrow 5). Competing uses are linked to externalities. Indeed, arrows 2, 3, 4, 7 and 1 in Figure 15.1 describe an externality in greater detail, by introducing the intervening variables, emissions and pollutants ambient in the environment.

In its role as environmental quality, the environment is a public good, that is, it is used to the same extent by all. Nobody can be excluded from the consumption of this good (non-excludability), and there is no rivalry in consumption (non-rivalry). In its role as an absorber of waste, the environment is not a public good, but a good for which exclusion rights can be defined (private good). With respect to environmental quality, the supply of a public good cannot be determined by the market system, because no institutional arrangement is available to aggregate the consumers' willingness to pay. Thus, the optimal supply of a public good must be determined in a political decision-making process. Once the desired quality of the environment is set, user rights can be defined for nature as an

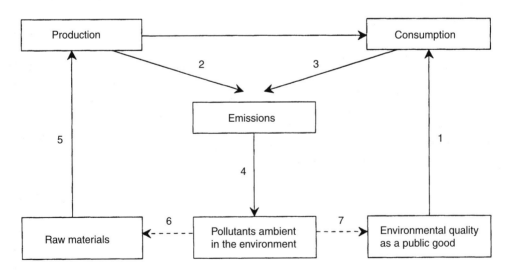

Figure 15.1 The economic system and the environment
Source: Siebert (1998b).

absorber of waste. With these user rights market processes can develop. In this way, prices can be put on emissions either by introducing transferable emission permits or by taxing the emissions. The public good should not be mixed up with a free good for which no price is charged. Historically, the environment was used as a free good in its capacity as an absorber of wastes; this implied a deterioration of environmental quality as a public good. Instead of the term 'free good', the term 'common property resource' ('the commons') is used for a situation in which no property rights are defined.

The spatial dimension of environmental goods

Environmental systems always have a spatial dimension. With respect to their dimension in space, environmental goods can be divided into three categories. The first comprises national environmental goods, i.e. those that fall completely within the borders of one nation as may a river system or the tributaries of a river. The second group is formed by cross-border environmental goods, which are shared by (at least two) countries like trans-frontier pollution (e.g. acid rain). The third category consists of global environmental goods, i.e. goods that pertain to the Earth as a whole like the ozone layer. Of course, environmental problems are mostly related to several environmental systems, but the separation into these three groups is very helpful for the analytical solution of the problem.[1]

The environmental problem is characterized by an extensive casuistry: pollutants are bound in products, they are emitted from stationary or mobile sources (like cars), they accumulate over time and, finally, there is a difference between the use of non-renewable and renewable resources (Siebert 1998b). All these issues pose specific problems for the international division of labor. In the following, we will assume that emissions originate from production processes by stationary sources and are delivered into air and water.

15.2 *Environmental abundance as a national factor endowment*

As far as the environment is a national good, its scarcity can be different from country to country owing to the following reasons:

- The absorption capacity of the environment as a receptacle for emissions may vary between countries because the assimilation capacity can differ owing to natural conditions.
- The population of one country may have stronger preferences for environmental quality than that of another country, consequently assigning a higher value to the environment. Even if international preferences are equal, a higher income per head can lead to a stronger demand for environmental quality. Finally, institutional rules also influence the demand for environmental quality, as they affect political decisions by which the desired state of the environment is determined.
- The demand for environmental assimilation services may be different because of the level and structure of consumption and production, but also due to abatement and disposal technologies for emissions and waste.

The different abundance of the environment means that the goals for environmental quality, set by the political process, differ. Defining U as environmental quality, the domestic environmental quality U is different from the foreign U^*, and thus $U \lessgtr U^*$. Different abundance also means that the absorption capacity for emissions E is not equal in

269

different regions of the world: $E \leqq E^*$. This holds even if environmental quality as a public good is identical.

Different environmental qualities have to be considered in the same way as differences in factor abundance. The Heckscher–Ohlin approach can thus be applied. Countries with a relative abundance in environmental quality will export commodities that use the environment intensively in their production. If the environmental endowment is not equal, prices will differ as well, owing to the differing scarcity. Through trade, prices will tend to become more equal over time, because in the country with the relatively abundant environment, the production of the good that uses the environment intensively will rise, and therefore the demand for assimilation services of the environment will increase. In the country where environment is relatively scarce, the production of the good that uses the environment intensively will fall, and therefore the prices for emissions will do so as well. If capital is mobile, these effects will occur through capital movements from one country to the other.

In so far as the environment is a national good and its scarcity can be expressed by market prices, environmental endowment and environmental policy signaling the preferences of the citizens are no reasons for international regulation. The environment must then be treated like any other factor endowment. When we consider the large casuistry on environmental problems, environmental political instruments can work as trade barriers (Chapter 16).

15.3 Global environmental problems

Looking at global environmental problems, the environment appears as a public good that covers the whole world and that everyone uses to the same degree. Examples are the atmosphere and the ozone layer. One of the current hypotheses of physicists is that the global climate is warming up owing, among other factors, to the increased concentration of carbon dioxide. Another hypothesis is that the emission of chlorofluorocarbons (CFCs) damages the ozone layer. These effects do not occur overnight; instead, it is a process that takes several decades to develop.

Let us consider two economies. The environmental quality U^W is a global public good, so that $U = U^* = U^W$. As environmental quality is a public good, it cannot be assigned to a single nation. The total emissions of the world E^W are composed of the emissions of both countries, $E + E^* = E^W$. They have a negative influence on global environmental quality, so that $U^W = G(E^W)$.[2]

The decision problem for allocating global environmental goods consists of two interwoven questions:

- Which environmental quality of the global environmental goods should we aim at?
- How should the costs of reaching the desired global environmental quality be divided among the individual countries?

Analytically, the approach to determining the target level for public environmental goods is to derive the aggregate willingness of nations to pay. The problem is that sovereign nations can behave as free-riders. The corresponding institutional difficulties surface when it comes to determining the benefits that arise from the protection of global environmental goods for individual countries, say the (monetary) value of prevented environmental damage, and to assigning the costs for the attainment of the protection, say the prevention of waste. According to the polluter-pays principle, cost assignment would be fair in terms of pollution caused. However, this principle requires a sovereign authority that does not exist for the world as a whole.

For these reasons, nations have to find mechanisms by which they bind themselves in using global environmental goods. In the end, this is a question of a contractual rule governing the use of global environmental goods in the way the Coase theorem on environmental agreements has suggested (Siebert 1998b), with the additional difficulty that sovereign states are doing the bargaining. In this process, the interests of important polluters and the preferences of countries with higher environmental awareness will play an important role, as well as income per head and a variety of other variables. Consider China, for example, a country with large coal reserves, that will want to use these resources for its development, without worrying too much about how this might influence the concentration of carbon dioxide in the world's atmosphere. As individual countries will behave strategically, it will be difficult to come to (and to implement) a self-restriction of sovereign states in using global environmental goods. Besides the problem of realizing multilateral solutions, another issue lies in the necessity that multilateral agreements should remain stable in the long run. Once a multilateral agreement is signed, it should be made sure that sovereign states have no interest in reneging and walking away from the contract.

Looking at possible institutional solutions, an example would be an agreement on a worldwide certificate system for carbon dioxide emissions. In such an agreement, the total quantity of worldwide allowed emissions is fixed. But difficulties arise when a consensus has to be reached on who will be entitled to these certificates, as they determine a user right, more precisely the right to use the global environment and indirectly the natural resources that generate carbon dioxide. Possibly, a proportional reduction rate for the given emissions is a starting point for industrial countries. This is the approach of the Kyoto Protocol. Developing countries will require that industrial countries reduce emissions at a higher rate. Unfortunately, such an approach starts from the current level of emissions and does not take into account that the level of emissions increases with the economic growth of the newly industrializing countries. Another example would be an international agreement on safeguarding biodiversity.

Notes

1 Cross-border environmental problems are not discussed in detail (Siebert 1998b, Chapter 12).
2 With cross-border environmental problems an interdependence exists such that the environment transports emissions from one country to another. The diffusion function is: $E = T(E^*)$ or $E^* = T^*(E)$.

Chapter 16

An institutional order for the world economy

••

What you will understand after reading this chapter

After having discussed several areas where national interests and world interests can clash, like trade policy, locational competition and environmental allocation, we now look at the institutional design for the world economy. The issue is how strategic and non-cooperative behavior of nation states can be channeled into a system of rules defining a global frame of reference. Countries can behave strategically in their national policies, in order to derive the greatest national benefit out of the international division of labor. In their trade policy, they can levy an optimal tariff or they can attempt to implement strategic trade policy in favor of certain sectors. Countries can also behave as free-riders towards global public goods. All these cases imply non-cooperative behavior of countries, which eventually leads to a welfare loss for the world as a whole and possibly even for the individual countries involved. Consequently, an institutional order has to be created that prevents countries from falling into the trap of non-cooperative behavior. Furthermore, mechanisms should be established that enable countries to get out of a situation of non-cooperative behavior. Strategic behavior in trade policy is explained in section 16.1; other areas of non-cooperative behavior or of externalities are discussed in section 16.2. The world economy needs a system of rules (section 16.3). We then look at the history of the WTO and how it works (section 16.4). A number of new problems have to be addressed, e.g. free market access versus national regulation, competition policy and aggressive trade policy (section 16.5). Moreover, as an implication of the paradigm of locational competition, rules for the mobility of production factors are receiving increasing attention in the discussion of economic policy (section 16.6). Social norms are a major matter of debate (section 16.7). The integration of the environment in the world trade order represents a specific problem (section 16.8). The mechanisms to stabilize and strengthen the world order are analyzed (section 16.9). The role of the IMF is discussed briefly in section 16.10. Finally, the main elements of the global economic order are summarized (section 16.11).

16.1 Strategic national behavior

States can behave strategically against other states. Trade policy is a major area where non-cooperative or strategic behavior of nation states can be observed. The goal is to influence the gains from trade.

Cooperative and non-cooperative trade policy

Countries can improve their terms of trade if they are sufficiently large. When one or several large countries implement such a strategic policy, the gains from the international division of labor dwindle for the other countries. For our analysis, we consider a two-country case and first introduce a situation of free trade as a reference point, in which both countries gain from international trade. As a simplification we assume that both countries are identical but are in different autarky positions before trade starts. In Figure 16.1 these autarky situations are depicted by points A and A^*. Gains from trade, i.e. the gains in welfare in comparison to autarky, will then be

equal for both countries. We assume that the trade benefits in a situation of free trade amount to $(17, 17^*)$. In the following, the first number of such a set denotes the domestic trade benefits, the second number indicates the foreign trade benefits. These numbers do not denote the level of utility, but the change in the level of utility in comparison to the autarky situation. In Figure 16.1, the free-trade situation is characterized by the point I $(17, 17^*)$, which is the tangential point of the indifference curves of the two economies. In point F_I, the transformation curves of both economies are tangent to each other, and the straight line p denotes the equilibrium world price ratio.

When the domestic country behaves strategically by levying an import duty or an export duty or intervenes in other ways, then the domestic gains from trade can be increased; the gains from trade of the foreign country decrease. Such a situation II can be achieved by using the optimal tariff. Point II $(20, 7^*)$ denotes the distribution of gains from trade. It is important to notice that the

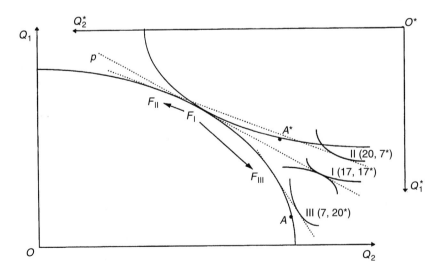

Figure 16.1 Gains from trade with strategic behavior

domestic production point moves to point F_{II}. The system of coordinates related to F_I of the foreign country is not valid any more.

Alternatively, the foreign country could raise an optimal tariff in order to increase its gains from trade, while the domestic gains from trade decrease. This is point III with bundle $(7, 20^*)$. The domestic production point moves to F_{III}. In this case again, the system of coordinates for the foreign country is not valid any more.

Also, a situation IV $(9, 9^*;$ not shown in Figure 16.1) can occur, in which both countries are implementing a tariff policy. Finally, in the extreme case in which both countries take protection to the limit and are in the autarky situation A and A^*, the gains from trade are (O, O^*).

Figure 16.2 depicts the trade benefits, that is the increase in benefits U, U^* relative to the autarky situation. The area within the curve through 0, II, I, III is the area of the possible gains from trade. Assume both countries to be in the initial position in situation IV, with trade benefits amounting to $(9, 9^*)$. Then the area between the curve and above point IV

defines the possible trade benefits for both countries.

In the initial position IV, both countries can benefit from the transition to free trade. If they cooperate, they will proceed to situation I, where each of them reaches a welfare maximum and where the gains in total utility are maximized. However, in the case of non-cooperative behavior, they will not reach the optimal situation I. Both countries strive for the positions II and III, but instead they remain in situation I or even move closer to the origin. This is the prisoners' dilemma. They cannot agree, because one country will always expect that it will have greater benefits in a situation different from situation I. The situation considered above corresponds to a game with four possible outcomes. In Table 16.1, the gains from trade represent a pay-off matrix for the players. In the case of free trade (situation I), both countries can benefit.

Trade benefits due to liberalization

A pay-off matrix with the welfare effects of liberalization and protectionism for the world

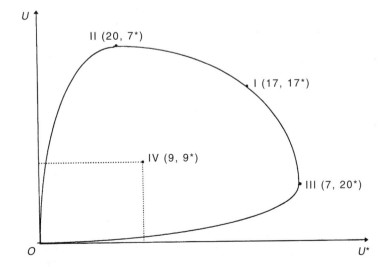

Figure 16.2 Trade benefits area

Table 16.1 The prisoners' dilemma: welfare levels with free trade and tariff policy

Domestic country		Foreign country			
		Free trade		*Tariff policy*	
Free trade	I	(17, 17*)	III	(7, 20*)	
Tariff policy	II	(20, 7*)	IV	(9, 9*)	

Table 16.2 Pay-off matrix of protectionism and liberalization of the EU and North America[a]

		North America is protectionist			North America liberalizes		
EU is protectionist	EU	−132			EU	42	
	Asia–Pacific	−18	World −214		Asia–Pacific	38	World 133
	North America	−64			North America	53	
EU liberalizes	EU	37			EU	211	
	Asia–Pacific	7	World 50		Asia–Pacific	63	World 397
	North America	7			North America	124	

[a] Change in gross domestic product in billion US dollars (in real values of 1988).

Source: Stoeckel *et al.* (1990).

as a whole and for the different regions was calculated before the conclusion of the Uruguay Round which took place from 1986 to 1994 (Table 16.2). The world would lose if North America or the European Union implemented a protectionist policy (US$214 billion a year). The protectionist region itself would also lose. If only one region liberalized trade unilaterally, not only would this region benefit from the policy as postulated in the free-trade-for-one theorem (Chapter 13) but the other regions would also benefit. Gains are considerably larger when both regions pursue free-trade policies. The gross world product could rise by about 5 percent.

Different concepts of trade policy

So far, we have outlined only two possible trade policies, i.e. free trade and tariff policy. However, in reality we can observe a great diversity of approaches to international trade

policies. In Figure 16.3, these approaches are ordered on a continuum that spans from free trade to autarky. In the situation of a centrally planned division of labor from above, as practiced in the former COMECON until the late 1980s, the allocation of production factors and goods was executed along political lines. Moreover, the economic area remained more or less closed to the outside world. Protectionism, import substitution and strategic trade policy intervene in different forms. Aggressive trade policy strives for the opening of foreign markets and is not afraid to use protectionist measures to achieve this goal. Regional integration approaches the free-trade situation.

16.2 Free-rider behavior, public goods and externalities

Strategic behavior in trade policy is possible when a country is large enough to acquire a

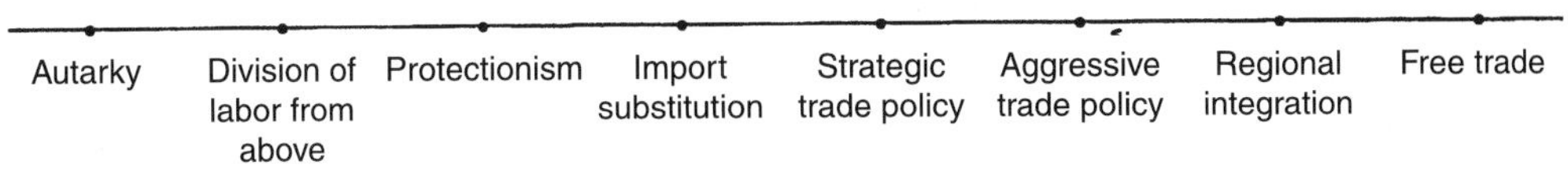

Autarky	Division of labor from above	Protectionism	Import substitution	Strategic trade policy	Aggressive trade policy	Regional integration	Free trade

Figure 16.3 Different concepts of trade policy

monopolistic position. Additionally, strategic behavior can occur when there are other interdependences apart from trade; for example, the case of global public goods, those goods that are consumed in equal amounts by all. An example of a worldwide public good is global environmental media. Public goods are strongly related to technological externalities. These interdependences do not represent interdependences via markets, but via 'technological' systems. Thus, in the case of global warming the global atmosphere is such a system. Technological external effects are interdependences in the output and input space of production and utility functions of economic agents.

If we consider strategic behavior towards public goods, then countries may behave as free-riders. They use a public good without contributing adequately to its production. A country could use the high quality of the global environmental good, but at the same time heavily burden this good through its emissions. In a similar way, a country could enjoy the stability of international trade rules, but break them at the same time, and in this way undermine this stability. Whenever global public goods are concerned, rules for the world economy have to be developed.

16.3 The world trade order as a system of rules

Nations autonomously pursue a trade policy in order to promote their welfare. Such an economic policy can get into conflict with a free international division of labor. Con-

sequently, a rule system is needed to reduce transactions costs, most prominently to diminish uncertainty arising from the behavior of market participants or originating from the non-cooperative conduct of sovereign nation states. The basic idea of such a world economic order for the trading system is to provide an institutional framework that allows the participating economies to capture the potential welfare gains from the international division of labor.

A system of rules for the behavior of governments takes the place of *ad hoc* negotiations between governments. A central element of such a rule-based institutional framework for the world economy is that sovereign states voluntarily commit themselves to respect rules which prevent strategic, i.e. non-cooperative, behavior by individual countries. The contractually binding commitments, made freely by governments, are ratified through domestic legislative processes. Strategic behavior of national governments would destroy the international order as a public good, representing a negative externality for the rule system. The rules must prevent such strategic behavior. Self-commitment by states limits national governments' choice of actions in the future and in this sense represents a 'negative catalogue', a restraint on government behaviour. It protects the international division of labor against national governments (Tumlir 1983). The self-commitment of states is also a shelter from the power of protectionist groups in the individual economies. Moreover, the rules must induce nation states to act cooperatively

277

in certain areas (Haggard and Simmons 1987) and to develop the system further. The World Trade Organization (WTO) is not only about respecting rules but also about making rules. An international order thus provides a skeleton of an international economic constitution for sovereign nation states in the area of international exchange.

Despite the game-theoretic character of international negotiations on rules for the division of labor and the related possibility of strategic behavior, countries have succeeded in concluding a multilateral agreement for trade for a variety of reasons. First of all, there is the historic experience that the way out of the prisoners' dilemma induces welfare gains to all, and that a tariff war is by no means advantageous for any single country. Second, an agreement on rules is not a solitary event, but only part of a sequence of agreements on rules. In such a repeated game with an infinite time horizon, gains are divided again and again. From this point of view, cooperation can pay off, because countries will care about their reputation. Finally, the uncertainty on future gains from new negotiations can lead to a less aggressive, more cooperative behavior.

16.4 The WTO: how it works

How the rules are set

The WTO practices decision making by consensus. It is attempted not to outvote members. If consensus cannot be reached, the 'one country–one vote' principle is applied. Unanimity is required whenever the core rules (most-favored-nation clause, decision procedure) are changed (Article X of the Agreement Establishing the World Trade Organization). A substantive change in the treaty must be approved by the national parliaments. Other changes of the multilateral treaty that affect the rights and obligations of member states require a two-thirds majority. The changes in the treaty bind only those who have agreed to the changes. Yet other changes that do not affect the rights and obligations of member states hold for all members when accepted by a three-quarters majority.

Rounds of liberalization

GATT succeeded in the course of eight liberalization rounds in significantly cutting tariffs and reducing other barriers (Table 16.4). In the years before the Geneva Round of 1947, the tariffs of the industrialized countries were as high as about 40 percent of the import value (on average). After the Uruguay Round, they were brought down to about 4.3 percent. The first five GATT rounds were concentrated on tariff cuts. The last rounds, all of them lasting several years, embraced new themes. The Kennedy Round, for example, developed an anti-dumping code, although this was not ratified by the US. In the Tokyo Round, a proposal for a new anti-dumping code saw daylight, but an improved code on subsidies was left aside. Finally, the Uruguay Round extended the agenda with new rules on services, intellectual property and property rights, and a dispute settlement procedure.

This tendency to liberalization was opposed by some developments that are rather protectionist. The United States obtained a waiver for agriculture in 1955; this then became very important for European agricultural policy. In 1961, the Short Term Arrangement on Cotton Textiles was introduced during the Dillon Round. It included the right for countries to impose unilateral import quotas. In 1988, the US introduced the 'Omnibus Trade and Competitiveness Act' (Super 301) and created the legal

A little bit of history

The first attempt to establish an International Trade Organization (ITO) in 1947 failed. As a compromise, the GATT (General Agreement on Tariffs and Trade) was founded in 1948 by 23 countries. In 1995 it was followed by the World Trade Organization (WTO). At the time when the GATT was established, after the protectionist experiences of the 1930s, the goal was to create a stable framework for international trade in order to provide the preconditions for growth and an increase of prosperity. Membership increased continuously over time (Table 16.3). As of November 2001, the WTO has 144 members, and 30 states are applying for membership, among them Russia. China and Taiwan have been members since the Doha meeting.

Table 16.3 GATT/WTO membership,[a] 1948–2001

1947	23
1960	38
1970	78
1980	85
1990	100
2001 (November)	144

[a] End of year.
Source for data: GATT, *International Trade* (several issues).

possibility of retaliating in the event of trade-restricting measures by other countries. The European Union developed its 'Trade Defence Instrument' in 1994 (see below).

Decision structure of the World Trade Organization

The WTO is an international organization based on a multilateral agreement. The central decision-making body, the ministerial conference, is responsible for general questions (Figure 16.4). The WTO Council, the General Director and the General Secretary are the operative bodies. They have a dispute settlement body and a trade policy review body at their disposal. The member countries of the WTO are legally bound by three multilateral agreements: GATT (General Agreement on Tariffs and Trade), GATS (General Agreement on Trade in Services) and TRIPs

(Trade-Related Aspects on Intellectual Property Rights). Three councils are assigned to the three multilateral agreements.

The WTO is different from GATT in several respects. First, member states have formally ratified the WTO agreements, whereas GATT was simply signed by governments. Second, GATT dealt only with trade in goods; in addition, the WTO covers services and intellectual property as well. Third, the dispute settlement mechanism is more effective. Note, however, that the GATT rules referring mainly to trade remain valid as an element of the WTO framework.

The basic principles

The world trade order is based on three main principles: the principle of liberalization, the principle of non-discrimination and the principle of reciprocity. More specific

Table 16.4 Liberalization rounds and protectionist counters

	Liberalization rounds	Average tariff reduction for industrial goods (in percent)		Protectionist arrangements
1947	Geneva Round	19		
1949	Annecy Round	2		
1950–1951	Torquay Round	3		
1955–1956	Geneva Round	2	1955	The US attains an exceptional arrangement for agriculture (waiver)
1960–1961	Dillon Round, Geneva Round (all five rounds on tariff cuts)	7	1961	Quantitative restrictions on trade in textiles
1963–1967	Kennedy Round, Geneva Round (anti-dumping code)	35		
1973–1979	Tokyo Round (new anti-dumping code, subsidy code)	34		
1986–1994	Uruguay Round (rules on services and intellectual property, dispute settlement)	40	1984	New trade policy instrument of the EU
			1994	Trade defence instrument
			1998	Omnibus Trade and Competitiveness Act of the US. Retaliation instrument
2000	Seattle Round failed			
2001	Doha Round started			

Source: GATT/WTO, annual reports.

principles support and specify those main principles.

Liberalization

The simple idea of GATT/WTO is to reduce trade barriers. This principle is a general point of reference. Nations have to abstain from raising existing tariffs or from levying new ones. In addition, quantitative restrictions or non-tariff barriers are forbidden. The eight liberalization rounds since the foun-dation of GATT in 1948 are proof that the concept of liberalization works.

Non-discrimination

Trade policy measures should not differenti-ate between countries, countries should be treated equally. In particular, there must be no discrimination between domestic and for-eign products. This principle can be explained very well with Thailand's cigarettes case, decided by GATT in 1990. Thailand had

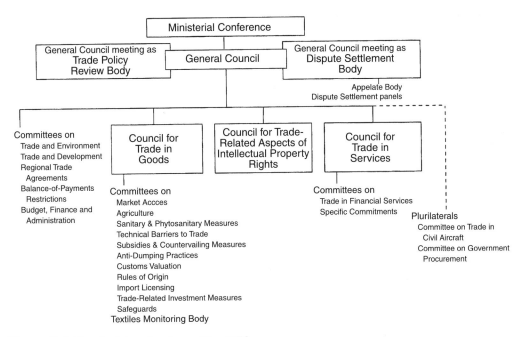

Figure 16.4 The decision structure of the WTO

raised a tariff on imported cigarettes, referring to health policy reasons, but without taxing domestically manufactured cigarettes. In the Thailand cigarettes case, it was ruled that it is consistent with the world trade order for a country to take measures for health reasons (Article XX), but it must not make a difference between domestic and foreign products and it should not discriminate against imports.

Most-favored nation

The most-favored-nation principle is an expression of the non-discrimination principle (favor one, favor all). The obligation towards a general, positive and unconditional most-favored treatment, which is included in Article I of the GATT treaty, implies that a tariff reduction that is granted to one country has to be granted to all countries. In this way bilateral tariff reductions are multilateralized.

While the non-discrimination principle is a negative mechanism banning discriminating behavior, the most-favored-nation principle is a positive mechanism strengthening free trade.

Reciprocity

The principle of reciprocity requires that concessions have to be granted mutually. This means that a tariff cut in one country has to correspond to an equivalent cut in another country. This is practiced by a bilateral demand–supply system. For example, a country will offer a concession x when another country has offered a concession y. However, a country can only ask for a concession for a specific product if it is in the position of the principal supplier, which means that it provides the main part of the imports of the partner country (principal supplier rule).

Bound tariffs

When countries agree on reduced tariffs, they bind their commitments. Changing the bindings requires negotiating with the trading partners and compensating them for loss of trade. Thus, binding creates opportunity costs of non-compliance.

The concept of reciprocity of concessions is based on the mercantilist idea, according to which the reduction of trade barriers is a sacrifice. This contradicts the theory of the international division of labor, according to which a country can raise its welfare by unilaterally reducing its tariffs. The notion of concession stems from the public opinion on international trade. It can possibly make the political realization of tariff cuts much easier.

Single undertaking

The single-undertaking nature of the WTO reflects the concept of packaging the benefits arising in different areas of the international division of labor. In the past, plurilateral agreements, introduced in the Tokyo Round, allowed a subset of GATT members to sign contracts for specific areas; for instance, the Agreement on Civil Aircraft and the Agreement on Government Procurement. Such a procedure, though easing a contract among at least some GATT members, represents an *à la carte* approach and entails the risk of fragmentation of the multilateral trading system. In principle, it can be expected that the single-undertaking nature of WTO will strengthen the rule system because it forces countries to swallow less favorable rules in one area if they are compensated by rules allowing higher benefits in other areas. The approach of packaging is also helpful in focusing bargaining when a liberalization round is being concluded. However, the 'offsetting' between the

advantages of suborders should not be carried too far. If in the course of time the advantages of countries shift asymmetrically in the individual suborders, a fragile structure of acceptance could collapse like a house of cards. To avoid domino effects, it makes sense that the suborders should basically legitimize themselves on their own and not be conditionally accepted.

Further rules of the WTO

Further rules relate to other aspects of trade barriers such as waivers, anti-dumping and subsidies. Other aspects refer to national regulation. The general aim is to restrain trade-restricting or trade-distorting activities of nations by a set of rules.

Voluntary export restraints

All voluntary export restraints that were used to circumvent tariff liberalization should be eliminated by the year 2000. No new forms of quantitative restrictions should be allowed.

Waivers

Within the framework of the international trade order there are a number of exceptions. A waiver from the non-discrimination principle and from the most-favored-nation clause holds for regional integrations according to Article XXIV, although they discriminate against third countries. It is assumed that regional integrations inducing free trade within a spatially limited area will eventually lead to global free trade. This exception relates to customs unions, free-trade areas and preference zones.

Another waiver is valid for agricultural products: market access may be restricted by

The most important articles of the WTO

The most important stipulations are:

Preamble: 'Recognizing that their relations in the field of trade and economic endeavour should be conducted with a view to raising standards of living, ensuring full employment and a large and steadily growing volume of real income and effective demand, developing the full use of the resources of the world and expanding the production and exchange of goods, . . .'

'Being desirous of contributing to these objectives by entering into reciprocal and mutually advantageous arrangements directed to the substantial reduction of tariffs and other barriers to trade and to the elimination of discriminatory treatment in international commerce, . . .'

Article I: '. . . any advantage, favour, privilege or immunity granted . . . to any product originating in or destined for any other country shall be accorded immediately and unconditionally to the like product originating in or destined for the territories of all other contracting parties . . .'

Article III: '. . . internal taxes and other internal charges, and laws, regulations and require-ments affecting the internal sale, . . . should not be applied to imported or domestic products so as to afford protection to domestic production . . .'

Article VI: '. . . dumping, by which products of one country are introduced into the com-merce of another country at less than the normal value of the products, is to be condemned . . .'

Article XI: 'No prohibitions or restrictions other than duties, taxes or other charges, whether made effective through quotas, import or export licences or other measures, shall be instituted or maintained . . .'

Article XII: 'Notwithstanding . . . Article XI, any contracting party, in order to safeguard its external financial position and its balance of payments, may restrict the quantity or value of merchandise permitted . . .'

Article XIII: 'No prohibition or restriction shall be applied . . . on the importation of any product . . . or on the exportation of any product . . . , unless the importation of the like product of all third countries or the exportation of the like product to all third countries is similarly prohibited or restricted . . .'

Article XX: '. . . nothing in this Agreement shall be construed to prevent the adoption or enforcement by any contracting party of measures: . . . necessary to protect human, animal or plant life or health; . . .'

Article XXIV: '. . . the provisions of this Agreement shall not prevent . . . the formation of a customs union or of a free-trade area . . .'.

import regulations and exports can be strengthened by subsidies. In the Uruguay Round variable levies and quantitative import restrictions were partly replaced by tariffs. This tariffication of quantitative restraints will allow the reduction of tariffs by a flat rate later on. Agricultural tariffs have been reduced by 38 percent in industrial countries and by 24 percent in developing countries.

New negotiations have to be launched in this area.

The third waiver is the world textile agree-ment (Multi Fiber Agreement). Bilateral agreements between individual countries (including tariffs, quantitative restrictions and voluntary export restraints) and trade restraints have been allowed internationally. Until the year 2005, the new world textile agreement shall be integrated into the WTO rules.

Anti-dumping and countervailing duty measures

Though defensible in a framework of theoretical models, these instruments can easily develop into a severe impediment for trade (administered protection). They are defined by national legislation and can be captured by national interest groups. They represent a way around bound tariffs and (now) forbidden quantitative restraints. Even if they are not actually applied, the threat of using them entails uncertainty and may already lead to the 'appropriate' export behavior. In economic categories, contingent protection represents effective protection. This 'administered protection' (Krueger 1998, p. 8) seems to have become more important as a protectionist device of US trade policy. The task for the WTO will be to contain the protectionist impact of this approach. Standards have to be defined that must be respected by national anti-dumping laws.

Country-of-origin versus country-of-destination

When product norms are applied, we distinguish between country-of-origin rules and country-of-destination rules. The country-of-origin principle accepts the rule of the country of origin whereas the country-of-destination principle leaves it to the importing country to set the domestic standard as the yardstick for its imports. The result would be a potpourri of diverging standards representing barriers to trade. Moreover, such regulations can easily be captured by interest groups. The attempt of GATT has been – and

the aim of the WTO must be – to push back the role of the country-of-destination principle. Which regulations are set for the production of goods should be left to the discretion of the country of origin. The different regulations of national countries of origin should rather have equal standing competing with each other. A weakening of the country-of-origin principle and a strengthening of the country-of-destination principle will inevitably harm the multilateral order. The goal of the world trade order is therefore that countries mutually accept the regulations of the country of origin for product quality and production processes in order to minimize transaction costs. Thus, competition between rules can thrive. Only in precisely demarcated cases, for example, public health protection, should the country of destination and its standards take precedence over the norms of the country of origin. But even then the measures adopted should involve neither discrimination nor protection.

National treatment

For services, the principle of national treatment is applied. Foreign suppliers have to be treated in the same way as domestic suppliers. This principle is much weaker than the principles applied in trade of products. For services, the country-of-origin principle has not been acceptable so far. It has found acceptance within the European Union, but not worldwide.

Dispute settlement

The member countries of the WTO have voluntarily agreed to a dispute-settlement system. If a country violates the rules, the WTO is allowed to demand a change in the trade policy decisions and to impose sanctions.

Relative to GATT, the dispute-settlement procedure has been strengthened. Whereas the ruling of a Dispute Panel can be appealed before the Appellate Body, the decision of the Appellate Body is binding unless all parties are against its adoption. When the Dispute Settlement Body has adopted the panel or the appellate report, the losing party must either propose a suitable implementation of the report's recommendations or negotiate compensation payment with the complaining party. If there is no agreement on compensation or if the losing party does not implement the proposed changes, the Dispute Settlement Body can authorize the other party to impose retaliatory measures such as counter-tariffs. The retaliation can occur in the same sector, in other sectors or even in other agreements.

The dispute settlement mechanism seems to have found acceptance. Since the formation of the dispute-settlement mechanism, WTO members have requested consultation 234 times in 180 distinct matters (if India, Malaysia, Pakistan and Thailand file a complaint about the import prohibition of shrimp products by the United States, this is counted as four requests and one distinct matter). Sixty-three of these consultation requests in 56 distinct matters were made by developing countries.

Thus, both developed and developing countries rely on the WTO settlement procedure. Developing countries file a rising share of cases. The United States and the European Union are the most frequent complainants to the WTO, often filing complaints against each other. Therefore, the WTO plays an important role in resolving conflicts in the transatlantic relationship. By and large, the dispute-settlement system has proved to be a successful device to address trade conflicts and enforce the rights and obligations of the WTO members. Nevertheless, some conflicts in which panel or appellate reports have been adopted by the Dispute Settlement Body (which would have required some kind of action to be taken by the respondent WTO member) have not been resolved. Eight such cases have been filed with the Dispute Settlement Body, since the complainant has not agreed with the actions taken by the respondent. The conflict between the United States and the EU about the EU import system for bananas is one of these cases. In the 'banana case', retaliation was requested by the United States. The dispute-settlement body authorized the United States to suspend tariff concessions on products of a value of US$191.2 million. The use of retaliation has been authorized by the Dispute Settlement Body in four instances.

Major trade conflicts in the world are: the closed Japanese internal market, anti-dumping measures of the EU and the US (for instance in steel) as an impediment for the developing countries (and for exporters in industrial countries as well) and agricultural protection. In the relationship between the United States and Europe the major areas of conflict are subsidization of airplane production, the US-Tax Treatment for Foreign Sales Corporation as a hidden subsidy for exports, hormone beef and EU import restrictions for bananas.

Trade policy review mechanism

The trade policy review mechanism scrutinizes the trade policy of each member state on a regular basis. The report on the four major trading partners (US, EU, Japan and Canada) are provided more frequently. This review is expected to exercise discipline on the trade policy of member states.

16.5   New areas for the world trade order

There are a number of new areas in the international division of labor for which rules have to be developed.

Strategic trade policy and subsidies

When tariffs and quantitative restraints eventually lose importance in the future, governments may be tempted to use subsidies in order to lower their producers' production costs, thus establishing an artificial price advantage and distorting the international division of labor. A conceivable response to this would simply be to ignore domestic subsidies, since a subsidizing country does not employ its resources optimally, and thereby accepts a loss of its own efficiency and welfare. This is especially revelant for old industries like the coal industry. One cannot, however, be too complacent about domestic subsidies. Subsidies by one country take market shares away from the corresponding sectors of other countries and lead to political demands for retaliation. Thus their effect resembles those of protectionist measures. Moreover, strategic trade theory could, in the future, become more appealing to practical politics and provide a rationale for subsidizing 'new' sectors, albeit on the basis of rather restrictive (and naive) models. We may see more of this interventionist approach in some European countries as a reaction to globalization. This may lead to political demands for retaliation. Thus, the effect of subsidies may be as detrimental to international trade as traditional protectionist measures. They may also be part of an aggressive bilateralism.

According to the WTO rules, trade-distorting subsidies for export goods and import substitutes are forbidden and product-and industry-specific subsidies are inadmissible if they harm the trade opportunities of other members. Even so, it is difficult to demarcate subsidy practices from other admissible policies such as research assistance and aid in adapting to new environmental technologies. It is likewise difficult to penalize and stop violations in the framework of monitoring processes. Furthermore, important sectors such as agriculture and the aviation industry either explicitly or implicitly still enjoy special treatment. Therefore, the existing subsidy code, of which the core is present in the world trade order, must be further developed in order to prevent subsidy competition between governments. How difficult it is to monitor subsidies is shown by the European Union's aid supervision.

Free market access and national regulation

The trade order is essentially oriented to denying governments (or integrated regions) tariff and non-tariff instruments with which the governments could directly intervene in trade flows at their borders. Such instruments have been outlawed through a negative catalogue. However, this still does not guarantee that there will be free access to markets. If we want to ensure free-market access, it will be necessary that national regulations do not limit access for goods and firms.

Therefore, multinational barriers, owing to national legislative and informal practices that effectively limit access to markets, should be dismantled. These barriers include policy measures in the broadest sense, such as licencing procedures for economic activities, for facilities and for products, technical standards, arrangements for public procurement and interlocking ties between firms (as with *keiretsu* in Japan) on the same or different levels of the vertical production structure, whereby outsiders are excluded (Ostry 1995). By accepting the country-of-origin principle instead of the country-of-destination principle, market access is made easier.

Open services markets

Services comprise an extensive and diverse spectrum. They include cross-border supply, consumption of a service abroad, commercial presence and presence of natural persons. The diversity of services becomes apparent by the WTO classification list with seven main categories and 62 subcategories (see Chapter 1). A rule system for the international exchange of services should hold for the whole variety of services. Since the phenomena to which rules are to be applied are so divergent, it is difficult to establish an all-encompassing international rule system. A major distinction is between border-crossing and local services analogous to that between tradable and non-tradable goods. Within these categories, another distinction becomes relevant, namely between 'person-dis-embodied' and 'person-embodied' services (Bhagwati 1984; Klodt *et al.* 1994). Disembodied services are not 'embodied' in persons; for example, detail engineering using computer-supported programs, the development of software and accounting. For the international trade order, disembodied cross-border services are not very different from material goods. Just as commodities are carried by the transport system, disembodied services cross national borders by means of communication media. As a consequence, markets must be open for them just as they must be open for commodities. Border-crossing disembodied services should be treated like commodities.

National treatment in the case of person-embodied services

In the case of person-embodied services (consumption abroad, commercial presence, presence of natural persons), non-discrimination can be obtained through national treatment, i.e. equal treatment for foreigners and one's own nationals.

The General Agreement on Trade and Services (GATS) establishes for the first time a framework for the notification of existing rules, but it has a long way to go before a rule system for all forms of international services with free-market access is fully developed (Snape 1998). Markets are yet to be opened in many respects: barriers discriminating against foreigners or non-discriminatory barriers erected by competition policy will have to be torn down, the product coverage must be extended. So far, these are exemptions to the most-favored-nation treatment. The conditionality of the most-favored-nation clause prevalent in services must be extended to an unconditional use. National treatment as a central principle applies only to services where a country has made a specific commitment; exemptions are allowed. Moreover, the present approach is to find agreements for specific services. For instance, in financial services a multilateral agreement was reached in December 1997 with 70 WTO members; other sector agreements relate to telecommunications and information technology. This sector-by-sector approach raises the risk that sector-specific aspects will dominate. It has the disadvantage that it does not sufficiently harness the export interests of the economy as a whole in order to dismantle barriers of trade (Krueger 1998).

International competition policy

Markets should not be closed through the market power of firms. Globalization makes markets more contestable, and in this sense free trade is the best competition policy. All measures that improve market access support competition policy. However, firms may try to create monopolistic positions in the global markets, if possible, and to exploit them by setting prices to the disadvantage of buyers.

In the past, competition policy was a national affair (and in the European Union it is an EU matter). In the new global environment, national competition policies face a new challenge. National competition policy should not be oriented towards the advantage of domestic firms or home-based multinationals and should not permit firms to build up or exploit monopolistic positions internationally. Competition policy should also oppose business practices intended to reduce global competition. It should prevent the exploitation of market power, and help to improve the contestability of the world product markets.

Therefore, it is necessary to change the orientation of national competition policies. Interactions between competition policies of different countries have to be taken into consideration. For instance, mergers in one country (Boeing and McDonnell-Douglas) have an impact on the market structure elsewhere (Airbus in Europe). Therefore, the competition policy of different authorities is involved and mergers need the agreement of different authorities (like the EU and the US). An example is the intended merger of General Electric and Honeywell (in 2001) that was approved by the US antitrust authority but stopped by the competition policy of the EU.

Another issue is the misuse of market power. Thus, the question arises whether a country harmed by another country's competition and antitrust policy should have the right to obtain changes in the objectionable policy or not. An institutional consultation and sanctioning mechanism must be created (Graham 1995). Under consideration are the effects doctrine with an international right to extra-territorial legal application (Immenga 1995), treaty agreements – including already existing bilateral treaties between the US and Europe – on the concession of mutual competencies (Ehlermann 1995), on the harmonization of international competition law (hard law) on the basis of national regulations (Fikentscher and Immenga 1995), and on the mutual recognition of institutional rules, that is a *Cassis-de-Dijon* approach with an international interpretation (Nicolaides 1994). An alternative proposal is to give parties injured by anti-competitive practices or competition policies a right to take their case to an international court or an international competition authority empowered to enforce competition rules (Scherer 1994).

Presently, it is not foreseeable that an international institutional framework for competition policy will be established that can effectively restrict the misuse of monopolistic market positions and discourage competition-limiting mergers. Thus, at present we can only expect to establish a few minimal competition policy rules for countries or regional integrations (such as the European Union), either in the framework of the World Trade Organization (Immenga 1995), in the OECD or in multilateral agreements, as between the EU and the US. We also have to consider the option that, initially, only some of the rules would be agreed upon by the most important OECD countries, because there are fundamental differences in their legal systems, as between Anglo-Saxon and Continental European law.

Aggressive trade policy versus the multilateral order

When important trading nations or regions of the world pursue an aggressive trade policy, they endanger the multilateral system. The US and the EU have built up an arsenal of new trade-political instruments, which they can use to open markets or as a retaliatory measure, without considering the mechanisms of the world trade order. The US, for instance, can react immediately on trade-restricting measures of other countries by imposing trade-restricting measures of its own with its powerful instrument 'Super 301'. Trade-barrier reductions already agreed on can be deleted, import restrictions can be imposed and bilateral export-restriction agreements can be pursued. Above all, trade policy restraints are supposed to serve as a lever for opening markets. With the 'Trade Defence Instrument' the European Union has created a similar apparatus, to counter the trade policy of other countries.

By creating these trade policy weapons, the two trading blocs, in the sense of result-oriented bilaterally conceived policies (Dornbusch 1990), have exempted themselves from the rules of the multilateral world trade order; they violate the most-favored-nation principle. The risk exists that bilateral measures will escalate. The two large players are forcing other countries to make concessions, and they threaten unilaterally by denying market access in the US and the EU. An aggressive trade policy of one country (unilateralism) and the reaction of other countries, or even the agreement of two countries at the cost of a third country (bilateralism) lead to a destabilization of the multilateral order. Therefore, unilateralism and bilateralism have to be limited. The trade policy instruments of such an aggressive market-opening policy have to be integrated in the rules of the world trade order. An outcome-oriented, bilaterally conceived aggressive trade policy for opening markets must not replace a rule-based multilateral order.

16.6 Rules for factor movements and locational competition

Besides the exchange of goods and services, factor mobility is a further important form of interdependence between economies. Countries compete for mobile technological knowledge, for mobile capital and for mobile qualified labor. This leads to locational competition (Chapter 14). The policy instruments governments can use in order to attract these mobile factors are institutional arrangements, taxes and infrastructure in the widest sense, including the educational and the university systems.

Property rights for mobile technological knowledge

When countries compete for mobile technological knowledge, property rights become important. These relate to all sorts of intellectual property, copyright and associated rights, trademarks, industrial design, patents, the layout designs of integrated circuits and geographical indications (like appellations of origin). Issues to be solved (and partly included in the Agreement on Trade-Related Aspects of Intellectual Property Rights (TRIPs)) are minimum standards of protection to be provided by the individual countries, enforcement of intellectual property rights and dispute settlements.

A global system of rules for new technology has to solve problems that are similar to those of structuring a national patent system. On the one hand, user rights to new technological knowledge must be secure, since otherwise there will be insufficient incentives to search for and adopt new technological knowledge. This means that property rights to new knowledge must be respected throughout the world. On the other hand, this property protection must not create permanently exclusive positions and make markets uncontestable. Rather, the diffusion of new knowledge must be possible after a certain passage of time. Accordingly, time limits should be set on the protective effect of user rights. The optimal duration of property rights depends among other things on product life-cycles and the time-frame of research and development phases; this can differ greatly from product to product. Since countries may have an interest in protecting their firms' technological knowledge for as long as possible (although this reduces the incentives for their own technological dynamics), the solution cannot consist simply in mutually recognizing national patent laws. Rather, it may be desirable to set time limits on the validity of national patents. With respect to the other types of property right such as trademarks and geographical indications there is no necessity to let protection run out.

National technology policy should be dealt with in the same way as national subsidies. Thus, the international subsidy code must set limits for industry-specific research subsidies. In contrast, there is no need for controlling the improvement of the general conditions for research and development, for example, when countries generally introduce more favorable tax conditions for research and development; innovation, investment and entrepreneurial activity, as well as organize basic research and further technology transfer so that they can be internationally competitive.

An investment code for capital mobility

It is in the best interest of each country to keep capital at home and to attract more capital from outside. Each country should therefore structure its institutional framework accordingly, i.e. provide for the security of property rights, avoid uncertainty about corporate taxes, develop a tax system and a general economic framework that make the country less risky and more attractive for foreign direct investments.

Even if it is the host country's responsibility to enhance its own attractiveness, it may be helpful to have an investment code in order to minimize disruptions. For instance, foreign direct investments should be protected against expropriation. Capital should be allowed to be repatriated and profits of capital invested should be allowed to be sent to the country of the capital owners. Multilateral agreements can make the direct investments of the sending country more secure. They can make a country appear less risky for direct investments. Moreover, uncertainty for investment may be a cause for uncertainty in trade. Consequently, an investment code is required which surpasses the Trade-Related Investment Measures (TRIMs). It is an open question whether a two-speed approach should be recommended for an investment code, with the OECD countries going ahead and the WTO following, or whether an investment code, has better chances to be accepted if it is initiated by the WTO (Krueger 1998, p. 408). Eventually, an investment code should be administered by the WTO.

Another important condition for an efficient international division of labor is that savings should not be prevented from seeking better opportunities abroad. Otherwise countries would force their savers to invest solely at home.

The right of exit for the migration of people

The right of individuals to leave a country, the exit option, can be interpreted as an important element of a liberal order. Every individual should have the right to choose to leave given living conditions that he or she finds unacceptable. This principle should hold even if the exit option conflicts with the claim that citizens of a state must fulfill their tax duties when they take their residence abroad. The freedom of the individual should be given priority to the tax claims of the state. A credible right to exit is a limit on the actions of the government and implicitly controls the government.

The exit option does not, however, imply the entry option, i.e. the right to migrate *into* a country. States define their identity by setting their immigration policy. This creates difficult ethical questions that can be more easily solved if potential countries of immigration – beyond the duty to accept the politically persecuted – are sufficiently open and if regional integrations such as the European Union, although only spatially limited from an international economic perspective, guarantee the freedom of movement within their territory.

For many reasons labor migration should be replaced by the movement of goods and capital mobility. The strengthening of an international economic order for the international exchange of goods and the openness of markets reduces the necessity of migration.

16.7 Social standards

Recently, there have been increased calls to equalize social norms worldwide (see Chapter 13), and this is supposed to be accomplished through trade policy measures. Countries that do not employ these standards are supposed to be denied access to markets elsewhere.

Except for some minimum standards as agreed upon by the members of the International Labor Organization (ILO), this is a misleading idea. By harmonizing social standards the developing countries would be negatively affected. Because of their lower labor productivity these countries are unable to pay the same wages that industrialized countries pay. For similar reasons, they cannot be expected to adopt the industrialized countries' labor standards or social norms because these standards increase the cost of production in the same way as higher wages do. The industrialized countries have no ethical right to ask the developing countries to implement the social norms of the industrialized countries. Therefore, harmonizing social norms cannot be a promising strategy of the rich countries against globalization. Also in this domain, the country-of-destination principle cannot be practiced in the world trade order. Which regulations are set for the production of goods should consequently be left to the discretion of the country of origin. Besides, trade policy is unsuitable as a means of harmonization. Social norms are not a public good.

16.8 The environment and the world trade order

In the past, the international frameworks for environmental issues and for the world trade order have been developed side by side. In the future, it will become increasingly important to consider more strongly the consistency of these frameworks.

National environmental policy and international rules

If the environment is an immobile national endowment factor, the different environmental scarcities of countries can be expressed by different prices of environmental services. This is relevant when the absorptive and regenerative capacities of national environments vary, when a high population density makes it more difficult to spatially separate residential and recreational areas from environmentally degrading transport and production activities and when the preferences of countries for environmental quality differ. Signaling different environmental scarcities by different prices does not require an international rule system but the pricing can be left to national policies. A market economy approach to environmental policy that taxes emissions or establishes prices for environmental services through licencing is consistent with an institutional framework for the international division of labor. The more successful the integration of the environment in the economic regulations of individual countries, and the more successful welfare can be defined by also taking into consideration nature and the environment, the better environmental policy can be integrated into the international trade order.

Protecting health and conserving natural resources

If prices for national environmental use are not (or cannot be) applied and other measures such as administrative approaches, emission norms or product standards are employed by countries in order to protect their citizens' health and life and to conserve natural resources (Article XX of the GATT treaty), those measures must be non-discriminatory. Non-discrimination requires that in the case of market entry restrictions, regulations through production permits, facility permits and product norms must not give preference to domestic producers and domestic goods. Thus it should not be permissible, for example, with the aim of reducing health hazards, as in the Thailand cigarettes case (1990), to restrict the import of goods or to tax them unless the same measures are simultaneously applied to similar domestic goods.

The similarity of products should be defined from the demand side, for example in terms of possible harmful effects, and not from the production side. As in the Mexican–American tuna fish case (1991), the principle of similarity should not be applied to the production methods (in the tuna case, methods of fishing are used that do not sufficiently protect dolphins). This means that the country-of-origin principle should apply. Non-discrimination should also satisfy the condition that policy instruments should accord to the proportionality principle. Measures must accordingly be necessary in the sense that otherwise environmental policy aims or the protection of natural resources could not be achieved. As a rule, these aims are, however, achieved in a better way through specific environmental policy measures rather than through trade policy.

The territorial principle as a restraint for national measures

Trade policy must not be employed to force national preferences on other countries. Any country's environmental policy should not apply to external effects outside its own territorial area. Externalities elsewhere would be emotional externalities. Since countries have different amounts of environmental resources and also different environmental preferences, those with stronger environmental preferences should not be entitled to impose their environmental preferences on other countries by means of trade-restricting measures (Siebert 1996). The thesis that the country-of-origin principle should be fundamentally recognized for national environments can be generalized. If harmful effects appear outside a country's territorial area, and if they do not affect a country's territory, i.e. if there are no cross-border externalities, countries should not have the right to use trade policy to influence the production methods of a country of origin. Also, the protective clauses for health, life and exhaustible resources found in Article XX should in the case of national environmental goods be applied only within a country's own territorial area. Thus countries should not have the right to employ unilateral measures to protect the environment in other countries. A different matter, however, is if trans-frontier pollution occurs. Then, a Coasian solution has to be found.

Global environmental goods

Global environmental goods, i.e. public goods with a worldwide spatial dimension, require an agreement of all countries as to what amount and what quality of these public goods should be supplied. It is not sufficient to decide about which emissions should be reduced; it is also necessary to decide about the appropriate distribution of costs of emission reduction among individual countries (see Chapter 15). It is difficult to reach an international consensus, because countries have different preferences and because they have different per capita incomes and thus have different willingness to pay. In addition, the cost functions for disposal differ from country to country.

Moreover, a nation can behave as a free-rider. Thus, implementing the polluter-pays principle for global goods runs into difficulties. To what extent a stable international environmental framework with voluntary commitments by states can be created under these conditions using compensatory payments is a complex issue and has been the subject of numerous studies (Siebert 1998b).

Consistency between the international environmental order and the international trade order

Environmental policy aims at protecting the natural living conditions, i.e. it deals with scarcity. An institutional order for the international division of labor attempts to make it possible to increase the prosperity of all countries through exchange, i.e. it also deals with scarcity. Both orders attempt to do away with distortions and they represent institutional frameworks dealing with allocation. Since environmental policy and international trade intersect at many points, the rules of the two frameworks should not come into conflict. In principle, the aims are not contradictory, since scarcity must be defined by taking the natural living conditions into account. If we start from the premise that the valuation of the goods on which affluence is based as well as the valuation of environmental quality must depend on national preference, a contradiction between the regimes can be avoided. The more successfully the environment as a scarce good is integrated into the economic order of individual countries and the more affluence is defined by taking into account nature and the environment, the sooner congruence of targets will be achieved between the two orders.

Compared to the administrative approach using regulations, the market economy approach to environmental policy provides more consistency between the two sets of rules. The sooner the polluter-pays principle is accepted as a guideline by all countries, the easier it will be to achieve consistency of the two orders in the case of global environmental concerns. This clearly holds for national environmental goods. For global goods, implementing the polluter-pays principle has to overcome the difficulties mentioned above like the differences in preferences, in willingness-to-pay and free-rider behavior. What would be needed is a consensus on the conditions under which the polluter-pays principle can be applied to global goods; this is equivalent to a consensus regarding the conditions under which compensations must be used.

Inconsistency between the two-rules system should be prevented. The following aspects can help to minimize conflicts:

- The group of countries signing international environmental agreements should not be too divergent from those who are members of the WTO.
- Even if the international environmental order and the international trade order have consistent aims in principle, the rules of the two orders should not be contingent upon each other. Making the rules mutually conditional would cause considerable uncertainty, not only in the international division of labor, but also in the production of environmental goods. Institutional orders should not be uncertain.
- It appears ill-advised to create a temporary waiver for the environment as an exception to the world trade order. One reason is that the previously created exemptions for the agricultural and textile sectors have become resistant to change and have led to a permanent infringement of the most-

favored-nation principle. If an exceptional regulation is questionable, even in the case of very specific and internationally declining sectors like agriculture, then a similar procedure appears still less desirable for an area like the environment that is pervasive in all sectors of the economy and that will become increasingly important in the future.

- The sets of instruments of the two orders should be kept separate. Trade policy instruments should not be employed for environmental policy purposes. Countries should not have the right to apply their environmental policy outside their own territory. Non-discrimination and the priority of the country-of-origin principle over the country-of-destination principle should be guiding principles.
- A similar mechanism to the WTO dispute settlement mechanism should be developed for the environmental domain.
- In the case of global environmental goods a consensus should be developed regarding the conditions under which the polluter-pays principle or compensations should be applied.

16.9 Stabilizing and strengthening the WTO

The WTO is a multilateral agreement of sovereign states. It is essential that sovereign states abide by the rules to which they have agreed and do not renege. A set of mechanisms stabilizes and strengthens the WTO.

Sanctions

An important mechanism in international contracts is sanctions which can be taken if rules are violated. The WTO dispute settlement procedure serves this purpose.

Positive mechanisms

Besides sanctions in dispute settlement, the world trading order contains mechanisms that attempt to strengthen the institutional arrangement and help to expand it. One such mechanism is the most-favored-nation clause which extends reductions of trade barriers to third parties and thus multilateralizes liberalizations. Another mechanism is reciprocity of concessions requiring that the tariff reduction of one country must be answered by other countries (even though the concept of reciprocity has its roots in a mercantilistic philosophy). Yet another mechanism is to bind tariffs so that the results of liberalization rounds are 'chiseled in stone' and countries cannot easily walk away from agreements that have been reached. A country that wants to raise the bound tariff has to negotiate with the countries most concerned. It has to compensate for the trading partners' loss of trade.

Strengthening support from private groups

In order to restrain national interest groups, the World Trade Organization needs the support of the private sector including the NGOs. In the past, export interests were harnessed against protectionist groups. Today, NGOs challenge the basis of the international division of labor by not accepting its mutual benefits for all countries. In order to attract the support of the private sector, it should be made clear what advantages households and enterprises can obtain from the international framework. New rules should be tailored such that they get the support of the private sector. Thus, strengthened intellectual property rights and improved exchange conditions for services can be attractive for the private sector.

The prospect of an increase in future benefits

An essential condition for an international economic order is that the institutional framework should be acceptable to all countries, that all countries can expect to gain from it. For each country the advantages of membership must exceed the advantages of non-membership. It is crucial that benefits are expected in the future. It pays to stick to the rules, because there will be a reward in the future. The individual country's cost–benefit calculations should not shift asymmetrically over time. The net advantage for each country should increase and in no case worsen. If this condition is not fulfilled, there will be an incentive not to honor the treaty, but instead to withdraw from it.

From an intertemporal perspective, the global rule system is a relational contract (MacNeil 1978), in which countries interact along a time axis and in which a strategic gain from non-cooperative behavior today must be confronted with the opportunity costs of retaliation in future periods. Honoring a rule system or violating it must be interpreted as a repeated game in which an agent accumulates or destroys reputation and in which the preparedness of the other agents to cooperate tomorrow is affected by the agent's behavior today. These intertemporal linkages help to prevent reneging on the contract and to give stability to the system.

Preventing institutional domino effects

An economic order may be conceived as existing of several suborders (Eucken 1940). The interdependence of suborders raises other issues. One is that the suborders may contradict each other. Clearly, they must be mutually consistent. One suborder must not lead to behavior on the part of economic agents which contradicts and undermines some other suborder. As a consequence, suborders must have the same or similar objectives or philosophies. An important example of this consistency issue is the relation between the world trade order and the world environmental order (see above). In any case, the interdependence of suborders must be taken into consideration when an overall rule system is developed.

Another issue is to what extent the withdrawal of benefits from one suborder can be used as a threat or sanction to abide by the rules of the other suborder. In a game-theoretic approach, threatening with the withdrawal of benefits from one rule system may be an effective inducement to join (and to respect) another rule system. However, this approach makes one suborder contingent on another suborder. If one institutional system falls, the other falls too. This raises the risk that the overall rule system is endangered. Therefore, the advantage of threatening with the withdrawal of benefits of one suborder must be weighed against the risk of destroying the overall rule system. If the WTO is understood as a single undertaking, suborders cannot be singled out for strategic purposes.

A possible approach to this question is to explicitly distinguish between two different stages, namely the creation of an institutional arrangement and the implementation of the rule system associated with it. In establishing a new institutional framework, withholding benefits to non-members from another subsystem is a strong sanction that is positive for establishing the new order. Once an institutional arrangement is established, however, the validity of one suborder should – as a principle – not be contingent on the functioning of some other suborder in order to prevent institutional domino effects. This means

that the instrumental levels should be clearly separated. As a rule, economic policy instruments available to an international organization should be limited to specific suborders. Trade policy instruments should not be employed for environmental policy purposes. The instrumental level should thus be subdivided into different modules which should be clearly demarcated.

Multilateralizing regional integrations

In order to prevent regionalism from becoming inward looking or degenerating into an aggressive bilateralism (Chapter 9), regional integrations should be multilateralized. An important precondition for multilateralizing regional integrations is to keep regional integrations open to new members. A strong mechanism for this is for members of integrated regions to grant concessions to third countries, in the sense of conditional most-favored-nation treatment where 'conditional' means that the third countries have to grant similar concessions to the integrated region in order to benefit from the trade barriers' reductions achieved within the integrated region (Klodt *et al.* 1994). This could be done on a voluntary basis, but the WTO could also agree on a timetable for multilateralization (Srinivasan 1998). Another approach is to link regional integrations by agreements going further than the WTO system (see below).

Drawing a line for which areas no rules should be developed

We have discussed several areas into which the WTO has to be expanded: services, investment and property rights. Other areas are debated such as competition policy, labor and social standards and the environment.

Quite clearly, the rule system has to respond to new issues, but somewhere must be a line where the WTO is not and should not be in charge.

A more theoretical answer is that the WTO should only be concerned about rules for the international division of labor, including trade of goods and services, international factor mobility and trade restrictions arising from national environmental policy for the national environment. Global environmental issues have to be solved by a different institutional arrangement. A basic principle is that differences in endowments are accepted as the starting point for the international division of labor arbitraged by trade and factor flows. This would exclude protectionism, harmonization and world wide redistribution. The WTO cannot possibly solve the issue of distribution between nation states. Introducing distributional constraints will make the world order ineffective. Such issues, including the alleviation of poverty, have to be solved in other ways.

A more practical answer is to look at which areas of rules nation states are prepared to hand over to the WTO and which new areas of rules the WTO can absorb into its rule system without losing efficacy.

Extending to new members

Enlarging the membership of the WTO club will generate additional benefits to the old members. The new members will have benefits as well. Enlargement of the membership is therefore an important mechanism to make the system more attractive.

In the long run, the optimal size of the WTO is the world as a whole because then all potential benefits of the international division of labor are exploited. In the short run, however, there is one important condition for the extension of membership. The system of rules should not be weakened but strengthened when a new member enters. The pending accessions of China and Russia illustrate that a new member can have a strong impact on the WTO rule system. New members must accept the rule system as a single undertaking. They must have a track record showing that they have followed the basic WTO philosophy for some time. Moreover, economic conditions in the potential new member countries must be such that the countries are fit to survive in the world market.

Extending the frontier by a WTO-Plus

Another positive mechanism is to allow new problems to be solved by a subset of WTO members. These countries could commit themselves to realize attempted results of the WTO rounds more quickly than planned, liberalize more than agreed and employ the permitted exceptions less often. Such a WTO-Plus, a two-speed world integration, could advance the integration process in the world economy. This also holds for dovetailing various regional blocs by establishing a free-trade zone between the blocs, for instance in a trans atlantic economic area. This mechanism, however, is in conflict with the single-undertaking nature of the WTO and the concept of packaging advantages in different areas. Care must be taken where each mechanism should have priority.

16.10 The role of the IMF once more

As discussed in Chapter 8, an institutional arrangement preventing financial crises is an important cornerstone of a multilateral order for the world economy. In this context, the IMF has to play its role. The IMF is caught between its short-term role of bridging balance-of-payments disequilibrium or preventing a run on a currency and its long-term task of establishing incentives that prevent a currency crisis from developing. The IMF has to provide more comprehensive information and to improve the early warning system. By signaling problems to the financial markets early on, larger problems can be prevented. Signaling problems is one way of reducing the moral hazards created by extensive costs of intervention by the IMF. Reducing the moral hazard problem also requires that private creditors (banks, bondholders) should be adequately involved in the losses of a financial crisis so that they anticipate the risk. The IMF should also address the issue that the size of its operation creates the wrong incentives for sovereign creditors.

16.11 The interdependence of the world institutional order: a summary

The institutional arrangements for the world economy vary with the different types of interdependence among countries. Traditionally, trade policy rules have been intended to facilitate international merchandise trade. Recently, these rules have been extended to services; other areas such as competition policy are discussed. Norms for the mobility of production factors–technology, physical capital and labor – are receiving increasing attention with locational competition between countries becoming more important. Norms for the use of the environment will also acquire greater significance in the future (Table 16.5). Finally, financial transactions, balance-of-payments disequilibria and exchange rate volatility are a matter of concern.

Looking at these and other problems, the institutional design of the world economy is in a process of continuous development. There has to be a division of labor between the international organizations. Trade and factor mobility is clearly the domain of the WTO. Improving structural conditions for long-run growth is the task of the World Bank. The Bank for International Settlements (BIS) in Basle is in charge of securing the functioning of the payment system. The IMF fluctuates between its short-run role of bridging international liquidity gaps or balance-of-payments crises and its long-run role of improving structural conditions. In fact, the assignment problem among international organizations seems to be unsolved.

Table 16.5 Elements of an institutional order for the world economy

Type of interdepence	Possible distortions, disturbances	Rules
Exchange of Goods	Protectionist trade policy (tariffs, import quotas, 'voluntary' export restraints, strategic trade policy, anti-dumping, subsidies, product standards)	Trade rules, above all against new forms of protectionist trade policy. Country-of-origin principle for product norms
	Social norms	No word-wide standardization possible
	Market power of firms	Competition rules. Free access to markets. Effects doctrine

Type of interdepence	Possible distortions, disturbances	Rules
Services	Discrimination against foreign suppliers	National treatment
Factor migration		
Capital	Risk of expropriation of foreign investments. Tax competition for mobile capital	Governments compete using their infrastructure, tax system and regulations for mobile capital. National self-interest implies countries to make themselves more attractive to outside capital. Investment code
Technology	Too low incentives for technological progress, owing to property rights not respected internationally	Property rights which protect new knowledge but permit gradual diffusion
Labor	Abrupt mass migrations	Free trade and free movements of capital as a substitute for labor migration. A right to emigrate (right of exit). Openness in immigration policy. Not achievable: a universal right of immigration
Diffusion of pollutants	Trans-frontier pollution, free-rider behavior of individual countries with regard to global environmental problems	International rules only for trans-frontier and global environmental problems. Trans-frontier pollution subject of agreement among countries concerned. National environmental problems are subject to national environmental policy. Separation between environmental policy and trade policy
Financial transactions	Volatility of exchange rates, currency runs	Each country must keep the value of its money stable. Discretionary macroeconomic coordination is not possible unless each country submits itself to rules giving up sovereignty similar to the gold standard

References

Alonso, W. (1964). *Location and Land Use*. Cambridge, MA: Harvard University Press.

Anderson, K., H. Norheim (1993). History, Geography and Regional Economic Integration. *Centre for Economic Policy Research. Discussion Paper*, 795. London.

APEC. http://www.apecsec.org.sg.

ASEAN. http://www.aseansec.org.

Axelrod, R. (1986). An Evolutionary Approach to Norms. *American Political Science Review*, 80: 1095–1111.

Baldwin, R.E., J.E. Francois, R. Portes (1997). The Costs and Benefits of Eastern Enlargement: The Impact on the EU and Central Europe. *Economic Policy*, 24: 125–176.

Baldwin R.E., E. Berglof, F. Giavazzi, M. Widgren (2001). Nice Try: Should the Treaty of Nice be Ratified? *Monitoring European Integration*, 11. CEPR.

Barro, R.J. (1992). Convergence. *Journal of Political Economy*, 100: 223–251.

Barro, R.J., X. Sala-i-Martin (1992). Convergence across States and Regions. *Brookings Papers on Economic Activity*, 15(1): 107–158.

——(1995). *Economic Growth*. New York: McGraw-Hill.

Bergsten, C.F. (1986). Gearing Up World Growth. *Challenge*, 29 (2): 35–40.

——(1988). *America in the World Economy: A Strategy for the 1990s*. Washington, DC: Institute for International Economics.

Bhagwati, J. (1984). Splintering and Disembodiment of Services and Developing Nations. *The World Economy*, 7: 133–143.

——(1989). Is Free Trade Passé After All? *Weltwirtschaftliches Archiv*, 125: 17–44.

——(1991). *The World Trading System at Risk*. New York: Harvester Wheatsheaf.

——(1992). Regionalism and Multilateralism. *The World Economy*, 15 (5): 535–555.

Bhagwati, J., A. Panagariya, T.N. Srinivasan (1998). *Lectures on International Trade*. 2nd edition. Cambridge, MA: MIT Press.

BIS (Bank for International Settlement) (1998). *The Maturity, Sectoral and Nationality Distribution of International Bank Lending. First Half 1997*. Basle: BIS.

Blackhurst, R. (1997). The WTO and the Global Economy. *The World Economy*, 20 (5): 527–544.

Blanchard, O.J., S. Fischer (1989). *Lectures on Macroeconomics*. Cambridge, MA: MIT Press.

Blanchard, O.J., L.F. Katz (1992). Regional Evolutions. *Brookings Papers on Economic Activity*, 15 (1): 1–75.

Blanchard, O.J., M. Watson (1982). Bubbles, Rational Expectations and Financial Markets: In: P. Wachtel (ed.), *Crises in the Economic and Financial Structure*. Lexington, MA: Lexington Books.

Bode, E. (1998). Lokale Wissensdiffusion und regionale Divergenz in Deutschland. *Kieler Studien*, 293. Tübingen: Mohr.

Bosworth, B.P. (1993). *Saving and Investment in a Global Economy*. Washington, DC: Brookings Institution.

Brander, J.A., B.J. Spencer (1985). Export Subsidies and International Market Share Rivalry. *Journal of International Economics*, 18: 83–100.

British Petroleum Company. *BP Statistical Review of World Energy*. London: BP.

Buch, C.M. (2002). *Globalization of Financial*

Markets: Causes of Incomplete Integration and Consequences for Economic Policy. Kiel Studies, Berlin: Springer (forthcoming).

Bucovetsky, S., J.D. Wilson (1991). Tax Competition with Two Tax Instruments. *Regional Science and Urban Economics*, 21: 333–350.

Bundesanstalt für Geowissenschaften und Rohstoffe (1995). *Reserven, Ressourcen und Verfügbarkeit von Energierohstoffen 1995.* Stuttgart: Schweitzerbart.

Calomiris, C. (1998). The IMF's Imprudent Role as a Lender of Last Resort. Cato Journal 17: 275–294.

Calomiris, C., A. Meltzer (1998). *Reforming the IMF.* New York: Columbia Business School. Unpublished manuscript.

Caves, R.E., J.A. Frankel, R.W. Jones (1996). *World Trade and Payments: An Introduction.* 7th edition. New York: HarperCollins.

Central Bank of the Russian Federation. *Bulletin of Banking Statistics.* Moscow.

Cline, W. (1995). Managing International Debt: How One Big Battle Was Won. *The Economist*, 18 February. London.

Coase, R.H. (1960). The Problem of Social Cost. *Journal of Law and Economics*, 3: 1–44.

Datastream.

David, P.A. (1999). The Determinants of Long-Run Economic Growth and Wealth Creation. *21st Century Economic Dynamics: Anatomy of a Long Boom.* Paris: OECD.

De Grauwe, P. (1997). *The Economics of Monetary Integration*, 3rd revd. edition. Oxford: Oxford University Press.

De Long, J.B. (1988). Productivity Growth, Convergence, and Welfare. [Comment (on W.J. Baumol (1986)): *Productivity Growth, Convergence, and Welfare*]. *American Economic Review*, 78 (5): 1138–1154.

Department of the Treasury of the United States Government. *Monthly Treasury Statement of Receipts and Outlays.* Washington, DC.

Deutsche Bundesbank. http://www.bundesbank.de/index_e.html.

—— *Balance of Payments Statistics.* Frankfurt am Main.

—— *Monthly Reports.* Frankfurt am Main.

Diamond, D., P. Dybvig (1983). Bankruns, Deposit Insurance, and Liquidity. *Journal of Political Economy*, 91: 401–419.

Dixit, A.K., V. Norman (1980). *Theory of International Trade.* Cambridge: Cambridge University Press.

Dornbusch, R. (1976). Expectations and Exchange Rate Dynamics. *Journal of Political Economy*, 84 (6): 1161–1176.

—— (1987). The Dollar is Down? Not Nearly Enough for America's Good. *International Herald Tribune*, 26 March.

—— (1990). Policy Options for Freer Trade: The Case of Bilateralism. In: R.Z. Lawrence, C.L. Schultze (eds.), *An American Trade Strategy: Options for the 1990s.* Washington, DC: Brookings Institution, pp. 106–134.

EBRD (European Bank for Reconstruction and Development). *Transition Report.* London: EBRD.

—— *Economics of Transition.* London: EBRD.

Economist Intelligence Unit (1999). *Country Report Brazil.* London: EIU.

Ehlermann, C.D. (1995). The Role of Competition Policy in a Global Economy. *New Dimensions of Market Access in a Globalizing World Economy.* Paris: OECD.

Eichengreen, B. (1997). *European Monetary Unification: Theory, Practice, Analysis.* Cambridge, MA: MIT Press.

—— (1999a). *Toward a New International Financial Architecture: A Practical Post-Asia Agenda.* Institute for International Economics.

—— (1999b). Involving the Private Sector in Crisis Prevention and Resolution. IMF Conference on Key Issues in Reform of the International Monetary and Financial Systems, 28–29 May, Washington, DC.

—— (2002). Capital Account Liberalization: What Do the Cross-Country Studies Tell Us? *The World Bank Economic Review*, March.

Ethier, W. (1995). *Modern International Economics*, 3rd edition. New York: Norton.

Eucken, W. (1940). *Die Grundlagen der Nationalökonomie.* Jena: Fischer. (English edition: *The Foundations of Economics: History and Theory in the Analysis of Economic Reality.* Berlin, 1992: Springer.)

European Central Bank. http://www.ecb.int.

European Union. http://europa.eu.int.

EUROSTAT. *Internal and External Trade of the EU.* Luxembourg.

Feldstein, M. (1997). The Political Economy of

European Monetary Union: Political Reasons for an Economic Liability. *Journal of Economic Perspectives*, 11: 23–42.

—— (1998). Refocusing the IMF. *Foreign Affairs*, 77 (2): 20–33.

Feldstein, M., C. Horioka (1980). Domestic Saving and International Capital Flows. *Economic Journal*, 90: 314–329.

Fikentscher, W., U. Immenga (eds.) (1995). Draft International Antitrust Code. *Kommentierter Entwurf eines internationalen Wettbewerbsrechts mit ergänzenden Beiträgen.* Baden-Baden: Nomos.

Finger, J.M., M.D. Ingco, U. Reincke (1996). *The Uruguay Round – Statistics on Tariff Concessions Given and Received.* Washington, DC: The World Bank.

Fischer, S. (1998). IMF and Crisis Prevention. *Financial Times*, 30 March.

Fischer, S. (1999). On the Need for an International Lender of Last Resort. *Journal of Economic Perspectives*, 13 (4): 85–104.

Fischer, S., R. Sahbay, C. A. Végh (1996). Stabilization and Growth in Transition Economies: The Early Experience. *Journal of Economic Perspectives*, 10: 45–66.

Frankel, J.A. (1997). *Regional Trading Blocs in the World Economic System.* Washington, DC: Institute for International Economics.

Freeman, R.B. (1995). Are Your Wages Set in Beijing? *Journal of Economic Perspectives*, 9 (3): 15–32.

Garber, P. M. (1989). Tulipmania. *Journal of Political Economy*, 97: 535–560.

—— (1990). Famous First Bubbles. *Journal of Economic Perspectives*, 4: 35–54.

GATT/WTO, *International Trade, Trends and Statistics*. Geneva.

Government of the Russian Federation. *Russian Economic Trends*: Monthly Update. London.

Graham, E.M. (1995). Competition Policy and the New Trade Agenda. In: OECD, *New Dimensions of Market Access in a Globalizing World Economy*. Paris: OECD.

Gros, D., A. Steinherr (1995). *Winds of Change: Economic Transition and Central and Eastern Europe.* New York: Longman.

Grossman, G.M., E. Helpman (1991a). *Innovation and Growth in the Global Economy.* Cambridge, MA: MIT Press.

—— (1991b). Trade, Knowledge Spillovers, and Growth. *European Economic Review*, 35: 517–526.

—— (1995). Trade Wars and Trade Talks. *Journal of Political Economy*, 103 (4): 675–708.

Gundlach, E. (1998). Das Wirtschaftswachstum der Nationen im zwanzigsten Jahrhundert. *Die Weltwirtschaft*, 1: 85–107.

Gundlach, E., P. Nunnenkamp (1998). Some Consequences of Globalization for Developing Countries. In: J.H. Dunning (ed.), *Globalization, Trade and Foreign Investment*. Amsterdam: Elsevier, pp. 153–174.

Haggard, S., B. Simmons (1987). Theories of International Regimes. *International Organization*, 41: 491–517.

Harcourt, G. (2001). Turn to the Tobin Alternative. *The Guardian* (www.guardian.co.uk/archive/article/0,4273,4262953).

Harris, J., M. Todaro (1970). Migration, Unemployment and Development; A Two-Sector Analysis. *American Economic Review, Papers and Proceedings*, 60: 126–142.

Hayek, F.A. von (1968). Der Wettbewerb als Entdeckungsverfahren. *Kieler Vorträge*, 56. Institut für Weltwirtschaft, Kiel.

—— (1973). *Law, Legislation and Liberty: A New Statement of the Liberal Principles of Justice and Political Economy. Volume I: Rules and Order.* London: Routledge & Kegan Paul.

Heitger, B. (1993). Comparative Economic Growth: East and West. In: B. Heitger, L. Waverman (eds.). *German Unification and the International Economy*. London: Routledge.

Helpman, E., P.R. Krugman (1990). *Market Structure and Foreign Trade.* Cambridge, MA: MIT Press.

Higgins, B.H. (1959). *Economic Development. Principles, Problems and Policies.* London: Constable.

Hillman, A.L. (1989). *The Political Economy of Protection.* Chur: Harwood.

—— (1994). The Political Economy of Migration Policy. In: H. Siebert (ed.), *Migration: A Challenge to Europe*. Tübingen: Mohr.

Hodrick, R.J., E.C. Prescott (1997). Postwar US Business Cycles: An Empirical Investigation. *Journal of Money, Credit, and Banking*, 29: 1–16.

Hoekman, B.M., P.C. Mauroidis (1994). Competition, Competition Policy and the GATT. *The World Economy*, 17 (2): 121–150.

Holtfrerich, C.E., O. Schötz (1988). *Vom*

Weltgläubiger zum Weltschuldner: Erklärungsansätze zur historischen Entwicklung und Struktur der internationalen Währungsposition der USA. Frankfurt am Main: Knapp.

Immenga, U. (1995). Konzepte einer grenzüberschreitenden und international koordinierten Wettbewerbspolitik. *Kiel Working Papers*, 692. Institut für Weltwirtschaft, Kiel.

International Monetary Fund. http://www.imf.org.

—— *Annual Report.* Washington, DC.

—— *Balance of Payments Statistics.* Washington, DC.

—— *Direction of Trade Statistics.* Washington, DC.

—— *International Financial Statistics.* Washington, DC.

—— (1999). *Involving the Private Sector in Forestalling and Resolving Financial Crises.* Washington, DC.

Ito, T. (1999). *The Role of IMF Advice.* Paper presented at the Conference on Key Issues in Reform of the International Monetary and Financial System, May 28–29. Washington, DC.

Jones, R.W., P.B. Kenen (eds.) (1984). *Handbook of International Economics.* Amsterdam: North-Holland.

Kindleberger, C.P. (1973). *The World in Depression 1929–1939.* London: Lane.

Klodt, H., J. Stehn, A. Boss, K. Lammers, J.O. Lorz, R. Maurer, A.O. Neu, K.H. Paqué, A. Rosenschon, C. Walter (1994). Standort Deutschland: Strukturelle Herausforderungen im neuen Europa. *Kieler Studien*, 265. Tübingen: Mohr.

Kornai, J. (1980). *Economics of Shortage.* Amsterdam: North-Holland.

—— (1982). *Growth, Shortage and Efficiency. A Macrodynamic Model of the Socialist Economy.* Oxford: Blackwell.

Krueger, A.O. (1996). *The Political Economy of Trade Protection.* Chicago: University of Chicago Press.

—— (ed.) (1998). *The WTO as an International Organization.* Chicago, IL: University of Chicago Press.

Krugman, P.R. (ed.) (1986). *Strategic Trade Policy and the New International Economics.* Cambridge, MA: MIT Press.

—— (1989). *Exchange-Rate Instability.* Cambridge, MA: MIT Press.

—— (1990). *Rethinking International Trade.* Cambridge, MA: MIT Press.

—— (1991). *Geography and Trade.* Leuven: Leuven University Press.

—— (1994). Competitiveness: A Dangerous Obsession. *Foreign Affairs*, 73 (2): 28–44.

Krugman, P.R., M. Obstfeld (1997). *International Economics, Theory and Policy*, 4th edition. Reading, MA: Addison-Wesley.

Langhammer, R.J. (1995). Regional Integration in East Asia: From Market-Driven Regionalisation to Institutionalised Regionalism? *Weltwirtschaftliches Archiv*, 131 (1): 167–201.

—— (1998). Europe's Trade, Investment and Strategic Policy Interests in Asia and APEC. In: P.D. Drysdale, D. Vines (eds.), *Europe, East Asia and APEC.* Cambridge: Cambridge University Press, pp. 223–253.

—— (1999). The WTO and the Millennium-Round: Between Standstill and Leapfrog. *Kiel Discussion Paper*, 352. Institute for World Economics, Kiel.

Langhammer, R.J., M. Lücke (1999). WTO Accession Issues. *The World Economy*, (22) 6: 837–873.

Lindbeck, A., P. Molander, T. Persson, O. Petersson, A. Sandmo, B. Swedenborg, N. Thygesen (1994). *Turning Sweden Around.* Cambridge, MA: MIT Press.

Lorz, O. (1997). Standortwettbewerb bei internationaler Kapitalmobilität: Eine modelltheoretische Untersuchung. *Kieler Studien*, 284. Tübingen: Mohr.

—— (1998). Capital Mobility, Tax Competition and Lobbying for Redistributive Capital Taxation. *European Journal of Political Economy*, 14(2): 265–279.

Lucas, R.E. (1981). *Studies in Business Cycle Theory.* Oxford: Blackwell.

MacNeil, I.R. (1978). Contracts. Adjustment of Long-Term Economic Relations under Classical, Neoclassical, and Relational Contract Law. *Northwestern University Law Review*, 72 (6): 854–905.

McKinnon, R.I. (1982). Currency Substitution and Instability in the World Dollar Standard. *American Economic Review*, 72 (3): 320–333.

Maddison, A. (1982). *Phases of Capitalist Development.* Oxford: Oxford University Press.

—— (1992). *Dynamic Forces in Capitalist Development.* Oxford: Oxford University Press.

—— (2001). *The World Economy: A Millennial Perspective.* Paris: Development Centre of the OECD.

Magee, S.P., W.A. Brock, L. Young (1989). *Black Hole Tariffs and Endogenous Policy Theory: Political Economy in General Equilibrium.* Cambridge: Cambridge University Press.

Mankiw, N.G. (1995). The Growth of Nations. *Brookings Papers on Economic Activity*, 18 (1): 275–326.

Marshall, A. (1890). *Principles of Economics. An Introductory Volume.* London.

Maurer, R. (1998). Economic Growth and International Trade with Capital Goods: Theory and Empiric Evidence. *Kieler Studien*, 289. Tübingen: Mohr.

Meltzer, A.H. (1998). Asian Problems and the IMF. Testimony. Prepared for the Joint Committee. February.

Messerlin, P.A. (1989). The EC Antidumping Regulations: A First Economic Appraisal, 1980–85. *Weltwirtschaftliches Archiv*, 125: 563–587.

Minton-Beddoes, Z. (1995). Why the IMF Needs Reform. *Foreign Affairs*, 74 (3): 123–133.

Mishkin, F.S. (1998). International Capital Movements, Financial Volatility, and Financial Instability. National Bureau of Economic Research. NBER Working Paper 6390. Cambridge, MA.

Mundell, R.A. (1961). A Theory of Optimum Currency Areas. *American Economic Review*, 51 (4): 657–665.

Mussa, M. (1997). IMF Surveillance. *American Economic Review*, 87 (2): 28–31.

Myrdal, G. (1956). *An International Economy.* New York: Harper.

National Institute of Statistics, Geography and Informatics. *Mexican Bulletin of Statistical Information.* Aguascalientes.

Nelson, R.R. (1956). A Theory of the Low-Level Equilibrium Trap in Underdeveloped Economies. *American Economic Review*, 46 (5): 894–908.

Nicolaides, P. (1994). Towards Multilateral Rules on Competition. The Problems in Mutual Recognition of National Rules. *World Competition*, 17 (3): 5–48.

Norheim, H., K.-M. Finger, K. Anderson (1993). Trends in the Regionalization of World Trade, 1928 to 1990. In: K. Anderson, R. Blackhurst (eds.), *Regional Integration and the Global Trading System.* New York: Harvester Wheatsheaf.

North, D. (1990). *Institutions, Institutional Change and Economic Performance.* Cambridge: Cambridge University Press.

Obstfeld, M., K. Rogoff (1996). *Foundations of International Macroeconomics.* Cambridge, MA: MIT Press.

OECD. http.//www.oecd.org.

—— *Economic Outlook.* Paris.

—— *International Trade by Commodities Statistics.* Paris.

—— *Main Economic Indicators.* Paris.

—— *National Accounts.* Paris.

—— *Short-Term Economic Indicators, Transition Countries.* Paris.

—— (1998). *Economic Surveys.* Japan, Paris.

Olson, M. (1969). The Principle of 'Fiscal Equivalence'. *American Economic Review*, 59: 479–487.

—— (1982). *The Rise and Decline of Nations. Economic Growth, Stagflation and Social Rigidities.* New Haven, CT: Yale University Press.

Ostry, S. (1995). New Dimensions of Market Access: Challenges for the Trading System. *New Dimensions of Market Access in a Globalizing World Economy.* Paris: OECD.

—— (1997). A New Regime of Foreign Direct Investment. Group of Thirty. *Washington Occasional Paper*, 53.

PlanEcon (Annual Reports). *Czech Economic Monitor PlanEcon Report.*

Popper, K.R. (1945). *The Open Society and its Enemies.* London: Routledge & Kegan Paul.

Prebisch, R. (1950). *The Economic Development of Latin America and its Principal Problems.* United Nations Publications, Economic Commission for Latin America, II G.2.

Radelat, S., J. Sachs (1999). *What Have We Learned, So Far, from the Asian Financial Crisis?* Unpublished manuscript.

Rauscher, M. (1997). *International Trade, Factor Movements, and the Environment.* Oxford: Clarendon.

Rawls, J. (1971). *A Theory of Justice.* Cambridge, MA: Belknap.

Rodrick, D. (1997). *Has Globalization Gone Too Far?* Washington, DC: Institute of International Economics.

Rogoff, K. (1996). The Purchasing Power Parity Puzzle. *Journal of Economic Literature*, 34 (2): 665–668.

Romer, P.M. (1986). Increasing Returns and Long-Run Growth. *Journal of Political Economy*, 94: 1002–1037.

Rubin, R. (1999). Remarks on Reform of the International Financial Architecture to the School of Advanced International Studies. *Treasury News*, April 21, RR–3093.

Sachs, J. (1994). The IMF and Economies in Crisis. Presented at the London School of Economics. July.

—— (1997). Limits of Convergence. Nature, Nurture and Growth. *The Economist*, 14 June. London.

Sachverständigenrat zur Begutachtung der gesamtwirtschaftlichen Entwicklung. Annual Reports. Stuttgart: Metzler-Poeschel.

Samuelson, P.A. (1954). The Pure Theory of Public Expenditure. *Review of Economics and Statistics*, 36 (4): 387–389.

Scherer, F.M. (1994). *Competition Policies for an Integrated World Economy*. Washington, DC: Brookings Institution.

Schulze, G.G., H.W. Ursprung (1999). Globalisation of the Economy and the Nation State. *The World Economy*, 22 (3): 295–352.

Schumpeter, J.A. (1934). *The Theory of Economic Development. An Inquiry into Profits, Capital, Credit, Interest and the Business Cycle*. Cambridge, MA: Harvard University Press.

Schweickert, R. (1994). Exchange Rate Based Stabilisation: Lessons from a Radical Implementation in Argentina. *The World Economy* 17 (2): 171–189.

Seidel, M. (1997). Between Unanimity and Majority. Towards New Rules of Decision-Making. In: H. Siebert (ed.), *Quo Vadis Europe?* Tübingen: Mohr, pp. 47–66.

Shiller, R.J. (2000). *Irrational Exuberance*. Princeton, NJ: Princeton University Press.

Siebert, H. (1983). *Ökonomische Theorie natürlicher Ressourcen*. Tübingen: Mohr.

—— (1987). Foreign Debt and Capital Accumulation. *Weltwirtschaftliches Archiv*, 123: 618–630.

—— (1989). The Half and the Full Debt Cycle. *Weltwirtschaftliches Archiv*, 125: 217–229.

—— (1991a). A Schumpeterian Model of Growth in the World Economy: Some Notes on a New Paradigm in International Economics. *Weltwirtschaftliches Archiv*, 127 (4): 800–812.

—— (1991b). German Unification, The Economics of Transition. *Economic Policy*, 13: 287–340.

—— (1991c). The Integration of Germany – Real Economic Adjustment. *European Economic Review*, 3: 591–602.

—— (1991d). *The New Economic Landscape in Europe*. Oxford: Basil Blackwell.

—— (1993). Internationale Wanderungsbewegungen – Erklärungsansätze und Gestaltungsfragen. *Schweizerische Zeitschrift für Volkswirtschaft und Statistik*, 129 (3): 229–255.

—— (1995). Eastern Germany in the Fifth Year. Investment Hammering in the Basement? *Kiel Discussion Papers*, 250. Institut für Weltwirtschaft, Kiel.

—— (1996). Trade Policy and Environmental Protection. *The World Economy*,: 19 (2): 183–194.

—— (1997a). *Weltwirtschaft*. Stuttgart: Lucius & Lucius.

—— (1997b). Die Weltwirtschaft im Umbruch: Müssen die Realeinkommen der Arbeitnehmer sinken? *Aussenwirtschaft*, 52: 349–368.

—— (1998a). An Institutional Order for a Globalizing World Economy. In: K. Jaeger, K.-J. Koch (eds.), *Trade, Growth, and Economic Policy in Open Economies – Essays in Honour of Hans-Jürgen Vosgerau*. Berlin: Springer, pp. 331–349.

—— (1998b). *Economics of the Environment. Theory and Policy*, 5th revd. edition. Berlin: Springer.

—— (1998c). The Future of the IMF – How to Prevent the Next Global Financial Crisis. *Kiel Working Paper*, 870. Institut für Weltwirtschaft, Kiel.

—— (1999). What Does Globalization Mean for the World Trading System? In: WTO, *The Global Trading System at Fifty*. The Hague: Kluwer.

—— (2000a). *Aussenwirtschaft*, 7th revd. edition. Stuttgart: Lucius & Lucius.

—— (2000b). The Paradigm of Locational Competition. *Kiel Discussion Papers*, 367. Kiel Institute of World Economics.

—— (2001a). How the EU Can Move to a Higher Growth Path – Some Considerations. *Kiel Discussion Papers*, 383. Kiel Institute of World Economics.

—— (2001b). *Der Kobra Effekt. Wie man Irrwege der Wirtschaftspolitik vermeidet*. München: Deutsche Verlags-Anstalt.

—— (2002). Europe – Quo Vadis? Reflections on the Future Institutional Framework of the European Union. *The World Economy*, 25 (1): 1–32.

Siebert, H., I. Collier (1991). The Economic Integration of Post-War Germany. *American Economic Review, Papers and Proceedings*, 81: 196–201.

Siebert, H., H. Klodt (1999). Towards Global Competition: Catalysts and Constraints. *21st Century Economic Dynamics: Anatomy of a Long Boom*. Paris: OECD.

Siebert, H., M. Koop (1990). Institutional Competition: A Concept for Europe? *Aussenwirtschaft*, 45: 439–462.

—— (1993). Institutional Competition versus Centralization: Quo Vadis Europe? *Oxford Review of Economic Policy*, 9 (1): 15–30.

Siebert, H., J. Eichberger, R. Gronych, R. Pethig (1980). *Trade and Environment. A Theoretical Enquiry*. Amsterdam: Elsevier.

Singer, H.W. (1950). The Distribution of Gains between Investing and Borrowing Countries. *American Economic Review*, 40 (2): 473–485.

Sinn, H.-W. (1997). The Selection Principle and Market Failure in Systems Competition. *Journal of Public Economics*, 66 (2): 247–274.

Sinn, S. (1992a). Saving–Investment Correlations and Capital Mobility: On the Evidence from Annual Data. *Economic Journal*, 102: 1162–1170.

—— (1992b). The Taming of Leviathan: Competition among Governments. *Constitutional Political Economy*, 3: 177–196.

Snape, R.H. (1998). Reading Effective Agreements Covering Services. In: A.O. Krueger (ed.), *The WTO as an International Organization*. Chicago: University of Chicago Press, pp. 279–295.

Solow, R.M. (1956). A Contribution to the Theory of Economic Growth. *Quarterly Journal of Economics*, 70: 65–94.

Srinivasan, T.N. (1998). Regionalism and the WTO: Is Nondiscrimination Passé? In: A.O. Krueger (ed.), *The WTO as an International Organization*. Chicago, IL: University of Chicago Press, pp. 329–349.

State Statistical Bureau, People's Republic of China. *China Statistical Yearbook*. Beijing.

Statistics Bureau, Management and Coordination Agency, Government of Japan. *Statistical Handbook of Japan*. Tokyo.

Statistics Canada. http://www.statcan.ca.

Statistisches Amt der DDR. *Statistisches Jahrbuch der Industrie der Deutschen Demokratischen Republik*. Berlin.

—— *Wirtschaftsbereich Industrie, Produktion und Auftragsbestand*. Berlin.

Statistisches Bundesamt. *Produzierendes Gewerbe* (Fachserie 4, Reihe 2.1/Reihe S. 17). Wiesbaden.

—— *Volkswirtschaftliche Gesamtrechnung* (Fachserie 18). Wiesbaden.

Stoeckel, A., D. Pearce, G. Banks (1990). *Western Trade Blocs: Game, Set or Match for Asia–Pacific and the World Economy*. Canberra: Centre for International Economics.

Stolpe, M. (1995). Technology and the Dynamics of Specialization in Open Economies. *Kieler Studien*, 271. Tübingen: Mohr.

Summers, R., A.W. Heston (1988). A New Set of International Comparisons of Real Product and Price Level Estimates for 130 Countries, 1950–1985. *Review of Income and Wealth*, 34 (1): 1–25.

—— (1991). The Penn World Table (Mark 5): An Expanded Set of International Comparisons, 1950–1988. *Quarterly Journal of Economics*, 106 (2).

Tangermann, S. (1997). Reforming the CAP. A Prerequisite for Eastern Enlargement. In: H. Siebert (ed.), *Quo Vadis Europe*? Tübingen: Mohr, pp. 151–179.

Thünen, J.H. von (1826). *Der isolierte Staat in Beziehung auf Landwirtschaft und Nationalökonomie*. Hamburg: Perthes.

Tiebout, C. (1956). A Pure Theory of Local Expenditures. *Journal of Political Economy*, 64: 416–424.

The New Palgrave (1987). *A Dictionary of Economics*, edited by J. Eatwell, M. Milgate, P. Newman, London.

Tobin, J. (1978). A Proposal for International Monetary Reform. *Eastern Economic Journal*, 4: 153–159.

Tumlir, J. (1979). Weltwirtschaftsordnung: Regeln, Kooperation und Souveränität. *Kieler Vorträge*, 87. Institut für Weltwirtschaft, Kiel.

—— (1983). International Economic Order and Democratic Constitutionalism. *ORDO*, 34: 71–83.

US Census Bureau. *International Data Base*. http://www.census.gov.

US Department of Commerce. *International Trade Administration*. http://www.ita.doc.gov/tradestats.

Viner, J. (1950). *The Customs Union Issue*. New York: Stevens.

307

Wade, R. (1996). Globalization and its Limits: Reports of the Death of the National Economy are Greatly Exaggerated, in S. Berger and R. Dore (eds) *National Diversity and Global Capitalism*. Ithaca, NY: Cornell University Press.

Williamson, J. (1983). *The Exchange Rate System. Policy Analysis in International Economics*. Cambridge, MA: MIT Press.

—— (1996). A New Facility for the IMF. *International Monetary and Financial Issues for the 1990s*, 7: 1–9.

World Bank. http://www.worldbank.org.

—— *Global Development Finance* (previously: *World Debt Tables*). Washington, DC.

—— *Global Economic Prospects and the Developing Countries*. Washington, DC.

—— *World Data*. Washington, DC.

—— *World Development Indicators*. Washington, DC.

—— *World Development Reports*. Oxford.

World Economic Forum (1998). *The Global Competitiveness Report 1998*. Davos.

World Trade Organization. http://www.wto.org.

—— *Annual Report*. Geneva.

—— (1995). *Regionalism and the World of Trading System*. Geneva.

Index

absorption 180
abstaining from consumption, cost of 55–8
access to markets 286–8
Africa 16–17, 165
aggressive trade policy 289
aging societies 91
Airbus consortium 45, 245, 288
anchor currencies 153–4, 157, 159
appreciation of currencies 101–2; in real terms 127–9, 179
arbitrage 29–30, 36, 102
Argentina 90, 96, 101, 141, 153, 168–70, 173–5, 178–9
Asia-Pacific Economic Cooperation (APEC) 202, 207
Asian financial crisis (1997–98) 71, 130–5, 141, 146
Asian Free Trade Area, proposed 202
Asian 'tigers' 4, 16, 83, 130–2
Association of South-East Asian Nations 202
asylum policy 215
asymmetric shocks 155, 227
Australia New Zealand Closer Economic Relations Trade Agreement 202–3
Austria 153
autarky 241, 243

balance of payments 100, 124, 251; *see also* current account balance
Baldwin, R. 217
bananas, trade in 285
Bangladesh 169–70
Bank of England 158
Bank for International Settlements 146, 298
banking crises 120–1, 140

banking sector, regulation of 141, 149
Barro rule 86–8
Basel Accords 141
beggar-thy-neighbour policies 236
Belgium 153
Bergsten, C.F. 116
Bertrand price competition 44, 245
Beta convergence 89
'big bang' 186–8, 194
Blanchard, O.J. 125
Boeing (company) 45, 245, 288
Brady Plan 173
Brander, J.A. 245
Brazil 104, 135–6, 168–70, 173–9
Bretton Woods system 157
Brownian motion 231
bubbles 111–16, 140, 157, 222; bursting of 114–15; historical examples of 112–13; impact of 115–16; modeling of 125; preconditions for 114; types 125
budget deficits 140, 167, 173, 188–90, 193, 224; monetization of 172
Bulgaria 231–2
Burundi 170
business cycles: turning points of 121; uniformity of 71

Cambridge equation 97
capital: excess demand for 60–2; as a growth factor 83–4; importers and exporters of 77–81; marginal productivity of 54, 57–60, 63–7, 71, 74–7, 84, 260–1
capital accumulation: 'golden rule' of 75; growth by means of 73–4; optimum level of 75
capital flight 150, 166, 173

capital flows 63, 102–5, 124, 191, 229–31, 259–60; controls on 143, 149–51; 'pecking order' of 151
capital formation in developing countries 167
capital market, global 54–60, 256
capital mobility 255–6, 290
carbon dioxide emissions 270–1
Caribbean Community 202
Cassis-de-Dijon case (1979) 210, 262, 288
central banks 96, 121, 154–5, 158; in Europe 219–21; independence of 140, 166, 172, 183–6
Central European Free Trade Area 200–1
centrally-planned economies 2–3, 41, 181–2, 185, 250, 262, 264; and division of labor 242
Chile 63, 150, 152, 168–70, 178, 265
China 7–8, 13, 32, 67, 169–70, 181, 188, 191, 195–6, 250, 271, 297
c–k diagram 75, 78–9
club-goods 263
coal, world supply curve for 26
Coase theorem 271, 293
Cobb–Douglas function 74
co-decision procedure (in the EU) 213, 215
Common Agricultural Policy 211, 232
common markets 200
common property resources 269
communication costs 8–9
communist system 2, 257
competition as a method of discovery 246, 250, 264
competition policy 211; international 288
competitiveness, international ranking of 17–18
conditionality 145–6
Congo, Democratic Republic of 169
contagion 125, 142–3
contestable markets 43–6, 243, 245
Contingent Credit Line (of the IMF) 142–3
convergence 84–8; absolute and conditional 89
convergence clubs 89
convertibility of currencies 149–50
cooperative trade policy 274
Corn Laws 236
country-of-destination principle 262–3, 284, 291
country-of-origin principle 210–11, 262–3, 284, 287, 291–4
coupon privatization 188
Cournot quantity competition 44, 245
'crawling peg' policy 153–4, 176–9, 193
creative destruction 89
credit crunches 115
credit expansion 114
crowding-out of private investment 189

currency, internal and external values of 223
currency boards 141, 153, 159, 173, 175
currency crises 140; financial mechanisms in 124–5; prevention of 145–6; recent examples of 130–7; role of IMF in 142
currency reform 183, 185
current account balance 61–2, 78, 124–6, 190
customs unions 200
cyclical fluctuations 70–1
Czech Republic 130–1, 174, 183–94 *passim*, 229, 231

debt crisis 173–4
debt cycle and half-cycle 63–5
decentralization of decision-making 9, 212
demand shifts and international trade 38–9
demand-supply diagram of world capital market 57–8
democratic deficit (in the EU) 217, 219
democratization 187
demonstration effects 257
deregulation, financial 125
deutsche mark, value of 106–9, 128–9; currencies anchored to 153–4
devaluation 101–4, 124–7, 156, 179–80, 191–4, 227, 236
developing countries 88, 152, 163, 180, 250–1; characteristics of 164–5; reasons for underdevelopment 165–8; shares of world exports 15–16
'development trap' 165–6
diffusion of knowledge 82
Dillon Round 278
discount rate 60, 79–81
discounting of future utility 56
divergence of economies 88
division of labor: in centrally-planned economies 242, 264; international 169, 236, 247–50
dollar, US, value of 105–8, 117, 128–9, 157
domino effects, institutional 296
Dornbusch, R. 117
dumping and anti-dumping measures 246, 278, 284

early warning systems 145, 147, 298
Eastern European states 2, 4, 41, 264–5; *see also* centrally-planned economies
economic development strategies 171–2
economic growth: benefiting from exports 81; driving forces of 73–7; history of 70; impulses of 71; international differentials in 2–4; as a process 89–91

economic unions 200
Edgeworth box 33–4
education 75, 263
efficiency gains: from capital movements 77–8; from foreign trade 191
employment, 'American' model of 37
employment policy 228
entrepreneurship 167
entry barriers 44
environmental goods 271, 293–4
environmental issues 6, 247, 251, 260–1, 267–71, 291–6; and the international trade order 293–4
equalization: of growth rates 84; of relative prices 36, 38
equilibrium 24–30; between capital imports and capital exports 77–8; between costs and benefits of abstaining from consumption 56–8; between savings and investments 54; in factor markets 68; in quantity of money 96–100; in real exchange rate 128–30
Erhard, Ludwig 184
Estonia 153, 185, 188, 197
euro, the 219
Europe Agreements 229
European Central Bank (ECB) 96, 154, 215, 219–25
European Commission 211, 214, 218
European Council 213–24 *passim*
European Court of Justice 210, 214, 262
European Economic Area 200
European Exchange Rate Mechanism 103, 106, 154–6, 262
European Free Trade Association 200–1, 210
European Monetary Union (EMU) 106, 201, 219–20, 223, 225, 228
European Parliament 213–14, 218, 220
European single market 209
European Union 88, 191, 200–1, 205, 207, 209–19, 222–5, 229–32, 260, 286; decision-making in 213–16; enlargement of 216–19, 229–32; exchange rate policy of 222–3; finances of 211–12; institutions of 214; monetary policy of 224–5; 'national treatment' principle in 284; Regulations and Directives of 213; stability pact 225; structural funds 232; trade agreements made by 240–1; Trade Defence Instrument 279, 289; Treaty of 213, 224–5; variable geometry in 219; and the WTO 285
exchange rates 47–9, 98–107, 262; defence of 104; and inflation 107; multiple 150; pegging of 141, 147; policy for 141, 183, 191–2, 222–3; real 126–30, 179–80, 193; stability of 222–3; stabilization of 152–9
expectations 77, 103–4, 112–15, 124–5, 262
export diversification 172
export enclaves 164–5
export subsidies 245
exports, real 48–9
Extended Fund Facility (of the IMF) 142

factor-price frontier 66–8
federalism 218
fiscal federalism 212
fiscal policy *see* taxation
foreign currency transactions, world volume of 104
foreign direct investment 10–11, 62–3, 151, 191, 229–31, 251, 290; as proportion of gross investment 65
foreign exchange controls 150
foreign exchange reserves 124–5, 146; auctioning of 150
France 104, 218, 262
free goods 269
free movement of goods, persons, services and capital 210–11
free-riding 270, 277, 293–4
free trade 236; benefits from 247
Free Trade Area of the Americas 202
free trade areas 200
free-trade-for-one theorem 30, 247, 276

gains from trade 30, 81, 242, 248, 274–6
General Agreement on Tariffs and Trade (GATT) 157, 206, 236, 246, 263, 278–84 *passim*
General Agreement on Trade in Services (GATS) 279, 287
General Electric 288
Germany 85, 106–9, 116, 120, 155, 184, 188, 218, 231–2, 236, 241; Trade Union Federation (DGB) 261; transformation in 194–5
Ghana 169–70
global warming 270, 277
globalization: of commodity markets 39–40; concerns about 250–1; and contestability 245, 288; and dependence on suppliers 241; economic impact of 8–10; of factor markets 32; of financial markets 158; and locational competition 257; reasons for 8; and technological progress 67; and wage bargaining 261
gold standard 97, 158–9, 236

gradual adjustment 186–8
Great Depression 4–5, 71, 113, 120, 149, 236
gross domestic product (GDP) 12
gross national product (GNP) 12; per capita
    169–71
growth equation 73
growth factors 77, 83–4
growth leaders 90
growth paths (of capital importers and exporters)
    78–80

Hansen, Alvin 90
Harberger triangle 52, 60
Harrod–Johnson diagram 35
Hayek, F.A. 246, 250, 264
Heckscher–Ohlin model 35–6, 38, 43, 255, 270
hedge funds 141
Higgins, B.H. 90
Honeywell (company) 288
Hong Kong 168
human capital 74–5, 167, 251
Hungary 63, 184, 188–93 passim, 229, 231, 257
hysteresis 167

IBM (company) 45
immigration policy 291
impatience of consumers 56
imperfect competition 40–2
import levies and tariffs 236, 240–1
import licenses 239
import quotas 278
import substitution 171–2, 238–9, 264–5
income distribution 165, 261
income effects 28, 31
income per capita 70
increasing returns to scale 40–3
India 169–70, 250
Indonesia 134–5, 170, 174
infant industries 171, 241–2, 265
inflation 98, 107, 166–7, 175–9, 182–3, 190, 193;
    targets for 140
infrastructure, provision of 257–60, 263
initial conditions 90
institutional arrangements 68, 77, 91, 140, 145,
    166, 172–3, 182, 184, 257–8, 262–3, 295–6; for
    the world economy 273, 277–8, 298–9
interdependence: of factor markets 10–11; of
    world institutional order 298–9
interest rate parity 101–4, 155
interest rate policy 104
interest rates 57–8; real 67

intergovernmental cooperation 213, 217, 219
International Labor Organization 246, 291
International Monetary Fund (IMF) 104, 141–8,
    157, 236, 297–8; bankruptcy procedure 143;
    credits 143–4; facilities of 142–3; information
    needs of 146
Internet, the 8, 82
intra-regional trade (as proportion of total) 207
intra-sectoral trade 42–3
investment codes 290
investment and growth 83–4
Ireland 265
Italy 106–7, 155, 224

J-curve 183–5, 195
Japan 2, 108, 116–19, 222, 240

Kennedy Round 278
Keynesian theory 225
Kindleberger spiral 3
knowledge capital 41, 76–7, 82
Kondratieff cycles 73
Korean War 71
Krugman, P.R. 116
Kyoto Protocol 271

labor, marginal productivity of 255
labor markets 11, 52–4, 82, 254–5; 'European'
    model of 36–7; and monetary union 225–9
labor supply 30–8
labor supply curve, world 52–3
Latin America 3, 71, 88–9, 140, 165, 167, 170–1,
    206, 242, 250, 264–5; macroeconomic instability
    in 174–5
Latin American Free Trade Association 202
Latin American Integration Association 202
law of one price 28–9, 32, 38, 99, 226
learning curves 41
lenders of last resort 148
liberalization: of banking sector and capital
    account 149, 157; of trade 206, 236, 275–80
Lithuania 184
localization factors 82–3
locational competition 254–5, 289; channels of
    255–7; impact on labor 261; instruments of
    257–8; inter-regional 264–5; relationship to
    national politics 261–2
Lomé Convention 200
long-run equilibrium 84–6, 103
Lorenz curve 165
'low-level equilibrium' 167

McDonnell-Douglas (company) 45, 288
McKinnon, R.I. 156
macroeconomic policies, coordination of 225
Maddison, A. 70, 86
Malaysia 135
marginal rate of transformation 24–8; in time
    54–7
market failure 172
Mercádo Común del Sur (MERCOSUR) 202,
    206
mercantilism 282
Mexico 3, 130, 132, 141, 168–70, 177–9
Microsoft 45
migration 52, 227–8, 231–2, 256–7, 262, 291
Mitterrand, François 104, 262
mobile factors of production 255, 261, 289
monetary crisis, types of 140
monetary equilibrium 96–8; with flexible exchange
    rates 99–100
monetary policy 98, 140–1, 211; of the EU 224–5;
    exchange-rate-oriented 153, 159, 222;
    international coordination of 156–7
monetary strategies 140
monetary unions 200, 224; and the labor market
    225–9
money, role of 95
money supply 96–103, 114, 121, 175–9, 222, 225,
    262; targets for 140
monopolies 11, 43–5, 243, 245, 288
moral hazard 143, 146–7, 298
'most-favored nation' principle 206, 281, 287, 289,
    294–6
Multi Fiber Agreement 283
multilateralism 206–7, 278, 281, 289–90, 296

national debt 167
'national treatment' principle 284, 287
natural resources 67–8, 91, 292
neoclassical growth theory 73, 90
Netherlands, the 153, 265
New Zealand 265
newly declining countries 91
newly industrialized countries 168–9
newly industrializing countries 32–3, 36, 46, 63
Nicaragua 169–70
Nice, Treaty of 213–18
Nikkei index 115, 117
non-discrimination principle of trade policy
    280–1, 292, 294
non-governmental organizations (NGOs) 295
non-renewable resources 68, 91, 269

non-tradable goods 39–40, 179–80, 227, 251
North American Free Trade Agreement (NAFTA)
    130, 200–2, 205, 207
North Sea oil 66

offer curves 27–8, 242
oil companies 46
oil prices 5–7, 25, 67, 71
oligopoly 43–5, 245
Olson, M. 91
Omnibus Trade and Competitiveness Act (US)
    278, 289
open economies 70, 81–2
open market operations 221–2
open societies 90–1
Organization for Economic Cooperation and
    Development (OECD) 168, 288, 290
Organization of Petroleum Exporting Countries
    (OPEC) 243
overshooting by exchange rates 102–3, 157
ozone layer 270

Pakistan 170
patents 290
path dependence 90
pay-off matrix 275–6
Phillips curve 222
Poland 185–8, 191–3, 229, 231
political unions 201
polluter-pays principle 270–1, 293–4
population growth 75, 165
portfolio equilibrium 101, 112, 124
portfolio investments 63
Poverty Reduction and Growth Facility (of the
    IMF) 143
Prebisch, R. 171, 264
preferences as between goods 38–9, 42–3
preferential trade agreements 200
price stability 141; *versus* employment 222
prisoners' dilemma of trade policy 247, 275–8
privatization 183–9 *passim*, 263
product cycle 82
production functions 66–7, 73–4, 77
production potential 98–9, 124, 140, 159
productivity, divergences in 226
profit expectations 77
property rights 182, 195; to knowledge 289–90
protectionist policies 171–2, 206, 236, 238, 241–2,
    263, 276
public goods 212, 255–60, 263, 268–9; global 264,
    270, 277, 293

purchasing power parity 99–103, 106, 109, 169, 262

qualified majority voting 213–15, 217
quantity theory of money 98
quotas 239–40, 278

'race to the bottom' 263
ratchet effect in economic growth 89
rate of return parity 124
reciprocity, principle of 281–2, 295
reference zones (for exchange rates) 154–5, 158
regional development banks 143
regional integration 200–7
regional structure: of world gross product 14–15; of world trade 15–17
regulation 125, 149, 257
rent creation and rent shifting 245
rent seeking 243, 245
repurchase agreements 221–2
reputations of countries 278, 295
research and development 45, 47, 77, 290
reserve requirements 150
resource shortage 91
revealed comparative advantage 47
Romania 231–2
Romer, P.M. 76–7
Russia 104–5, 145, 184–93 *passim*, 297
Rybczinski theorem 34, 38

Sala-i-Martin, X. 86
savings in relation to investment 64
Schumpeterian processes 89
segmentation of labor markets 52–4
services, trade in 10, 287
shadow prices 59
Short Term Arrangement on Cotton Textiles 278
Sigma convergence 89
Singapore 168
Singer, H.W. 171, 264
single currency for the world 96
Sinn, S. 64
Slovak Republic 184, 190
Slovenia 231
social security 229, 264
social standards 246, 291
social union (in Europe) 228
soft budget constraints 185
South Korea 104–5, 115, 132–4, 168, 173–4
sovereignty 218

Soviet Union 181, 196–7
specialization by countries 47
Spencer, B.J. 245
spillovers 41, 212, 225
Sri Lanka 170
stabilization: macroeconomic 182–4, 262; monetary 185, 190
Stackleberg leadership position 245–6
stagnation thesis 90
Stand-by Arrangements (of the IMF) 142
stationary state 74, 76
steady state 74, 84–6, 89
Stolper–Samuelson theorem 38
strategic trade policy 44, 244–6, 276–7, 286
subsidiarity 212
subsidies 211, 238–9, 245, 286, 290
substitutability of resources 28, 92
Sudan 169–70
sunk costs 44, 83, 256
'Super 301' 278, 289
Supplemental Reserve Facility (of the IMF) 142
supply risk 241
sustainable development 92
Sweden 104, 125, 149

Taiwan 168
target zones (for exchange rates) 154
tariff wars 278
tariffs 236–9, 244; binding of 282, 295; optimal 242–4, 274–5
taxation 185–6, 218, 224, 258–64, 292
technological externalities 277
technological knowledge 289–90
technological progress 68, 76–7, 81, 167
technology intensity 47
terms of trade 32, 242–3, 274
terrorism 264
Thailand 125, 131, 134–5, 149, 174, 280–1, 292
Tiebout, C. 255, 257
time preference, rate of 56–8, 77
Tobin tax 149–52, 158
Tobin's *q* 58–9
Tokyo Round 278, 282
trade barriers 29, 206, 262–3, 280–4
trade creation and trade diversion 203–5
trade deficits 100–1, 142, 167, 180
trade policy, continuum of concepts of 276–7
Trade-Related Aspects of International Property Rights (TRIPs) 279, 289
Trade-Related Investment Measures (TRIMs) 290
trade triangle 238–9, 243

trade unions 261
transaction costs 46, 152, 277
Trans-Atlantic Free Trade Area, proposed 202
transfer mechanisms 229
transformation curve: in time 54–7; world 24–31
transformation processes 183–4, 189–90; foreign trade aspects of 191–4
transport costs 8–9, 82
tulipomania 112–13
tuna fishing 292
Turkey 104, 136–7

unemployment 227–8
United Kingdom 66, 155
United States: competitiveness of 49; debt cycle 66; Federal Reserve 120, 221; financial exuberance in (1985–91) 119–20; growth factors 77; and locational competition 265; size of GNP 13; transfers in 229; and the WTO 285
Uruguay Round 241, 276, 278, 283

vertical integration 46
Vietnam War 71, 157
Viner, J. 203

Visegrad countries 183, 201
voluntary export restraints 240, 282

wage policy 228
wages, real 67, 186, 225
waivers (from trading principles) 282–3
Watson, M. 125
working conditions 246
World Bank 143, 168–9, 236, 298
World Economic Forum 17
world gross product 11–15
world trade: regional structure of 15–17; volume of 104
world trade order, new areas for 286–91
World Trade Organization (WTO) 8, 10, 200, 240, 246, 263, 278–84 *passim*, 288, 290, 298; classification of services 287; dispute settlement system 284–5; principles of 283, 286; stabilizing and strengthening of 294–7
'WTO-Plus' 297

yen, the, value of 108

Zambia 170